HISTORY
of
ATHENS COUNTY
OHIO

and

Incidentally of the Ohio Land Company
and the
First Settlement of the State at Marietta

WITH

PERSONAL AND BIOGRAPHICAL SKETCHES OF THE EARLY SETTLERS, NARRATIVES OF PIONEER ADVENTURES, ETC.

By
Charles M. Walker

"Forsam et hæc olim meminisse juvabit."—Virgil

WITH MAP AND PORTRAITS

HERITAGE BOOKS
2008

HERITAGE BOOKS
AN IMPRINT OF HERITAGE BOOKS, INC.

Books, CDs, and more—Worldwide

For our listing of thousands of titles see our website
at
www.HeritageBooks.com

A Facsimile Reprint
Published 2008 by
HERITAGE BOOKS, INC.
Publishing Division
100 Railroad Ave. #104
Westminster, Maryland 21157

Entered according to Act of Congress in the year 1869,
by Robert Clarke & Co.
In the Clerk's Office of the District Court of the
United States for the Southern District of Ohio

— Publisher's Notice —
In reprints such as this, it is often not possible to remove blemishes from the original. We feel the contents of this book warrant its reissue despite these blemishes and hope you will agree and read it with pleasure.

International Standard Book Numbers
Paperbound: 978-0-7884-0582-2
Clothbound: 978-0-7884-7513-9

PREFACE.

THIS unpretending book is a record of but narrow interest and of purely local events. Its preparation was undertaken at the instance and request of some of the old citizens of Athens county—a county which, one of the earliest organized in Ohio, contains, perhaps, a greater number of surviving pioneers than any other in the state except Washington. The desire, on the part of these pioneers, to see preserved in a somewhat connected form the annals of the first settlement of the county and of their own labors and struggles in founding society here, is not an unnatural one. "Near is thy forgetfulness of all things," said Marcus Aurelius, in one of his aphorisms, "and near the forgetfulness of thee by all." With something of this feeling, it is, perhaps, that the old always dwell with such keen pleasure on the events and associations of their early life. Conscious of approaching change and of waning strength, they love to linger on the honorable achievements and labors of that period when the eye was bright, the brain active, and the step elastic. There is, also, a feeling among men that the record of a well-spent and useful life, even if humble, deserves to be remembered. They derive a pardonable pleasure from the thought that posterity will not wholly ignore nor forget them.

It is in recognition of this feeling that these pages have been written. To preserve some account of the lives and labors of the early settlers, who bore so honorable a part in converting a wilderness into a great commonwealth, and to rescue from total oblivion some matters that seem worthy of being narrated, is the modest object of this sketch concerning the history of Athens county.

In endeavoring to accomplish faithfully what was undertaken, it has been found that the work, notwithstanding its narrow scope, involved considerable labor and difficulties. Much of the information touching the first settlement of the county has passed out of reach and is lost forever. Nearly three-quarters of a century have elapsed since the first band of pioneers came into Athens and Ames townships, and that generation has disappeared. If this work had been undertaken by some one fifteen or twenty years since, a vastly greater amount of oral and traditional history could have been gained from the then surviving pioneers. But they have passed away, and it is from their sons and successors that many of the facts herein have been obtained. It is evident that much of the material so acquired would be more or less vague, confused, and difficult to arrange. The writer has, however, labored diligently to overcome these obstacles, and hopes that he has been mainly successful. He is well aware that there will be found errors both of omission and of commission in the book, but it is impossible, in a work of this sort, to eliminate all such. The writer is very conscious, too, of the literary deficiencies of the book. It has been prepared hurriedly, amid the constant pressure of other duties, and the marks of haste are apparent; could he have had more time, he would have improved and greatly condensed it. Such as it is, however, if it shall afford any gratification to the good people of the county, where he was born and passed the early portion of his life, the writer will feel pleased and well rewarded. Doubtless it will be discovered that some prominent early settlers, or leading men among recent citizens, have not been mentioned at all, while comparatively too great prominence will be thought to have been given to others; but the best has been done that could be, under the circumstances, and it is hoped such inequalities and defects will be overlooked.

In seeking requisite facts and information, the writer has met with valuable assistance from so many quarters, that it is entirely impossible to name here the numerous persons to whom he is thus indebted, however agreeable it would be to his own feelings to do so. He is forced, therefore, to adopt the unsatisfactory mode of thus thanking them, one and all, indiscriminately, for their marked and constant courtesy.

C. M. W.

May, 1869.

CONTENTS.

	PAGE
CHAPTER I.	
Indian Occupation of Ohio, - - - - -	1
CHAPTER II.	
The Ohio Company, - - - - - - -	21
CHAPTER III.	
From 1787 to 1796, - - - - - -	76
CHAPTER IV.	
From 1797 to 1805, - - - - - - -	109
CHAPTER V.	
Athens County, - - - - - - - -	143
CHAPTER VI.	
Town and Township of Athens, - - - -	197
CHAPTER VII.	
The Ohio University, - - - - - -	309
CHAPTER VIII.	
Alexander Township, - - - - - -	351
CHAPTER IX.	
Ames Township, - - - - - - -	363
CHAPTER X.	
Bern Township, - - - - - - - -	434

Contents.

	PAGE
CHAPTER XI.	
Canaan Township,	*441*
CHAPTER XII.	
Carthage Township,	*451*
CHAPTER XIII.	
Dover Township,	*460*
CHAPTER XIV.	
Lee Township,	*472*
CHAPTER XV.	
Lodi Township,	*481*
CHAPTER XVI.	
Rome Township,	*488*
CHAPTER XVII.	
Trimble Township,	*519*
CHAPTER XVIII.	
Troy Township,	*526*
CHAPTER XIX.	
Waterloo Township,	*534*
CHAPTER XX.	
York Township,	*541*
Appendix,	*549*
Index,	*583*

HISTORY

OF

Athens County, Ohio.

CHAPTER I.

Indian Occupation of Ohio.

EIGHTY years ago the territory included within the limits of the present State of Ohio was an almost unbroken wilderness. The beautiful river that forms its southern boundary had, indeed, been threaded by a few eager explorers; but the white man had not yet established himself upon its banks. So too Lake Erie, on the north, had long before been furrowed by the adventurous craft of civilized men; but on all its borders there was not a hamlet nor a house. Over the whole region, now so thickly populated, brooded the silence of savage life. The rivers were ploughed only by the swift canoe of the Indian, the forests echoed no sound of productive industry, and the virgin earth waited for the race that was to develop its riches and its beauty.

To-day, in wealth and population Ohio ranks third among the states of the Union. Large cities, flourishing towns, peaceful hamlets, and smiling farms enliven and beautify the scene. Huge steamers, laden with passengers and with wealth, ply upon the rivers and lakes which, less than three generations ago, were silent and desolate. Railroads traverse the state in all directions; busy manufactories give employment to thousands; institutions of learning and charity abound, and, in all respects, the state ranks as a prosperous and powerful commonwealth.

History does not elsewhere record such an extraordinary case of rapid development, and the political philosopher finds abundant food for thought in tracing, from their first beginning, the causes that have contributed to so great a growth. We propose, in these pages, to chronicle some of the events and to sketch some of the individuals connected with the settlement and development of one small portion of this great state, viz: *Athens County.*

Before entering, however, upon matters purely local, let us take a general view of the country and its inhabitants prior to its first settlement by the whites, and thus enable ourselves more clearly to appreciate the wildness of the region to which the early settlers came.

Whatever curious speculations may be indulged as to the origin of the Indian races that once inhabited the northwestern territory, it is certain that we have no clear knowledge of them farther back than the middle of the seventeenth century. Beyond that, they disappear in the mists of the pre-historic period, and, even long after that, much that is written concerning them rests on vague tradition. Whether they were sprung from some of the oriental tribes, or what their origin and whence their travels, are questions that will probably never be answered; they belong to the class of ethnological mysteries which will, in all times, furnish themes for the ingenious researches of learned men, but which will never be solved. It is not proposed to enter into this broad and interesting topic, but merely to glance at the condition of the country and the character of the aboriginal inhabitants of Ohio before its first settlement by the whites.

In 1650, Ohio was an unbroken forest, occupied principally by a tribe of Indians called the *Eries*, who had their villages and hunting grounds near the shores of the lake of that name, and whose wanderings were chiefly confined to the present northern portions of the state. The *Wyandots* (or *Hurons*) held the peninsula between Lakes Huron, Erie, and Ontario, and their hunting excursions extended as far south as the regions about the mouths of the Maumee and Sandusky, while a tribe called the *Andastes* possessed the valleys of the Allegheny and the upper Ohio.

During the latter half of the seventeenth century, frequent and terrible incursions were made among these tribes of the west by the more warlike and powerful *Iroquois*, from New York. These *Iroquois*, so called by the French, were the noted Five Nations, viz: the *Mohawks, Oneidas, Onondagas, Cayugas,* and *Senecas,* and they formed the strongest confederation known in Indian history. Tradition relates with what relentless fury and unwearying tenacity the hostile *Iroquois* warred upon the western tribes until finally the latter were wiped out—either massacred, driven away, or merged into other tribes.

Thus, at the beginning of the eighteenth century, Ohio was almost unclaimed and uninhabited by human beings save as it was used as a hunting ground by the *Iroquois,* or crossed and recrossed by them in their long war expeditions. But they were not able to maintain complete supremacy over so vast a region, and between 1700 and 1750 Ohio again became occupied by different tribes of savages, which, the active warfare of the *Iroquois* having measurably ceased, took possession of the whole region as weeds take possession of a neglected field. They probably sprung from the surviving members of the tribes that had been overcome and dispersed by the *Iroquois,* and a mere enumeration of them will answer our present purpose. They were,

1. The *Wyandots*, who were descended, doubtless, from the undestroyed remnant of the once powerful tribe of that name, which, half a century before, had been driven off by the *Iroquois*. Freed from the vindictive pursuit of their ancient enemies, this tribe returned to their old hunting grounds, and by the middle of the eighteenth century their right was undisputed to the northern part of the state.

2. The *Delawares*, whose principal settlements were on the Muskingum river, where they flourished and became a powerful tribe, asserting a possession over nearly one-half of the state.

3. The *Shawanese* (written also *Shawanoese* and *Shawnees*), who are supposed to have come from the distant south — perhaps from the country bordering on the Gulf of Mexico. They occupied the Scioto and Miami country, and for a long distance eastward, including the present county of Athens and adjacent region, though the *Wyandots* and *Delawares* were also frequently found in this section on hunting or war expeditions. The *Shawanese* had four tribes, or subdivisions, two of which were the *Piqua* and the *Chillicothe* tribes; hence the names of those towns. Powerful and warlike, they were among the most efficient allies of the French during the seven years war, and subsequently took an active part against the Americans

during the revolution and the Indian war which followed. Their hostility was terminated by the treaty at Greenville in 1795, by which they ceded nearly the whole of their territory. A portion of them, however, again made war against the United States, having, with Tecumseh, joined the British standard during the war of 1812.

4. The *Ottawas* (or as they were called by the early white settlers, the *Tawas*), who dwelt in the valleys of the Sandusky and Maumee rivers, and who, together with the *Wyandots*, occupied portions of northern Ohio.

The foregoing enumeration conveys an idea, sufficiently accurate for our purpose, of the Indian tribes that inhabited Ohio during the middle and latter part of the eighteenth century, and up to the time of the first white settlement, under the auspices of the "Ohio Company." These tribes were roving and active, and in the power to make war by no means contemptible. The long and bloody struggle which they made to keep possession of the country, sufficiently attests their tenacity of purpose and their capacity for concerted action.

There is reason to believe that in some former age, though how remote can only be conjectured, what is now Athens county was a favorite resort of the Indians. Indeed, remarkable traces of their existence are still to be found here. In Athens and Dover townships, on the level plateau called "the Plains," are several of those Indian mounds which, found in various parts of the Mississippi valley, have so long interested American archæologists. A still more interesting Indian relic in the same township, is the remains of an ancient earthwork or fortification.* Considerably more than an acre is included by an embankment which, though it has been plough ' over for a third of a century, is still very marked with its rude bastions, ramparts, and curtains. It is probable that on this spot, some hundreds of years since, a battle was fought between warring tribes of savages for the possession of the inviting plains of Dover and the lower valley of the Hockhocking. Numerous skeletons have been found in these mounds, together with Indian hatchets and other weapons of stone.

Such, then, were the occupants of Ohio in the middle of the eighteenth century, and such, at least, approximately, were the limits of their homes and haunts. During the half century that followed, while the white men were building up a civil society in the East, and events were slowly drifting toward the collision and war which resulted in American independence, the possessory rights of these savages were but little disturbed in Ohio. Here they roamed, and hunted, and made

---

* On the farm now owned by David Zenner.

love or war at their pleasure, little conscious of their approaching troubles and doom. It is no part of the purpose of this narrative to treat in detail of the history of this period, of the intrigues and wars of the French and English for the possession of this Western country, and of the fitful and treacherous alliances of the Indians now with one side and now with the other. Our aim is merely to call attention to the character of the Indian tribes that occupied the country by way of showing in some degree the dangers and the obstacles with which the pioneers had to deal; this being cursorily accomplished, we pass to events more nearly connected with our subject.

Dunmore's War.

Probably but few of the present inhabitants of Athens county are aware that a fort was established within its limits, and an army marched across its borders, led by an English earl, before the Revolutionary war. The building of *Fort Gower* at the mouth of the Hockhocking river, in what is now Troy township, and the march of Lord Dunmore's army across the county, thirty years before its erection as a county, forms an interesting passage in our remote history before the earliest settlement by the whites.

"Dunmore's war" was the designation applied to a series of bloody hostilities between the whites and Indians during the year 1774. It was the culmination of the bitter warfare that had been waged with varying success between the frontier population of Pennsylvania and Virginia, and the *Delawares*, *Iroquois*, *Wyandots*, and other tribes of Indians. One of the most noted of the many massacres of that period was that of Logan's family by the whites, and, in retaliation, the swift vengeance of the *Mingo* chief upon the white settlements on the Monongahela, where, in the language of his celebrated speech, he "fully glutted his vengeance."

In August, 1774, Lord Dunmore, then royal Governor of Virginia, determined to raise a large force and carry the war into the enemy's country. The plan of the campaign was simple. Three regiments were to be raised west of the Blue Ridge, to be commanded by General Andrew Lewis, while two other regiments from the interior were to be commanded by Dunmore himself. The forces were to form a junction at the mouth of the Great Kanawha and proceed under the command of Lord Dunmore to attack the Indian towns in Ohio.

The force under Lewis, amounting to eleven hundred men, rendezvoused at Camp Union, now Lewisburg, Greenbriar county, West Virginia, whence they marched early in September, and reached Point Pleasant on the 6th of October. Three days later, Lewis received dispatches from Dunmore informing him that he had changed his plan of operations; that he (Dunmore) would march across the country against the *Shawanese* towns on the Scioto, situated within the present limits of Pickaway county, and Lewis was ordered to cross the Ohio river at once and join Dunmore before those towns.

This movement was to have been made on the 10th of October. On that day, however, before the march had begun, two men of Lewis's command were fired upon while hunting a mile or so from camp. One was killed and the other came rushing into camp with the alarm that Indians were at hand. General Lewis had barely time to make some hasty dispositions when there began one of the most desperate Indian battles recorded in border warfare—the battle of Point Pleasant. The Indians were in great force, infuriated by past wrongs and by the hope of wiping out their enemy by this day's fight, and were led on by their ablest and most daring chiefs. Pre-eminent among the savage leaders were Logan and "Cornplanter" (or "Cornstalk"), whose voices rang above the din, and whose tremendous feats performed in this day's action have passed into history. The contest lasted all day and was not yet decided. Toward evening General Lewis ordered a body of men to gain the enemy's flank, on seeing which movement about to be successfully executed the Indians drew off and effected a safe retreat. The force on both sides in this battle was nearly equal —about 1,100. The whites lost half their officers and

52 men killed. The loss of the Indians, killed and wounded, was estimated at 233.* Soon after the battle Lewis crossed the river and pursued the Indians with great vigor, but did not again come in conflict with them.

Meanwhile, Lord Dunmore, in whose movements we are more interested, had, with about twelve hundred men, crossed the mountains at Potomac Gap, reviewed his force at Fort Pitt (now Pittsburg), and descended the Ohio river as far as the mouth of the Hockhocking, within the present limits of Athens county. Here he landed, formed a camp, and built a fortification which he called *Fort Gower.* It was from here that he sent word to General Lewis of the change in his plan of campaign, and he remained here until after the battle of Point Pleasant. Abraham Thomas, formerly of Miami county, Ohio, who was in Dunmore's army, has stated in a letter published many years ago in the *Troy Times,* that by laying his ear close to the surface of the river on the day of the battle, he could distinctly hear the roar of the musketry more than twenty-five miles distant.

Leaving a sufficient force at Fort Gower to protect the stores and secure it as a base, Lord Dunmore marched up the Hockhocking toward the Indian country. There is a tradition that his little army

---

*Amer. Archives, vol. 1, p. 1018.

encamped a night successively at Federal creek, and at Sunday creek, in Athens county.

He marched across the present limits of the county and up the Hockhocking as far as where Logan now stands; and from there westward to a point seven miles from Circleville, where a grand parley was held with the Indians. It was at this council, by the way, that the famous speech of the Mingo chief was made, beginning "I appeal to any white man to say, if ever he entered Logan's cabin hungry and he gave him not meat," etc. After the execution of a treaty with the Indians (for we do not propose to detail the movements of General Lewis or the operations of the campaign, except as they had some connection with what is now Athens county), Lord Dunmore returned to Fort Gower by nearly the same route he had pursued in his advance, viz: across the country and down the valley of the Hockhocking to its mouth. It is probable that his army was disbanded at this point, and returned in small parties to their homes.

Charles Whittlesey, in *Fugitive Essays*, says:

"In 1831 a steamboat was detained a few hours near the house of Mr. Curtis, on the Ohio, a short distance above the mouth of the Hockhocking, and General Clark, of Missouri, came ashore. He inquired respecting the remains of a fort or encampment at the mouth of the Hockhocking river. He was told that there was evidence of a clearing of several acres in extent, and that pieces of guns and muskets had been found on that spot; and also that a collection of several hundred bullets had been discovered on the bank of the Hockhocking, about twenty-five miles up the river. General Clark then stated that the ground had been occupied as a camp by Lord Dunmore who came down the Kanawha with three hundred men in the spring of 1775, with the expectation of treating with the Indians here. The chiefs not making their appearance, the march was continued up the river twenty-five or thirty miles, where an express from Virginia overtook the party. That evening a council was held and lasted till very late at night. In the morning the troops were disbanded, and immediately requested to enlist in the British service for a stated period. The contents of the dispatches, received the previous evening, had not transpired when this proposition was made. A major of militia, named McCarty, made an harangue to the men against enlisting, which seems to have been done in an eloquent and effectual manner. He referred to the condition of the public mind in the colonies, and the probability of a revolution which must soon arrive. He represented the suspicious circumstances of the express, which was still a secret to the troops, and that appearances justified the conclusion that they were required to enlist in a service against their own countrymen, their own kindred, their own homes.

"The consequence was that but few of the men re-enlisted, and the majority, choosing the orator as leader, made the best of their way to Wheeling. The news brought out by the courier proved to be an account of the opening combat of the Revolution, at Lexington, Mass., April 20, 1775.

"General Clark stated that himself (or his brother) was in the expedition."

Of this account, Mr. Whittlesey says it was related to him "by Walter Curtis, Esq., of Belpre, Washington county, Ohio, and transmitted by me in substance to the secretary of the Ohio Historical Society. Mr. Curtis received it from General Clark, an eminent citizen of Missouri, a brother of General George Rogers Clark, of Kentucky." Mr. Whittlesey admits that, "though it comes very well authenticated, it seems to contradict other well-known facts." We are decidedly of opinion that General Clark's statement was erroneous in respect of the time, nature, and object of Lord Dunmore's expedition up the Hockhocking, and that he never made but one expedition to that region, which was the one we have already described. In the first place, there is not a scrap nor particle of history extant to show that Dunmore made any western expedition in the "spring of 1775." Secondly, we know that he *was* there in the summer and autumn of 1774, that Fort Gower was built at that time, and, probably, the buried bullets, etc., were deposited at the same time. Thirdly, hostilities with the mother country had begun in the spring (April) of 1775; Lord Dunmore was one of the most active and determined royalists in the colonies, and it is not likely that he was spending his time chasing after the Indians when his master's empire in America was crumbling to pieces. Finally, we know that Dunmore was at Williamsburg, Virginia, on the 3d day of May,

1775, for on that day he issued a proclamation to "the disaffected persons of the Colony," calling on them to return to their allegiance.* There is evidence that he was there in April of the same year; and in June, 1775, a letter written from Baltimore says: "A gentleman who last night came here from Williamsburg, which he left on Friday last, June 9th, brings an account of Lord Dunmore having the day before gone on board a man-of-war at York, with his lady and family, for safety."† These considerations we think, render it quite clear that Lord Dunmore did not make an expedition to the Hockhocking country in the spring of 1775, and doubtless the one made in the summer of 1774 was the only one he ever made to this region.

As a matter of historical curiosity we give the following:

"*Proceedings of a Meeting of Officers under Earl Dunmore.*

"At a meeting of the officers under the command of his Excellency, the Right Honorable the Earl of Dunmore, convened at Fort Gower, situated at the junction of the Ohio and Hockhocking rivers, November 5, 1774, for the purpose of considering the grievances of British America, an officer present addressed the meeting in the following words:

"'Gentlemen: Having now concluded the campaign, by the assistance of Providence, with honor and advantage to the colony

---

*Amer. Archives, vol. 2, p. 466.   † *Idem*, p. 975.

and ourselves, it only remains that we should give our country the strongest assurance that we are ready, at all times, to the utmost of our power, to maintain and defend her just rights and privileges. We have lived about three months in the woods, without any intelligence from Boston or from the delegates at Philadelphia. It is possible, from the groundless reports of designing men, that our countrymen may be jealous of the use such a body would make of the arms in their hands at this critical juncture. That we are a respectable body is certain, when it is considered that we can live weeks without bread or salt; that we can sleep in the open air without any covering but the canopy of heaven, and that our men can march and shoot with any in the known world. Blessed with these talents, let us solemnly engage with one another, and our country in particular, that we will use them to no purpose but the honor and advantage of America in general, and of Virginia in particular. It behooves us then, for the satisfaction of our country, that we should give them our real sentiments, by way of resolves, at this very alarming crisis.'

"Whereupon the meeting made choice of a committee to draw up and prepare resolves for their consideration, who immediately withdrew; and after some time spent therein, reported that they had agreed to and prepared the following resolves, which were read, maturely considered, and unanimously adopted by the meeting:

"*Resolved*, That we will bear the most faithful allegiance to his Majesty King George the Third, whilst his Majesty delights to reign over a brave and free people; that we will, at the expense of life and everything dear and valuable, exert ourselves in support of the honor of his Crown and the dignity of the British Empire. But as the love of liberty, and attachment to the real interests and just rights of America, outweigh every other consideration, we resolve that we will exert every power within us for the defense of *American liberty*, and for the support of her just rights and privileges; not in any precipitate, riotous, or tumultuous manner, but when regularly called forth by the unanimous voice of our countrymen.

"*Resolved*, That we entertain the greatest respect for his Excellency the Right Honorable Lord Dunmore, who commanded the expedition against the Shawanese; and who, we are confident, underwent the great fatigue of this singular campaign from no other motive than the true interest of this country.

"Signed, by order and in behalf of the whole corps,

BENJAMIN ASHBY, *Clerk.*"*

On his return to Virginia, Lord Dunmore received the congratulations of various towns, and the thanks of the Assembly, on the successful issue of his expedition and his execution of a treaty with the Indians. He at once ardently espoused the cause of the King, was one of his most influential and obstinate adherents in the colonies, and spent the remainder of his brief stay in this country in the vain effort to resist the consummation of American independence. But the doom of the cause which Lord Dunmore thus earnestly espoused was as clearly written in the book of fate as was that of the savage race, against whose towns he had marched up the banks of the Hockhocking. †

---

* Amer. Archives, vol. I, p. 962.

† *Hockhocking* is a Delaware (Indian) name, and meant, in their language, *Bottle river*. In the spring of 1765, George Croghan, a

sub-commissioner of the British government, embarked at Pittsburg, with some friendly Indians, intending to visit the Wabash and Illinois country, and conclude a treaty with the Indians. Five days from Pittsburg, he notes in his journal that "we passed the mouth of *Hochocen*, or *Bottle River*." This translation of the word Hochocen or Hockhocking, is also given by Heckewelder and Johnson, and is undoubtedly correct. The Shawanese called the river *Weathak-agh-qua*, which meant, in their dialect, the same as Hockhocking; and one of the other tribes called it by a name signifying *Bow river*. All of these names had reference to the winding, crooked course of the stream. The origin of the name Hockhocking—Bottle river—is thus explained by a writer in an old number of the *American Pioneer*, who says: "About six or seven miles northwest of Lancaster, there is a fall in the Hockhocking of about twenty feet; above the falls, for a short distance, the stream is very narrow and straight, forming a neck, while at the falls it suddenly widens on each side, and swells into the appearance of the body of a bottle. The whole, when seen from above, appears exactly in the shape of a bottle, and from this fact arose the Indian name of Hockhocking."

It is to be regretted that the name of the river is now almost invariably abbreviated to *Hocking*. True, it takes longer to write or pronounce the real name—Hockhocking; but the whites have never rendered such distinguished favors or services to the Indian race as to entitle them to mutilate the Indian language by altering or clipping the few words that cling to the geography of the country. Some of these Indian names are not only expressive in their original signification, but are really musical. The following verses, written many years ago, by a former editor of Cincinnati—Mr. William J. Sperry, of the *Globe*—though not highly poetical, are worth insertion in this connection:

The Last of the Red Men.

Sad are fair Muskingum's waters,
    Sadly, blue Mahoning raves;
Tuscarawas' plains are lonely,
    Lonely are Hockhocking's waves.

From where headlong Cuyahoga
    Thunders down its rocky way,
And the billows of blue Erie,
    Whiten in Sandusky's bay;

Unto where Potomac rushes
    Arrowy from the mountain side,
And Kanawha's gloomy waters
    Mingle with Ohio's tide;

From the valley of Scioto,
    And the Huron sisters three,
To the foaming Susquehanna,
    And the leaping Genesee;

Over hill, and plain, and valley,
    Over river, lake, and bay—
On the water, in the forest,
    Ruled and reigned the Seneca.

But sad are fair Muskingum's waters,
    Sadly, blue Mahoning raves;
Tuscarawas' plains are lonely,
    Lonely are Hockhocking's waves.

By Kanawha dwells the stranger,
    Cuyahoga feels the chain;
Stranger ships vex Erie's billows,
    Strangers plough Scioto's plain.

And the Iroquois have wasted
    From the hill and plain away;
On the waters, in the valley,
    Reigns no more the Seneca.

Only by the Cattaraugus,
    Or by Lake Chautauqua's side,
Or among the scanty woodlands
    By the Allegheny's tide:

There, in spots, like sad oases,
    Lone amid the sandy plains,
There the Seneca, still wasting,
    Amid desolation reigns.

CHAPTER II.

The Ohio Company.

ALL of the present county of Athens was included in the original "Ohio Company's Purchase." It formed a part of Washington county until the year 1805, so that for a period of sixteen years, or until the date of its severance from Washington and erection into a separate county, their histories were, in some sense, identical. The fortified and well-protected settlement of Marietta, begun in 1788, very soon pushed its outposts into the interior, and many of those who first located within the limits of Washington, died within the limits of Athens county. The number of instances is still greater in which the second generation of pioneer families is found to have removed from one county to the other. In view of these facts we may with propriety introduce into this narrative some account of the formation of "The Ohio Company" and its founders, and of the first colony planted under its auspices at Marietta in 1788, by which Washington and Athens counties became the site of the earliest white settlement made in the territory of the Northwest.

The conclusion of the Revolutionary war, as of all earnest and protracted wars, witnessed the sudden throwing-out of employment of a great many men. There were patriotic officers who had risked their lives and sacrificed their property in the contest, and no less patriotic soldiers who, though they had not sacrified so much, found themselves at the end of the war with an abundance of liberty but no property, and their occupation gone. The eastern states abounded with these men. They were men of character, energy, and enterprise, full of patriotism and true democratic ideas, proud of their manhood and of their ability to labor. Nor were they in every case men of merely physical resources; in many instances they had enjoyed the advantages of scholastic training, and had mingled the culture of science with the profession of arms. Others of them, though not educated, in the usual acceptation of the term, had that strong native sense and "mother wit" which avail far more in the world than the knowledge of mere pedants however extensive. Bold, active, and adventurous, they had the fullest confidence in the future of their country, and longed to bear a further part in its history and development. Added, doubtless, to such considerations was a desire to rebuild their shattered fortunes, and to regain, under the large liberty and equal laws of the new republic, some portion of the wealth they had sacrificed in fighting for it. The following sketch of one of these retired warriors will revive the memory of a good and pure man, who was for many years very closely identified with the first settlement of Washington and Athens counties.

Rufus Putnam.

RUFUS PUTNAM was born at Sutton, Massachusetts, on the 9th of April, 1738. His father, Elisha Putnam, was the great-great grandson of John Putnam who emigrated from Buckinghamshire, England, and settled at Salem, Massachusetts, in 1634, just fourteen years after the landing at Plymouth Rock. Rufus was the youngest of six children. His father, who is spoken of as "a very useful man in the civil and ecclesiastical concerns of the town" where he lived, died in 1745. Thus orphaned at the tender age of seven, the boy Rufus was sent to live with his maternal grandfather, Mr. Jonathan Fuller, in Danvers, Massachusetts, where he remained less than two years. While here he had such school advantages as the place and times afforded, and learned to read. These advantages, however, meager as they were, were quickly ended; for about this time his mother married again, and Rufus went home and lived there till he was fifteen years old. His stepfather was not only an illiterate man, but despised learning and scouted at the idea of studying books. He not only did not aid his stepson in his efforts to learn, but denied him all opportunities for instruction. The boy was not allowed to go to school, was refused the means of adding to his little store of books, and was even denied a candle at night by which to study. But, he verified the adage "Where there is a will there is a way," and proved anew that a youth with a thirst for learning was never yet baffled in his resolve to quench it. The stepfather kept a kind of public house, and Rufus, by diligently waiting on chance travelers, acquired a few pence of his own. With these he bought powder and shot, and, being something of a sportsman, raised money enough by the sale of game to purchase a spelling book and arithmetic. With these invaluable aids he made fair progress, teaching himself meanwhile to write and compose sentences.

When nearly sixteen years old he was apprenticed to a millwright in Brookfield, Massachusetts, with whom he remained four years. Here he learned the purely mechanical parts of the trade, but he had no further instruction. He pursued, however, his course of self instruction, getting such books as he could, and toiling painfully along in the study of arithmetic and geography. His working hours were devoted to acquiring the practical art of the millwright and to farm labor, and his leisure time to reading and the study of such books as he could procure. Thus, by the time he was eighteen years old, he was, physically, a thoroughly developed and powerful man, and, in mental culture, had laid a good foundation for future acquisitions, and gained a stock of ideas by no means despicable.

At the age of nineteen his apprenticeship was completed. The war between Great Britain and France had then (1757) been in progress about three years, and young Putnam was no sooner free to choose his own course than he enlisted as a private soldier in the provincial army. His patriotic instincts at that time led him to fight for, as in later life they forced him to fight against, the King. The company to which he belonged joined the army in the vicinity of Lake George, New York, in May, 1757. He served from this time in all of the campaigns till the close of the war, undergoing with patient heroism all the toils and dangers of the service, and discharging his duty with fidelity and zeal. At the close of the war, in December, 1760, he returned to his home in New Braintree, and in the following spring, April, 1761, married Miss Ayres, of Brookfield, who died in childbed in the ensuing winter.

For seven or eight years after the conclusion of the French war, Mr. Putnam devoted himself exclusively to his trade as millwright. Being now master of his own time, he habitually gave certain portions of it to self improvement, especially in the practical branches of mathematics, in which he felt himself deficient. By persevering industry, he so far acquired the principles of surveying and navigation as to be able to practice them. Later in life his knowledge of surveying was of the greatest value to him. In January, 1765, being then twenty-seven years old, he married a second time. His wife was Miss Persis Rice, of Westborough, Massachusetts. They lived together more than fifty-five years, and raised a numerous family of children.

We have very little record of Mr. Putnam's life during the next ten years. It is probable that he pursued the joint vocations of farmer and millwright, rearing his family, meanwhile, according to the thrifty code of New England. These were the piping times of peace, from 1765 to 1775, and the crisis had not yet arrived when men of action like Putnam showed to advantage. We are, however, informed of one undertaking in which he engaged during this interval, which indicates that he was full of enterprise and alive to the movements of the day. This was an effort to colonize in Florida, by an association styled "The Military Company of Adventurers." It was composed of those who had served in the provincial army during the French war, and the association expected to obtain grants of land in "West Florida" (now Mississippi), from the British government. Mr. Putnam was chosen one of the explorers. The necessary preparations for the voyage and service having been completed, the party sailed from New York in January, 1773. After a long voyage they arrived at Pensacola, and there, to their great disappointment and chagrin, found that the

Governor had no authority to grant them lands as had been represented. Considerable time was spent in negotiations on the subject, and exploring the rivers and adjacent country; but no settlement was made, and Mr. Putnam finally returned to Massachusetts.

The contest between England and her American colonies had now reached the acme of bitterness. On one side was evinced a disposition to oppress, and on the other a determination to resist. Reconciliation was out of the question, and what shrewd men had long foreseen was now to become a reality. War began. On the 19th of April, 1775, the battles of Lexington and Concord were fought, and immediate and open hostilities followed. Among the first to take up arms in defense of the country was Mr. Putnam. He received a commission as lieutenant-colonel in Brewer's regiment, one of the first that was raised. From this time till the close of the war, he was ardent, active, and efficient in his support of the colonial cause. In August, 1776, he received from Congress an appointment as engineer, with the rank of colonel, in which rank he served several years with great efficiency. In 1782 there were two vacant brigadier-generalships in the Massachusetts line, to one of which Col. Putnam felt that his long and meritorious service entitled him to be promoted. Owing, however, to certain local intrigues, not necessary to be detailed, no promotion was made, and the places were kept vacant for a considerable time, much to Col. Putnam's annoyance and disgust. Washington, whose entire confidence Putnam enjoyed, and who fully appreciated his services and ability, interested himself in the Colonel's behalf. Hearing that Putnam thought of quitting the army in disgust, he wrote him as follows:

"*Headquarters, Newburg, Dec.* 2, 1782.

"SIR: I am informed you have had thoughts of retiring from service, upon an arrangement which is to take place on the 1st of January. But as there will be no opening for it unless your reasons should be very urgent indeed, and as there are some prospects which may, perhaps, make your continuing more eligible than was expected, I have thought proper to mention the circumstances, in expectation that they might have some influence in inducing you to remain in the army. Col. Shepherd having retired, and Brig.-Gen. Patterson being appointed to the command of the first brigade, you will, of consequence, be the second colonel in the line, and have the command of a brigade, while the troops are brigaded as at present. Besides, I consider it expedient you should be acquainted that the question is yet before Congress, whether there shall be two brigadiers appointed in the Massachusetts line. Should you continue, you will be a candidate for this promotion. The Secretary at War is of opinion the promotion will soon take place; whether it will or not I am not able to determine, and, therefore, I would not flatter you too much with expectations which it is not in my power to gratify. But if, upon a view of these circumstances and prospects, the state of your affairs will permit you to continue in the present arrangement (which must be completed immediately), it will be very agreeable to, sir,

Your most humble servant,

G. WASHINGTON."

"COL. PUTNAM."

On receipt of this letter, Col. Putnam, who was at the time absent on furlough, immediately repaired to camp and reported for duty. On the 8th of January following, he was commissioned a brigadier-general, which position he held during the brief remainder of the war.

The friendship of Washington was extended to Gen. Putnam after he retired from the military service, as was evidenced by his appointment to various offices at different times.

In the summer of 1783, just before the final reduction of the army took place, some two hundred and fifty officers petitioned Congress for a grant of land in the Western country. Gen. Putnam, who was himself personally interested in the measure, and was revolving ideas of emigration, addressed a letter to Washington on the subject, setting forth the plan in some detail, and requesting the latter to use his influence with Congress in favor of the grant. It is an interesting document, as illustrating the difficulties that had then to be dealt with in the subjugation of the Western wilderness, and shows decided ability and foresight on the part of the writer. The letter is as follows:

"*New Windsor*, June 16, 1783.

"SIR: As it is very uncertain how long it may be before the honorable Congress may take the petition of the officers of the army, for lands between the Ohio river and Lake Erie, into consideration, or be in a situation to decide thereon, the going to Philadelphia to negotiate the business with any of its members, or committee to whom the petition may be referred, is a measure none of the petitioners will think of undertaking. The part I have taken in promoting the petition is well known, and, therefore, needs no apology, when I inform you that the signers expect that I will pursue measures to have it laid before Congress. Under these circumstances, I beg leave to put the petition in your Excellency's hands, and ask, with the greatest assurance, your patronage of it. That Congress may not be wholly unacquainted with the motives of the petitioners, I beg your indulgence while I make a few observations on the policy and propriety of granting the prayer of it, and making such arrangements of garrisons in the western quarter as shall give effectual protection to the settlers, and encourage emigration to the new government; which, if they meet your approbation, and the favor be not too great, I must request your Excellency will give them your support, and cause them to be forwarded, with the petition, to the President of Congress, in order that, when the petition is taken up, Congress, or their committee, may be informed on what principles the petition is grounded. I am, sir, among those who consider the cession of so great a tract of territory to the United States, in the western world, as a very happy circumstance, and of great consequence to the American empire. Nor have I the least doubt but Congress will pay an early attention to securing the allegiance of the natives, as well as provide for the defense of the country; in case of a war with

Great Britain or Spain. One great means of securing the allegiance of the natives, I take to be, the furnishing them with such necessaries as they stand in need of, and in exchange receiving their furs and skins. They have become so accustomed to the use of fire-arms, that I doubt if they could gain a subsistence without them, at least they will be very sorry to be reduced to the disagreeable necessity of using the bow and arrow as the only means of killing their game; and so habituated are they to the woolen blanket, etc., etc., that absolute necessity alone will prevent their making use of them.

This consideration alone, is, I think, sufficient to prove the necessity of establishing such factories as may furnish an ample supply to these wretched creatures; for unless they are furnished by the subjects of the United States, they will undoubtedly seek elsewhere, and, like all other people, form their attachment where they have their commerce; and then, in case of war, will always be certain to aid our enemies. Therefore, if there were no advantages in view but that of attaching them to our interests, I think good policy will dictate the measure of carrying on a commerce with these people; but when we add to this the consideration of the profit arising from the Indian trade in general, there can not, I presume, be a doubt that it is the interest of the United States to make as early provision for the encouragement and protection of it as possible. For these and many other obvious reasons, Congress will no doubt find it necessary to establish garrisons in Oswego, Niagara, Michilimackinac, Illinois, and many other places in the western world.

The Illinois, and all the posts that shall be established, on the Mississippi, may undoubtedly be furnished by way of the Ohio, with provisions at all times, and with goods whenever a war shall interrupt the trade with New Orleans. But in case of a war with Great Britain, unless a communication is open between the river Ohio and Lake Erie, Niagara, Detroit, and all the posts seated on the great lakes, will inevitably be lost without such communication; for a naval superiority on Lake Ontario, or the seizing on Niagara, will subject the whole country bordering on the lakes to the will of the enemy. Such a misfortune will put it out of the power of the United States to furnish the natives, and necessity will again oblige them to take an active part against us.

Where and how this communication is to be opened, shall next be considered. If Capt. Hutchins, and a number of other map-makers, are not out in their calculations, provisions may be sent from the settlements on the south side of the Ohio, by the Muskingum or Scioto to Detroit, or even to Niagara, at a less expense than from Albany by the Mohawk, to those places. To secure such communication (by the Scioto, all circumstances considered, will be the best), let a chain of forts be established; these forts should be built on the banks of the river, if the ground will admit, and about twenty miles distant from each other, and on this plan, the Scioto communication will require ten or eleven stockaded forts, flanked by block-houses, and one company of men will be a sufficient garrison for each, except the one at the portage, which will require more attention in the construction, and a larger number of men to garrison it. But besides the supplying the garrisons on the great lakes with provisions, etc., we ought to take into consideration the protection that such an arrangement will give to the frontiers of Virginia, Pennsylvania, and New York. I say New York, as we shall undoubtedly extend our settlements and garrisons from the Hudson to Oswego. This done, and a garrison posted at Niagara, whoever will inspect the map must be convinced that all the Indians living on the waters of the Mohawk, Oswego, Susquehanna, and Alleghany rivers, and in all the country south of the lakes Ontario and Erie, will be encircled in such a manner as will effectually secure their allegiance and keep them quiet, or oblige them to quit their country.

Nor will such an arrangement of posts from the Ohio to Lake Erie be any additional expense; for, unless this gap is shut, notwithstanding the garrisons on the lakes and from Oswego to the Hudson, yet the frontier settlers on the Ohio, by Fort Pitt to the Susquehanna, and all the country south of the Mohawk will be exposed to savage insult, unless protected by a chain of garrisons which will be far more expensive than the arrangement proposed, and, at the same time, the protection given to these states will be much less complete; besides, we should not confine our protection to the present settlements, but carry the idea of extending them at least as far as the lakes Ontario and Erie.

These lakes form such a natural barrier, that when connected with the Hudson and Ohio by the garrisons proposed, settlements in every part of the states of New York and Pennsylvania may be made with the utmost safety; so that these states must be deeply interested in the measure as well as Virginia, who will, by the same arrangement, have a great part of its frontier secured, and the rest much strengthened; nor is there a state in the Union but will be greatly benefited by the measure, considered in any other point of view, for, without any expense, except a small allowance of purchase money to the natives, the United States will have within their protection seventeen million five hundred thousand acres of very fine land, to dispose of as they may think proper. But I hasten to mention some of the expectations which the petitioners have respecting the conditions on which they hope to obtain the lands. This was not proper to mention in the body of the petition, especially as we pray for grants to all members of the army who wish to take up lands in that quarter.

The whole tract is supposed to contain about seventeen million four hundred and eighteen thousand two hundred and forty acres, and will admit of seven hundred and fifty-six townships of six miles square, allowing to each township three thousand and forty acres for the ministry, schools, waste lands, rivers, ponds, and highways; then each township will contain, of settlers' lands, twenty thousand acres, and in the whole, fifteen million one hundred and twenty thousand acres. The land to which the army is entitled, by the resolves of Congress, referred to in the petition, according to my estimate, will amount to two million one hundred and six thousand eight hundred and fifty acres, which is about the eighth part of the whole. For the survey of this, the army expect to be at no expense, nor do they expect to be under any obligation to settle these lands, or do any duty to secure their title in them; but in order to induce the army to become actual settlers in the new government, the petitioners hope congress will make a further grant of lands on condition of settlement, and have no doubt but that honorable body will be as liberal to all those who are not provided for by their own states, as New York has been to the officers and soldiers that belong to that state; which, if they do, it will require about eight million acres to complete the army, and about seven million acres will remain for sale. The petitioners, at least some of them, are much opposed to the monopoly of the lands, and wish to guard against large patents being granted to individuals, as, in their opinion, such a mode is very injurious to a country, and greatly retards its settlement; and whenever such patents are tenanted, it throws too much power into the hands of a few. For these, and many other obvious reasons, the petitioners hope that no grant will be made but by townships of six miles square, or six by twelve, or six by eighteen miles, to be subdivided by the proprietors to six miles square, that being the standard on which they wish all calculations to be made; and that officers and soldiers, as well as those who petition for charters on purchase, may form their associations on one uniform principle, as to number of persons or rights to be contained in a township, with the exception only, that when the grant is made for services already done, or on condition of settlement, if the officers petition, with the soldiers, for a particular township, the soldier shall have one right only to a captain's three, and so in proportion with commissioned officers of every grade.

These, sir, are the principles which gave rise to the petition under consideration; the petitioners, at least some of them, think that sound policy dictates the measure, and that congress ought to lose no time in establishing some such chain of posts as have been hinted at, and in procuring the tract of land petitioned for, of the natives; for, the moment this is done, and agreeable terms offered to the settlers, many of the petitioners are determined not only to become adventurers, but actually to remove themselves to this country; and there is not the least doubt, but other valuable citizens will follow their example, and the probability is that the country between Lake Erie and the Ohio *will be filled with inhabitants*, and the faithful subjects of the United States so established on the waters of the Ohio and the lakes, as to banish forever the idea of our western territory falling under the dominion of any European power; the frontiers of the old states will be effectually secured from savage alarms, and the *new* will have little to fear from their insults.

I have the honor to be, sir, with every sentiment, your Excellency's most obedient and very humble servant,

RUFUS PUTNAM."

" GEN. WASHINGTON."

It will be noted that Gen. Putnam, in the foregoing letter, suggests townships of six miles square, and the allowance to each township of "3040 acres for the ministry, schools, waste lands, rivers, ponds, and highways." This was, it is believed, the first suggestion of these points, and to Gen. Putnam belongs the honor of devising and first urging these practical and beneficent measures. His advice as to the size of townships was subsequently adopted, and has continued to be the standard of a surveyed township ever since. The other suggestion as to school and ministerial lands was applied to the Ohio Company's and to Symmes's Purchase (on the Miami), but never became of general application.

Washington addressed a communication to congress, strongly approving Gen. Putnam's letter and the application of the officers for a land grant, but no definite action was taken by that body.

In the spring of 1784, Gen. Putnam, who was deeply interested in the matter and anxious to open the way for the settlement of the Ohio country, again addressed Washington as follows:

"*Rutland, April* 5*th*, 1784.

"Dear Sir: Being unavoidably prevented from attending the general meeting of the *Cincinnati* at Philadelphia, as I had intended, where I once more expected the opportunity in person of paying my respects to your Excellency, I can not deny myself the honor of addressing you by letter, to acknowledge with gratitude the ten thousand obligations I feel myself under to your goodness, and most sincerely to congratulate you on your return to domestic happiness; to inquire after your health, and wish the best of Heaven's blessings may attend you and your dear lady.

The settlement of the Ohio country, sir, engrosses many of my thoughts, and much of my time, since I left the camp, has been employed in informing myself and others, with respect to the nature, situation, and circumstances of that country, and the practicability of removing ourselves there. And, if I am to form an opinion on what I have seen and heard on the subject, there are thousands in this quarter who will emigrate to that country as soon as the honorable congress make provisions for granting lands there, and locations and settlements can be made with safety, unless such provision is too long delayed; I mean till necessity turn their views another way, which is the case with some already, and must soon be the case with many more. You are sensible of the necessity, as well as the possibility of both officers and soldiers fixing themselves in business somewhere, as soon as possible, as many of them are unable to lie longer on their oars, waiting the decision of congress, on our petition, and, therefore, must unavoidably settle themselves in some other quarter; which, when done, the idea of removing to the Ohio country will probably be at an end, with respect to most of them. Besides, the commonwealth of Massachusetts have come to a resolution to sell their eastern country for public securities, and should their plan be formed, and propositions be made public before we hear anything from congress respecting our petition and the terms on which the lands petitioned for are to be obtained, it will undoubtedly be much against us, by greatly lessening the number of Ohio associates.

Another reason why we wish to know, as soon as possible, what the intentions of congress are respecting our petition, is the effect such knowledge will probably have on the credit of the certificates we have received on settlement of accounts; those securities are now selling at no more than three shillings and six pence, or four shillings on the pound, which, in all probability, might double, if not more, the moment it was known that government would receive them for lands in the Ohio country. From these circumstances, and many others which might be mentioned, we are growing quite impatient, and the general inquiry now is, when are we going to the Ohio? Among others, Brig. Gen. Tupper, Lieut. Col. Oliver, and Maj. Ashley, have agreed to accompany me to that country, the moment the way is open for such an undertaking. I should have hinted these things to some member of congress, but the delegates from Massachusetts, although exceeding worthy men, and, in general, would wish to promote the Ohio scheme, yet, if it should militate against the particular interest of this state, by draining her of inhabitants, especially when she is forming the plan of selling the eastern country, I thought they would not be very warm advocates in our favor; and I dare not trust myself with any of the New York delegates, with whom I was acquainted, because that government is wisely inviting the eastern people to settle in that state; and as to the delegates of other states, I have no acquaintance with any of them.

These circumstances must apologize for my troubling you on this subject, and requesting the favor of a line, to inform us in this quarter, what the prospects are with respect to our petition, and what measures have been or are likely to be taken, with respect to settling the Ohio country.

I shall take it as a very particular favor, sir, if you will be kind enough to recommend me to some character in congress acquainted with and attached to, the Ohio cause, with whom I may presume to open a correspondence.

I am, sir, with the highest respect,

Your humble servant,

RUFUS PUTNAM."

"GEN. WASHINGTON."

In reply to this communication Gen. Putnam received the following letter from Washington:

"*Mount Vernon, June* 2d, 1784.

"DEAR SIR: I could not answer your favor of the 5th of April, from Philadelphia, because Gen. Knox, having mislaid, only presented the letter to me in the moment of my departure from that place. The sentiments of esteem and friendship which breathe in it, are exceedingly pleasing and flattering to me, and you may rest assured they are reciprocal.

"I wish it was in my power to give you a more favorable account of the officers' petition for lands on the Ohio, and its waters, than I am about to do. After this matter and information respecting the establishment for peace, were my inquiries, as I went through Annapolis, solely directed; but I could not learn that anything decisive had been done in either.

On the latter, I hear congress are differing about their powers; but as they have accepted of the cession from Virginia, and have resolved to lay off ten new states,* bounded by latitudes and longitudes, it should be supposed that they would determine something respecting the former before they adjourn; and yet I very much question it, as the latter is to happen on the 3rd, that is to-morrow. As the congress who are to meet in November next, by the adjournment will be composed from an entire new choice of delegates in each state, it is not in my power, *at this time*, to direct you to a proper correspondent in that body. I wish I could; for persuaded I am, that to some such cause as you have assigned, may be ascribed the delay the petition has encountered, for *surely, if justice and gratitude* to the army, and general policy

---

* The plan reported by the committee (consisting of Mr. Jefferson, Mr. Chase, and Mr. Howell) on the 19th of April, 1784, provided for the division of the northwestern territory into ten states, by parallels of latitude and meridian lines. The names of the new states, beginning at the northwest and proceeding southwardly, were to be Sylvania, Michigania, Chersonasus, Assonisipia, Metropotamia, Illinoia, Saratoga, Washington, Polypotamia, and Pelisipia. (Journals of Congress, April 23d, 1784.) The report of the committee was debated for several days, during which it underwent very essential changes. Looking at the foregoing list of horrible names, the innocent people of the western states may well tremble at their narrow escape.

of the Union were to govern in this case, there would not be the smallest interruption in granting its request. I really feel for those gentlemen, who, by these unaccountable delays (by any other means than those you have suggested), are held in such an awkward and disagreeable state of suspense, and wish my endeavors could remove the obstacles. At Princeton, before congress left that place, I exerted every power I was master of, and dwelt upon the argument you have used, to show the propriety of a speedy decision. Every member with whom I conversed, acquiesced in the reasonableness of the petition. All yielded, or seemed to yield to the policy of it, but plead the want of cession of the land, to act upon; this is made and accepted; and yet matters, as far as they have come to my knowledge, remain in *statu quo.* * * *

I am, dear sir, with very sincere esteem and regard,
Your most obedient servant,
G. WASHINGTON."

Though his favorite scheme for an organized emigration to the western country failed in 1784, Gen. Putnam was destined not only to witness its success a few years later, but to live to see the most marvelous results of civilization follow the accomplishment of his sagacious policy.

The next few years were spent by Gen. Putnam in part attending to his private affairs and in part discharging the duties of public surveyor and land agent of the state of Massachusetts, in which position he gave entire satisfaction. From 1788 his career was in a great degree identified with the operations of the

Ohio Company, and the colony at Marietta; and we shall, in that connection, obtain further insight into the excellence of his character and the simplicity of his life. He died at Marietta, beloved and mourned by the whole community in May, 1824, at the age of eighty-six.

Timothy Flint, who knew Gen. Putnam personally, said of him, writing in 1828:

" He was probably the member of the Ohio Company who had the greatest influence in imparting confidence to emigration from New England to Ohio. When he moved there it was one compact and boundless forest. He saw that forest fall on all sides under the axe; and, in the progress of improvement, comfortable and then splendid dwellings rise around him. He saw his favorite settlement survive the accumulated horrors of an Indian war. He saw its exhaustless fertility and its natural advantages triumph over all. He saw Marietta making advance toward an union of interest with the Gulf of Mexico by floating down to its bosom a number of sea vessels built at that place. He saw such a prodigious increase of navigation on the Ohio as to number a hundred large boats passing his dwelling within a few hours. He heard the first tumult of the steamboats as they began to be borne down between the forests. He had surrounded his republican mansion with orchards bending with fruit. In the midst of rural abundance and endeared friends who had grown up around him; far from the display of wealth, the bustle of ambition and intrigue, the father of the colony, hospitable and kind without ostentation and without effort, he displayed in these remote regions the grandeur, real and intrinsic, of those immortal men who achieved our revolution. He has passed away. But the memory of really great and good men, like Gen. Putnam, will remain as long as plenty, independence, and comfort shall prevail on the shores of the Ohio." *

Benjamin Tupper.

Contemporary with Gen. Putnam, and a companion in arms and friend of his, was *Gen. Benjamin Tupper.* Born in 1738 at Stoughton, Massachusetts, of parents whose immediate ancestors came from England, he reached manhood in time to bear arms during the French war, in which he served as a subaltern in the provincial army. In November, 1762, he married Miss Huldah White at Easton, Massachusetts. At the commencement of the Revolutionary war, Tupper, who was then a lieutenant of militia at Chesterfield, ardently espoused the cause of the colonies. The first act of his military career was arresting and adjourning the supreme court, in 1776, which was sitting at Springfield under the royal authority. From this time he served continuously till the close of the war, rendering efficient service to the cause in the various grades which he successively filled, of major, colonel, and brigadier general.

In 1785, after the return of peace, Gen. Tupper sought employment of the government as a surveyor

---

* Flint's Western States, vol. 2, p. 364.

of public lands in the West, under the ordinance of May 20th, 1785, providing for the execution of that work. This appointment had been tendered to Gen. Putnam, who, for private reasons, declined it. He, however, used his influence to secure the office for his friend Tupper, who was appointed by the following resolution of congress:

"*July 18th*, 1785.
"On motion of the delegates from Massachusetts,—
Whereas, Mr. Rufus Putnam, appointed a surveyor under the ordinance of the 20th of May, from public engagements with the commonwealth of Massachusetts, can not attend to the business of his appointment during the year: *Resolved*, that Mr. Benjamin Tupper be and hereby is appointed a surveyor, with authority to perform the duties of that office, until Mr. Putnam shall actually join the geographer and take the duties upon himself." *

In the autumn of the same year Gen. Tupper started for the northwest, intending to prosecute the land surveys of that region, but, owing to Indian troubles, did not proceed further than the present site of Pittsburg. In the summer of 1786, after the Indians had been temporarily quieted by treaty made in January previous, Gen. Tupper made a second journey to the west, and completed, during that season, the survey of "the seven ranges."

---

* Journals of Congress, vol. 4, p. 547.

On his return to Massachusetts from his *first* visit to the northwest, during the winter of 1785-6, Gen. Tupper's mind was filled with the idea of removing to the Ohio country — an idea which appeared so visionary to most of his friends that they could not regard it as serious. He, however, was thoroughly in earnest, and knew where to find a person who would enter into his plan. This was his friend Gen. Putnam. Tupper visited him at his residence in Rutland; and thus were brought together again, after the war, the two men who originated the idea of the famous Ohio Company. What they talked of the night of Tupper's visit, history does not wholly record. We fancy them sitting before a blazing fire in the old-fashioned open fire-place, where hickory logs were steaming and sparks flying up the chimney. Putnam's sword and spurs, perhaps, hung on the wall, relics of the late war, and mute reminders of common perils. If the little Putnams were permitted to sit up that evening later than usual, to listen to the conversation, it may, with tolerable certainty, be conjectured that they dreamed of strange western countries, wild men and beasts. Perhaps the elders recounted the trials and adventures of the war; doubtless, they discussed the politics of the day, and the perils that beset the cumbrous and rickety government of the liberated colonies (for the constitution was not yet framed, and those were the dark days of the "confederation"); but one thing we know of which they discussed long and thoroughly, and that was western land and emigration. The next day their ideas on this subject were so far matured that they united in an advertisement which was published in the newspapers of the state, on the 25th of January, 1786, as follows:

"INFORMATION.

" The subscribers take this method to inform all officers and soldiers who have served in the late war, and who are, by a late ordinance of the honorable congress, to receive certain tracts of land in the Ohio country—and also all other good citizens who wish to become adventurers in that delightful region; that from personal inspection, together with other incontestible evidences, they are fully satisfied that the lands in that quarter are of a much better quality than any other known to New England people; that the climate, seasons, products, etc., are in fact equal to the most flattering accounts that have ever been published of them; that being determined to become purchasers and to prosecute a settlement in this country, and desirous of forming a general association with those who entertain the same ideas, they beg leave to propose the following plan, viz: That an association by the name of *The Ohio Company* be formed of all such as wish to become purchasers, etc., in that country who reside in the commonwealth of Massachusetts only, or to extend to the inhabitants of other states as shall be agreed on. In order to bring such a company into existence, the subscribers propose that all persons who wish to promote the scheme, should meet in their respective counties at 10 o'clock A. M. on

Wednesday, the 15th day of February next, and that each county meeting then assembled choose a delegate or delegates, to meet at the Bunch of Grapes Tavern in Boston on Wednesday, the first day of March next at 10 o'clock A. M., then and there to consider and determine on a general plan of association for said company; which plan, covenant, or agreement being published, any person (under condition therein to be provided), may by subscribing his name become a member of the company.

RUFUS PUTNAM,
BENJAMIN TUPPER."

In response to this call county meetings were held and delegates appointed, who convened at the Bunch of Grapes Tavern, in Boston, March 1st, 1786. The delegates were Winthrop Sargent and John Miles from Suffolk county; Manasseh Cutler from Essex; John Brooks and Thomas Cushing from Middlesex; Benjamin Tupper from Hampshire; Crocker Sampson from Plymouth; Rufus Putnam from Worcester; John Patterson and Jelaliel Woodbridge from Berkshire, and Abraham Williams from Barnstable.

Gen. Rufus Putnam was chosen chairman of the meeting, and Major Winthrop Sargent secretary. We quote from the records of the company:

"From the very pleasing description of the western country given by Generals Putnam and Tupper and others, it appearing expedient to form a settlement there, a motion was made for choosing a committee to prepare the draft of a plan of an association into a company for the said purpose, for the inspection and approbation of this convention. Resolved in the affirmative.

Also, resolved that this committee shall consist of five. Gen. Putnam, Manasseh Cutler, Col. Brooks, Major Sargent, and Capt. Cushing were elected.

On Friday, the 3d of March, the convention met, and the committee reported as follows:

Articles of Agreement entered into by the Subscribers for constituting an Association by the name of the Ohio Company.

PREAMBLE. The design of this association is to raise a fund in continental certificates, for the sole purpose and to be appropriated to the entire use of purchasing lands in the Western Territory belonging to the United States, for the benefit of the Company, and to promote a settlement in that country.

Article 1st. That the fund shall not exceed one million of dollars, in continental specie certificates, exclusive of one year's interest due thereon (except as hereafter provided), and that each share or subscription shall consist of one thousand dollars, as aforesaid, and also ten dollars in gold or silver, to be paid into the hands of such agents as the subscribers may elect.

Article 2d. That the whole fund of certificates raised by this association, except one year's interest due thereon mentioned under the first article, shall be applied to the purchase of lands in some one of the proposed states northwesterly of the river Ohio, as soon as those lands are surveyed, and exposed for sale by the commissioners of congress according to the ordinance of that honorable body passed the 20th of May, 1785, or on any other plan that may be adopted by congress, not less advantageous to the company. The one year's interest shall be applied to the purpose of making a settlement in the country and assisting those who may be otherwise unable to remove themselves thither. The gold and silver is for defraying the expenses of those persons employed as agents in purchasing the lands, and other contingent charges that may arise in the prosecution of the business. The surplus, if any, to be appropriated as the one year's interest on the certificates.

Article 3d. That there shall be five directors, a treasurer and secretary, appointed in manner and for the purposes hereafter provided.

Article 4th. That the prosecution of the Company's designs may be the least expensive, and at the same time the subscribers and agents as secure as possible, the proprietors of twenty shares shall constitute one grand division of the Company; appoint their agent, and, in case of vacancy by death, resignation, or otherwise, shall fill it up as immediately as can be.

Article 5th. That the agent shall make himself accountable to each subscriber for certificates and monies received, by duplicate receipts, one of which shall be lodged with the secretary; that the whole shall be appropriated according to these articles of association, and that the subscriber shall receive his just dividend according to quality and quantity of lands purchased, as near as possibly may be, by lot drawn in person or through proxy, and that deeds of conveyance shall be executed to individual subscribers, by the agent, similar to those he shall receive from the directors.

Article 6th. That no person shall be permitted to hold more than five shares in the Company's funds, and no subscription for less than a full share will be admitted; but this is not meant to prevent those who can not or choose not to adventure a full share, from associating among themselves, and by one of their number subscribing the sum required.

Article 7*th.* That the directors shall have the sole disposal of the Company's fund for the purposes before mentioned; that they shall, by themselves, or such person or persons as they may think proper to entrust with the business, purchase lands for the benefit of the Company, where, and in such way, either at public or private sale, as they shall judge will be most advantageous to the Company. They shall also direct the application of the one year's interest, and gold and silver, mentioned in the first article, to the purposes mentioned under the second article, in such way and manner as they shall think proper. For those purposes, the directors shall draw on the treasurer from time to time, making themselves accountable for the application of the moneys, agreeably to this association.

Article 8*th.* That the agents, being accountable to the subscribers for their respective divisions, shall appoint the directors, treasurer and secretary, and fill up all the vacancies which may happen in these offices respectively.

Article 9*th.* That the agents shall pay all the certificates and moneys received from subscribers into the hands of the treasurer, who shall give bonds to the agents, jointly and severally, for the faithful discharge of his trust; and also, on his receiving certificates or moneys from any particular agent, shall make himself accountable therefor, according to the condition of his bonds.

Article 10*th.* That the directors shall give bonds, jointly and severally, to each of the agents conditioned that the certificates and moneys they shall draw out of the treasury shall be applied to the purposes stipulated in these articles; and that the lands purchased for the Company shall be divided among them within three months from the completion of the purchase, by lot, in such manner as the agents or a majority of them shall agree; and that, on such division being made, the directors shall execute deeds to the agents, respectively, for the proportions which fall to their divisions, correspondent to those the directors may receive from the commissioners of congress.

Article 11*th. Provided,* That whereas a sufficient number of subscribers may not appear to raise the fund to the sums proposed in the first article, and thereby the number of divisions may not be completed, it is therefore agreed that the agents of divisions of twenty shares each, shall, after the 17th day of October, next, proceed in the same manner as if the whole fund proposed had been raised.

Article 12*th. Provided, also,* That whereas it will be for the common interest of the Company to obtain an ordinance of incorporation from the honorable congress, or an act of incorporation from some one of the states in the Union (for which the directors shall make application), it is therefore agreed that, in case such incorporation is obtained, the fund of the Company (and, consequently, the shares and divisions thereof) may be extended to any sum, for which provision shall be made in said ordinance or act of incorporation, anything in this association to the contrary notwithstanding.

Article 13*th.* That all votes under this association may be given in person, or by proxy, and in numbers justly proportionate to the stock holden, or interest represented."

The foregoing report was adopted March 3, 1786, and subscription books were opened at once. A year passed before a sufficient number of shares were subscribed to justify further steps. On the 8th of March, 1787, a called meeting of the shareholders was held at Brackett's Tavern, in Boston, and Samuel H. Parsons, Gen. Rufus Putnam, and Dr. Manasseh Cutler were appointed directors to make proposals to congress, "for a private purchase of lands, and under such descriptions as they shall deem adequate for the purposes of the Company." Major Winthrop Sargent was elected secretary of the Company. The election of the other two directors (five being the number required) and treasurer was postponed till a future meeting. The directors employed Dr. Manasseh Cutler* to make a contract with congress for a body of land in the "Great Western territory of the Union."

---

* In an original memorandum concerning the transactions of the Ohio Company, in the handwriting of Dr. Cutler, now before us, he says: "In April, 1787, the directors empowered Gen. Parsons, of Connecticut, to apply to congress for the purchase of lands on the Muskingum river. He petitioned congress, and a committee was appointed to confer with him. To that committee he proposed a purchase on the Scioto river. The proprietors here were generally dissatisfied with the situation and lands on the Scioto, and much preferred the Muskingum. The directors then appointed Sargent and myself agents to go on to congress, and, if possible, make the purchase on Muskingum—which we did. This business was precipitated through fear of other purchasers taking the lands we wished to purchase, as several other companies were making applications to congress at that time. This circumstance occasioned an earlier appointment of a majority of directors, and less formality than there would otherwise have been."

Dr. Cutler left his home in Hamilton, Massachusetts, in June, 1787, for New York, where the congress was then sitting. The constitutional convention, engaged in framing the Federal constitution, was sitting at the same time in Philadelphia, and Dr. Cutler bore letters of introduction to leading men in both cities. His Journal of this trip is before us, and we insert, at length, those portions of it which relate to his negotiations with congress, as a part of the chronicles of the Ohio Company.* The good Doctor's Journal shows that the art of "lobbying" was not altogether unknown even at that early period of our history. The portions omitted are entirely personal or have no relation whatever to the negotiation.

Dr. Cutler's Journal.
"*Sunday, June* 24, 1787.—Exchanged with Mr. Parsons, of Lynn. After meeting, called on John Carnes, Esq., to receive his commands, if any, for New York. Rode to Cambridge. Spent the evening at Dr. Williams's, in company with Mr. Winthrop, the librarian. Proposed going to President Wil-

---

* For this very interesting document, as for other valuable material, we are indebted to Mrs. Sarah Cutler Dawes, of Washington county, Ohio, a granddaughter of Dr. Cutler. The Journal ought to be published entire; our space only allows such extracts as are here inserted touching the history of the Ohio Company.

lard's (of Harvard College), but the Doctor insisted on my lodging with him, which I did.

Monday, June 25th.—Waited on Dr. Willard this morning, who favored me with a number of introductory letters to gentlemen at the southward. Received several from Dr. Williams, and went with him to Boston. Received letters of introduction from Gov. Bowdoin, Mrs. Winthrop, Dr. Warren, Dr. Dexter, Mr. Guild, Mr. Belknap, etc.; conversed with Gen. Putnam; received letters; settled the principles on which I am to contract with Congress for lands on account of the Ohio Company."

* * * * * * * *

He arrived at Middletown, Connecticut, the residence of Gen. Parsons, on the 30th of June, and the next day, Sunday, preached in that town.

"*Monday, July 2.*—It was nine o'clock this morning before Gen. Parsons and I had settled all our matters, with respect to my business with Congress. He favored me with a large number of letters to members of Congress and other gentlemen in New York.

* * * * * * * *

July 5th. * * * About three o'clock I arrived at the city (New York) by the road that enters the Bowery. Put up my horse at the sign of the Plough and Harrow, in the Bowery Barns. After dressing myself, I took a walk into the city. When I came to examine my letters of introduction, I found them so accumulated that I hardly knew which to deliver first. As this is rather a curiosity to me, I am determined to preserve a catalogue, although only a part are to be delivered at New York."

Here follows a list of over fifty names, some of them very celebrated, which we omit.

"The first letter I delivered was to Mr. Hugh Henderson. He is a wholesale merchant, and lives in a genteel style on Golden Hill street, New York. Mr. Henderson received me very politely. After tea, he proposed a walk about the city, but first gave me a specimen of Scotch generosity—urged me to take lodgings with him while I tarried in the city, assigned me one of the front chambers, and ordered his servant, Starling, to attend me. After finding that no apology would avail, I accepted his invitation, and his servant was sent for my baggage. We rambled over a considerable part of the city before dark, delivered a number of my letters, and returned and spent the evening very agreeably at Mr. Henderson's.

Friday, July 6th.—This morning delivered most of my introductory letters to members of Congress. Prepared my papers for making my application to Congress for the purchase of lands in the western country for the Ohio Company. At eleven o'clock, I was introduced to a number of members on the floor of Congress chamber, in the City Hall, by Colonel Carrington, member from Virginia. Delivered my petition for purchasing lands for the Ohio Company, and proposed terms and conditions of purchase. A committee was appointed to agree on terms of negotiation, and report to Congress. Dined with Mr. Dane.
*   *   *   *   *   *   *   *

July 7th.—Paid my respects this morning to Dr. Holton

and several other gentlemen. Was introduced, by Mr. Ewing and Mr. Rittenhouse, to Mr. Hutchins, geographer to the United States. Consulted him where to make our location. Dined with Gen. Knox.

*   *   *   *   *   *   *   *

Monday, July 9*th.*—Waited this morning, very early, on Mr. Hutchins. He gave me the fullest information of the western country, from Pennsylvania to the Illinois, and advised me, by all means, to make our location on the Muskingum, which was decidedly, in his opinion, the best part of the whole western country. Attended the committee before Congress opened, and then spent the remainder of the forenoon with Mr. Hutchins.

*   *   *   *   *   *   *   *

Attended the committee at Congress chamber; debated on terms, but were so wide apart that there appears little prospect of closing a contract.   *   *   *   Called again on Mr. Hutchins, consulted him further about the place of location. Spent the evening with Dr. Holton, and several other members of Congress, in Hanover square.

July 10*th.*—This morning, another conference with the committee. As Congress was now engaged in settling the form of government for the Federal territory, for which a bill has been prepared and a copy sent to me (with leave to make remarks and propose amendments), which I had taken the liberty to remark upon, and propose several amendments, I thought this the most favorable time to go on to Philadelphia. Accordingly, after I had returned the bill with my observations, I set out, at seven o'clock."

*   *   *   *   *   *   *   *

The visit to Philadelphia consumed a week. After his return, the Journal continues:

"*July* 18*th.*—Paid my respects, this morning, to the President of Congress, Gen. St. Clair. Called on a number of my friends. Attended at the City Hall on members of Congress and their committee. We renewed our negotiations.

*　　*　　*　　*　　*　　*　　*　　*

July 19*th.*—Called on members of Congress very early in the morning, and was furnished with the ordinance establishing a government in the western Federal territory. It is, in a degree, new modeled. The amendments I proposed have all been made except one, and that is better qualified. It was, that we should not be subject to continental taxation, unless we were entitled to a full representation in Congress. This could not be fully obtained; for it was considered in Congress as offering a premium to emigrants. They have granted us representation, with the right of debating but not of voting, upon our being first subject to taxation. As there are a number in Congress opposed to my terms of negotiation, and some to any contract, I wish now to ascertain the number for and against, and who they are; and must then, if possible, bring the opponents over. This I have mentioned to Col. Duer, who has promised to assist me. Grayson, R. H. Lee, and Carrington are certainly my warm advocates. Holton, I think, may be trusted. Dane must be carefully watched, notwithstanding his professions. Clark, Bingham, Yates, Kearney, and Few are troublesome fellows. They must be attacked by my friends at their lodgings. If they can be brought over, I shall succeed; if not, my business is at an end. Attended the committee this morning. They are determined to make a report to-day, and try the spirit of Congress. Dined with Gen. Knox and about forty-two gentlemen, officers of the late continental army, and among them Baron Steuben. Gen. Knox gave us an entertainment in the style of a prince. I had the honor to be seated next the Baron, who is a hearty, sociable old fellow. He was dressed in his military uniform, and with the ensigns of nobility, the star and garter. Every gentleman at the table was of the 'Cincinnati,' except myself, and wore his appropriate badges. Spent the evening at Dr. Holton's with Col. Duer and several members of Congress, who informed me that an ordinance was passed in consequence of my petition, but, by their account of it, it will answer no purpose.

July 20*th*.—This morning the Secretary of Congress furnished me with the ordinance of yesterday, which states the conditions of a contract, but on terms to which I shall by no means accede. I informed the committee of Congress that I could not contract on the conditions proposed; that I should prefer purchasing lands from some of the states, who would give incomparably better terms; and therefore proposed to leave the city immediately. They appeared to be sorry no better terms were effected, and insisted on my not thinking of leaving Congress until another attempt was made. I told them I saw no prospect of contracting, and wished to spend no more time and money in a business so unpromising. They assured me that I had many friends in Congress, who would make every exertion in my favor; that it was an object of great magnitude, and that I must not expect to accomplish it in less than two or three months. If I desired it they would take the matter up that day on different grounds, and did not doubt they should obtain terms agreeable to my wishes. Col. Duer came to me with proposals from a number of the principal characters of the city, to extend our contract and take in another company—but that it should be kept a profound secret.* He explained the plan they had concerted, and offered me generous conditions if I would accomplish the business for them. The plan struck me agreeably; Sargent insisted on my undertaking, and both urged me not to think of giving the matter up so soon. I was convinced it was best for me to hold up the idea of giving up a contract with Congress, and making a contract with some of the states, which I did in the strongest terms, and represented to the committee and to Duer and Sargent the difficulties I saw in the way, and the improbability of closing a bargain when we were so far apart; and told them I conceived it not worth while to say anything further to Congress on the subject. This appeared to have the effect I wished. The committee were mortified, and did not seem to know what to say; but still urged another attempt. I left them in this state, but afterward explained my views to Duer and Sargent, who fully approved my plan. Promised Duer to consider his proposal. We had agreed last evening to make a party to Brooklyn, on Long Island, which is a small village opposite New York, divided from it by East river. Duer, Webb, Hammond, Sargent, with others, were of the party. When we landed, we ordered a dinner of fried oysters at the Stone House tavern. We took a walk on the highlands, and viewed several of the old forts

---

* This refers to the "Scioto Company," whose French settlement at Gallipolis was one of the most disastrous episodes of the day. The confused and mysterious accounts of it can not, even at this distance of time, be read without lively pity for the sufferings of the poor Frenchmen, and indignation at the authors of their misfortunes. With this, however, neither Dr. Cutler nor the Ohio Company had anything to do. Their action was all in good faith.

erected by the British. Our dinner was elegant. I spent the evening closeted with Colonel Duer, and agreed to purchase more land, if terms can be obtained, for another company, which will probably forward the negotiation.

Saturday, July 21*st.*—Several members of Congress called on me early this morning. They discovered much anxiety about a contract, and assured me that Congress, on finding I was determined not to accept their terms, and had proposed leaving the city, had discovered a much more favorable disposition, and believed, if I renewed my request, I might obtain conditions as reasonable as I desired. I was very indifferent, and talked much of the advantages of a contract with one of the states. This I found had the desired effect. At length I told them that if Congress would accede to the terms I proposed, I would extend the purchase from the tenth township from the Ohio and to the Scioto inclusively; by which Congress would pay more than four millions of the public debt; that our intention was *an actual, a large and immediate settlement* of the most robust and industrious people in America; and that it would be made systematically, which must instantly enhance the value of Federal lands, and prove an important acquisition to Congress. On these terms I would renew the negotiation, if Congress was disposed to take the matter up again. Dined with Gen. Webb, at the Mess House, in Broadway, opposite the Play House. Spent the evening with Mr. Dane and Mr. Milliken. They informed me that Congress had taken up my business again.

July 23*d.*—My friends had made every exertion, in private conversation to bring over my opponents in Congress. In order to get at some of them so as to work powerfully on their minds, we were obliged to engage three or four persons before we could get at them. In some instances we engaged one person, who engaged a second and he a third, and so on to the fourth before we could effect our purpose. In these maneuvers I am much beholden by the assistance of Col. Duer and Major Sargent. The matter was taken up this morning in Congress and warmly debated until three o'clock when another ordinance was obtained.* This was not to the minds of my friends, who were considerably increased in Congress, but they conceived it to be better than the former, and they had obtained an additional clause empowering the Board of Treasury to take order upon this ordinance and complete the contract on the general principles contained in it, which still left room for negotiation.

Spent the evening with Col. Grayson, and members of Congress from the southward, who were in favor of a contract. Having found it impossible to support Gen. Parsons as a candidate for Governor, after the interest that Gen. St. Clair had secured, and suspecting this might be some impediment in the way (for my endeavors to make interest for him were well known) and the arrangements for civil officers being on the carpet, I embraced this opportunity frankly to declare that for my own part—and ventured to engage for Major Sargent—if Gen. Parsons could have the appointment of First Judge, and Sargent, Secretary, we would be satisfied ; and that I heartily wished that His Excellency Gen. St. Clair might be Governor, and that I would solicit the Eastern members to favor such an arrangement. This I found rather pleasing to the Southern members and they were so complacent as to ask repeatedly what office would be agreeable to me in the Western country. I assured them I wished for no appointment in the civil line. Col. Grayson proposed the office of one of the Judges, which

---

* Ordinance of July 23d.

was seconded by all the gentlemen present. The obtaining an appointment, I observed, had never come into my mind, nor was there any civil office I should, at present, be willing to accept. This declaration seemed to be rather surprising, especially to men who were so much used to solicit or to be solicited for appointments of honor or profit. They seemed to be the more urgent on this head. I observed to them although I wished for nothing for myself, yet I thought the Ohio Company entitled to some attention; that one of our Judges, besides Gen. Parsons, should be of that body, and that Gen. Putnam was the man best qualified, and would be most agreeable to the Company, and gave them his character. We spent the evening very agreeably until a late hour.

July 24*th.*—I received this morning a letter from the Board of Treasury inclosing the resolutions of Congress which passed yesterday and requesting to know whether I was ready to close a contract on those terms. As the contract had now become of much greater magnitude than when I had only the Ohio Company in view, I felt a diffidence in acting alone, and wished Major Sargent to be joined with me, although he had not been formally empowered to act, for the commission from the directors was solely to me. It would likewise take off some part of the responsibility from me if the contract should not be agreeable. After consulting Duer, I proposed it to Sargent who readily accepted. We answered the letters from the Board as jointly commissioned in making the contract. We informed the Board that the terms in the Resolve of Congress were such as we could not accede to, without some variation. We therefore begged leave to state to the Board the terms on which we were ready to close the contract, and that those terms were our *ultimatum*. This letter * was sent to the Board, but the packet

---

* See Appendix.

having just arrived from England and another to sail next morning, it was not in their power to attend any further to our business for the day. Dined with Mr. Hillegas, Treasurer of the U. S. I spent the evening with Mr. Osgood, President of the Board of Treasury, who appeared very solicitous to be fully informed of our plan. No gentleman has a higher character for planning and calculating than Mr. Osgood; I was therefore much pleased with having an opportunity of fully explaining it to him. We were, unfortunately, interrupted with company; we, however, went over the outlines and he appeared to be well disposed.

July 25*th.*—This morning the Board of Treasury sent our letter to the Secretary of Congress, requesting him to lay it before Congress for their approbation or rejection. But the dispatches from Europe, received yesterday by the British packet, occupied the attention of Congress for the day. Mr. Osgood desired me to dine with him, assuring me that he had purposely omitted inviting any other company, that we might not be interrupted in going over our plan. I had been repeatedly assured that Mr. Osgood was my friend, and that he had censured Congress for not assenting to the terms I had offered; but, such is the intrigue and artifice often practiced by men in power, I felt very suspicious and was as cautious as possible. Our plan, however, I had no scruple to communicate and went over it in all its parts.

Mr. Osgood made many valuable observations. The extent of his information astonished me. His views of the continent of Europe were so enlarged that he appeared to be a perfect master of every subject of this kind. He highly approved of our plan, and told me he thought it the best formed in America. He dwelt much on the advantages of system in a new settlement—said system had never before been attempted; that we might depend on accomplishing our purposes in Europe, and that it was a most important part of our plan. If we were able to establish a settlement as we proposed, however small in the beginning, we should then have surmounted our greatest difficulty; that every other object would be within our reach, and, if the matter was pursued with spirit, he believed it would prove one of the greatest undertakings ever yet attempted in America. He thought Congress would do an especial service to the United States even if they gave us the land, rather than that our plan should be defeated, and promised to make every exertion in his power in my favor. We spent the afternoon and evening alone and very agreeably.

July 26th.—This morning I accompanied Gen. St. Clair and Gen. Knox on a tour of morning visits, particularly to the Foreign Ministers.

* * * * * * * *

It being now eleven o'clock Gen. St. Clair was obliged to attend Congress. After we came into the street, Gen. St. Clair assured us he would make every possible exertion to prevail with Congress to accept the terms contained in our letter. He appeared much interested and very friendly, but said we must expect opposition. I was fully convinced that it was good policy to give up Parsons, and openly to appear solicitous that St. Clair might be appointed Governor. Several gentlemen have told me that our matters went on much better since St. Clair and his friends had been informed that we had given up Parsons, and that I had solicited the Eastern members in favor of St. Clair's appointment. I immediately went to Sargent and Duer. We now entered into the true spirit of negotiation with great bodies. Every machine in the city that it was possible to set to work we now put in motion. Few, Bingham, and Kearney are our principal opposers. Of Few and Bingham there is hope, but to bring over that stubborn mule of a Kearney is beyond our power. The Board of Treasury, I think, will do us much service, if Dr. Lee is not against us—though Duer assures me that I have got the length of his foot, and that he calls me a frank, open, honest New England man, which he considers as an uncommon animal; yet from his jealous, cautious make, I feel suspicious of him, especially as Mr. Osgood tells me that he has made every attempt to learn his sentiments but is unable to do so. His brother, Richard Henry Lee, is certainly our fast friend, and we have hopes he will engage him in our interests. Dined with Sir John Temple in company with several gentlemen. Immediately after dinner I took my leave of them and called on Dr. Holton. He told me Congress had been warmly engaged in our business the whole day; that the opposition was lessened, but our friends did not think it prudent to come to a vote, lest there should not be a majority in favor. I felt much discouraged and told Dr. Holton I thought it in vain to wait any longer, and should certainly leave the next day. He cried out on my impatience; said if I obtained my purposes in a month from that time, I should be far more expeditious than was common in getting much smaller matters through Congress; that it was of great magnitude for it far exceeded any private contract ever made before in the United States; that if I should fail now I ought still to pursue the matter, for I should most certainly finally obtain the object I wished. To comfort me, he assured me it was impossible for him to conceive by what kind of address I had so soon and so warmly engaged the attention of Congress; for since he had been a member of that body he assured me, on his honor, that he never knew so much attention paid to any one person who made application to them on any kind of business, nor did he ever know them more pressing to bring it to a close. He could not have supposed that any three men from New England, even of the first characters, could have accomplished so much in so short a time. This, I believe, was mere flattery, though it was delivered with a very serious air; but it gave some consolation. I now learned very nearly who were for and who against the terms. Bingham has come over, but Few and Kearney are stubborn. Unfortunately there are only eight states represented, and, unless seven of them are in favor, no ordinance can pass.* Every moment of this evening until two o'clock was busily employed. A warm siege was laid on Few and Kearney from different quarters, and, if the point is not effectually carried, the attack is to be renewed in the morning. Duer, Sargent, and myself have agreed that if we fail, Sargent shall go on to Maryland, which is not at present represented, and prevail on the members of that state to come on, and interest themselves, if possible, in our plan. I am to go on to Connecticut and Rhode Island to solicit the members from those states to go on to New York, and to lay an anchor to windward with them. As soon as those states are represented, Sargent is to renew the application, and I have promised Duer that, if it be found necessary I will then return to New York again.

Friday, July 27th.—I rose very early this morning, and after adjusting my baggage (for I was determined to leave New York this day), I set out on a general morning visit and paid my respects to all the members of Congress in the city, and

---

* At this time the vote in Congress was taken by states, each state having but one vote.

informed them of my intention to leave the city that day. My expectations of forming a contract, I told them, were nearly at an end. I should, however, wait the decision of Congress, and if the terms which we had stated and which I considered to be very advantageous to Congress, considering the state of the country, were not accepted, we must turn our attention to some other part of the country. New York, Connecticut, and Massachusetts would sell us lands at half a dollar an acre, and give us exclusive privileges beyond what we had asked of Congress. The speculating plan concerted between the British of Canada and the New Yorkers was now well known. The uneasiness of the Kentucky people with respect to the Mississippi was notorious. A revolt of that country from the Union, if a war with Spain took place, was universally acknowledged to be highly probable; and most certainly a systematic settlement in that country, conducted by men strongly attached to the Federal Government and composed of young, robust, hardy, and active laborers, who had no idea of any other than the Federal Government, I conceived to be an object worthy of some attention. Besides, if Congress rejected the terms now offered, there could be no prospect of any application from any other quarter. If a fair and honorable purchase could now be obtained, I presumed contracts with the natives similar to that made with the Six Nations, must be the consequence, especially as it might be much more easily carried into effect. These, and such like, were the arguments I urged. They seemed to be fully acceded to, but whether they will avail is very uncertain. Mr. R. H. Lee assured me he was prepared for one hour's speech, and he hoped for success. All urged me not to leave the city so soon, but I assumed an air of perfect indifference and persisted in my determination, which had, apparently, the effect I wished. Passing the City Hall as the members were going into Congress, Col. Carrington told me he believed Few was secured; that little Kearney was left alone, and that he was determined to make one trial of what *he* could do in Congress. Called on Sir John Temple for letters to Boston. Bid my friends good bye, and, as it was my last day, Mr. Henderson insisted on my dining with him and a number of his friends whom he had invited.

At half past three, I was informed that an ordinance had passed Congress on the terms stated in our letter, without the least variation, and that the Board of Treasury was directed to *take order and close the contract.* This was agreeable but unexpected intelligence. Sargent and I went immediately to the Board, who had received the ordinance, but were then rising. They urged me to tarry the next day, and they would put by all other business to complete the contract; but I found it inconvenient, and after making a general verbal adjustment, left it with Sargent to finish what was to be done at present. Dr. Lee congratulated me, and declared he would do all in his power to adjust the terms of the contract, so far as was left to them, as much in our favor as possible. I proposed three months for collecting the first half million of dollars, and for executing the instruments of contract, which was acceded to. By this ordinance we obtained the grant of near five millions of acres of land, amounting to three and a half million dollars. One million and a half acres for the Ohio Company, and the remainder for a private speculation, in which many of the principal characters in America are concerned. Without connecting this speculation, similar terms and advantages could not have been obtained for the Ohio Company. On my return through Broadway, I received the congratulations of a number of my friends in Congress, and others, with whom I happened to meet."

Dr. Cutler left New York on the evening of this day—the 27th of July. On his homeward journey, he again called on Gen. Parsons at his home in Connecticut.

"When I had informed the General of my negotiations with Congress, I had the pleasure to find it not only met his approbation, but he expressed his astonishment that I had obtained terms so advantageous, which, he said, were beyond his expectation. He assured me he preferred the appointment of first judge to that of governor, especially if Gen. St. Clair was governor. He proposed writing to Gen. St. Clair and his friends in Congress, that they would procure an appointment for me on the same bench; but I absolutely declined, assuring him I had no wish to go in the civil line." *

On the 26th of July, Dr. Cutler and Mr. Sargent

---

* In an original memorandum, now before us, written by Dr. Cutler many years later, he says:

"On the 29th of August, 1787, I made a report to the directors and agents at a meeting in Boston, of the purchase and terms agreed upon by the Board of Treasury, and Sargent and myself. At this meeting a great number of the proprietors attended, all of whom fully approved of the proposed contract. Gen. Varnum was elected a director, and Richard Platt treasurer. Sargent and myself were directed to proceed to New York immediately, to make the first payment and complete the contract. At this meeting, Gen. Parsons and Gen. Varnum, two gentlemen eminent in the law, were requested to prepare the bonds for the directors and treasurer to execute. They did so."

had addressed a letter to the Board of Treasury, proposing to enter into a contract for the purchase of the lands described in the ordinance of July 23d.* On the 27th, their letter was referred by Congress to the Board of Treasury "to take order," but the contract was not finally executed till October 27th, 1787.

Of the grant thus obtained, amounting to nearly five million acres of land, only one million and a half were for the Ohio Company; and, owing to certain embarrassments in its affairs, the company finally became possessed of only nine hundred and sixty-four thousand two hundred and eighty-five acres. The whole tract bargained for by the Ohio Company for themselves is thus described: "From the seventh range of townships, extending along the Ohio southwesterly to the place where the west line of the seventeenth range of townships would intersect that river; thence northerly so far that a line drawn due east to the western boundary of said seventh range of townships would, with the other lines, include one million and a half acres of land, besides the reserves." These reserves were two townships for the purposes of a university, and the school and ministerial sections in each township. †

There has been a good deal of criticism about the alleged bad location of the Ohio Company's purchase,

---

* See Letter, Appendix.

† For what they finally came in possession of, see Appendix.

and some have held that they showed great lack of judgment in the matter. Why, it has been asked, did they choose the hilly and unattractive lands lying on the Hockhocking and the Raccoon, when they might as easily have selected the broad and fertile plains in the southwestern part of the state?

There were weighty considerations at the time of the purchase to justify the wisdom of their location. First, they had the protection of Fort Harmar, a well-established military post, garrisoned by government troops. Secondly, they were influenced by the remoteness of the Indian tribes, who had no fixed habitations in this region, and whose visits thither, though full of danger to the settlers and much dreaded, might be expected to be comparatively rare. They were also contiguous to Western Virginia, where the whites had some settlements pretty well advanced. Moreover, there is evidence that they knew of the existence, to some extent, of coal, salt, and iron, within the territory selected; and, finally, it was then believed that the communication between the Ohio river and Lake Erie, would be through the Cuyahoga and Muskingum rivers, and that a great trade would eventually grow up, flowing westwardly from the Potomac and James rivers, across the mountains and down the Kanawha. It is needless to say that not all of these considerations were well founded.

It is entirely clear from Dr. Cutler's Journal, that Thomas Hutchins, the "government geographer," had a great deal to do in deciding the location, if, indeed, his advice was not conclusive. He had formerly been a captain in the army, and had accompanied Col. Bouquet's celebrated expedition against the Indians, in 1764, as a military engineer. He wrote "A Description of the Ohio, Scioto, Kanawha, Wabash, and Illinois Rivers," which was published in London in 1778; also, "An Account of Florida, Louisiana, the Mississippi," etc., published at Philadelphia, 1784. He had traveled much through the western country, and had closely noted the comparative advantages of different regions. He advised Dr. Cutler, "by all means to make the location on the Muskingum." Mr. Hutchins's recommendation probably referred to the rich bottom lands on the upper Muskingum, a region at that time greatly exposed to Indian depredations. His advice was, however, followed to the extent of locating the Company's chief town at the mouth of the Muskingum, and extending the purchase from there southwestwardly into the interior and along the Ohio river.

The writer of a "View of Ohio" (Am. Quar. Rev. for March, 1833, p. 100), referring to this subject, says:

"The Ohio Company had their first choice within this rich and ample domain, but unfortunately selected the poorest tract in its whole compass. An anecdote is told, which, if true, would seem to indicate that their shrewdness, for once, over-reached itself. " It is said that when the party arrived at Wheeling, on their way to the settlement, they met with Ebenezer Zane, afterward the proprietor of Zanesville, and at that time familiar with the Ohio country. They asked his opinion as to the best place of location, and he, in honest simplicity, named several, either of which would have verified his recommendation. He did *not*, however, mention the tract about the mouth of the Muskingum. What could be the reason? Possibly he had an eye to it himself, and, if so, it must be the best. The party at once took up their line of march, and, without looking further, planted themselves there."

Thus, according to this writer, securing the region coveted because old Zane had not mentioned it.

This anecdote is quite incredible, for the palpable reason that the location had been decided upon, and even the plan for a city at the mouth of the Muskingum adopted, before the party left New England, or ever met Col. Zane.

Another version is given of Col. Zane's possible influence in fixing the location. General Samuel H. Parsons, one of the Ohio Company's directors, who strongly urged the location between the Muskingum and Scioto, had been appointed by the old congress a commissioner to treat with the Indian tribes of the west, and in the discharge of this duty, visited that country in 1785 and.'6. A writer in the North American Review (vol. 47), who states that his information was received direct from Gen. Putnam, says:

"After Gen. Parsons had examined the country immediately about the junction of the Muskingum with the Ohio, he proceeded up the valley of the former that he might have a view of the interior. Having gone many miles, he met one of the Zanes, four of which family were among the most noted of the frontier rangers. Zane was probably engaged in salt making, at Salt creek, which runs into the Muskingum about ten miles below the present town of Zanesville. Parsons, well knowing that the man he had chanced upon knew, from an acquaintance of fifteen years or more, the whole of what now forms the state of Ohio, asked his advice touching the location of the purchase which the Ohio Company proposed to make. Zane, having pondered the matter, and consulted with some of the old Delaware Indians that lived thereabout, recommended the General to choose either the Miami country or the valley of the Scioto, in preference to that which he was then examining. What it was that made Parsons doubt the good faith of the pioneer, we know not; but he came to the conclusion that Zane really preferred the Muskingum to any other point, and wished to purchase it himself, when the sales should begin, in a few months. This impression did away what little doubt still remained in his mind; and returning to the east, he laid his proposal to contract with Congress for all the land along the Ohio, between the seventh range of townships and the Scioto, and running back as might be afterward agreed upon, before the directors of the Company of Associates."

There may be some foundation for this anecdote, thus reiterated, but it appears doubtful.

After all, the location was not the worst that might have been made. The purchase undoubtedly included a large amount of rough and broken land; but it also included many tracts of beautiful farming country, well watered, well timbered, healthful, and fertile. And whatever reasons were wanting fifty years ago to justify the wisdom of the location, have been furnished in later days by the solid agricultural growth of the counties included in the purchase, and by their great and rapidly developing mineral wealth. Agricultural interests are ever the earliest to be developed; but, in the long run, the mineral resources of a country are equally important to its wealth and supporting power. The vast deposits of coal and iron in Athens county and adjacent regions, are but just beginning to be utilized, and the time may yet come when the "Ohio Company's Purchase," which they were laughed at for selecting, and which, in later years, has been stigmatized as the "Huckleberry Knobs," will support a swarming population. Those hills will some day smoke with forges, foundries, and manufactories of iron. They will be honey-combed with innumerable tunnels, from which will be taken the precious deposits of coal there concealed, and a million freemen may yet inhabit those counties, which, while their wealth lay hidden, were disregarded for more fertile parts, but which, when developed, will furnish forth the wealth of an empire.

CHAPTER III.

From 1787 to 1796.

THEIR purchase being now fully consummated and the Company having been put in immediate possession of seven hundred and fifty thousand acres, they at once began to arrange details and prepare for emigration. A meeting of the directors and agents of the Company was held at Brackett's Tavern, in Boston, on the 21st of November, 1787, at which it was

"*Resolved,* That the lands of the Ohio Company may be alloted and divided in the following manner, anything to the contrary in former resolutions notwithstanding, viz: four thousand acres near the confluence of the Ohio and Muskingum rivers for a city and commons, and, contiguous to this, one thousand lots of eight acres each, amounting to eight thousand acres.

Upon the Ohio, in fractional townships, one thousand lots of one hundred and sixteen acres and $\frac{43}{100}$, amounting to one hundred and sixteen thousand four hundred and eighty acres.

In the townships on the navigable rivers, one thousand lots of three hundred and twenty acres each, amounting to three hundred and twenty thousand acres.

And in the inland towns, one thousand lots of nine hundred and ninety-two acres each, amounting to nine hundred and ninety-two thousand acres, to be divided and allotted as the agents shall hereafter direct.

Resolved, further, That there be the following reservations, viz: one township at the falls of the Great Hockhocking river; one township at the mouth of the Great or Little river of that name; and one township opposite to the mouth of the Great Kanawha river; which reservations may hereafter be allotted and divided as the directors and agents shall see fit.

Resolved, That the army bounty rights be considered in part payment of the shares of military associates in the ratio of one dollar to every acre to which they are entitled; and that this rule be observed by the agents of the subscribers in rendering their returns, and by the agents appointed by the directors for the second payment to the Board of Treasury.

Resolved, That no further subscriptions be admitted after the 1st day of January next, and that all interest arising on sums paid since the payment of the first half million to the Board of Treasury, until the second payment be completed, shall accrue to the benefit of the Company's funds; and that the agents pay all the money they may have in their possession into the treasury of the Company by the 1st day of March next.

Resolved, That the eight-acre lots be surveyed and a plat or map thereof be made, with each lot numbered thereon, by the first Wednesday in March next, and that a copy thereof be immediately forwarded to the secretary and the original retained by the Company's superintendent; that the agents meet on the same Wednesday in March, at Rice's Tavern, in Providence, State of Rhode Island, to draw for said lots in numbers as the same shall be stated upon the plat; that a list of the drawings be transmitted by the secretary to the superintendent, and a copy thereof preserved in the secretary's office.

Resolved, That this meeting of the directors and agents of the Ohio Company be and it is hereby adjourned to the first Wednesday in March, 1788, to be then holden at Rice's Tavern in the town of Providence and State of Rhode Island."*

Much of the foregoing resolutions relative to the allotments, division, and reservations of land, became of no effect, because, as before stated, the Company finally came in possession of only nine hundred and sixty-four thousand two hundred and eighty-five acres.

Prior to the March meeting, above ordered, a meeting was held on the 23d of November at Brackett's Tavern, when it was

" *Ordered,* That four surveyors be employed under the superintendent hereinafter named ; that twenty-two men shall attend the surveyors ; that there be added to this number twenty men, including six boat-builders, four house-carpenters, one blacksmith and nine common workmen :

That the boat-builders shall proceed on Monday next, and the surveyors shall rendezvous at Hartford, the 1st day of January next, on their way to the Muskingum :

That the boat-builders and men, with the surveyors, be proprietors in the company ; that their tools and one axe and

---

*Journals of the Ohio Company.

one hoe to each man and thirty pounds weight of baggage, shall be carried in the company's wagons, and the subsistence of the men on their journey be furnished by the company.

That upon their arrival at the places of destination, and entering on the business of their employment, the men shall be subsisted by the company and allowed wages at the rate of four dollars each, per month, until discharged.

That they be held in the company's service until the first day of July next, unless sooner discharged, and that if any of the persons employed shall leave the service, or willfully injure the same, or disobey the orders of the superintendent, or others acting under him, the person so offending shall forfeit all claim to wages.

That their wages shall be paid the next autumn, in cash, or lands, upon the same terms as the company purchased them. That each man furnish himself with a good small arm, bayonet, six flints, a powder-horn and pouch, priming-wire and brush, half a pound of powder, one pound of balls, and one pound of buckshot. The men so engaged shall be subject to the orders of the superintendent, and those he may appoint, as aforesaid, in any kind of business they shall be employed in, as well for boat building and surveying, as for building houses, erecting defences, clearing land, and planting, or otherwise, for promoting the settlement; and, as there is a probability of interruption from enemies, they shall also be subject to orders as aforesaid in military command, during the time of their employment.

That Col. Ebenezer Sproat, from Rhode Island, Mr. Anselm Tupper and Mr. John Matthews, from Massachusetts, and Col. R. J. Meigs, from Connecticut, be the surveyors.

That Gen. Rufus Putnam be the superintendent of all the business aforesaid, and he is to be obeyed and respected accordingly; that he be allowed for his services forty dollars a month and his expenses, to commence from the time of his leaving home."

The next meeting was held March 5th, 1788, at Rice's Tavern, in Providence, Rhode Island. At this meeting, the drawing for lots in the new city took place, as had been previously ordered. A committee was also appointed, consisting of the Rev. Dr. Cutler, Col. May, and Gen. Varnum, "to consider and report upon the expediency of employing some suitable person as a public teacher at the settlement now making by the Ohio Company." The committee reported:

"That the directors be requested to pay as early attention as possible to the education of youth and the promotion of public worship among the first settlers; and that, for these important services, they employ, if practicable, an instructor eminent for literary accomplishments and the virtue of his character, who shall also superintend the first scholastic institutions and direct the manner of instruction; and to enable the directors to carry into execution the intentions expressed in this resolution, the proprietors, and others of benevolent and liberal minds, are earnestly requested to contribute, by voluntary donation, to the forming of a fund to be solely appropriated thereto."

The report being approved, the directors authorized Dr. Cutler to employ some suitable person, who should discharge the double functions of preacher and teacher. Thus early and clearly did the founders of the new state recognize the fact that republican institutions are based on the intelligence and virtue of the people, and that there can be no liberty without light. Dr. Cutler engaged the Rev. Daniel Story, a young minister then preaching at Worcester, Massachusetts; and to him belongs the distinguished honor of being *the first regularly ordained Congregational minister* in all the territory northwest of the Ohio river.*

---

*See ordination sermon, preached by the Rev. Dr. Cutler, Aug. 15, 1798. Appendix, H.

The following extract is from a letter of Dr. Cutler to Gen. Putnam, now before us:

"*Ipswich, November* 18, 1788.

"DEAR SIR: This will be handed you by Mr. Daniel Story, whom I beg leave to introduce to your acquaintance in character of a preacher, and who, I hope, will be very agreeable to you and to the people. He has ever supported a respectable character in private life and as a minister of the Gospel. The terms on which he goes into the country are, that his board be given him; that he draw from the funds, raised to support preaching four dollars, in silver, per week; that he be permitted to improve, if he pleases, a part of the lands, near the city, granted for religious purposes; that the people be requested to assist in clearing and cultivating, so far at least as shall render his pay equal to five dollars per week; and that he be allowed a reasonable compensation for his expenses in going into the country. These were the lowest terms on which he would consent to go. He could have his board and five dollars a week here, and constant employ. As he must lose several Sabbaths in going into the country, he conceived it reasonable that he should have a consideration for his expenses. There was no other person of respectable character, whom I could engage on better terms. This is to be

Pursuant to the orders of the directors, the boat-builders and mechanics, under the command of Major Haffield White, rendezvoused at Danvers, Massachusetts, in December, 1787. The party consisted of twenty-two men. The arrangements being completed they set out for Sumrill's Ferry, on the Youghiogheny river, about thirty miles above Pittsburg, where it was intended to build boats, and proceed thence by water. After a long and difficult journey, they reached this point toward the last of January, and immediately began their work of boat building.

Meanwhile, the surveyors with their attendants, and the remainder of the pioneer party, having met at Hartford, Connecticut, early in January, 1788, commenced their march westward, under the command of Gen. Rufus Putnam, assisted by Col. Ebenezer Sproat. When they reached the mountains, it was found that the great depth of snow there rendered the crossing impossible, save by the use of sleds, which were accordingly constructed, and the baggage by this means transported over the Alleghanies, and on to Sumrill's

---

his pay until other terms shall be agreed on between him and the directors, or the people, or till he shall continue no longer to preach to them.

*　*　*　*　*　*　*　*　*　*　*

I have requested Col. Platt to forward a sum raised for the support of preachers and schoolmasters, to the directors at Muskingum, of two hundred dollars, if he has so much on hand, which will enable you to pay the preacher and schoolmaster for the present. I have advanced to Mr. Story six dollars and two thirds, on account, which you will deduct from his wages."

Ferry, the general rendezvous, where Putnam's party arrived about the middle of February.

With the working force thus largely increased, and urged on by the energetic superintendence of Gen. Putnam in person, the boat building, which had lagged somewhat, owing to the severity of the weather, now progressed rapidly.

On the 2d of April, 1788, the largest boat was launched, and the pioneers left Sumrill's. In addition to the large boat, forty-five feet long and twelve wide, which was roofed over, and had an estimated capacity of fifty tons, there were a flatboat and three canoes. Laden with the emigrants, their baggage, surveying instruments, weapons, and effects, the little flotilla glided down the Youghiogheny into the Monongahela, and finally out upon the broad bosom of the Ohio, which stream was to bear them to their new home. For several days and nights they pursued their solitary travel, urged along only by the current of the beautiful river, whose banks gave no signs of civilized life, nor of welcome to the pioneers. Occasionally, a flock of wild turkeys in the underbrush, or a startled deer, drinking at the water's edge, would draw the fire of the riflemen from the boats; and now and then the dusky form of an Indian would be seen darting into the forest. But the emigrants met with no interruption.

On the fifth day they approached their destination. It was cloudy and raining as they drew near the mouth of the Muskingum, and Capt. Jonathan Devol suggested to Gen. Putnam that a close look-out be kept as they must be near their landing-place. In a few moments they came within sight of Fort Harmar (a U. S. fort erected in 1785), located at the mouth and on the right bank of the Muskingum. The hanging branches of the trees on the bank of the river, combined with the foggy atmosphere, that day, partially obscured the river's mouth, so that the boat floated almost beyond it before it was discovered. They could not regain the upper bank of the Muskingum, and were obliged to make fast a little way below Fort Harmar. The commander of the fort sent some soldiers to their aid, and the boat was towed back with ropes and across the Muskingum, where it landed, at the upper point, about noon on the 7th of April, 1788, and from that day Ohio dates her existence.

The pioneers immediately began to unload their effects. The boards which they had brought with them for the erection of temporary huts were landed and properly disposed, and a comfortable tent was at once set up for the use of Gen. Putnam. In this tent he had his headquarters and transacted the business of the colony for several months, until the block-houses were ready for occupancy.

The following is a list of the first party of emigrants to the territory northwest of the Ohio, who became the founders of Marietta, and the first settlers of Washington and Athens counties, viz:

Gen. Rufus Putnam, superintendent; Col. Ebenezer Sproat, Col. R. J. Meigs, Maj. Anselm Tupper, and Mr. John Matthews, surveyors; Maj. Haffield White, steward and quartermaster; Capt. Jonathan Devol, Capt. Josiah Munroe, Capt. Daniel Davis, Peregrine Foster, Capt. Jethro Putnam, Capt. William Gray, Capt. Ezekiel Cooper, Jervis Cutler, Samuel Felshaw, Hezekiah Flint, Hezekiah Flint, jr., Amos Porter, Josiah Whitridge, John Gardiner, Benjamin Griswold, Elizur Kirkland, Samuel Cushing, Oliver Dodge, Isaac Dodge, Jabez Barlow, Daniel Bushnell, Ebenezer Corry, Phineas Coburn, Allen Putnam, David Wallace, Joseph Wells, Gilbert Devol, jr., Israel Danton, Jonas Davis, Theophilus Leonard, Joseph Lincoln, William Miller, Earl Sproat, Josiah White, Allen Devol, Henry Maxon, William Maxon, William Moulton, Edmund Moulton, Simeon Martin, Benjamin Shaw, and Peletiah White.

The situation of the colonists was now interesting and critical. Lodged in the midst of a vast wilderness, many hundred miles from home and from the protecting care of government, surrounded by bands of hostile savages, who, though quiet at present, were apt to become deadly foes at any moment; and but scantily supplied with the means of living, the brave pioneers had need of all their energies to prepare for the future. No time was lost in providing for the protection and comfortable subsistence of the colony. General Putnam immediately began the erection of a fort, near the Muskingum river, comprising a block-house, and other means of defense, which was afterward, during periods of Indian hostilities, crowded with families, and became of the utmost importance. The gigantic trees of the forest were girdled and deadened, the rich soil easily prepared for seeding, and about one hundred and thirty acres of corn were planted this first spring. The rivers abounded with fish; game of every sort was found in the greatest plenty; herds of buffaloes and deer roamed the forests, and innumerable flocks of wild turkeys were added to supply the settlement with fresh meat.

The day after their landing, the surveyors commenced laying off lots, and preparing for the expected arrival of other emigrants. The officers of the territory not having yet arrived, a series of regulations or laws for the temporary government of the community was prepared and promulgated by being nailed to the trunk of a large tree on the river bank. This code was rigidly observed till other laws were regularly enacted, and under it the peace of the settlement was never once disturbed. All was energy, industry, prosperity, and hopefulness for the future. Well might Washington write:

"No colony in America was ever settled under such favorable auspices as that which has just commenced at the Muskingum. Information, property, and strength will be its characteristics. I know many of the settlers personally, and there never were men better calculated to promote the welfare of such a community." *

The little city at the mouth of the Muskingum was first called *Adelphia*. There were some men of classical education among the directors, and a harmless pedantry was evinced in some of the names adopted by them. Thus the large public square was called *Quadranaon*, and the smaller one the *Capitolium*. The wide road, leading up from the river landing to the square, was named *Sacra via*, and the fort, with its inclosure of block-houses, etc., was called *Campus Martius*. At a meeting of the directors, held on the 2d of July, 1788, which was the first convened west of the mountains, the name of the city was changed by the following resolution: †

---

* Sparks's Washington, vol. 9, p. 385.

† The original name was suggested by Dr. Cutler. In a letter to Gen. Putnam, dated Ipswich, December 3, 1787, after speaking of the affairs of the company, and the best means of forwarding letters to and from the settlement, Dr. Cutler says:

"Saying so much about conveying of letters, reminds me of the necessity of a name for the place where you will reside. I doubt not you will early acquire the meaning of Muskingum; or you may meet with some other name that will be agreeable. At present, I must confess, I feel a partiality for the name proposed at Boston, and think it preferable to any that has yet been mentioned. I think that *Adelphia* will, upon the whole, be the most eligible. It strictly means *Brethren*, and I wish it may ever be characteristic of the Ohio Company."

"*Resolved*, That the city near the confluence of the Ohio and Muskingum be called *Marietta;* that the directors write to his Excellency, the Count Moustiers (French Minister), informing him of their motives in naming the city, and request his opinion whether it will be advisable to present to her Majesty of France a public square."

The name is compounded from that of the unfortunate young queen of France, Marie Antoinette, who had manifested a constant friendship for the United States during the Revolutionary war.

While the infant colony of the Ohio Company is being thus auspiciously planted, and the herculean task of subduing the wilderness well begun, let us glance at the measures taken by congress to establish government, law, and order within the territory.

The settlement at the mouth of the Muskingum was made before the arrival in the territory of the governor and judges. Congress, however, had organized the territorial government soon after the passage of the ordinance of 1787. Gen. Arthur St. Clair was appointed governor, his commission bearing date February 1, 1788, and to run for three years. He was a citizen of Pennsylvania, had been a distinguished officer in the Revolutionary army, and president of congress, and stood high in the confidence of Washington.

Samuel H. Parsons, of Connecticut, James M. Varnum, of Massachusetts (both of whom were directors in the Ohio Company), and John Cleves Symmes, of New Jersey, were appointed judges; and Winthrop Sargent, of New Hampshire (secretary of the Ohio Company), was appointed secretary of the territory. The judges arrived in June, and on the 9th of July, 1788, Governor St. Clair reached Marietta. He was escorted by a detachment of troops, under Major Doughty, who had gone up to Pittsburg, from Fort Harmar, some days before to meet the governor, and was received at the fort with military honors and salute. Joseph Buell, who was an orderly sergeant at the time, in one of the companies of United States troops in the fort, kept a journal, in which he says:

"*July 9th.*—Governor St. Clair arrived at the garrison. On landing, he was saluted with thirteen rounds from the field-piece. On entering the garrison the music played a salute, and the troops paraded and presented their arms. He was also saluted by a clap of thunder and a heavy shower of rain as he entered the fort; and thus we received our governor of the western frontiers."

After a few days of repose, the governor, on the 18th of July, made his first public appearance before the citizens of the territory. At three o'clock in the afternoon he came over from Fort Harmar in the government barge, escorted by the officers of the garrison, and accompanied by Mr. Sargent, the secretary. He was received in the grove by Gen. Putnam, the judges of the territory, and the principal inhabitants of the settlement, with congratulations and expressions of welcome. The secretary then proceeded to read the ordinance of July 13, 1787, for the government of the territory, and also the commissions of the governor, the judges, and himself. The governor then delivered an inaugural address, to which a response was made "in the name of all the people," and the ceremonies concluded with cheers and congratulations.

We may here digress, a few moments, to remark upon the unique form of civil government thus inaugurated, and formally established in the territory, and which was continued for a period of ten years. It was the first territorial government ever organized by Federal authority, and was, in some respects, crude and anomalous. The people had no part whatever in the government. The governor and judges derived their appointments first from congress, and, after the adoption of the Federal constitution, in 1789, from the president. There were no elective officers. The whole power, legislative, judicial, and executive was vested in the governor and judges, and in its exercise they were responsible only to the remote central government. A portion of the expenses of the government were borne by the United States, but the principal part were drawn from the people of the territory by heavy taxes.

This temporary system, however, crude as it now

seems, worked reasonably well in most respects, and though in some points it was unfriendly to the large liberty of the people, we must never forget the noble principles that were secured to the embryo states of the northwest by the famous ordinance of 1787. In language whose dignity befits the lofty theme, it provides "for extending the fundamental principles of civil and religious liberty, which form the basis whereon these republics, their laws and constitutions, are erected; and for fixing and establishing those principles as the basis of all laws, constitutions, and governments, which forever hereafter shall be formed in said territory." It secured for all time civil and religious liberty, *habeas corpus*, and other fundamental rights. It enacts that, "religion, morality, and knowledge being necessary to good government and the happiness of mankind, schools, and the means of education, shall forever be encouraged." Finally, it provided that, in the vast area over which it extended, slavery should never exist. Thus, perpetual freedom was secured to the states of the northwest. The borders of Ohio were consecrated while the wilderness was yet unbroken, and long before the state was formed; and the pioneers who landed at the mouth of the Muskingum trod upon a soil which could bear up none but free men.

By the ordinance of 1787, the governor and judges, or a majority of them, were empowered to adopt and publish in the district, such laws of the old states, civil and criminal, as they saw fit, and were to report them to congress from time to time. But they did not confine themselves very strictly to the letter of the ordinance in this regard; for when they could not find laws of the old states suited to the wants and condition of the territory, they made enactments of their own—all of which were, a few years later, ratified and confirmed by the first territorial legislature.

The first law enacted for the territory was passed July 25th, 1788, and was thus entitled:

"A LAW for regulating and establishing the MILITIA in the Territory of the United States northwest of the river Ohio, published at the city of Marietta upon the twenty-fifth day of July, in the thirteenth year of the Independence of the United States, and of our Lord one thousand seven hundred and eighty-eight, by his Excellency, ARTHUR ST. CLAIR, Esquire, Governor and Commander-in-chief, and by the Honorable SAMUEL HOLDEN PARSONS and JAMES MITCHELL VARNUM, Esquires, Judges." *

Almost the first public act of the governor, was creating the county of Washington, the first county estab-

---

* Laws passed in the territory of the United States, northwest of the river Ohio, from the commencement of the government to the 31st of December, 1791. Published by authority. Philadelphia, 1792, p. 3.

lished in the great northwestern territory, and, as its boundaries were then fixed, comprising about one half of the present state of Ohio. The proclamation is as follows:

"*By his Excellency, Arthur St. Clair, Esq., Governor and Commander-in-Chief of the territory of the United States, northwest of the river Ohio.*

"A PROCLAMATION.

To all persons to whom these presents shall come, Greeting:

WHEREAS, By the ordinance of Congress of the thirteenth of July, 1787, for the government of the territory of the United States northwest of the river Ohio, it is directed that for the due execution of process, civil and criminal, the governor shall make proper divisions of the said territory and proceed from time to time, as circumstances may require, to lay out the part of the same, where the Indian title has been extinguished, into counties and townships, subject to future alterations as therein specified. Now, know ye, that it appearing to me to be necessary, for the purposes above mentioned, that a county should immediately be laid out, I have ordained and ordered, and by these presents do ordain and order that all and singular the lands lying and being within the following boundaries, viz.: Beginning on the bank of the Ohio River, where the western boundary line of Pennsylvania crosses it, and running with that line to Lake Erie; thence along the southern shore of said lake to the mouth of the Cuyahoga river; thence up said river to the portage between that and the Tuscarawas branch of the Muskingum; thence down the branch to the forks, at the crossing place above Fort Laurens; thence with a line to be drawn westerly to the portage of that branch of the Big Miami, on which the fort stood that was taken by the French in 1752, until it meets the road from the lower Shawanese town to the Sandusky; thence south to the Scioto river, thence with that river to the mouth, and thence up the Ohio river to the place of beginning; shall be a county, and the same is hereby erected into a county named and to be called hereafter the county of Washington; and the said county of Washington shall have and enjoy all and singular, the jurisdiction, rights, liberties, privileges and immunities whatever to a county belonging and appertaining, and which any other county, that may hereafter be erected and laid out, shall or ought to enjoy, conformably to the ordinance of Congress before mentioned. In witness whereof, I have hereunto set my hand and caused the seal of the territory to be affixed, this twenty-sixth day of July, in the thirteenth year of the Independence of the United States, and in the year of our Lord, one thousand seven hundred and eighty-eight.

[Signed]   A. St. Clair."

The "Law for establishing General Courts of Quarter Sessions of the Peace," published at Marietta August 23d, 1788,* provided that that court should be held at Marietta four times in every year by justices of the peace appointed and commissioned by the governor. There were to be "a competent number" of these justices in each county, not less

---

* Laws of North West Territory, p. 7.

than three nor more than five of whom (to be specially named by commission), should hold the courts of quarter sessions. Any three of them, one being of the quorum specifically named, might hold special sessions when occasion required.

The county court of common pleas was to be held semi-annually by not less than three nor more than five judges to be appointed in each county and commissioned by the governor. A sheriff was to be appointed in each county by the governor.

The "General Court of the Territory of the United States northwest of the river Ohio,"* composed of the judges appointed and commissioned by the Federal authority, was to hold four terms yearly in such counties as the judges should from time to time deem most conducive to the general good. Only one term yearly was to be held in any one county; and all processes, civil and criminal, were returnable to said court wheresoever it might be in the territory.

The first judges of the court of common pleas were Rufus Putnam, Benjamin Tupper and Archibald Crary. Return J. Meigs was appointed clerk of the court, and Col. Ebenezer Sproat sheriff, which office he held for fourteen years till the formation of the state government. The first judges of the courts of general quarter sessions were Rufus Putnam and Benjamin Tupper (justices of the quorum), and

---

* Laws of North West Territory, p. 11.

Isaac Pierce, Thomas Lord and Return J. Meigs, assistant justices.

General Putnam resigned his position as judge of the quorum in 1790, and Joseph Gilman, formerly of New Hampshire, was appointed in his place; and on the death of Judge Tupper, in June 1792, Robert Oliver was appointed judge of the quorum to fill the vacancy.

Meanwhile, notwithstanding the difficulties and dangers attending western emigration, and the perils that surrounded the little settlement, there began to be some arrivals from the east. During the month of August, 1788, eight families arrived from New England, which increased the population of the colony to one hundred and thirty-two men, with some women and children. At the beginning of the year 1789, there was not a single white family within the present bounds of Ohio save those in this settlement. The settlement at Cincinnati did not begin till the spring of 1789. Flint, himself a pioneer, in his "Indian Wars of the West," thus speaks of early emigration:

"The writer of this distinctly remembers the wagon that carried out a number of adventurers from the counties of Essex and Middlesex in Massachusetts, on the second emigration to the woods of the Ohio. He remembers the black canvas covering of the wagon; the white and large lettering in capitals '*To Marietta on the Ohio!*' He remembers the food which, even then, the thought of such a distant expedition furnished to his imagination. Some twenty emigrants accompanied the wagon. The Rev. Dr. Manasseh Cutler, he thinks, had the direction of this band of emigrants.

*   *   *   *   *   *   *   *   *   *   *

General Putnam seems to have been the only one who preceded him in claims to be the patriarch of the Marietta settlement. Dr. Cutler, at the time of his being engaged in the speculation of the Ohio Company's purchase, had a feud—it is not remembered whether literary, political, or religious—with the late learned and eccentric Dr. Bentley, of Salem, Massachusetts. Dr. Bentley was then chief contributor to a paper (*Salem Register*) which he afterward edited. The writer still remembers and can repeat doggerel verses by Dr. Bentley upon the departure of Dr. Cutler on his first trip to explore his purchase on the Ohio.

The first travelers to explore Ohio, availed themselves of the full extent of the traveler's privilege in regard to the wonders of this new land of promise, and the unparalleled fertility of the soil. These extravagant representations of the grandeur of the vegetation, and the fertility of the land, at first excited a great desire to emigrate to this new and wonderful region. But some returned with different accounts, in discouragement, and the hostility of the savages was painted in the most appalling colors. A reaction took place in the public mind. The wags of the day exercised their wit in circulating caricatured and exaggerated editions of the stories of the first adventurers, that there were springs of brandy, flax that bore little pieces of cloth on the stems, enormous pumpkins, and melons, and the like. Accounts the most horrible were added of hoop snakes of such deadly malignity that a sting which they bore in their tails, when it punctured the bark of a green tree, instantly caused its leaves to become sear and the tree to die. Stories of Indian massacres and barbarities were related in all their horrors. The country was admitted to be fertile; but was pronounced excessively sickly, and poorly balancing by that advantage all those counterpoises of sickness, Indians, copperheaded and hoop snakes, bears, wolves, and panthers.

The tendency of the New England mind to enterprise and emigration thus early began to develop. For all these horrors, portrayed in all their darkness, and with all the dreadful imaginings connected with the thought of such a remote and boundless wilderness, did not hinder the departure of great numbers of the people, following in the footsteps of Gen. Putnam and Dr. Cutler. They were both men of established character, whose words and opinions wrought confidence. Dr. Cutler was a man of various and extensive learning. He was particularly devoted to the study of natural history, and was among the first who began scientifically to explore the botany of our country. He had great efficiency in founding the upper settlement (the Ohio Company's) in Ohio, and his descendants are among the most respectable inhabitants of the country at present."

During the year 1789 there were added to the colony one hundred and fifty-two men and fifty-seven families.

Thus the love of adventure and the migratory instincts of the New England people, year after year impelled little bands of pioneers to set their faces toward Ohio, and the settlements steadily, though slowly, increased. By long and toilsome journeys, carrying their effects in wagons, camping out at night, and subsisting chiefly on the game which they killed by the way, these brave emigrants crossed the mountains to the head waters of the Ohio, whence they proceeded in large canoes or small flatboats down that river to their various destinations. Arrived there, they were beset with perils and difficulties of the most serious character. There were perils of famine which they more than once bitterly experienced, perils of flood, of Indians, and exposure of every sort. Yet the resolute New Englanders not only successfully combated all these enemies, but, in the midst of the struggle, found time to secure civil rights, establish law and order, introduce a pure religion, and provide for universal education.

"The most exalted sentiments arise on the consideration of the nature of those men who first broke in upon the forest-world of the West, and successfully planted civilization in the midst of the fiercest barbarism. Their like is never to be known again. In the progress and mutations of human affairs such a concourse of circumstances will never arise. There can never be another such revolution as that of 1776. If that was possible, will there be again such patriots, such men? Then came the weakness of their country and their own impoverishment; afterward the offer of the western lands in compensation for military service, but requiring the protection of military force. The never-lessening patience, perseverance, and piety of those stern characters have no parallel. With all these traits we behold the hourly exercise of courage, the cool contemplation of danger, acuteness of design, and vigor of execution." *

By the year 1790 a perceptible current of emigration had began to set from the older states to the western country, and Marietta and Cincinnati, the only two points yet settled, promised to become the nuclei of prosperous colonies. The inroad on the wilderness commenced, and, little by little, civilization was making good its advance. The sound of the pioneer's axe was heard, though in but few and widely-separated localities, and the smoke of his cabin chimney ascended from more than one peaceful settlement. Clearings were made, crops and families began to be raised, and the new-comers were taking root in the soil.

But from this peaceful dream there came a sudden and terrible awakening, in the Indian war which now burst upon the settlements with great fury. Indian aggressions had been growing in frequency during the past year or more. The Marietta settlers were peaceable men, who desired to treat the natives justly, and, if possible, to avoid warfare. But the frontier population of Virginia, the "Longknives," as they were called by the Indians, and those of Kentucky, were a different class of men. Born and bred hunters, and

---

*Whittlesey's Fugitive Essays, p. 24.

always ready for a deadly conflict, they regarded the Indians as vermin, or wild beasts, who were to be shot on sight. This treatment had engendered with the savages a mortal hatred of the whites, and the Ohio Company's settlers were, to some extent, included in their bitter hostility. They regarded the white men as their natural enemies, and, notwithstanding treaty stipulations, resented their settlement on the ancient hunting grounds as an intrusion, and cause of war. Thus, for a year or two past, the incursions and attacks of the Indians had become so frequent as to cause apprehension of a general war. They had announced their purpose of destroying every settlement, and putting out every white man's fire north of the Ohio river. To avert the impending danger, the government first tried negotiations; but, these proving futile, and the depredations growing more frequent and disastrous, General Harmar was directed to attack their towns.

In September, 1790, with thirteen hundred men, he marched from Cincinnati, through the wilderness, to the Indian villages on the Miami, which he burned. On his homeward march he was attacked by a superior force of savages, and, after a desperate battle, was totally defeated. Harmar was barely able to make good his retreat to Cincinnati. His expedition was a failure, and so far from restraining only served to embolden the Indians.

From this time, for four years, there was uninterrupted war with the Indians, and sad, indeed, were the calamities of the settlers. Wherever the settlements extended, the whole frontier was lighted by the flames of burning cabins and improvements. The first blow struck at the Ohio Company's purchase was on the 2d of January, 1791. On that day, it being a Sunday, the little settlement at Big Bottom, in Washington county, on the Muskingum river, was the scene of one of those bloody episodes, with which pioneer history abounds. We have not space to recount the event in its details; it was characterized by the usual horrible features of stealth and sudden surprise by the savages, of quick massacre and scalping of the victims, and of hasty retreat into the wilderness. In this attack twelve persons were killed, and five carried into captivity. [Hildreth's Pioneer History, pp. 431-439.]

The tidings of this bloody affair were borne to Marietta by special messenger, who reached there the morning after the massacre. The general court of quarter sessions was sitting, and had just convened, when the news arrived. The town was at once thrown into the utmost consternation. It was supposed that Marietta would be the next point attacked, and instant measures of safety were taken. The court hurriedly adjourned. Many of the jurors and witnesses in attendance, who were from Waterford, Belpre, and other exposed settlements, hastened at full speed to their homes, each one expecting, or, at least, fearing, to find his dear ones slaughtered, and his cabin reduced to ashes.

General Putnam, who was always the master spirit in important crises and whose foresight had prepared for such an emergency as this, instantly put Marietta in a state of defense. All the families within reach were summoned thither, and securely placed in the block-houses of the garrison. The defenses were strengthened, guards doubled, and four sentinels placed at each of the bastions of the fort. The garrison was kept under the strictest discipline. The ammunition was inspected and made accessible at a moment's notice, and four-pounder cannon were placed at two of the corners of the fort. The present safety of the people being secured, Gen. Putnam immediately wrote urgent letters to President Washington and to Gen. Knox, the secretary of war, informing them that the storm of Indian war had burst upon the frontiers, and imploring them, by every consideration, to send troops for the protection of the settlers.

At Belpre and at Waterford, the panic caused by the massacre was even greater, as their means of defense were less. Quite a number of families had joined these settlements during the years 1789 and '90, and there were several women and little children. The news was brought to the latter settlement about ten o'clock P. M. of January 2d. Men, women, and children were roused from their sleep by the fearful cry of "Indians," and woke to hear the story repeated with numberless exaggerations, to which, in their terror, they gave ready credence. It was believed, and not without reason, that the savages would fall upon them before daylight. All the inhabitants, amounting to about thirty souls, were hurriedly gathered into the largest and strongest cabin. Their most valuable portable property and necessary cooking utensils were brought in. A supply of water was hastily procured. The doors and windows were strongly barred. Interstices were made in the sides of the cabin, by punching out the chinking between the logs, for the men to fire through. Thus prepared, the rest of the night was passed in painful anxiety, and momentary expectation of attack. About daylight the Indians approached the cabin. Their forms were dimly seen by the sentinel, gliding among the trees, as if reconnoitering the position. The alarm was given, and the settlers awaited the onslaught with such firmness and composure as they could. The women and children were huddled into the safest corner of the cabin, and the men stood with finger on the trigger, prepared to fight it out.

But the attack did not come. Finding the inhabitants of the settlement awake and prepared for them, the Indians refrained from attacking the place. Having spent some time in reconnoitering, as day fairly dawned, they made off into the woods, and the settlement escaped.

Everywhere, throughout the territory, the same consternation prevailed. The exposed out-posts were abandoned, and the people rushed for safety to the block-houses and garrisons. This state of things filled President Washington with the utmost anxiety for the vigorous prosecution of the Indian war. A second army, in all respects superior to Harmar's, was assembled at Cincinnati. Governor Arthur St. Clair was placed in command. His force consisted of three regiments of infantry, two companies of artillery, one of cavalry, and about six hundred militia. With this army he marched toward the Indian towns on the Maumee.

Disaster followed St. Clair from the beginning. On the march, a considerable portion of the militia deserted in a body. A whole regiment was detached— a portion to pursue the deserters, and a portion to save the expeditionary stores, which it was feared the deserters intended to plunder. With his force thus weakened by desertion and details, St. Clair advanced into the enemy's country. On the morning of the 4th of November, 1791, just before daylight, he was attacked with great fury by the combined army of the northwestern tribes. The battle was short and the result decisive: St. Clair was totally defeated, with a loss of more than six hundred men.

The government had hitherto prosecuted the war with little vigor and weak determination. In fact, there was opposition to the Indian war, and reluctance to enter on a difficult and dangerous campaign. The country had, as yet, hardly begun to recover from the prostration that followed the revolutionary struggle. Industry was paralyzed, the debt burdensome, and the currency disordered. But no alternative was now left. The existence of all the western settlements, and, perhaps, even our possession of the territories already acquired from the Indians, depended on a vigorous prosecution of the war. President Washington made new appeals to congress, and, in spite of violent opposition from certain quarters, the necessary supplies were voted, and the Indian war went on.

General Anthony Wayne was now appointed to the command. He was an officer of revolutionary experience, great energy, personal enthusiasm, and executive ability. He arrived at Cincinnati in the spring of 1793, and began the work of organizing a third army. It was not, however, till July, 1794, that, with a force of about thirty-five hundred men, he marched against the Indians. They had collected their whole force, amounting to about two thousand men, at the Maumee rapids. Wayne encountered the Indians on the 20th of August. The battle which ensued resulted in the utter defeat of the Indians, and was the beginning of their downfall in the northwestern territory.

Wayne followed up his victory, and gathered all its fruits. He burned their villages, destroyed their growing crops, and laid waste their whole country. Forts were erected in the heart of their territory, and they were made to feel, as they had never felt before, the energy and power of the government. Convinced, at last, of their inability to maintain the contest, or resolved, perhaps, to accept their inevitable doom, they sued for peace. A general council was convened at Greenville (now in Darke county), at which Gen. Wayne represented the United States, and the following tribes were represented by their chiefs, viz: the Wyandots, Delawares, Shawanese, Ottawas, Chippewas, Putawatomies, Miamis, Eel-rivers, Kickapoos, Weeas, Piankashaws, and Kaskaskias. By the treaty here made, it was declared that "henceforth all hostilities shall cease; peace is hereby established and shall be perpetual; and a friendly intercourse shall take place between the said United States and Indian tribes." Prisoners were given up, boundary lines established, large cessions of land made, annual allowances of money to the Indians assured, certain hunting privileges granted, and provisions for trading agreed upon. *

This treaty was signed August 3, 1795, and became

---

* U. S. Stat. at Large, vol. 7, p. 49.

the basis of a permanent peace in this part of the country. The tomahawk was buried, the Indians gave up their ancient hunting grounds and the graves of their fathers, and the white man's title to the lands of Ohio was never again seriously contested.

The following anecdotes of Gen. Wayne are furnished to the author by the venerable Dr. C. F. Perkins, of Erie, Pennsylvania, formerly a resident of Athens:

Some time after the conclusion of the treaty above named, Gen. Wayne was stationed at Erie, Pennsylvania. During his last illness his distress was greatly augmented and his nerves much excited by clouds of smoke from an ill-constructed chimney in his military cabin. Sending for the unfortunate mason who had built the chimney (a worthy man by the name of Hughes), Gen. Wayne berated him with considerable violence, and threatened to severely chastise him on the morrow. But the mason escaped punishment, for the brave general died before the dawn of the next day.

The body of Gen. Wayne was interred in the military ground near the block-house at Erie and on the bay of Presque Isle. After it had rested for at least a few years undisturbed, his son came from Wyoming to Erie to look after the body of his deceased parent. It was exhumed and found to be undecayed and almost entire. The son wished to convey the body to Wyoming for interment, but he had traveled on horseback and had no vehicle. Beside, no wheeled vehicle could be drawn through the unbroken forest without the greatest labor. The question was what could be done? It was solved by an army surgeon, who suggested that if the bones were divested of their covering, the young man might take them home with him in a portmanteau. Though uncongenial to the son's feelings, this proposition was acted upon. The osseous frame work was denuded by cutting away the solid flesh, and finally by boiling it in water and scraping thoroughly. Thus cleansed the bones were separated and carefully placed in the two ends of a large portmanteau and carried on horseback to Wyoming. The above was related to Dr. Perkins by an old citizen of Erie, who held a candle for and saw the entire operation.

CHAPTER IV.

From 1797 to 1805.

THE first permanent settlement within the present limits of Athens county was made in the early part of the year 1797 (eight years before the organization of the county), at the site of the present town of Athens. At this time the state of Ohio was practically an unknown region, and from the river to the lakes was almost an unbroken wilderness. Cincinnati had been laid out, on paper, a few years before, but was not settled till 1789, and did not begin to be a growing village till 1802. The sites of the cities of Columbus, Cleveland, etc., had not been thought of. The settlements on the Ohio Company's purchase and about Cincinnati, in the Miami valley, comprised nearly the whole population of the northwestern territory. The treaty of Greenville, and the cessation of the Indian war, removed the last obstacle to the peopling of this extensive region. The active spirit of emigration, restrained during the years of hostilities, was now set free, and the living column began its westward movement with an impetus that was destined steadily to increase till the whole vast area should be possessed and populated. Every part of New England furnished its quota, and New York and Pennsylvania contributed to swell the tide of emigration as it rolled across their borders to the promised land of the West.

"Never," says an early writer, "since the golden age of the poets, did 'the syren song of peace and of farming' reach so many ears, and gladden so many hearts, as after Wayne's treaty at Greenville in 1795. 'The Ohio,' as it was called, seemed to be, literally, a land flowing with milk and honey. The farmer wrote home of a soil 'richer to appearance than can possibly be made by art;' of 'plains and meadows without the labor of hands, sufficient to support millions of cattle summer and winter;' of wheat lands that would vie with the island of Sicily; and of bogs from which might be gathered cranberries enough to make tarts for all New England; while the lawyer said that as he rode the circuit, his horse's legs were dyed to the knee with the juice of the wild strawberry. At that time the diseases and the hardships of frontier life were not dwelt upon; the administration of Washington had healed the divisions among the states; the victory of Wayne had brought to terms the dreaded savages; and as the dweller on the barren shore of the Atlantic remembered these things and the wonderful facts, in addition, that the inland garden to which he was invited was crossed in every direction by streams even then counted on as affording means for free commercial intercourse, and that it possessed besides nearly seven hundred miles of river and lake coast, the inducements for emigration became too strong to be resisted; the wagon was tinkered up at once, the harness patched anew, and a few weeks found the fortune seeker looking down from the Chestnut Ridge or Laurel Hill upon the far-reaching forests of the West."

During the year 1796, nearly one thousand flatboats or "broadhorns," as they were then called, passed Marietta laden with emigrants on their way to the more attractive regions of southwestern Ohio. Reports as to the comparative sterility of the lands of the Ohio Company's purchase had been widely bruited, and, at that time, were generally credited. Yet, though thousands passed its barren hills scoffing as they guided their keels to the richer regions about the Miami, its progress in population, etc., was of the most encouraging kind. Those who stopped here were willing to work hard and content to earn independence and moderate fortunes by economy, thrift, and laborious effort.

In the early part of 1797, a considerable number of newly arrived emigrants were assembled in Marietta, eager to obtain lands on the best terms they could and to form settlements. · The two townships of land appropriated by the Ohio Company for the benefit of a university had been selected in December, 1795. They were townships Nos. eight and nine in the fourteenth range, constituting at present Athens and Alexander townships. The township lines were run in 1795, and the sectional surveys made in 1796, under the supervision of General Putnam, the Company's surveyor, who, from the first took an ardent interest in the selection of these lands and the founding of the university. His policy (in which he was seconded by the other agents) was to encourage the early settlement of the college lands, make them attractive and productive, and so begin the formation of a fund for the institution.

"These lands," says Ephraim Cutler, "with a large surrounding region, were one of the most favorite portions of the hunting ground which the Indians had surrendered in their several treaties; and the treaty of 1795 seemed to close the last fond hope of ever after enjoying them. Yet the hunters living about Sandusky, and on the different branches of the Muskingum not only continued to visit there, but until the winter of 1810–11, they were in large parties during the hunting season, coursing through that extensive range of country comprising the lands watered by the Raccoon, Monday, Sunday and the heads of Federal creek. It was here that they formerly found the buffalo, the elk, and the bear. The buffalo and the elk were not exterminated until the year 1800. The bear continued in considerable abundance until the last great hunt of the Indians in the winter of 1810–11. That winter was a favorable season for them to effect the object they seemed to have in view, which was to destroy the game, the weather being cold with several falls of snow. The carcasses of many deer were found in the woods bordering the settlements in Washington and Athens counties, which appeared to be wantonly destroyed by the savages. A young buffalo, believed to be the last seen in this part of the country, was captured a few miles west of Athens, on a branch of Raccoon, in the spring of 1799, brought to the settlement, and reared by a domestic cow."

In 1795 a man named Gillespie and two of the Fleeharts, noted frontiersmen, came up the Hockhocking to hunt. Landing at the mouth of Federal creek just at dark they found Indian signs so abundant and recent that they were afraid to proceed or remain. They built up a large fire, supplied it well with logs and hung up a blanket and one or two other articles to signify that they would soon be back, and leaving this to deceive the Indians, and throw them off their track, they hurriedly embarked again and returned down the river to Virginia whence they came. The next autumn (1796), the same party came up the river again to hunt. There was now not much fear of Indians, and they landed again at the mouth of Federal, where they camped and hunted for two days. The third day they agreed to explore the country somewhat; one of the Fleeharts kept the camp, the other went up Federal, and Gillespie up Hockhocking. He camped the first night at the mouth of Sunday creek. The next morning he crossed the river there, and came down on the other side to the ripple about where Bingham's mill was afterward built. Here he rested and removed his moccasins to recross the river. At the water's edge he noticed the track of a large animal which seemed to have crossed recently. Tracing it over the shallow stream and up the opposite bank he found the peavines still wet from the animal's dripping legs, and from the broken underbrush and size of the path it had made concluded it was a buffalo. He followed on about a quarter of a mile, and coming upon a little rise just where the present Fair ground west of Athens is, he saw a very large male buffalo grazing there. Gillespie immediately fired and hit the animal, but not being fatally wounded it dashed off through the woods with Gillespie's dog in close pursuit, and himself at the best pace he could make. He followed the buffalo to the present site of Athens, and found him not far from where the court house now stands—a few rods south—(Gillespie frequently visited Athens in after years) tearing in great rage and pain at the roots of a fallen tree, and charging furiously at the dog, who was safely ensconced under the trunk. Gillespie lost no time in getting a second shot and this time killed the brute, whose tongue and choice parts he carried into camp with him the same night.*

---

*This incident is related to the writer by Mr. John P. Thompson, who was born in Athens township in 1808, and who, while on a visit to Crawford county in 1832, where he hunted with the Wyandot Indians, made the acquaintance of Gillespie. Gillespie after the settlement of Athens became familiar with its localities, and told the story to Thompson as we have set it down.

Encouraged by Gen. Putnam, who wished to introduce permanent settlers as soon as possible, a number of the emigrants who had stopped at Marietta decided to locate on the college lands. Among these were Alvan Bingham, Silas Bingham, Isaac Barker, William Harper, John Wilkins, Robert Linzee, Edmund, William and Barak Dorr, John Chandler, and Jonathan Watkins. They made their way down the Ohio and up the Hockhocking in large canoes early in the year 1797. Having ascended as far as the attractive bluff where the town of Athens now stands, they landed and sought their various locations. A few of them fixed on the site of the present town, but most of them scattered up and down the adjacent bottoms. The surrounding country was then covered with dense forests, and the echo of their axes was the first sound of civilized industry heard in all this region. The bluff and bottoms were heavily timbered with hickory, walnut, ash, poplar, and other trees indicative of good soil; while the course of the tortuous Hockhocking was marked as far as the view extended by the gigantic sycamores that grew thick-set and lofty along its edge.

The first business of each settler was to make a little clearing and erect a log cabin, which was built with unhewed logs, poles, clapboards, puncheons, and, in those days, wooden pins instead of nails. In its erection, no tools were necessary except an axe, an auger, and, perhaps, a cross-cut saw. Straight trees of the proper size were cut down, and either drawn by a team, or carried with the assistance of neighbors, to the building spot. The logs being cut of proper lengths were notched and laid up somewhat as children build cob-houses. If a large, or "double," cabin was desired, the logs were laid up to form two square pens, with an open space between, connected by a roof above and a floor below, so as to form a parallelogram, nearly three times as long as wide. In the open space, the family sometimes took their meals in pleasant weather, and it served the triple purpose of kitchen, lumber room, and dining room. The roof was covered with thin splits of oak, something like staves, about four feet long, from four to six inches wide, and about one-third of an inch thick. Instead of being nailed, these staves or clapboards were generally confined in their place by heavy timbers, laid at right angles across them, giving the roof a unique and rough appearance. A door-way and windows were made by chopping out the logs of proper length and hight before laying them up, so as to make suitable apertures. The doors were made of thin clapboards, split, like the roofing, from fresh-cut timber, and were generally hung, in an ingenious fashion, on large wooden hinges, and fastened with a substantial wooden latch. Frequently the latch was raised from the outside by a small leather string attached to it, and passing through a hole from within. When this string was drawn in, the latch could not be raised from the outside, nor the door opened; hence the western expression to signify hospitality, that "the latch string is always out." Into the window apertures, small pieces of wood were fitted for sash, and upon them paper was pasted, and rendered translucent by oiling. Wooden shutters, made of staves, like the doors, were attached to the windows and closed at night. The floors (when any were used) were made of short, thick plank, split from poplar, walnut, or oak. In some cases, the more wealthy settlers had the logs hewed on the inside, and the puncheon floor hewed and planed. For a fire place and chimney, a space about six feet square was cut out of the end of the cabin, the lower part of the chimney built of rough stones, and the rest laid up with small logs and flat pieces, like laths, cemented with clay mortar, well intermixed with short cut straw or hay. The chimney had a huge aperture, and tapered upward like a pyramid. The hearth was made with clay mortar, or sometimes a large slab of sandstone. Finally, the spaces between the logs were filled with timber, split like fire wood, from some soft tree, and made impervious to wind and rain by daubing the cracks with mud. A few chairs and stools, a bedstead of poles interlaced with bark, and furnished with plenty of bear skins, a table split from a large log, and some cooking and eating utensils, constituted, perhaps, the bulk of the furniture within; and the pioneer's home was completed.

Many of our readers, early settlers, are familiar with cabins of this sort, not a few of which are still to be found in the less thickly settled parts of the county, and very generally throughout the west. Though rude in structure and limited in accommodations, no one will read the description with contempt who has had any experience of new countries. Such cabins as those described have formed the germ of all the powerful and prosperous communities of the west. Not only have their rough walls sheltered rural plenty, manly independence, guileless honesty, contentment, and happiness, but they have been the birth-place of men and women who have left their impress on the age in which they lived. No more charming picture of honest industry and unalloyed happiness can be imagined than is sometimes afforded by the interior of these rude cabins. When the wintry wind blows and the shutters are barred, and the walls of hewed logs show the white lines of plaster which mark the interstices; when the fire blazes high in the wide, open chimney, illuminating the stores of dried meats or vegetables which hang from the rafters, and the rustic table, around which are gathered the happy and healthy family, smokes with woodland plenty—at such a time no one could doubt that even these primitive log cabins are compatible with real and profound enjoyment.

The pioneers soon opened up several clearings about Athens, and a little corn, for corn bread, was put in the first spring. The clearings, however, were irregular and scattered, and no effort was made, as yet, to lay out a town. Early in 1798 a number of emigrants arrived, among whom were Solomon Tuttle, Christopher Stevens, John and Moses Hewitt, Cornelius Moore, Joseph Snowden, John Simonton, Robert Ross, the Brooks, and the Hanings. Some of these had families. Some settled in Athens and some in Alexander township. Mrs. Margaret Snowden, wife of Joseph Snowden, was honored by having "Margaret's creek" named after her, she being the first white woman who reached this central point in the county.

For the enforcement of laws and preservation of order, Alvan Bingham had been commissioned a magistrate, and his brother, Silas, a deputy sheriff. One of their most difficult duties was to prevent illegal entries and occupations of land by new comers; but this, and their other duties, sometimes delicate and accompanied with danger, they discharged with firmness and general acceptance. Ephraim Cutler, who came in a little later than the Binghams, and settled in Ames township, was also a magistrate, and in a certain class of land cases, which required two magistrates and a jury, he and Judge Bingham held court together. In those early times, notwithstanding the primitive state of society, the judges had proper ideas of the sanctity of law, and the dignity of a court. It is related that at one of these trials of forcible entry, the leaders of the disorderly class came forward and threatened violence; the magistrates ordered them to leave the room, which they did, but uttering threats to put a stop to such courts. The judges, determined to vindicate their judicial dignity, instantly issued warrants, and ordered the sheriff to arrest the parties immediately, and take them to Marietta. They were arrested accordingly, and it is not easy to conceive of men more frightened; the idea of being taken to Marietta, to be tried by a court that had established a reputation throughout the territory for firmness and strict justice, filled them with terror. Silas Bingham (who, to great shrewdness and dispatch in business, united an unconquerable humor) did nothing to allay their fears, but told them the better way would be to come into court, and, on their knees, ask forgiveness and promise amendment. The ringleader of the offending party replied that "it was too bad to be compelled to kneel down and ask forgiveness of two Buckeye justices;" but he concluded to submit, rather than be taken to Marietta, and the penitential ceremony was accordingly performed. [E. Cutler's Sketch.] During the first year of the county, the court was held in a private house, obtained for the occasion. In December, 1806, Silas Bingham was allowed twelve dollars for the use of a room occupied by the courts during that year, and an allowance of six dollars was made by the county commissioners to "Edmund Dorr and Baruch Dorr, for guarding and victualling John Farmer one month." The two Binghams, Judge Alvan and his brother Silas, were natives of Litchfield county, Connecticut, and had both served in the revolutionary army. The former was a man of strong common sense, and his judicial mind and well-trained conscience, admirably qualified him for the position of judge, which he filled for many years. He is said to have been a person of quiet and dignified manners, stern and uncompromising in his sense of right. Silas was "full of anecdote and humor, social and kind in his feelings, a man of excellent sense, and a terror to evil-doers." The promptness with which these men acted in enforcing the laws had the effect to rid the settlement of nearly all disorderly persons. Alvan Bingham was the first treasurer of Athens county, and Silas was for several years a constable.

One of the greatest troubles that the pioneers had to contend with was the extreme scarcity of salt, and the high price of that essential article often caused severe privation. At the time of the first settlement of Athens and Ames, it was sold for six dollars a bushel, and had to be packed on horseback a great distance. As early as 1788, when the first colony arrived at Marietta, it had been rumored that salt springs existed on a stream, since called Salt creek, which flows into the Muskingum river near Duncan's falls, Muskingum county, and even during the Indian war a party was sent up the river from Marietta to search for them. The exploration was made at great risk, but the springs were not found. White men, held as prisoners by the Indians, had seen them make salt at these springs, and had noted their locality. An accurate description of the country having been gained from these persons, another exploring party of hunters and experienced woodsmen was sent out, a year or two later, to find the springs. This time they were successful, and brought back with them a small supply of the precious article. In 1796, a joint stock company was formed of fifty shareholders, at one dollar and a half each, making a capital of seventy-five dollars, with the object of buying castings, erecting a furnace, and manufacturing salt. Twenty-four kettles were bought at Pittsburg, and transported by water to Duncan's falls, and thence, on pack-horses, to the salt springs, seven miles further. A well was dug, near the edge of the stream, about fifteen feet deep, to the bed rock, through the crevices of which the salt water oozed and rose, though not very abundantly. The trunk of a hollow sycamore tree was fixed in the well to exclude the fresh water. A furnace was built, of two ranges with twelve kettles each. The water was raised from the well by a sweep and pole. The company was divided into ten sections of five men each, who worked, in turn, for two weeks at a time, and the works were thus kept in operation day and night, the men standing regular watches. They were thus able to make about one hundred pounds of salt in twenty-four hours, using about sixteen hundred gallons of water. This was the first attempt to manufacture salt in Ohio, and the product was a very inferior and costly article. For several years, all of the salt used by the pioneers of Athens county was brought from these works, and afterward from the Scioto salt licks,* in Jackson county, on pack horses. It was both a great luxury and a prime necessity, and every grain of it was carefully husbanded.

The settlement was about two years old when an act was passed by the territorial assembly, relative to laying off the town of Athens. At this time only one town had been incorporated in the northwestern territory, viz: Marietta, the act incorporating which was passed less than three weeks previously. (Cincinnati was not incorporated till January 1, 1802. In the year 1800, the population of Cincinnati was 750; in 1805,

---

* These salt licks, in Jackson county, were considered of so much value, that, on the organization of the state, in 1802, a tract of land six miles square containing them was reserved from sale. The salines were worked for several years under state supervision, and were not sold until 1826, when the proceeds went into the state treasury.

it was 960; in 1810, it was 2,300; in 1813, it was 4,000; and in 1820, it was 10,500.)

The act relative to laying off the town of Athens is as follows:

"WHEREAS, In the county of Washington, within this territory, the townships Nos. eight and nine in the fourteenth range have been appropriated and set apart for the purpose of endowing an university, and, *whereas*, the application of the same to the purpose aforesaid has been entrusted to the legislature of this territory; therefore, to enable the said legislature the better to determine the situation whereon to establish the said university:

Be it resolved by the Legislative Council and House of Representatives in General Assembly, That Rufus Putnam, Benjamin Ives Gilman and Jonathan Stone, esquires, be requested to lay off, in the most suitable place within the townships aforesaid, a town plat which shall contain a square for the college, also lots suitable for house lots and gardens, for a president, professors, tutors, etc., bordering on or encircled by spacious commons, and such a number of town lots adjoining the said commons and out-lots as they shall think will be for the advantage of the university, who are to make a return of the said town plat and lots, describing their situation within the said townships, to the legislature at their next session, and shall receive such compensation for their services as the legislature shall and may direct and allow.

EDWARD TIFFIN,
Speaker of the House of Representatives.
H. VANDERBURGH,
President of the Council."

"Approved December 18th, 1799.
ARTHUR ST. CLAIR."

Pursuant to this act the town plat was surveyed and laid off by Messrs. Putnam, Gilman, and Stone in the summer of 1800, and a copy thereof returned to the legislature, as required.

In December, 1800, the following act was passed by the territorial legislature:

"*An act confirming and establishing the town of Athens in the county of Washington.*

"WHEREAS, By a resolution of the legislature of this territory, of the 18th day of December, 1799, Rufus Putnam, Benjamin Ives Gilman and Jonathan Stone, esquires, were requested to lay off a town in the most convenient place within the townships numbered eight and nine, in the fourteenth range of townships as set apart by the agents and directors of the Ohio Company, for the uses and purposes of an university, which should be so laid off as to contain a square for colleges, and lots suitable for house-lots and gardens for a president, professors and tutors, with out-lots and commons. And, *whereas*, the said Putnam, Gilman and Stone in conformity to the said resolution, have laid off the said town within the ninth, tenth and fifteenth, sixteenth and twenty-second sections of the aforesaid ninth township, and have returned a plat of the same; therefore, to establish and confirm the same:

SECTION I. *Be it enacted by the Legislative Council and House of Representatives in General Assembly*, And it is hereby enacted by the authority of the same, that the return and report of the said Putnam, Gilman and Stone be accepted and approved, and that the said town be confirmed and established by the name of the town of *Athens; Provided,* that the trustees of the university therein to be established shall have power to alter the plan of the said town, by extending the house-lots into the commons or out-lots, which adjoin the town, or by altering the streets, when, on actual survey, they may find it necessary or convenient. *Provided, also,* that such alterations be made and a plat of the town, out-lots and commons, with a designation of the uses of the commons, be recorded in the office of the recorder of the proper county prior to the offering to lease of any of the said lots.

SEC. 2. *And be it further enacted,* That the house-lots numbered fifty-five and fifty-six in the said town of Athens, or some other two lots therein equally well situated, to be designated and set apart by the trustees of the said university when appointed, shall be reserved for the accommodation of public buildings that may be necessary to be erected for the use of said town and the county in which it may be situated; which two lots, when agreed upon by said trustees, shall be particularly noted on the plat of said town and vest in the county to and for the uses designed thereby.

EDWARD TIFFIN,
Speaker House of Representatives.
ROBERT OLIVER,
President of the Council."

"Approved December 6th, 1800.
ARTHUR ST. CLAIR,
Governor."

At this time there were not more than five or six cabins occupied on the town plat. A Mr. Earhart lived on the brow of the hill near where Bing's carriage shop now is. Othniel Tuttle had a cabin on the S. W. corner of the old graveyard. In 1800 Dr. Perkins bought his cabin and moved it down the road and added it to his own, near where Dr. E. G. Carpenter now lives. Solomon Tuttle lived in a cabin near where Love's grocery now is—opposite the Currier homestead. Christian Stevens had a cabin just back of the college green, and a man by the name of Brakefield lived 20 or 30 rods east of the S. E. corner of the green. Alvan Bingham lived half a mile N. E., where widow Bingham now lives.

During the next four or five years the settlement at Athens, though increasing but slowly, received the addition of numbers of valuable citizens, sketches of some of whom will be found elsewhere. About this time John Hewitt built the first grist mill in the county (in 1800), on Margaret's creek, about a mile above its mouth, where Timothy Goodrich afterward built a saw mill. Hewitt's mill was much resorted to by the settlers for grinding their breadstuffs. Previous to this the nearest mills were in Washington county, on the Ohio and Muskingum rivers, which could only be reached by tedious journeys. Soon after this a small mill was built by Charles Shepard, in Alexander township, on the place now owned by Samuel Armstrong. The horse mill below Athens, built by Capt. Silas Bingham, is believed to have been the next in order of time. During this period Henry Cassel, an ingenious man, manufactured small hand mills which ground corn tolerably well. The stone from which they were made was found on the old Shepard place in Alexander township, now owned by John S. Miller. These hand mills of Cassel's were visited by the neighboring settlers almost daily, each taking his turn and grinding one quart, when he would yield the mill to some one else. Some families were provided with a private "hominy block," in which the corn was pounded and broken as with a pestle.

The first house was erected on the town plat in 1798, by Capt. John Chandler, a brother-in-law of Judge Alvan Bingham, on lot No. 1, near where Bing's carriage shop now stands. John Havner built a hewed log house on the opposite side of the street, very soon after. Dr. Perkins lived in a log cabin on State street, near where Dr. Carpenter now resides. Dr. Leonard Jewett, who came in 1804 or '5, occupied a hewed log house, previously erected by Capt. Silas Bingham, on the lot now occupied by Geo. W. Norris, on College street. Joel Abbott succeeded Captain Chandler, and erected one of the earliest brick houses, in 1803 or '4. William McNichol built, and occupied as a tavern, a hewed log house nearly opposite to Abbott's. About this time, William Dorr built, and occupied as a store, a double, hewed log house, on the lot where Judge Barker now resides. Afterward the house was occupied as a tavern. John Johnston built and occupied a log house, on the corner where Crippen's grocery now is. Jared Jones built a log house on the lot now occupied by Mr. Topky. One of the first brick houses was built, and occupied as a store and dwelling, by Joseph B. Miles, near the corner known as "Brown's Corner."

Meanwhile the settlement had grown to a size that entitled it, in 1803, to the honor of mention by, probably, the first professional tourist who visited the northwest,* and who said: "Athens, on the Great Hockhocking river, forty miles by water from the Ohio, lies in the election district of Middletown. This settlement commenced in the year 1797. The town is regularly laid out, on elevated ground, of easy ascent, round which the river forms a graceful bend. The situation is healthy, and the prospect delightful beyond description. The town is abundantly supplied with never-failing springs of excellent water, and the adjacent country is thought to be superior to any in the state for pleasantness and fertility."

---

* The Rev. Thaddeus M. Harris, a Massachusetts clergyman, who made a trip to the western country in 1803, in search of health and pleasure, an account of which he published in 1805. His book is, and has long been, a very rare one. Dr. Pierce said of it, nearly fifty years ago:

"The celebrated John Foster, of London, author of *Essays on Decision of Character*, etc., employed me to find or procure it for him. As it could not be found in any book store, I reluctantly parted with my own copy, to satisfy the curiosity of this learned man."

At this time, and for many years after the county was organized, various kinds of game were abundant in the forests, and deers, bears, wild turkeys, etc., were killed in great numbers. Wolves and panthers were a great annoyance, and, to the sheep growers, a great scourge. The first board of county commissioners, in June, 1805, ordered that a bounty of three dollars be paid for the scalp of every wolf or panther killed within the county, under six months old, and four dollars for every one over six months. This rate was continued for six years. June 11, 1811, the board resolved that from and after that date, the county would pay, for every wolf and panther scalp, one dollar, in addition to the state bounty, which was then two dollars for those under six months old, and four dollars if over six months. December 4, 1811, the commissioners ordered that, from and after that date, they would pay, in addition to the state bounty, two dollars per scalp. In September, 1813, the bounty was suspended till further ordered, but in June, 1814, it was renewed, and fixed at two dollars per scalp. June 5, 1817, the commissioners resolved, "that the bounty on wolf scalps be discontinued from and after the 5th day of June, 1818." The bounty on panther scalps was discontinued not long afterward.

The following persons, in addition to those already named, were residents of the town or township of Athens in 1805, viz: John Simonton, Andrew Higgins, Cornelius Moore, Moses Bean, Henry Bartlett, James Jolly, Daniel Mulford, Simon Speed, Samuel Luckey, John, Samuel, William, and Robert Lowry, John Green, Garret Jones, Uriah Tippee, Joel Abbott, Jacob Wolf, Ignatius Thompson, William and Aaron Young, Samuel Pickett, Samuel Smith, Josiah Coe, Francis Whitmore, Isaac and Michael Barker, Jonathan and Timothy Wilkins, William and Charles Harper, and Jehiel Gregory—the last named represented the county in the legislature, in 1805 and '6, and built one of the earliest mills on the Hockhocking, east of Athens.

The names of some of the pioneer settlers, mentioned in these pages, are preserved in different parts of the county, as follows: Moore's run, in Athens township; Brown's branch, Ewing's branch, Wyatt's branch, Walker's branch, Linscott's branch, and Brawley's branch, in Ames; Ross run, in Alexander; Pilcher's branch, Hoskinson's branch, Buckley's branch, and Mansfield's branch, in Canaan; Guthrie's branch, Davis's branch, and Lottridge P. O., in Carthage; Bailey's branch and Jackson run, in Dover; Cassel's run and Shidler's branch, in Lee; Thompson's fork, Pratt's fork, Dailey run, Dinsmore branch, and Douglas branch, in Lodi; Stewart's run, Case run, Herrold run, Hatch branch, Rowell branch, and Green branch, in Rome; Frost branch, Washburn branch, Ross branch, and Devol's run, in Troy; Woodbury run and McCune run, in Trimble; Hewitt's branch, in Waterloo; and Meeker's branch, in York township.

The settlement of the county was now fairly begun, and the population was receiving steady additions. The time was approaching when they would divide from Washington county, and begin a separate career. Before speaking, however, of the organization of Athens county, let us, in order to complete our view of this period, and gain a better understanding of some points in the early annals of the county, glance at

Some Political Events from 1798 to 1805.

The ordinance of 1787 provided that, as soon as there should be 5,000 free male inhabitants of full age, in the territory, and on proof thereof being made to the governor, the people should be authorized to elect representatives to a territorial legislature. The requisite population being reached in 1798, an election of representatives was ordered by proclamation of Governor St. Clair, to be held on the third Monday in December of that year. The lower house of the territorial assembly was to consist of one member for every five hundred voters, but the total not to exceed twenty-five members. The privilege of voting was confined to free-holders, in fee simple, of fifty acres of land within the district; and none but free-holders, in fee simple, of five hundred acres, were eligible as representatives. The upper house, corresponding now to the senate, was to consist of a council of five members, each of whom should be a free-holder of not less than five hundred acres, to be chosen by the representatives from their own number, and to be confirmed and appointed by congress. At this election (the first ever held in the state), Col. Robert Oliver, Return J. Meigs, and Paul Fearing were chosen representatives from Washington county, receiving the hearty support of the voters of Athens and Ames, or, as it was then called, the Middletown district. The representatives elect assembled, according to the governor's proclamation, at Cincinnati, on the 4th of February, 1799, to transact certain business, preliminary to their regular meeting. After due deliberation, they nominated for the legislative council of five, Henry Vanderburg, of Vincennes, Robert Oliver, of Marietta, James Findlay and Jacob Burnet, of Cincinnati, and David Vance; all of whom were subsequently confirmed and appointed by Federal authority. Col. Oliver was chosen president of the council and held that position until the formation of the state government. The following is from a letter, written in 1837, by Jacob Burnet,* of Cincinnati, himself a member of the territorial legislature.

---

*Jacob Burnet, one of the ablest among the early lawyers of the territory, was born at Newark, N. J., February 22, 1770, graduated at Princeton College, studied law under Judge Boudinot, was admitted to

We quote:

"On the 16th of September, 1799, both branches of the territorial legislature assembled at Cincinnati, and organized for business. The governor met the two houses in the representatives' chamber, and in a very elegant address recommended such measures as he thought were suited to the condition of the country, [and would advance the safety and prosperity of the people. The body continued in session till the 19th of December, when, having finished their business, the governor prorogued them, at their request, till the first Monday in November.

This being the first session it was necessarily a very laborious one. The transition from a colonial to a semi-independent government, called for a general revision as well as a considerable enlargement of the statute book. Some of the adopted laws

---

practice in 1796, and immediately emigrated to Cincinnati, where he passed the rest of his life. He says:

"At this time, the country to which I united myself, and with which it was my purpose to rise or fall, was, literally, a wilderness. The entire white population, between Pennsylvania and the Mississippi, from the Ohio to the lakes, was estimated at fifteen thousand. Cincinnati was a small village of log cabins, including perhaps a dozen of coarse frame houses, with stone chimneys, most of them unfinished. Not a brick had been seen in the place. It may aid in forming an idea of the appearance of the place at this time, to state that, at the northeast corner of Main and Fifth streets (now—1837—the centre of business and tasteful improvements), and contiguous to a rough, half finished frame house, in which our courts were held, there was a pond, filled with alder bushes, in which the frogs serenaded us regularly, from spring to autumn. The morass extended so far into Main street, that it was necessary to construct a causeway of logs, in order to pass it with convenience; and it remained in its natural state, filled with alder bushes and frogs, three or four years after my residence there began. The population of the town, including officers and followers of the army, was about five hundred."

were repealed, many others altered and amended, and a long list of new ones added to the code. New offices were to be created and filled, the duties attached to them prescribed, and a plan of ways and means devised to meet the increased expenditures, occasioned by the change which had just taken place. As the number of members in each branch was small, and a large portion of them either unprepared or indisposed to partake largely of the labors of the session, the pressure fell on the shoulders of a few. Although the branch to which I belonged was composed of sensible, strong-minded men, yet they were unaccustomed to the duties of their new station, and not conversant with the science of law. The consequence was that they relied chiefly and almost entirely on me to draft and prepare the bills and other documents, which originated in the council. One of the important duties which devolved on the legislature, was the election of a delegate to represent the territory in congress. As soon as the governor's proclamation made its appearance, the election of a person to fill that station excited general attention. Several persons were spoken of, and among them myself. Many of my friends solicited me to become a candidate, and ventured to give strong assurance of my election if I would consent to serve; but being at that time engaged in an extensive and lucrative practice, and not wealthy, I could not afford to quit my profession, or to abstract from it as much time and attention as the duties of the station would require. In addition to this, it appeared to me that I could be more useful to the people of the territory in their own legislature, than in congress. For these reasons I declined to be a candidate; and, before the meeting of the legislature, public opinion had settled down on William Henry Harrison and Arthur St. Clair, Jr., who were eventually the only candidates. On the 3d of October, 1799, the two houses met in the representatives' chamber, according to a joint resolution, and proceeded to an election. The ballots being taken and counted, it appeared that William Henry Harrison had eleven votes, and St. Clair ten votes; the former was therefore declared to be duly elected. Having received his certificate of election, General Harrison resigned the office of secretary of the territory, proceeded forthwith to Philadelphia, and took his seat, congress being then in session. Though he represented the territory but one year, he obtained some important advantages for his constituents. He introduced a resolution to subdivide the surveys of the public lands and to offer them for sale in small tracts, which measure he succeeded in getting through both houses, in opposition to the interests of speculators who were, and who wished to be, the retailers of land to the poorer classes of the community. His proposition became a law, and was hailed as the most beneficent act that congress had ever done for the territory. It put it in the power of every industrious man, however poor, to become a freeholder, and to lay a foundation for the future support and comfort of his family.

"Congress at that session (1799–1800), divided the northwestern territory, by establishing the new territory of Indiana, of which Mr. Harrison was appointed governor. By the division of the territory, Mr. Vanderburg (one of the legislative council) became a citizen of Indiana, and Solomon Sibley, of Detroit, was appointed to fill the vacancy in that body. The office of secretary, vacated by the election of Mr. Harrison as delegate in congress, was filled by the appointment of Charles Willing Byrd, who was afterward district judge of the United States for the district of Ohio.

"After the close of the first session of the territorial legislature, a law was passed by congress (May 7, 1800), removing the seat of government from Cincinnati to Chillicothe. On the 3d of November, 1800, the general assembly convened at that place. The governor met and addressed them, recommending, specifically, the measures to which he desired their attention. On the 6th of November the two houses met for the purpose of filling the vacancy made by the resignation of Gen. Harrison in congress and also to elect a delegate for the next succeeding term. William McMillan, of Cincinnati, was elected to fill the vacancy and Paul Fearing, of Marietta, for the term to begin on the 4th of March then next. On the 2d of December (as the governor's term of office expired on that day) the assembly adjourned *sine die.*"

Governor St. Clair was soon reappointed by President Adams, and a new assembly was elected by the people, which convened at Chillicothe on the 24th of November, 1801. It remained in session till the 23d of January, 1802, when it was adjourned by the governor to be reopened at Cincinnati, on the fourth Monday of November, 1802. This removal of the seat of government from Chillicothe to Cincinnati was (says Burnet), "in consequence of the violent and disgraceful proceedings of a mob, which assembled on two successive evenings for the purpose of insulting the governor and several of the members of the legislature, without any steps being taken by the town authorities to repress it, or to punish the leaders." But the territorial assembly never convened again. Before the day of its adjournment arrived, delegates had been elected to a constitutional convention, and preparations were being made for admission as a state into the Federal Union. This step was the theme of a great deal of discussion at that day, and was the most absorbing topic of the times.

The territorial government was of brief duration, lasting less than three years, when the contest between those who desired and those who opposed the formation of a state government, resulted in favor of the former; not, however, without a sharp popular struggle and considerable excitement. Indeed, the contest was for some time an active and bitter one. The opponents of a state government (*i. e.* of forming one *at this time*), argued that such a measure would be especially injurious to the inhabitants of the Ohio Company's purchase; that they had been struggling with the hardships of opening the wilderness since the year 1788, and for a large part of the time pressed by the merciless savage to the extremes of want, danger, and even death; that the population was sparse and generally poor; that the expenses of a state government would be heavy in proportion to the inhabitants, while the advantages to them in their present situation would be few, perhaps none, over a territorial government; and, finally, that the taxes to support a state government would fall on the actual settlers and land-holders, as the Ohio Company's lands would all be brought on the tax list, while congress lands, daily becoming more valuable by the improvements of the settlers, were to be free from taxation. The people of Washington county were so much opposed to the formation of a state government at that time, that they determined to hold a convention and give formal expression to their views. Delegates were accordingly chosen by the different settlements in the purchase, as follows: for Marietta, Paul Fearing and Elijah Backus; for Belpre, Isaac Pierce and Silas Bent; for Waterford, Robert Oliver and Gilbert Devol; for Adams, Joseph Barker; for Newport, Philip Witten and Samuel Williamson; for Middletown (or Athens), Alvan Bingham; and for Gallipolis, Robert Safford. Gilbert Devol was chosen chairman of the convention, and Joseph Barker secretary. The foregoing arguments were presented, in a paper prepared by Joseph Barker, and after mature deliberation the convention adopted the following:

" *Resolved*, That, in our opinion, it would be highly impolitic and very injurious to the inhabitants of this territory, to enter into a state government, *at this time*. Therefore, we, in behalf of our constituents, do request that you will use your best endeavors to prevent, and steadily oppose the adoption of any measures that may be taken for the purpose."

Which, being properly attested, was sent to their representatives in the territorial assembly.

In the assembly, also, the measure met with determined opposition. But those who expected office, or preferment of some sort, under the new government, outnumbered the more sober and cautious representatives. The measure was carried, and it was decided to form a state government. So eager were the ambitious friends of the project for a change, that they relinquished the right of taxing the lands owned by congress, until five years after they had been sold and in the possession of the purchaser; whereas, in equity, they should have been liable to taxation as soon as they were in his possession. The apprehensions of the injurious results to the inhabitants of the Ohio Company's purchase, were soon realized, as the taxes for the support of the new government fell very heavily on them. This inequality remained until the year 1825, when the *ad valorem* system was introduced, and removed the long continued injustice. [Hildreth.]

The next step in the transition from territorial to state government, was the passage of an act by congress, on the 30th of April, 1802, "to enable the people of the eastern division of the territory northwest of the river Ohio, to form a constitution and state government." This act provided for the election of delegates to frame a constitution, and fixed the qualifications of electors. It also fixed the present boundaries of Ohio, reserving the territory west and north of it for other states. Delegates to the constitutional convention were elected in the summer of

1802. The inhabitants of Athens (a part of Washington county) were represented by Ephraim Cutler, Rufus Putnam, John McIntire, and Benjamin Ives Gilman. The convention assembled at Chillicothe on the 1st day of November, 1802, and remained in session about three weeks. The constitution being formed, was ratified and signed by the members on the 29th of November. It was never submitted to the people, but became the organic law of the state by the act of the convention alone.

Certain important changes, concerning the school lands, were made by the convention, in the proposition of congress, under which the state was to come into the Union. Congress assented to the proposed modifications by act of March 3, 1803, thus completing the compact and accepting Ohio as a state and a member of the Federal Union.

Governor St. Clair and most of the leading men during the period of the territorial government, were federalists; but by the time the territorial legislature was chosen (in 1799), democratic or Jeffersonian ideas were becoming popular, and the assembly, which met at Cincinnati in September, 1799, was possessed of some of the democratic temper then prevalent. This, together with the rather arbitrary use of the veto power by Governor St. Clair, caused some clashing between them. The result was that an impetus was given to the growth of democratic ideas in the territory, the constitutional convention, which met in 1802, was strongly Jeffersonian, and the constitution which they formed was a thoroughly democratic one. Its excellencies and defects, for it had both, were those of a truly popular form of government.

And now began the contest between "federalism" and "democracy"—the one school represented by Hamilton and his coadjutors, who believed in a powerful and splendid central government; and the other by Jefferson and his followers who advocated the largest liberty to the individual, and regarded with the utmost jealousy what they stigmatized as the centralization of power. "There were giants in those days," and their political and intellectual contests were admired and repeated in the remotest parts of the republic. By these opposing ideas, the actors in the little political arena of Athens county, like those of many other greater or smaller arenas throughout the country, were for many years to come excited and educated.

The time had now arrived when for various reasons, chiefly political perhaps, it was deemed advisable to form a new county on the west of Washington, and to be carved out of it.

CHAPTER V.

Athens County.

The county of Athens was established by the following act:

"*An act establishing the County of Athens.*

Section I. *Be it enacted, etc.,* That so much of the county of Washington as is contained in the following boundaries, be and the same is hereby erected into a separate county, which shall be known by the name of Athens, viz: beginning at the southwest corner of township number ten, range seventeen; thence easterly with the line between Gallia and Washington counties, to the Ohio river; thence up said river to the mouth of Big Hockhocking river; thence up the said Hockhocking river to the east line of township number six, of the twelfth range; thence north on said line to the northeast corner of the eighth township, in the said twelfth range; thence west to the east line of Fairfield county; thence south on said county line and the line of Ross county, to the place of beginning.

Sec. II. That from and after the first day of March next, the said county of Athens shall be vested with all the powers, privileges, and immunities of a separate and distinct county: *provided always,* that all actions and suits which may be pending on the said first day of March next, shall be prosecuted and carried into final judgment and execution, and all taxes, fees, fines, and forfeitures, which shall be then due, shall be collected in the same manner as if this act had never been passed.

SEC. III. That the seat of justice for said county, is hereby established in the town of Athens, any law to the contrary not withstanding. This act shall take effect and be in force from and after the first day of March next."

[Passed February 20th, 1805.]

The county as thus established in 1805, contained one thousand and fifty-three square miles, or about thirty regular surveyed townships, and included five townships now belonging to Meigs county, viz: Columbia, Scipio, Bedford, Orange, and Olive townships; two now belonging to Morgan county, viz: Homer and Marion; three now belonging to Hocking county, viz: Ward, Green, and Starr; and seven now belonging to Vinton, viz: Brown, Swan, Elk, Madison, Knox, Clinton, and Vinton townships; and a strip of land about ten miles long and one mile wide now belonging to Washington county. By an act passed January 30th, 1807, entitled "an act to alter the boundary line between the counties of Athens and Gallia," a strip about ten miles long and one mile wide, was added to the southeast corner of Athens county as it then existed. By an act passed February 18th, 1807, entitled "an act altering the line between the counties of Washington and Athens," the boundary of Athens was changed so as to take in the portion of Troy township lying east of the Hockhocking river; and the same act detached a strip one mile wide and fifteen miles long, lying along the eastern border of Rome, Bern, and Marion townships, from Athens county, and added it to Washington. By an act passed February 10th, 1814, sections thirty-one and thirty-two in township number six, range eleven (Rome) were detached from Washington and added to Athens, and sections eleven and twelve in township number eight, range twelve (now Marion township, Morgan county), were detached from Athens and added to Washington. The creation of the county of Jackson by act of January 12, 1816, took township number ten, range seventeen (now Clinton township, Vinton county), from Athens. The creation of the county of Hocking by act of January 3, 1818, took parts of three townships (Green and Starr, of Hocking, and Brown, of Vinton county), from Athens; and by an act of March 12th, 1845, entitled "an act to attach part of the county of Athens to the county of Hocking," the residue of those townships was stricken off. The creation of the county of Meigs, January 21, 1819, took five townships from Athens and reduced our southern boundary to its present limits. By an act passed March 11, 1845, the townships of Homer and Marion were detached from Athens and added to Morgan county. Finally, the erection of the county of Vinton by act passed March

23, 1850, took the remainder of our outlying possessions in that direction, and the same act detached Ward township from Athens and gave it to Hocking, thus reducing our boundaries all around to their present limits. The present boundaries of the county include about four hundred and eighty-four square miles.

An act of the legislature, passed February 13th, 1804, entitled "an act establishing boards of commissioners," provided that the election for commissioners should be held on the first Monday of the next April. The first election in Athens county resulted in the choice of Silas Dean, William Howlett and John Corey, commissioners. We quote from the record of the first board of commissioners:

"*County of Athens, State of Ohio,*
April 16*th*, 1805.

Agreeably to an act entitled 'an act establishing boards of commissioners,' passed February the 13th, 1804,

We, Silas Dean, Wm. Howlett and John Corey, being elected commissioners for the county of Athens on the 13th day of April, 1805, Silas Dean and John Corey, agreeably to appointment, met this day in order to proceed to business, and have made choice of John Corey for clerk, and then proceeded to divide the county into the following townships:

The township of *Ames* begins at the N. E. corner of the county, thence running W. to the N. W. corner of said county; thence S. to the S. W. corner of township No. 12 in the 16th range; thence E. to the S. E. corner of township No. 7 in the 12th range; thence N. to the place of beginning.

The township of *Athens* begins at the N. W. corner of township No. 12 in the 17th range, thence S. to the S. W. corner of township No. 12; thence E. to the S. E. corner of township No. 5 in the 13th range; thence N. to the N. E. corner of the aforesaid township No. 5; thence West to the place of beginning.

The township of *Alexander* begins at the N. W. corner of township No. 11 in the 17th range, thence South to the S. W. corner of township No. 10 in the aforesaid 17th range; thence E. to the S. E. corner of township No. 3 in the 13th range; thence N. to the N. E. corner of township No. 4 in the 13th range; thence W. to the place of beginning.

The township of *Troy* begins at the S. W. corner of township No. 4 in the 12th range, thence East on the south line of the county until it intersects with Shade river; thence down Shade river to its junction with the Ohio; thence up the Ohio to the mouth of the Great Hockhocking; thence up the Hockhocking to where the eastern line of the 12th range crosses said river; thence N. to the N. E. corner of township No. 6 in the 12th range; thence W. to the N. W. corner of the aforesaid 6th township; thence S. to the place of beginning.

By a majority of the board of commissioners Alvan Bingham was appointed treasurer for the county of Athens. April 17th, said Bingham's bonds executed and accepted."

[Here follow proposals and specifications for the building of a log jail and jailor's house, the jail to be 24 feet long in the clear and 13 feet wide, with minute descriptions of every part; but our space does not allow their insertion.]

"The board of commissioners have appointed John Armstrong's house as the first place of meeting for the electors of Alexander township; John Havner's house as the first place of meeting for the electors of Athens township; Ebenezer Buckingham's house as the first place of meeting for the electors of

Troy township, and Sylvanus Ames' house as the first place of meeting for the electors of Ames."

[This session of the board lasted from the 16th to the 19th of April. William Howlett joined the other commissioners on the 17th. Their compensation was $1.50 per day, and the expense of this, the first meeting of the board, was $19.25. They adjourned till the second Monday of June, 1805.]

"The board met agreeably to adjournment on the second Monday of June and proceeded to levy the county tax, and made out one duplicate for the township of Ames, one for Athens and Alexander, and one for Troy.

In conformity to the 11th section of an act for granting tavern licenses, ferriages, &c., passed at Chillicothe the 1st day of February, 1805,

Resolved by the Board of Commissioners, That the price of licenses for ferries crossing the Ohio within this county shall be two dollars. The rates for crossing said river shall be as the law prescribes in the aforesaid 11th section.

Resolved, That the license for ferries crossing the Great Hockhocking river shall be two dollars. The rate of ferriage of the same shall be as follows, viz: For each foot passenger, three cents; for man and horse, ten cents; for loaded wagon and team, fifty cents; for every other four-wheeled carriage, or empty wagon and team, thirty-seven and one-half cents; for every loaded cart and team, thirty-seven and a half cents; for every loaded sled, or sleigh, or empty cart and team, twenty-five cents; for every empty sled, or sleigh and team, twelve and a half cents; for every horse, mare, mule, or ass, and every head of neat cattle, six cents; for sheep and hogs, three cents.

Resolved, That all other ferries within the county shall be one dollar for license, and the rates of ferriage shall be as above prescribed on the Hockhocking.

Resolved, That the license for taverns in the town of Athens shall be eight dollars; for the township of Ames, four dollars; for the township of Troy, five dollars; and for the township of Alexander, four dollars and a half. For the township of Athens, the price of a tavern license shall be six dollars.

The tax assessed on the township of Ames is thirty-nine dollars, as appears by the duplicate; the tax assessed on the townships of Athens and Alexander is ninety-six dollars and forty cents, as appears by the duplicate; the tax assessed on the township of Troy is twenty-two dollars and twenty cents, as appears by the duplicate. The total amount of all the taxes assessed in the county of Athens is one hundred and fifty-seven dollars and sixty cents.

The petition of David Watkins and others for a road, after being read, was rejected, it not being according to law. The petition of William Young and others for a road, after being read, was rejected, it not being according to law. The petition of H. Castle and others praying for a road, after being read, was rejected, not being according to law. The petition of Daniel Weethee and others for the division of the township of Ames was not acceded to. The petition of Elijah Hatch and others praying for the erection of a new township in this county was not acceded to.

County of Athens to Josiah True. Dr.
For services by him done in the township of Ames, listing taxable property in the year 1805, - - - - $5 30

County of Athens to Stephen Buckingham. Dr.
For services done in listing taxable property in the township of Troy, in the year 1805, - - - - - 5 00

County of Athens to George Shidler. Dr.
For services done in listing taxable property in the townships of Athens and Alexander, in the year 1805, - - - 8 00

The total amount for listing and returning is $18 30.

Resolved, by the Board of Commissioners, that John Corey shall receive twelve dollars for his services as clerk for this board during the time the said board elected him for.

WHEREAS, It appears by a more mature deliberation to the board, that the resolution passed by them the 19th of April last, fixing the place for the first meeting of the electors of the township of Ames, is a grievance, and that the same should be changed, and for that purpose it is *Resolved*, by the board, that the place for the first meeting of the electors of the aforesaid township of Ames, is the dwelling house of Nathan Woodbury.

The County of Athens. Dr.
To William Howlett, Silas Dean, and John Corey for four days' services, each, as commissioner, seven dollars each, - $28 00

Adjourned till the second Tuesday of July.

July 9th, 1805.—William Howlett and John Corey met, pursuant to adjournment, and proceeded, after a more mature deliberation, to strike out the price of license for the town plat of Athens.

WHEREAS, It appears on more mature deliberation by the Board of Commissioners that the petition of David Watkins and others praying for a road to be laid out from Asahel Cooley's to Henry Cassel's mill was done according to law, the said board have appointed George Shidler, Henry Shidler, and Charles Weeks to view said road.

The petition of William Young and others praying for a road to be laid out from Athens toward Lancaster, that was rejected, is now considered according to law, and the Board of Commissioners have appointed Arthur Coates, George Shidler, and Robert Ross to view said road.

It appearing to the board on more mature deliberation that the petition of Henry Cassell and others praying for a road to be laid out from Athens toward Salt Lick, which was rejected, was done agreeably to law, they now appoint Robert Linzee, Samuel Moore, and Joel Abbott to view out said road.

Resolved, by the Board of Commissioners, that Daniel Stewart be appointed collector for the township of Troy, in the room of Stephen Buckingham, delinquent.

This day, George Shidler came forward, and gave his bond as collector for the townships of Athens and Alexander.

Adjourned.

November 4th, 1805.—[An election having occurred in October.] Agreeably to an act entitled 'an act establishing Boards of Commissioners,' passed February 13th, 1804, We, William Howlett, William Barrows, and Samuel Moore, being elected commissioners for the county of Athens, have met this day in order to do business.

A petition, bearing date May 30th, 1805, having been presented to the board by David Watkins and others, of the township of Alexander, praying for a road beginning at the range line between the 12th and 13th ranges, thence onward to the Salt Lick, and George Shidler, Charles Weeks, and Henry Shidler having been appointed to view said road, now report the same useless.

The County of Athens to Ebenezer Barrows. Dr.
For carrying the returns of the election for the town of Athens to Marietta, - - - - - - - - $3 00

County of Athens to Henry Shidler. Dr.
For carrying returns of election for the township of Alexander to Marietta, - - - - - - - - 3 50

County of Athens to Henry Bartlett. Dr.
For services rendered in attempting to get a list of nonresidents' lands within said county, - - - - - 5 00

We, the Commissioners, at our first meeting, cast lots, as the law directs, and drew as follows, viz: Samuel Moore to stand three years, William Howlett to stand two years, and William Barrows to stand one year.

County of Athens to Alexander Stedman. Dr.
For carrying the returns of election for the township of Troy, for the year 1805, to Marietta, - - - - $2 00

County of Athens to Abel Miller. Dr.
To two days' attendance as judge of the court of common pleas
at November term, 1805, - - - - - $6 00

To Alexander Stedman. Dr.
To two days' attendance as judge, etc. (as above), - - 6 00

To Silvanus Ames. Dr.
To one day's attendance, and going and returning, - - 6 00

Adjourned.

December 21, 1805.—Josiah True came forward and gave bonds as collector of the township of Ames.

County of Athens. Dr.
To postage on letter taken out of the postoffice and paid 12½ cents by A. Stedman and 12½ cents by Samuel Moore - 25 cts.

May 19*th*, 1806.—We agreed with Joel Abbott for vacant house for a temporary prison to receive the body of John Fleehart for the present.

June 2*d*, 1806.—William Barrows and Samuel Moore met in order to do business at the house of Silas Bingham. Silas Dean and Samuel Brown presented a petition for a road beginning at the Twenty-five mile tree on the state road, and ending at or near the Thirty-four mile tree on the Lancaster road.

Robert Linzee presented a petition for the road to be altered from Samuel Moore's to Stroud's run. Alvan Bingham, Arthur Coats and Jehiel Gregory are appointed to view said road the third Saturday in July, and Abel Miller is appointed surveyor.

County of Athens to Joseph Guthrie, Jun. Dr.
To services done in listing and making out duplicates for the
township of Troy, eight days, - - - - $8 00

To Martin Boyles. Dr.
To services in listing, appraising, and making out duplicates for
the township of Ames—seven days and a half, - - 7 50

To Robert Fulton. Dr.
To services as lister and making out returns—six days, - 6 00

To Thomas Armstrong. Dr.
To services as lister and making out returns, - - - 6 00

Resolved, by the Board of Commissioners, that the bounty on wolves' and panthers' scalps for this year shall be as follows, viz: For any wolf or panther under six months old, three dollars, and for all above that age, four dollars per scalp.

June 5th.—We have appointed William Harper treasurer for this year, and this day he came forward and gave bonds as the law directs.

We have received Robert Linzee's bond as sheriff as the law directs.

Athens township licenses for taverns for this year, *i. e.*, from the State road toward the Salt works are fixed at six dollars and fifty cents, and license on the State road, in said township, at four dollars each. Tavern licenses for the township of Ames are five dollars and fifty cents each. Tavern licenses for Troy and Alexander are five dollars each.

Ferry licenses on the State road, for this year, are two dollars, and other ferries on the Hockhocking, one dollar and fifty cents. Rates of ferriage across said river for man and horse, twelve and a half cents; and all the other rates the same as last year.

Athens County to Henry Bartlett. Dr.
For services done the county, - - - - - $27 75
For making out duplicates for state and county taxes, - - 6 00

Athens County to Jehiel Gregory. Dr.
To services done said county as an associate judge by notifying an election for sheriff, coroner, and county commissioners, and receiving and making returns thereof; also for time spent with Judge Ames appointing and making bonds with Henry Bartlett as clerk *pro tem.* for the court of common pleas, - - - - - - - - 4 50

Athens County to Abel Miller. Dr.
To laying out jail bounds, - - - - - - 75
To chainmen, - - - - - - - - 75

Athens County to Silas Bingham. Dr.
For a room for one session of commissioners, June, 1806, - 4 00

Athens County to Samuel Beaumont. Dr.
To one wolf scalp, - - - - - - - 4 00

To Joseph Guthrie. Dr.
To one wolf scalp, - - - - - - - $4 00

To Robert Linzee. Dr.
To viewing a road from Athens toward the Salt Lick, twelve days and a half, - - - - - - - 12 50
To pack horse twelve and a half days, for the use of the company, - - - - - - - - 3 12½

Athens County to Alvan Ogden. Dr.
To viewing a road from near Asahel Cooley's, in Troy township, through Alexander, to intersect with the Salt Lick road at or near Wheelabout—nine days, - - 9 00

To Charles Weeks. Dr.
To viewing above road—nine days, - - - - 9 00

To Daniel Mulford. Dr.
To boxes for grand and petit juries, - - - - 1 50

To William Howlett. Dr.
To panther scalp, over six months, - - - - 4 00

To William Barrows. Dr.
To three days' services in reforming (planning?) a jail and forming a courthouse, and advertising the same, $5 25.
[Ordered by the associate judges that this amount be docked down and carried out, - - - - - - 3 50]

September, 1, 1806. A petition being presented by William Green and others, praying for a road from John Brown's to Reuben Davis's, and from thence to Moses Hewitt's, the board appoint Ephraim Cutler, Joshua Wyatt, and Jason Rice viewers for said road, to meet the 9th day of September, at the house of John Brown; and they appoint Thomas M. Hamilton surveyor of said road.

A petition being presented by Eliphaz Perkins and others, praying for a road from the town of Athens to the house of Frederic Foughty, in Ames township, John Corey, Abel Mann, and Nicholas Phillips are appointed viewers, and Abel Miller surveyor of said road.

Athens County to Ebenezer Carrier. Dr.
To one quire of paper, - - - - - - - 45 cts.

Athens County to Azel Johnson. Dr.
To three wolf scalps, over 6 months old, - - - $12 00

Athens County to Henry Bartlett. Dr.
To posting the commissioners' books, - - - - 2 00

Athens County to Abel Miller. Dr.
To surveying a road from Athens to the county line, towards Scioto Salt Lick, and his chainmen and markers, - 21 00
To surveying a road from No. 5, in Troy, through the township of Alexander to intersect the Salt Lick road, on the waters of Wheelabout, and his chainmen and markers, - 22 50

Athens County to Joseph Guthrie. Dr.
To one wolf scalp, - - - - - - - 4 00

To Stephen Buckingham. Dr.
To one day's service in returning poll-book of election held in Troy township, - - - - - - - 1 00

The acc'ts in this book audited to this date, Nov. 13, 1806.
SILVANUS AMES,
ALEXANDER STEDMAN,
ABEL MILLER,
Associate Judges.

County of Athens to Silvanus Ames. Dr.
To five days' service as judge at November term, - - $15 00

To Alexander Stedman. Dr.
To five days' service as judge, - - - - - 15 00

To Abel Miller. Dr.
To four days' service as judge, - - - - - - 12 00

To Silas Bingham. Dr.
For a court house one year, - - - - - - 12 00

December 1, 1806. At a meeting of the County Commissioners on Monday, the 1st day of December, 1806, present Alvan Bingham and Samuel Moore, commissioners, the board appointed Henry Bartlett clerk for the term of one year, and agreed to pay him thirty dollars for his services, payable quarterly.

Personally appeared before me Abel Miller, one of the associate judges of the court of common pleas for the county of Athens, the above-named Henry Bartlett, who was sworn according to law, for the faithful discharge of his duties as clerk to the commissioners.

  (Signed)   ABEL MILLER, *Asso. Judge.*

December 2. Present as yesterday, and William Howlett, who also appeared and took his seat as commissioner.

Ordered by the commissioners that their clerk sign all orders issued by them, as clerk of the commissioners.

Notice issued to the trustees of Athens township to open a road, leading from Samuel Moore's to Stroud's run, agreeably to law.

Also, to open a road leading from the town of Athens to the county line toward the Scioto Salt Lick, *i. e.*, so much of said road as lies in the township of Athens, as surveyed by Abel Miller.

Notice issued to the trustees of the township of Alexander to open a road, leading from Athens toward the Scioto Salt Lick, *i. e.*, so much of said road as lies in the township of Alexander.

Also, to open a road leading from the line of the township of Alexander to the waters of Wheelabout, toward the Scioto Salt Lick.

Adjourned to 25th December.

December 25, 1806. The board met agreeably to adjournment, at the house of Leonard Jewett; adjourned to the house of Joel Abbott.

Ordered by the commissioners that the sum of ten dollars be appropriated for the purpose of purchasing blank county orders, stationery, paying postage on letters, etc., and that an order be given to Henry Bartlett, as their clerk for that purpose.

   County of Athens to Robert Linzee. Dr.
To summoning grand jury July and November terms, - $ 4 00
   County of Athens to Thomas Armstrong. Dr.
To collecting taxes and delinquencies, - - - - 6 57

Ordered that Joel Abbott receive orders to the amount of $65.50, being the balance of his contract for building a jail.

Adjourned to the 10th of January next, at the house of Joel Abbott.

County of Athens to Asahel Cooley, Jun. Dr.
To three wolf scalps, - - - - - - - $12 00

To Milton Buckingham. Dr.
To two wolf scalps, - - - - - - - 8 00

To Hiram Howlett. Dr.
To one wolf scalp, - - - - - - - 4 00

Want of space forbids further extracts; we append, however, a statement of the tax assessed in 1808.

Tax assessed in the County in 1808.

June 16, 1808. The Board of Commissioners appointed the following persons collectors for the present year, viz:

For Athens township, Michael Barker; for Ames township, John Brown, 2d; for Troy township, Asahel Cooley; for Alexander township, Amos Thompson.

Amount of duplicates of taxes assessed for the year 1808:

Athens.—	Land,	- - - -	$37 85
	Taxable property,	- - -	90 47
Ames.—	Land,	- - - -	68 80
	Taxable property,	- - -	49 67
Troy.—	Land,	- - - -	62 38
	Taxable property,	- - -	51 20
Alexander.—	Land,	- - - -	6 46
	Taxable property,	- - -	59 60
			$426 43

Athens County.

County Commissioners from the Organization of the County.

1805	Silas Dean,	William Howlett,	John Corey—(At special election.)
1805	William Barrows,	"	Samuel Moore—(At regular election.)
1806	Alvan Bingham,	"	Samuel Moore—(At regular election.)
1807	"	Caleb Merritt,	Samuel Moore—(At regular election.)
1808	"	"	Ebenezer Currier.
1809	Asahel Cooley,	"	"
1810	"	Zebulon Griffin,	"
1811	"	"	Seth Fuller.
1812	Ebenezer Currier,	"	"
1813	"	Caleb Merritt,	"
1814	"	"	Robert Linzee.
1815	Daniel Stewart,	Levi Stedman,	"
1816	Caleb Merritt,	Asahel Cooley,	Daniel Stewart.
1817	"	"	Levi Stedman.
1818	George Walker,	Stambro P. Stancliff,	
1819	"	"	James Gillmore.
1820	"	"	"
1821	"	Edmund Dorr,	"
1822	"	"	"
1823	"	"	"
1824	"	"	"
1825	"	Daniel Stewart,	"
1826	"	"	Justus Reynolds.
1827	"	Harry Henshaw,	"
1828	"	"	"
1829	"	"	"
1830	"	Absalom Boyles,	"
1831	Joshua Hoskinson,	"	"
1832	"	"	"
1833	"	David Jones,	"
1834	"	"	"
1835	"	"	Frederic Abbott.
1836	"	Alfred Hobby,	"
1837	"	"	"
1838	"	"	William R. Walker.
1839	"	Elmer Rowell,	"
1840	"	"	Benj. M. Brown.
1841	"	"	"
1842	"	Arnold Patterson,	"
1843	Silas M. Shepard,	"	"
1844	"	"	Alfred Hobby.
1845	"	Ziba Lindley,	"
1846	"	"	"
1847	"	"	"
1848	James Dickey,	"	"
1849	"	"	"
1850	"	"	Pearley Brown.
1851	"	"	John Elliott.

History of Athens County, Ohio. 159

1852	L. D. Poston,	Ziba Lindley,	John Elliott.
1853	"	"	"
1854	"	William Mason,	"
1855	John Brown,	"	Daniel B. Stewart.
1856	"	"	"
1857	"	Joseph Jewett,	"
1858	"	"	"
1859	John T. Winn,	"	John E. Vore.
1860	"	John Dew,	"
1861	John Brown,	"	"
1862	"	"	G. M. McDougall.
1863	"	Hugh Boden,	"
1864	"	W. F. Pilcher,	"
1865	"	"	"
1866	"	"	"
1867	"	"	"
1868	Thomas L. Mintun,	"	"

County Auditors.

The first constitution of Ohio provided for the election by the people of only two county officers, viz.: sheriff and coroner; other county officers were, during the first eighteen years of the state's history, appointed by the county commissioners or by the associate judges of the respective counties. The office of county auditor was created by act of the legislature, at the session of 1820–21. Before that time the principal duties of the auditor were performed by the county clerk, who was appointed by the commissioners. Henry Bartlett, so long known in the county as "Esquire Bartlett," was clerk, and *ex officio* auditor, from 1806 till March 1821. From this time the successive auditors were:

Joseph B. Miles, appointed by commissioners in 1821, and served nine months.
Gen. John Brown, appointed and served till March, 1827.
Norman Root, elected 1827   "   "   1839.
Leonidas Jewett,   "   1839   "   "   1843.
Abner Morse,   "   1843   "   "   1845.

Leonidas Jewett, elected 1845 and served till March, 1847.
E. Hastings Moore, " 1847 " " 1861.
Simeon W. Pickering, " 1861 " present time.

County Sheriffs.

Robert Linzee, appointed April, 1805; Silvanus Ames, appointed November, 1807; Robert Linzee, appointed November, 1809; Thomas Armstrong, elected October, 1813; Isaac Barker, elected October, 1817; Jacob Lentner, elected October, 1821; Calvary Morris, elected October, 1823; Robert Linzee, elected October, 1827; John McGill, elected October, 1829; Amos Miller, elected October, 1831; Joseph Hewitt, elected October, 1835; Joseph H. Moore, elected October, 1839; William Golden, elected October, 1843; J. L. Currier, elected October, 1847; Joseph L. Kessinger, elected October, 1851; Leonard Brown, elected October, 1855; H. C. Knowles, elected October, 1857; Frederic S. Stedman, elected October, 1861; John M. Johnson, elected October, 1863; William S. Wilson, elected October, 1867, and is still in office.

County Recorders.

	In office.			Recorded what volumes.
Dr. Eliphaz Perkins,	From	1806 to July	1819,	Nos. 1, 2, 3, 4.
Chauncey F. Perkins,	" July	1819 to May	1826,	" 4, 5.
A. G. Brown,	" May	1826 to Aug.	1833,	" 5, 6.
Robert E. Constable,	" Aug.	1833 to Nov.	1835,	" 6, 7.
A. G. Brown,	" Nov.	1835 to Oct.	1841,	" 7, 8, 9, 10.
Enos Stimson,	" Oct.	1841 to "	1844,	" 10, 11, 12.
John Boswell,	" "	1844 to "	1847,	" 12, 13, 14.
A. J. Van Vorhes,	" "	1847 to "	1850,	" 14, 15, 16.
W. H. Bartlett,	" "	1850 to Dec.	1854,	" 17, 18, 19, 20, 21.
Frank E. Foster,	" Dec.	1854 to Nov.	1855,	" 22.
George H. Stewart,	" Nov.	1855 to June	1861,	" 23, 24, 25, 26.
Norman Root,	" June	1861 to Jan.	1862,	" 26, 27.
Daniel Drake,	" Jan.	1862 to "	1868,	" 28, 29, 30, 31, 32.
Josiah B. Allen,	" "	1868, still in office.		33, 34, 35.

County Treasurers.

Alvan Bingham, appointed April, 1805; William Harper, appointed June, 1806; Ebenezer Currier, appointed June, 1807; Eliphaz Perkins, appointed March, 1808; William Harper, appointed June, 1809; Eliphaz Perkins,* appointed June, 1811; Amos Crippen, appointed June, 1815; Isaac Barker, appointed June, 1825, elected October, 1825; Amos Crippen, elected October, 1829; Isaac Barker, elected October, 1831; Isaac N. Norton, elected October, 1835, died in December, 1836. Abram Van Vorhes acted first year, and Isaac Barker, second year, by appointment. Isaac Barker, elected October, 1837; Amos Crippen, elected October, 1839; Robert McCabe, elected October, 1841; William Golden, elected October, 1847; Samuel Pickering, elected October, 1853; Leonard Brown, elected October, 1857; Joseph M. Dana, elected October, 1859; Leonard Brown, elected October, 1861; A. W. S. Minear, elected October, 1863; George W. Baker, elected October, 1867, and is still in office.

County Court.

The first court of common pleas, July 8, 1805, consisted of Robert F. Slaughter, president judge, and Silvanus Ames and Elijah Hatch, associate judges. Henry Bartlett was appointed clerk. Since that time the following judges have acted:

1806—Levin Belt, president judge, and Silvanus Ames, Alexander Stedman, and Abel Miller, associate judges.

In 1807, Judge Ames became sheriff, and Elijah Hatch became judge.

---

* Extract from county records:

"June 9, 1809. Completed the settlement with Eliphaz Perkins, county treasurer

Amount of money received by him, as per his book		$1,622 36
Received of him in county orders	$1,619 16	
His commissions on same, at 3 per cent. . . .	48 58	
Balance due E. Perkins		45 38
	$1,667 74	$1,667 74

1807 to 1812—William Wilson, president judge, and Alexanander Stedman, Abel Miller, and Elijah Hatch, associate judges.
1813—William Wilson, president judge, and Jehiel Gregory, Silvanus Ames, and Elijah Hatch, associate judges.
1814—William Wilson, president judge, and Jehiel Gregory, Silvanus Ames, and Ebenezer Currier, associate judges.
1815 to 1818—William Wilson, president judge, and Silvanus Ames, Ebenezer Currier, and Elijah Hatch, associate judges.
1819—Ezra Osborne, president judge, and Robert Linzee, Ebenezer Currier, and Silvanus Ames, associate judges.
1824—Alvan Bingham, associate judge, *vice* Silvanus Ames, deceased.
1825—Amos Crippen, associate judge, *vice* Robert Linzee.
1826—Edmund Dorr, associate judge, *vice* Ebenezer Currier, and Thomas Irwin, president judge, *vice* Osborne.
1827—Elijah Hatch, associate judge, *vice* Amos Crippen.
1838—George Walker, associate judge, *vice* Alvan Bingham.
1833—Ebenezer Currier, associate judge, *vice* Edward Dorr.
1834—David Richmond, associate judge, *vice* Elijah Hatch.
1840—John E. Hanna, president judge, *vice* Thomas Irwin.
1840—Samuel B. Pruden, associate judge, *vice* Ebenezer Currier.
1841—Isaac Barker, associate judge, *vice* D. Richmond.
1845—Robert A. Fulton, associate judge, *vice* George Walker.
1847—Arius Nye, president judge, *vice* John E. Hanna.
1847—Samuel H. Brown, associate judge, *vice* S. B. Pruden.
1850—Norman Root, associate judge, *vice* Samuel H. Brown.
1850—A. G. Brown, president judge, *vice* Arius Nye.
1852—Simeon Nash, elected first judge under new constitution, when associate judges were dispensed with.
1862—John Welch elected.
1865—Erastus A. Guthrie, appointed, *vice* John Welch, elected supreme judge.
1866—E. A. Guthrie elected, and is still in office.

County Clerks.

Henry Bartlett, appointed December 1, 1806; served till February 8, 1836.

Joseph M. Dana, appointed February 8, 1836; elected February 22, 1843; served till 1857.

Louis W. Brown, elected 1857, and is still in office.

Probate Court (Organized in 1852).

Jacob C. Frost, elected 1852.

Nelson H. Van Vorhes, elected October, 1855; resigned September, 1855.

Daniel S. Dana, appointed September, 1855.

Calvary Morris, elected October, 1855, and is still in office.

Prosecuting Attorneys.

1806 to 1809, E. B. Merwin; 1809 to 1810, Benjamin Ruggles; 1810 to 1812, Artemas Sawyer; 1812 to 1813, Alexander Harper; 1813 to 1815, Artemas Sawyer; 1815 to 1816, J. Lawrence Lewis; 1816 to 1817, Thomas Ewing; 1817 to 1820, Joseph Dana, sen.; 1820 to 1822, Samuel F. Vinton; 1822 to 1824, Thomas Ewing; 1824 to 1826, Thomas Irwin; 1826 to 1830, Dwight Jarvis; 1830 to 1835, Joseph Dana, jun.; 1835 to 1839, John Welch; 1839 to 1841, Robert E. Constable; 1841 to 1843, John Welch; 1843 to 1845, Tobias A. Plants; 1845 to 1847, James D. Johnson; 1847 to 1851, Lot L. Smith; 1851 to 1855, Samuel S. Knowles; 1855 to 1857, George S. Walsh; 1857 to 1861, Erastus A. Guthrie; 1861 to 1863, Lot L. Smith; 1863 to present time, Rudolph de Steiguer.

Population.

By the census of 1800, Washington county (then including Athens, etc.) had 5,427 inhabitants.

Athens County.

By the census of 1810, Athens county had,

561	males	and	517	females	under	10	years.	
234	"	"	210	"	over	10	and under 16 years.	
241	"	"	260	"	"	16	" " 26	"
283	"	"	235	"	"	26	" " 45	"
144	"	"	102	"	"	45	years.	
1,463			1,324					

Total population of the county in 1810, - - - - 2,787.

Population by Townships in 1820.

	Males.	Females.	Total.
Ames, - - - - -	388	333	721
Athens, - - - -	582	532	1,114
Alexander, - - - -	421	433	854
Canaan, - - - -	193	163	356
Carthage, - - - -	175	145	320
Dover, - - - -	330	277	607
Elk, - - - - -	274	271	545
Homer, - - - -	101	100	201
Lee, - - - - -	185	157	342
Rome, - - - -	266	231	497
Troy, - - - - -	295	246	541
York, - - - -	183	158	341
Aggregate, - -	3,393	3,046	6,439

NOTE.—It must be borne in mind that the boundaries of some of the townships underwent changes from time to time till March, 1850, since when there have been no changes.

History of Athens County, Ohio. 165

Population by Townships in 1830.

Athens village	729
Residue of Athens township	974
Alexander	882
Ames	857
Bern	223
Canaan	375
Carthage	395
Coolville village	84
Residue of Troy	565
Dover	550
Lee	418
Lodi	276
Elk	822
McArthurstown village	69
Residue of Vinton	109
Homer	636
Rome	522
Trimble	190
Nelsonville village	73
Residue of York	798
Waterloo	216
Total	9,763

Population by Townships in 1840.

	Male.	Female.	Total.
Alexander	728	723	1,451
Ames	718	713	1,431
Athens	1,178	1,104	2,282
Bern	196	185	381
Brown	132	125	257
Canaan	421	379	800
Carthage	397	337	734
Dover	679	611	1,290
Elk	647	614	1,261
Homer	451	461	912
Lee	440	408	848
Lodi	394	360	754
Marion	569	510	1,079
Rome	427	425	852
Trimble	385	377	762
Troy	546	510	1,056
Ward	179	157	336

POPULATION BY TOWNSHIPS IN 1840.—*Continued.*

Waterloo	382	359	741
Vinton	108	119	227
York	863	737	1,600
Total, white	9,840	9,214	19,054
Colored persons			55
Aggregate population			19,109

STATISTICS OF THE COUNTY FOR THE YEAR 1850.

Population.

	White males.	White fem.	Total.	Colored.	Aggregate.
Alexander	869	859	1,728	7	1,735
Ames	780	702	1,482	—	1,482
Athens	1,151	1,179	2,330	30	2,360
Bern	432	387	819	—	819
Canaan	589	553	1,142	—	1,142
Carthage	554	533	1,087	—	1,087
Dover	628	604	1,232	—	1,232
Lee	480	477	957	4	961
Lodi	678	655	1,333	3	1,336
Rome	650	627	1,277	32	1,309
Trimble	482	442	924	—	924
Troy	686	735	1,421	—	1,421
Waterloo	511	487	998	18	1,016
York	745	634	1,379	12	1,391
Total	9,235	8,874	18,109	106	18,215

Churches, etc., 1850.

	No. of Churches.	Value.
Baptist	2	$ 1,100
Methodist	12	8,250
Presbyterian	8	7,000
Roman Catholic	1	800
Universalist	1	800
	24	$17,950

Agricultural Statistics, 1850.

Acres of land, improved, in farms	82,168
" " unimproved	103,109
Cash value of farms	$2,125,967
Value of farming implements and machinery	92,283
Number of horses	3,345
" milch cows	4,302
" working oxen	1,331
" other cattle	6,260
" sheep	359,45
" swine	15,675
Value of live stock	$314,894
" slaughtered animals	75,551

PRODUCED DURING YEAR ENDING JUNE 1, 1850.

Bushels of wheat	72,146
" rye	395
" Indian corn	443,546
" oats	74,255
Pounds of tobacco	58,356
" wool	92,990
Bushels of Irish potatoes	34,447
" sweet potatoes	2,328
" buckwheat	7,095
Value of orchard products	$6,199
Pounds of butter	257,302
" cheese	58,170
Tons of hay	12,188
Bushels of clover seed	375
Bushels of other grass seeds	229
Pounds of flax	7,618
Bushels of flax seed	348
Pounds of maple sugar	28,665
Gallons of maple molasses	2,052
Pounds of beeswax and honey	9,983
Value of home made manufactures	$28,325

STATISTICS OF THE COUNTY FOR THE YEAR 1860.

White Population by Age and Sex.

	Males.	Females.	Total.
Under 1 year of age	324	282	606
1 year and under 5	1,334	1,343	2,677
5 years " 10	1,470	1,514	2,984
10 " " 15	1,422	1,354	2,776
15 " " 20	1,263	1,225	2,488
20 " " 30	1,778	1,737	3,515
30 " " 40	1,213	1,150	2,363
40 " " 50	835	748	1,583
50 " " 60	523	503	1,026
60 " " 70	338	289	627
70 " " 80	134	119	253
80 " " 90	41	31	72
90 " " 100	2	5	7
Above 100	1		1
Total	10,678	10,300	20.978
Total colored population			386
Aggregate			21,364

Population by Townships, 1860.

	White males.	White fem.	Total.	Colored.	Aggregate.
Alexander	816	843	1,659	16	1,675
Ames	675	657	1,332	3	1,335
Athens	1,413	1,394	2,807	45	2,852
Bern	482	472	954	68	1,022
Canaan	639	633	1,272	—	1,272
Carthage	579	548	1,127	—	1,127
Dover	722	699	1,421	2	1,423
Lee	565	562	1,127	174	1,301
Lodi	818	780	1,598	—	1,598
Rome	787	749	1,536	45	1,581
Trimble	574	536	1,110	2	1,112
Troy	876	871	1,747	—	1,747
Waterloo	765	701	1,466	17	1,483
York	969	853	1,822	14	1,836
Aggregate					21,364

Churches, etc., 1860.

	No. of Churches.	Value.
Baptist	1	$ 650
" free-will	5	4,600
Christians	3	1,825
Episcopal	2	700
Methodist	42	23,565
Presbyterian	5	10,550
Cumberland Presbyterian	1	1,000
Roman Catholic	1	800
Union	1	600
Universalist	1	600
Total number	62	$44,890

The valuation of estate, real and personal, in the county, for the year 1860, was:

Real	$6,467,950
Personal	2,600,677
	$9,068,627

Agricultural Statistics, 1860.

Acres of land, improved, in farms	129,531	
" " unimproved	123,170	
Cash value of farms		$4,980,034
Value of farming implements and machinery		156,646
Number of horses	5,731	
" asses and mules	33	
" milch cows	5,658	
" working oxen	1,558	
" other cattle	11,597	
" sheep	36,498	
" swine	21,447	
Value of live stock		748,589
Bushels of wheat produced	120,082	
" rye	721	
" Indian corn	641,605	
" oats	66,104	
Pounds of tobacco	275,789	
" wool	88,968	

Bushels of peas and beans	2,428	
" Irish potatoes	57,261	
" sweet potatoes	3,600	
" barley	476	
" buckwheat	14,930	
Value of orchard products		$17,799
Pounds of butter	634,872	
" cheese	89,213	
Tons of hay	19,278	
Bushels of clover seed	104	
" grass seeds	1,098	
Pounds of hops	356	
Tons of hemp	79	
Pounds of flax	2,774	
Bushels of flax seed	118	
Pounds of maple sugar	22,778	
Gallons of maple molasses	2,549	
" sorghum molasses	28,335	
Pounds of beeswax	554	
" honey	19,540	
Value of home made manufactures		15,978
" animals slaughtered		122,375

Manufactures, 1860.

	Capital Invested.	Annual value of Products.
Blacksmithing	$1,750	$ 4,452
Boots and shoes	3,700	16,794
Carriages	8,200	4,113
Clothing	7,100	12,150
Coal	49,450	49,700
Flour and meal	70,400	263,938
Furniture	3,950	4,030
Leather	26,815	29,028
Lumber	32,200	46,944
Machinery	3,000	7,100
Marble and stone work	800	3,500
Pottery ware	1,000	800
Printing	3,000	2,400
Provisions—pork and beef	10,000	12,000
Saddlery and harness	2,700	6,141
Salt	96,000	59,050

History of Athens County, Ohio.

MANUFACTURES, 1860.—*Continued.*

Tin, copper, and sheet iron ware	$1,000	$2,585
Wagons, carts, etc.	1,400	1,700
Wool carding	1,500	9,860
Total	$331,665	$545,002

Products of Athens County, in the Year 1865-6.

No. of acres of wheat	13,176,	Number of bushels	104,893
" " rye,	153,	" "	1,450
" " buckwheat,	243,	" "	2,450
" " oats	3,403,	" "	56,445
" " corn	15,422,	" "	546,791
" " meadow	15,188,	Tons of hay	18,206
" " potatoes	514,	Number of bushels	40,462
" " tobacco	168,	" pounds	136,460
" " clover	755,	" tons hay	799
" " sorghum	526,	" galls. sirup	80,253
No. of lbs. of maple sugar	14,347,	" "	1,391
" " butter	327,480.		
" " cheese	27,705.		

Number of sheep in the county, year ending July 1, 1866	75,406
Value	$221,585
Number of hogs in the county, year ending July 1, 1866	12,191
Value	$60,342
Amount of wool produced, year ending July 1, 1866, lbs.	189,183
Number of dogs in the county, " " "	1,082
Number of sheep killed by dogs year ending July 1, 1866	304
" deeds and leases recorded " "	713
" mortgages recorded " "	144
Amount of money secured by mortgage " "	$124,658
Number of crimes indicted during year ending July 1, 1866,	
Against the person	16
Against property	11
Statutory offenses	15
Number of convictions	27
Number of marriages during same year	352
" divorces	15
" dwellings erected during same year	50
" barns " " "	9
" factories " " "	1
" school houses " "	2
" civil judgments rendered during same year	91
Amount of " " " " "	$55,026 03

The following statement shows the number and value of certain live stock, in the respective townships, as listed by the assessors for taxation, in 1867:

	MULES.		SHEEP.		HORSES.		CATTLE.	
	No.	Value.	No.	Value.	No.	Value.	No.	Value.
Athens town					98	$7,815	115	$3,149
Athens township	2	$125	7,208	$16,235	414	26,803	1,021	18,320
Alexander	2	100	7,808	18,287	520	32,445	1,455	33,265
Ames	9	670	14,139	42,093	552	38,976	1,513	37,176
Bern	7	352	5,090	15,843	324	25,404	796	19,494
Canaan	2	50	3,775	9,003	407	16,806	1,004	20,733
Carthage	3	75	6,976	18,737	377	2,230	936	18,934
Dover	8	516	6,384	14,746	324	21,338	995	22,511
Lee	9	620	3,544	9,355	214	15,050	602	13,880
Albany village	10	470	1,067	2,559	123	9,415	263	6,405
Lodi	9	585	5,217	13,247	564	36,869	1,917	28,691
Rome	9	600	3,142	7,981	431	26,882	1,527	23,732
Troy	4	260	4,364	10,006	336	20,300	917	18,915
Coolville village	11	670	523	1,172	59	4,080	116	2,494
Trimble township	7	210	4,227	10,124	367	21,537	717	14,459
Waterloo	7	489	7,436	22,507	369	24,225	756	16,335
York	8	510	3,098	8,425	338	20,565	768	18,690
Nelsonville village	6	435	17	41	122	8,035	122	2,825
Total	113	$6,737	84,018	$220,757	5,939	$388,675	15,540	$320,008

Statement showing the Vote of Athens County at various Elections from 1836 to 1868.

	Whig.		Democrat.	
1836—President	Harrison,	1,098	Van Buren,	957
" Governor	Vance,	966	Baldwin,	736
1838—Governor	Vance,	1,086	Shannon,	732
1840—President	Harrison,	2,094	Van Buren,	1,322
1842—Governor	Corwin,	1,519	Shannon,	1,278
1844—President	Clay,	2,050	Polk,	1,425

(At this election, Birney, Abolitionist, received 220 votes.)

1844—Governor	Bartley,	1,742	Tod,	1,267

(King, Abolitionist, 266.)

1846—Governor	Bebb,	1,189	Tod,	1,007

(Lewis, Abolitionist, 209.)

1848—Congress	Vinton,	1,580	Tucker,	859
" President	Taylor,	1,846	Cass,	1,509

(Van Buren, Abolitionist, 320.)

1850—Congress	Welch,	1,602	Daniels,	1,208
1851—Governor	Vinton,	1,294	Wood,	1,162

(Lewis, Abolitionist, 114.)

1852—President	Scott,	1,750	Pierce,	1,383

(Hale, Abolitionist, 366.)

1853—Governor	Barrere,	849	Medill,	1,272

(Lewis, Abolitionist, 735.)

1854—Congress	Horton,	1,628	Smith,	919

History of Athens County, Ohio.

Vote of Athens County—*Continued.*

Year / Office	Republican	Votes	Democrat	Votes
1855—Governor	Chase,	1,634	Medill,	974
(Trimble, Whig, 98.)				
1856—President	Fremont,	2,299	Buchanan,	1,350
(Fillmore, American, 154.)				
1856—Congress	Horton,	2,183	Medill,	1,270
1857—Governor	Chase,	1,723	Payne,	1,319
(Van Trump, American, 14.)				
1858—Congress	Van Vorhes,	2,143	Martin,	1,303
" Supreme judge	Peck,	2,105	Bartley,	1,354
1859—Governor	Dennison,	1,843	Ramsey,	1,237
1860—President	Lincoln,	2,526	Douglas,	1,491
(Bell, American, 36; Breckenridge, 43.)				
1861—Governor	Tod,	2,405	Jewett,	642
1862—Secretary of state	Kennon,	1,954	Armstrong,	1,194
" Congress	Cutler,	1,965	Morris,	1,185
1863—Governor—home vote	Brough,	2,788	Vallandigham,	1,008
soldiers' vote		609		16
		3,397		1,024
1864—Secretary of state—home vote	Smith,	2,289	Armstrong,	1,175
soldiers' "		442		27
		2,731		1,202
1864—President—home vote	Lincoln,	2,474	McClellan,	1,246
soldiers' vote		566		72
		3,040		1,318
1864—Congress—home vote	Plants,	2,280	Morris,	1,178
soldiers' vote		435		14
		2,715		1,192
1865—Governor—home vote	Cox,	2,541	Morgan,	1,160
soldiers' vote		50		10
		2,591		1,170
1866—Secretary of state	Smith,	2,647	LeFever,	1,210
" Congress	Plants,	2,640	Follett,	1,212
1867—Governor	Hayes,	2,598	Thurman,	1,701
" Constitutional amendment	"Yes,"	2,278	"No,"	1,904
1868—Congress	Moore,	2,807	Follett,	1,590
" President	Grant,	2,908	Seymour,	1,592

Post Offices.

Prior to the year 1794, there was no mail route to the northwestern territory, nor any post office north of the Ohio river west of Pittsburg. The only communication the Ohio Company's settlers had with the east was by private hands, and the receipt of letters or papers was a rare and interesting occurrence. In the year 1794, a route was established from Pittsburg, *via* Washington, Pennsylvania, West Liberty, Virginia, and Wheeling, to Limestone (now Maysville, Kentucky), and Fort Washington (Cincinnati). From Pittsburg to Wheeling the mail was carried by land, and from Wheeling down the Ohio river in small boats, about twenty-four feet long, built much like a whale-boat, and steered with a rudder. Each boat was manned by five persons, well armed and provided against attacks by the Indians. Though not covered, each of the little craft was furnished with a large tarpaulin, which, in case of storm or other necessity, was used to cover the arms, mail bags, etc. The boats, ascending and descending the river, met and exchanged mails at Marietta, Gallipolis, and Maysville. The time consumed was about twelve days from Cincinnati to Wheeling, and about half that time from Wheeling to Cincinnati.* By this route, the inhabitants of

---

*Though not strictly germane to the subject, we may be excused for presenting some facts concerning the early postal operations of the government, showing the very small beginnings of our present vast and beneficent system.

On the 1st of January, 1790, there were only seventy-five post offices in the United States. There are now more than twenty-four thousand. For the quarter ending December 13, 1789, the total receipts of the post office at New York were $1,067 08; the emoluments of the post master amounted to $327 32, and the incidental

Washington county, and afterward those of Athens, received their mail matter once in two or three weeks. In the year 1800, the only post route in southern Ohio was from Zanesville to Marietta. In 1802, a route was established from Marietta, by way of Athens and Chillicothe, to Cincinnati; and in 1804, the route from Marietta to Zanesville was discontinued.

The first post office in the county of Athens, was established at Athens in January, 1804, and the first post master was Jehiel Gregory. The office was kept at his house, across the river, east of Athens, where D. B. Stewart's woolen factory is now situated. The office changed hands in the spring of the same year, and Dr. Eliphaz Perkins was appointed post master,

---

expenses of the office were $36 89. At the Philadelphia post office, the receipts for the same period were $1,530 73; post master's emoluments, $315 28, expenses of office, $77 84. The mail was carried from Philadelphia to Pittsburg once in two weeks. The contracts for carrying the mail to the southward of New York city, for that year, amounted to $14,973 75; and to the eastward of the same place to $6,003 15. From New York to Albany, the contractors received all the postage for carrying the mail. The route from Boston to Providence, New London, and New Haven, was an expense to the department of $520, for that year. The route from Philadelphia to Pittsburg, was an expense of $800. The department fell in debt $34 84 for the quarter. In the year 1825, the mail was carried from Wheeling to Zanesville, Ohio, three times a week; from Zanesville to Lancaster, three times a week; from Lancaster to Cincinnati, twice a week; from Marietta to Zanesville, once a week; from Marietta to Chillicothe, twice a week, and from Marietta to Lancaster, once in two weeks. [American State Papers.]

and kept the office for a short time, on State street, near D. M. Clayton's late residence, and afterward, for many years, in the brick building now known as Ballard's corner.

The second post office established in the county was in Ames township, in the year 1821. Loring B. Glazier was the first post master there, and the office received the name of Amesville. Previous to the establishment of this office, Judge Ames, Judge Walker, Doctor Walker, Abel Glazier, Judge Cutler, and other citizens of the neighborhood, taking the Marietta paper, received their papers from the mail carrier, who brought them in a way-bag for distribution, for which service each person was required to pay fifty cents a year to the carrier. During the early years of this century, several copies of the *National Intelligencer* were taken in the Ames settlement. It was received every two weeks, and was at once the great news bringer from the outer world to the little community, and the political gospel of all its readers. The writer has heard an aged relative, herself a staunch adherent of the Jeffersonian school of politics, relate with what eagerness the *Intelligencer* was awaited during the war of 1812, and how its narratives of events, political and military, were devoured by those who could read, and read aloud to those who could not.

The following is a list of the post offices now in operation in the county, in the order of their establishment, with the names of those who have acted as post masters, from the first to the present:

Athens. Established in 1804.

Jehiel Gregory, post master	from	1804	1 quarter.
Eliphaz Perkins		1804	till 1821
John Perkins		1821	1839
Amos Crippen		1839	1841
John Perkins		1841	1845
Amos Crippen		1845	1849
Wm. Loring Brown		1849	1853
R. DeSteiguer		1853	1858
Lot L. Smith		1858	1861
David M. Clayton		1861	1865
E. C. Crippen		1865	1866
John F. Mahon		1866	1867
William Golden		1867	present time.

Amesville. Established in 1821.

Loring B. Glazier, post master	from	1821	till 1829
Robert Henry		1829	1834
Hiram Cable		1834	1837
N. Dean		1837	1841
Loring B. Glazier		1841	1842
Hiram Cable		1842	1846
Evert V. Phillips		1846	1849
Lorenzo Fulton		1849	1861
A. W. Glazier		1861	1862
Lorenzo Fulton		1862	present time.

Coolville. Established in 1822.

Jacob S. Miller, post master	from	1822	till 1824
Alfred Hobby		1824	1840
In 1840, name changed to Hocking City.			
R. B. Blair		1840	1841
Eps Story		1841	1842
James M. Miller		1842	1843
John Pratt		1843	1857
In 1844, name changed back to Coolville.			
Joseph K. Davis		1857	1862
W. F. Pilcher		1862	present time.

Nelsonville. Established in 1825.

Daniel Nelson, post master	from 1825	till 1834
James Knight	1834	1836
John Lillabridge	1836	1839
Henry Parkson	1839	1840
L. D. Poston	1840	1848
John H. Tucker	1848	1850
Charles Cable	1850	1852
Alfred Couden	1852	1855
C. A. Cable	1855	1857
M. A. Stuart	1857	2 quarters.
Joseph Brett	1857	1862
T. L. Mintun	1862	1866
John F. Welch	1866	present time.

Federalton. Established in 1829.

Elijah Hatch, post master	from 1829	till 1835
Alexander Stewart	1835	1837
Peter Beebe	1837	1846
Sydney S. Beebe	1846	1858
Blanford Cook	1858	present time.

Lee. Established in 1829.

Jacob Lentner, post master	from 1829	till 1836
James Wilson	1836	1837
Lucius R. Beckley	1837	1840
J. McCully	1840	1841
Jonathan Winn	1841	1846
John V. Brown	1846	1847
John Earhart	1847	1849
Peter Morse	1849	1853
J. M. Gorsline	1853	1861
Peter Morse	1861	1865
W. W. Kurtz	1865	1866
Augustus Palmer	1866	present time.

Canaanville. Established in 1834.

Stephen Pilcher, post master	from 1834	till 1839
Nehemiah O. Warren	1839	1866
J. Warren Baird	1866	present time.

Hebbardsville. Established in 1834.

A. Stearns, post master	from 1834	till 1835
Abraham Van Vorhes	1835	1839
Samuel Earhart	1839	1843
Peter Morse	1843	1845
Samuel Earhart	1845	1848
Almus Lindley	1848	1853
Samuel W. Crabbe	1853	1858
George Six	1858	1861
N. L. Wilson	1861	1865
John J. Coe	1865	present time.

Millfield. Established in 1834.

John Pugsley, post master	from 1834	till 1836
Josiah True	1836	1837
William Larue	1837	1841
David Nesmith	1841	1848
Joel Sanders	1848	1851
Henry Brown	1851	1862
Chester Woodworth	1862	present time.

Calvary. Established in 1838.

Sylvanus Howe, post master	from 1838	till 1863
William Watson	1863	1865
George Curfman	1865	present time.

Chauncey. Established in 1838.

Henry Clark, post master	from 1838	till 1841
Eli House	1841	1842
Benjamin P. Hubbard	1842	3 quarters.
G. S. Williams	1842	1844
Charles R. Smith	1844	1845
Robert Sharp	1845	1849
Thomas Anderson, jr	1849	1851
William M. Edwards	1851	1853
Robert Sharp	1853	1855
William M. Edwards	1855	present time.

Athens County.

Guysville. Established in 1839.

Guy Barrows, post master	from 1839	till 1847
Elvira Barrows	1847	1852
Edward D. Dalbey	1852	1855
Abraham Parrell	1855	1859
Aratus Buckley	1859	1862
E. R. Minear	1862	1864
L. C. Heath	1864	1866
David M. Burchfield	1866	present time.

Hockingport. Established in 1839.

(Big Hocking from 1836 till '39.)

Ferdinand Paulk, post master	from 1836	till 1846
Erastus H. Williams	1846	1861
David P. Scott	1861	1865
Erastus H. Williams	1865	present time.

Shade. Established in 1839.

J. M. Waterman, post master	from 1839	till 1841
John Cather	1841	1845
Charles D. Martin	1845	3 quarters.
Nathan Axtell	1845	1847
James C. Burson	1847	1853
Asbury Cremer	1853	1863
John Burson	1863	present time.

Trimble. Established in 1841.

Samuel Porter, post master	from 1841	till 1849
John S. Dew	1849	1851
Lewis W. Russell	1851	1866
George A. Russell	1866	present time.

Hulls. Established in 1851.

Isaac B. Dudley, post master	from 1851	till 1853
F. R. Stacey	1853	1855
Isaac B. Dudley	1855	1857
B. R. Pierce	1857	1860
John Kinney	1860	1861
S. W. Hull	1861	1866
Windell Shott	1866	present time.

Lottridge. Established in 1851.

Edward Lawrence, post master - from 1851 till present time.

Pleasanton. Established in 1851.

Franklin Burnham, post master -	from 1851	till 1855
Nelson Lord - - - - - -	1855	1862
D. Drake - - - - - -	1862	1865
Henry Logan - - - - -	1865	present time.

Torch. Established in 1851.

Nicholas Baker, post master - -	from 1851	till 1861
Sherman Brewster - - - - -	1861	1866
Edgar Hallet - - - - -	1866	present time.

Woodyards. Established in 1851.

Robert Figley, post master - -	from 1851	till 1855
Leven Oliver - - - - -	1855	present time.

Garden. Established in 1853.

John O. Fox, post master - -	from 1853	till 1855
Daniel S. Johnson - - - - -	1855	1857
J. R. Evans - - - - -	1857	1859
John Buck - - - - - -	1859	1861
A. H. Brill - - - - -	1861	1865
N. F. Woodworth - - - - -	1865	present time.

Hartleyville. Established in 1853.

Martin Shaner, post master - -	from 1853	till 1855
Benjamin Norris - - - - -	1855	1866
Samuel Banks - - - - -	1866	present time.

Athens County.

New England. Established in 1857.

T. R. Rider, post master	from 1857	till 1859
L. R. Jarvis	1859	1865
Daniel F. Wyatt	1865	present time.

Rock Oak. Established in 1857.

S. D. Workman, post master	from 1857	till 1866
Joseph Miller	1866	present time.

Marshfield. Established in 1859.

Hugh Baden, post master	from 1859	till 1865
A. G. Patterson	1865	1866
David Mayhugh	1866	present time.

Salina. Established in 1866.

George T. Gould, post master - from 1866 till present time.

Big Run. Established in 1866.

Thomas Lucas, post master - from 1866 till present time.

Kings. Established in 1866,

Irwin R. King, post master - from 1866 till present time.

Agricultural Society.

The earliest legislation in Ohio relative to the organization of agricultural societies, and designed to encourage that branch of industry, was an act passed February 25, 1832, entitled "an act to authorize and encourage the establishment of agricultural societies in the several counties of this state, and for other purposes therein set forth." The farmers of Athens county had, however, already perceived their interests in this regard, and a society had been formed and a fair held some years before the passage of this act. The society was organized May 19, 1828. The preamble to the constitution recites that,

"We, whose names are annexed, convinced of the benefits resulting to communities from the operations of well regulated agricultural societies, in the means and facilities afforded by them for the attainment and diffusion of useful practical information, and the spirit of emulation and improvement in the culture of the soil, and the domestic manufacture of its products; do form oursélves into an association for the above mentioned purposes, to be called the *Athens County Agricultural Society*, of which the following shall be the constitution."

The constitution provides for the government of the society, by the usual officers and a board of six directors; for terms of membership, annual meetings, and the awarding of premiums "to members and their families for distinguished merit, exertion, discovery, or improvement in the various branches of husbandry and agricultural economy, household manufactures, etc." At the first meeting, the following persons were appointed and requested to act as agents in soliciting subscriptions to the constitution:

Athens.—S. B. Pruden, R. J. Davis, Charles Shipman.
Alexander.—Ziba Lindley, jr., Asa Stearns, Daniel Dudley.
Ames.—Col. A. Boyles, Geo. Walker, Jacob Boarman.
Bern.—James Dickey, Wm. T. Brown, Robert Henry.
Canaan.—Parker Carpenter, Martin Mansfield, Harry Henshaw.
Carthage.—Francis Caldwell, B. B. Lottridge, Milton Buckingham.
Dover.—Josiah True, Daniel Herrold, John Pugsley.
Elk.—Thomas Johnson, James Bothwell, Edward Dodge.
Homer.—R. S. Lovell, Selah Hart, Wm. Hyde.
Lee.—Jacob Lentner, Michael Canny, Wm. Brown.
Lodi.—Joseph Thomson, Rufus Cooley, Elam Frost.
Rome.—Elijah Hatch, Daniel Stewart, John Thompson.
Troy.—Charles Devol, Alfred Hobby, Wm. Barrows.
Trimble.—Wm. Bagley, Samuel B. Johnson, James Bosworth.
Vinton.—Daniel H. Horton, Isaac Hawk, Samuel Zinn.
Waterloo.—Joseph Hewitt, Nathan Robinett, Alexander Young.
York.—James Knight, Joseph J. Robbins, Robert Terry.

The next meeting of the society was held at Athens, in July, 1828, and arrangements were made for an exhibition, which was accordingly held, in October of that year, and which was the first agricultural fair held in southern Ohio.

The next annual meeting of the society, for the choice of officers, etc., was announced by A. G. Brown, secretary, to be held "at the court house in Athens, on Thursday, April 16th, at one o'clock, P. M." The secretary, then editing and publishing the *Athens Mirror*, accompanied the call with some judicious remarks as to the importance of sustaining the movement, which would, however, "assuredly flag and fall into disuse, without the frequently renewed and strenuous efforts of those who were convinced of its utility, and friendly to its objects."

In the *Mirror* of April 18, 1829, we are informed that,

"The meeting, though not large, was respectable, and made up in zeal what it wanted in numbers. The peculiarity of this season, by which the advance of vegetation, and, consequently, of the farmer's labor, has been delayed, doubtless prevented the attendance of many who would have wished to be present. The meeting was, notwithstanding, very interesting, and hopes are now entertained of the most beneficial results."

The following officers were elected for the ensuing year, each of whom was requested and expected "to take an active part in promoting the objects of the society."

President, Ziba Lindley, jr.; vice presidents, Christopher Wolf, Athens; Samuel McKee, Alexander; Abel Glazier, Ames; James Dickey, Bern; Joshua Hoskinson, Canaan; Fr. Caldwell, Carthage; John B. Johnson, Dover; Justus Reynolds, Elk; H. Alderman, Homer; Jacob Lentner, Lee; J. Thompson, Lodi; Daniel Stewart, Rome; Wm. Barrows,

Troy; Wm. Bagley, Trimble; Geo. Utsler, Vinton; Joseph Hewitt, Waterloo; James Knight, York; treasurer, Thomas Brice; secretary, A. G. Brown; directors, Levi Booth, Col. Absalom Boyles, Robert Linzee, Calvary Morris, S. B. Pruden, Isaac Baker.

A week later, April 25th, the directors met at the same place, and resolved that "seventy-five dollars be appropriated, to be awarded as premiums for the encouragement of industry, enterprise and skill, during the present year," and made out their premium list. The premiums were of course small. The largest was for the best stallion, owned and kept by a member of the society, four dollars. The next largest, for the best pair of working oxen and yoke, three dollars. For the best six merino ewes, two dollars; best beef animal, two dollars, etc. In the list were the following:

"To the person producing evidence of having killed the greatest number of wolves, two young ones to be counted as one old one, three dollars.

Best specimen of sewing silk	$1 00
Best five yards fulled cloth, 3-4 wide	1 00
Best ten yards linen	1 50
Best straw or grass bonnet	1 00
Best grass scythe	50

On motion, it was

"*Resolved*, That the next annual exhibition be held on the last Thursday in October next (1829)."

Several annual exhibitions were held after this, but in the course of a few years the interest began to flag, local dissensions crept in, and finally the fairs ceased to be held. A lapse of nearly twenty years occurred before the society was revived. In December, 1850, the county commissioners issued a call for a meeting of citizens, to be held on the 13th of January, 1851, for the purpose of organizing an agricultural society. At that meeting, a constitution and by-laws were adopted, and Sabinus Rice was chosen president; Ziba Lindley, vice president; George Putnam, recording secretary; A. B. Walker, corresponding secretary; Joseph M. Dana, treasurer; and Henry Brawley, Eleazur Smith, Hiram Stewart, P. W. Boyles, and James Dickey, managers. Since that time, several annual fairs have been held, and there has been a steady and gratifying growth of interest in the society. The present officers are, Charles L. Wilson, president; Peter Long, vice president; Nelson H. Van Vorhes, treasurer; A. W. Glazier, secretary; and Joseph Higgins, George Putnam, A. W. Glazier, A. S. Tidd, A. N. Vorhes, N. Warren, Cyrus Blazer, and Charles R. Smith, directors.

Topography and Minerals.

The county contains about four hundred and eighty-four square miles of land, some portions of which are admirably adapted for grazing and agricultural purposes, while others are rich in minerals. It is well watered by the Hockhocking river and its tributaries, Sunday creek, Monday creek, Margaret's creek, Federal creek, Shade river, etc. The Hockhocking, entering at the northwestern corner of York township, traverses the county diagonally for a distance of about fifty miles, flowing into the Ohio river in Troy township. The average width of the stream throughout the county is about fifty yards. The region drained by its numerous tributary streams, and which may be called its valley, will average about twenty miles in width. The whole extent of the valley (in Athens county) is hilly and broken, the hills rising from two hundred to three hundred feet above the beds of the neighboring streams, which, in times past, appear to have worn their way through the strata, so as to give the surface of the country, once a plain, the features which we now observe. The alluvial lands of the Hockhocking and its tributaries are very rich, though liable to occasional overflow from the sudden floods that take place in all the streams of this region. The hill lands are covered with a fertile soil, and clothed with a heavy growth of forest trees.

Coal.

Of this wonderful product of nature—so mysterious in its origin, and so incalculably useful to the comfort and industries of men—vast deposits exist within the county, there being at least eight or ten beds, or veins, varying in thickness from a few inches to several feet.

It is probable that the most valuable vein is that one which, as it has been most extensively worked in the vicinity of Nelsonville, has been called the "Nelsonville coal." This bed is unquestionably one of the most, if not the most, valuable in the state; not only on account of its superior quality and its proximity to canal and railroad facilities, but also for the comparative ease with which it can be obtained. The average thickness of the vein may be rated at six feet, but it varies from five to nine. As we descend the river from Nelsonville, it gradually dips and finally disappears below the bed of the Hockhocking, about five miles below Nelsonville, on section eight, in York township. Taking into account the fall of the river, the dip between the two places is between twenty and twenty-five feet per mile, in a south or southeast direction. West of Nelsonville, it extends up the river, gradually becoming more elevated until it runs out on the tops of the hills, three or four miles above the town. The same vein has been traced over to the head waters of Raccoon, in Waterloo township.

About a mile and a half northeast from the point where the vein above described dips *below* the river, occurs a bed of coal about forty feet *above*. It is found in the eastern part of Dover township. This vein, sometimes called the "Denman vein," has been opened in several places east of this point, as far as Sunday creek, at the mouth of which it is found near the bed of the stream. North of this it extends into Trimble township.

Another bed, sometimes designated as the "Federal creek coal," occupies an area, from north to south through the county, of from six to ten miles in width, embracing the townships of Lodi, Carthage, Rome, Canaan, Ames, and Bern. Several shafts have been opened near Big run, in Rome township, and from seven hundred to a thousand bushels of excellent coal have been shipped from that point daily during most of the last year. This vein is best disclosed along Federal creek and its branches, and from a point about two miles above the mouth of Federal, it can be found upon almost every section to the north part of the county, varying in thickness from four to eight feet, while its average is not perhaps over five. This vein has not been so extensively worked as the Nelsonville, but of its existence in vast quantities, of its good quality, and of the potent influence which at some future day it will exert on the wealth and prosperity of this section of country, there can be no doubt. The aggregate amount of coal that may be mined within the county has been estimated, by competent authority, at two thousand five hundred millions of tons.

Thus the Creator, working 'through the agencies of

nature, has deposited, where the industry of future generations will make it available, this incalculable store of fossil fuel which will not only supply, for ages, the region it pervades, but will form an article of extensive commerce with other sections and states. Heretofore only about one hundred thousand tons of coal have been annually mined in the county; but the greatly increased railroad facilities which the coal region will soon enjoy, must give a powerful impetus to this important branch of industry. The Mineral railroad, now nearly finished, from Mineral station, on the Marietta and Cincinnati railroad, northerly, some five miles into the coal region, commands access to very extensive deposits, and ample preparations are making for placing the coal in market. The Hocking Valley railroad, also, extending from the capital of the state to Athens, seventy-three miles, will soon be completed, thus opening up the central and northern parts of the state, and even the great northwest, to be supplied with cheap fuel from the hills of Athens county. Already, and more and more each successive year, the industry of the county feels the healthful effects of the growing coal business. But who can say — what imagination shall dare to conceive — the influence which will probably be exerted by these exhaustless coal fields on the society of a hundred years hence? Then, when the population of the state of Ohio may be twenty million souls; when the commercial metropolis of the state may exceed in population the present city of New York; when the smoke of many great manufacturing cities shall roll over the land; when almost every acre shall support its family, and the ground shall be tilled up to the edges of the railroad tracks, *then* this rich mineral region of southern Ohio, will have taken its proper place in the march of progress.

Iron.

In natural sequence to coal, without which it can not be utilized, comes *iron*—the weapon, the utensil, the lever, the support of modern civilization. Of this metal, which, in its countless uses, enters so largely into the demands of agriculture, commerce, science, and art, there are very extensive deposits in the county. Though, as yet, the manufacture of iron has never been undertaken in the county, excellent iron ore exists here in great abundance, and in close proximity to the great coal mines in the northwestern part of the county. The most continuous and probably the most valuable deposit, is a few feet below the Nelsonville coal. This is a heavy, compact ore, of a bluish color, and the vein varies in thickness from eight to twelve inches. In explorations for this ore, the Nelsonville coal affords a sure guide. It is found on the head waters of Monday creek, in Trimble township; on Meeker's run, in York township, and along the branches of Raccoon, in Waterloo. The vein is well exposed at other points, and probably extends through the southeast part of the county. There are also exposures of other veins in different parts of the county, affording conclusive evidence that iron ore, suitable for smelting, exists here in large quantities.

Salt.

The production of *salt* in the county, has been long and successfully tested. For more than twenty years about fifty thousand barrels of excellent salt have been annually produced in the county. Salt water, varying in strength from six to nine per centum, is found in several localities, by boring from six hundred to eight hundred feet; and the brine thus obtained is speedily reduced to salt by the use of coal, which is generally conveniently at hand, and is found to be the cheapest fuel known for the purpose.

The principal operators are M. M. Greene & Co., at Salina; Messrs. Ewing & Vinton, in Chauncey; Mr. Joseph Herrold, near Athens; and Pruden Brothers, at Harmony, two miles below Athens, in Canaan township.

During the War of the Rebellion.

During the terrible four years, from 1861 to 1865, in which the government waged a tremendous war to preserve its own existence, and the union of the states, Athens county was not behind any portion of the loyal north, in the promptness and zeal of her responses to every call. According to the United States census report of 1860, the number of male inhabitants of the county in that year, between the ages of fifteen and fifty, both inclusive, was five thousand and eighty-nine. The county furnished to the government during the war, in all, two thousand six hundred and ten soldiers,* or more than fifty per cent. of her men able to bear arms. In other words, of the able-bodied men in the county, every other one left his business and his family to assist in suppressing the rebellion. This is a record of which the county may well be proud—a record which *no county in the state of Ohio*, and, we dare say, few counties in all the northern states, can surpass. And it should be added that no draft was ever made in the county. What she did was done voluntarily, and stands as a lasting monument of her patriotism. During this trying period, the mass of her people, women not less than men, were profoundly stirred, and a loyal zeal pervaded all. For directing that zeal and organizing it into acts, for keeping up the patriotic fervor, and giving it practical, constant, and continuous expression, great credit belongs to the military committee of the county. During nearly the whole of

---

* This is the number that served in the army, and does not include one thousand nine hundred and sixty-seven men who volunteered and served in repelling the "Morgan raid," in 1863, nor one hundred and sixty "squirrel hunters," who hurried to the defense of Cincinnati, in 1862.

the war that committee consisted of Henry T. Brown, M. M. Greene, James W. Bayard, Lot L. Smith, Simeon W. Pickering, Joseph M. Dana, E. H. Moore, and W. R. Golden.

But even far more deserving than these of lasting remembrance and perpetual honor, were the men of the county who volunteered and served the country in the field. If it were possible, we should have liked to record here, as a small tribute to their patriotism, the name of every Athens county volunteer, officers and privates. It would have been a list of heroes. Our efforts, however, to obtain such a complete list have proved unavailing, and we can only present the following exhibit, which is accurate.* These figures furnish but a bald outline of the stirring and tragic history of the war period. It is easy to write that Athens county contributed two thousand six hundred and ten men to fight for the Union, but this statement conveys not even a suggestion of the events that were transpiring in her borders during those years. Meetings were held by day and night in all parts of the county, local

---

* The materials for such a perfect list probably exist in the war department, at Washington, and among the state records, at Columbus, but at present in such a scattered and confused shape, as to render it entirely out of our power to present a complete list, and a partial one would have been worse than none. Some of the states have published a complete list, giving the name of every volunteer furnished by them during the war, with his county and residence. It is to be hoped that Ohio will eventually do this.

committees appointed in every township, christian commission and aid societies organized, and all these appliances again and again started, with renewed energy as the government repeated its calls for help. Scarcely a family but contributed its quota, and the vacant places in many a one remain unfilled to-day. Some families gave all their men; one widow gave five sons,* and grim-visaged war crossed nearly every threshold, claiming the services of the bravest and best. All these things, with many others, and the names of those who enlisted, would properly appear in a history of the county during the rebellion; but that would form a volume of itself.

Abstract of Soldiers in the United States and State Service, furnished by Athens County, in the War of the Great Rebellion.

Townships.	No. in U. S. army.	No. of 100 days' men.	Total.
Athens	267	96	363
Alexander	162	58	220
Ames	142	—	142
Bern	108	—	108
Carthage	112	—	112
Canaan	117	10	127
Dover	154	30	184
Lee	117	68	185
Lodi	143	39	182
Rome	156	54	210
Trimble	143	27	170
Troy	181	—	181
Waterloo	162	—	162
York	226	38	264
Total	2,190	420	2,610

* Mrs. Anna Barrows, of Rome township.

CHAPTER VI.

Town and Township of Athens.

THE records of the Ohio Company show that on the 9th of November, 1790, a committee of three was appointed to reconnoiter and survey the lands of the Company lying on the upper Hockhocking. This committee consisted of Jonathan Devol, Robert Oliver and Haffield White, and was styled "the reconnoitering committee." Owing, however, to Indian hostilities, the work was deferred some years and the regular survey of Athens and adjoining townships was not begun till January, 1795. The surveying party, which came up the Hockhocking river in canoes, was accompanied by a guard of fifteen men, as the Indian war had hardly closed and it was feared that bands of the savages might be found lurking in these deep forests. But none were met with, and the survey was completed during the ensuing spring and summer.*

---

* We quote from the records of the Ohio Company, December

Some account of the first settlement of the town of Athens and of its history up to the organization of the county is given in Chapter IV. The township as established by the county commissioners at their first meeting included territory which now forms five townships, viz: Swan and Brown, of Vinton county, and Waterloo, Canaan and Athens of Athens county. Thus though not so extensive as Alexander or Ames, Athens township nevertheless included a large extent of country. It was, for that period, a fair two days' journey across the township; and although the country was now emerging from the condition of an unbroken wilderness,

> "Where beasts with men divided empire claim,
> And the brown Indian marks with murderous aim,"

8th, 1795, the following report of the committee for examining the lands on the Hockhocking, suitable for fifth division lots:

"We, the subscribers, being appointed a committee by a resolve of the agents of the Ohio Company of the 9th of November, 1790, and for the purpose expressed in said resolve, but being prevented from attending to that business by the Indian war, until a treaty took place, since which (in company with Jeffrey Matthewson, a surveyor appointed by the superintendent of surveys), having measured and very minutely examined the lands of the Hockhocking, report: That in range 14, township 10, the following sections or mile squares, viz: No. 13, 19, 20, 25, 31, and 32; in range 15, township 12, sections No. 2, 3, 4, 9, 10, 17, 23, 24, 30, 35, and 36; in range 16, township 12, sections No. 5, 12, and 18; in range 16, township 13, sections No. 13, 14, 20, 21, 26, 27, 28, 33 and 34, we find are suitable to be laid out in fifth division lots agreeably to a map herewith exhibited. Having also examined and surveyed the land at the mouth of the great Hockhocking we find it very suitable for house lots and in quantity according to the map herewith exhibited.

JONATHAN DEVOL,
ROBERT OLIVER, } Committee."
HAFFIELD WHITE, it was still very wild and thinly populated. The Rev. James Quinn, a pioneer Methodist preacher who died in Highland county at an advanced age in 1847, settled in Ohio in 1804. The same year he and the Rev. John Meek were appointed to the "Hockhocking circuit," which embraced not only the Hockhocking valley but also the settlements on the Muskingum and on the Scioto from the high bank below Chillicothe up to the neighborhood of where Columbus now stands. In 1805 Mr. Quinn was returned to the same circuit with the Rev. Joseph Williams as his colleague. A camp-meeting, probably the first ever held in the county, was held by Bishop Asbury and Mr. Quinn near the town of Athens in 1810. Mr. Quinn states that it lasted four days, and that Bishop Asbury preached two powerful sermons. In his autobiography, published many years since, Mr. Quinn says:

My first missionary excursion up the Hockhocking valley was performed in December, 1799. Leaving the vicinity of Marietta I ascended the Muskingum to the mouth of Wolf creek and then took the trace to Athens and the falls of Hockhocking. But, taking the right hand trace I left Athens to the left and passing through Amestown, struck the Hockhocking at the identical spot where Nelsonville now stands. There, at the foot of a large beech tree, I stopped and prayed. Having given my horse his mess of corn, and eaten my piece of pone and meat, I cut my name on the beech, mounted poor Wilks and went on. Between sundown and dark I reached the old Indian town near the falls. Here I found three families. They came together and I preached to them. I passed on up the river as far as there were any settlements, spending nearly a week with the people in the vicinity of where Lancaster now is. I then returned by the way I had come and stopped again at my beech tree. Saturday night found me at Athens and in comfortable lodgings at the house of a Mr. Stevens. The people came together the next day, which I think was the first sabbath of January, 1800. I took for my text St. Paul's language to the Athenians of old, 'Of this ignorance,' etc. There were a few Methodists in the region round about, and we had a refreshing time."

This Mr. Quinn was ordained by Bishop Whatcoat, who was ordained by Wesley himself.

Between this time and the organization of the county in 1805 steps were taken by the trustees of the university toward establishing the town.

On the 6th of June, 1804, they passed an "ordinance providing for the sale of lots in the town of Athens." Sec. 1 appointed Rufus Putnam and Samuel Carpenter to survey and lay off the town of Athens agreeably with the rule of the resolution of the legislature of December 18th, 1799. Sec. 2 directed the treasurer of the university to have the town plat recorded. Sec. 3 directed Putnam and Carpenter, after due notice, to sell on the first Monday of November, 1804, at public auction, twenty-seven house-lots and an equal number of out-lots at their discretion, excepting and reserving house-lots number 57 and 58. The remaining sections related to the form of certificate and lease to be given.

The sale took place November 5th, 1804, and with the following result:

No. of lot.	Purchaser.	Price.	Purchaser's residence.
1	John Havner,	$132 00	Athens.
4	Wm. McNichol	46 00	Salt works.
7	Silas Bingham	40 50	Athens.
10	Jarrett Jones	27 00	Middletown.
13	Silas Bingham	62 00	Athens.
16	Silvanus Ames	51 00	Ames.
19	Moses Hewitt	61 00	Middletown.
23	Wm. McNichol	25 00	Salt works.
26	Eliphaz Perkins	30 00	Athens.
28	"	101 00	"
29	Rufus Putnam	59 00	Marietta.
32	John Simonton	27 00	Middletown.
36	John Johnson	20 00	Wheeling.
40	Rufus Putnam	20 00	Marietta.
43	"	30 00	"
46	Henry Bartlett	17 00	Middletown.
49	Canaday Lowry	14 00	"
52	Daniel Mulford	13 00	"
55	Jehiel Gregory	42 00	"
59	Timothy N. Wilkins	22 00	"
63	John Wilkins	10 00	"
65	Rufus Putnam	30 00	Marietta.
68	Wm. McNichol	23 00	Salt works.
71	"	30 00	"
73	"	101 00	"
74	Wm. Dorr	65 00	Middletown.
77	Wm. McNichol	42 00	Salt works.

On the 2nd of April, 1806, Rufus Putnam and Dudley Woodbridge were appointed a committee to conduct a second sale of town lots, which took place November 25, 1806. Some of the lots previously sold were sold again, payments having not been made. The following is the report of the second sale:

Town and Township of Athens.

No. of lot.	Purchaser.	Price.	No. of lot.	Purchaser.	Price.
1	Joel Abbott,	$72 00	24	Moses Hewitt,	$11 00
2	"	40 50	25	Rufus Putnam,	16 00
3	Ebenezer Currier,	36 50	27	Samuel Luckey,	14 00
4	Wm. Skinner,	15 00	29	Wm. Skinner,	16 00
5	Silvanus Ames,	15 00	30	Joseph Buell,	15 00
6	Leonard Jewett,	15 00	31	B. Seamans,	20 00
8	"	15 00	32	Joseph Buell,	11 00
9	"	13 00	33	Wm. Skinner,	35 00
10	John Walker,	12 50	34	Rufus Putnam,	26 00
11	Wm. Skinner,	7 50	36	Moses Hewitt,	18 00
12	John Walker,	26 00	38	David Boyles,	17 00
14	Silvanus Ames,	35 00	39	Timothy Wilkins,	14 00
15	Wm. Dorr,	18 00	40	Dudley Woodbridge,	11 00
16	Silvanus Ames,	15 00	41	Timothy Wilkins,	17 00
17	Ebenezer Currier,	52 00	42	Dudley Woodbridge,	10 00
19	Moses Hewitt,	35 00	43	Benajah Seamans,	12 00
20	"	40 00	44	Jehiel Gregory,	6 00
21	Silas Bingham,	15 00	45	Henry Bartlett,	6 00
22	"	22 00	47	Jehiel Gregory,	6 00
23	Rufus Putnam,	10 00	48	Moses Hewitt,	6 00

The first act passed by an Ohio legislature relative to the navigability of any stream was passed February 15, 1808, and entitled "An act for the navigation of the Hockhocking." It declared that stream to be navigable from its mouth to Rush creek and affixed penalties for obstructing its channel. The first act passed in the state authorizing the construction of a mill dam conferred this privilege on two citizens of Athens. It was passed February 21, 1805, and entitled "An act authorizing Jehiel Gregory, and John Havner, their heirs and assigns, to erect a mill dam across the Hockhocking river."

Sec. 1, authorized these persons "to build a mill on the Hockhocking river, and erect a mill dam across said river opposite to out-lot number ten (10) in the town of Athens, which mill and dam when completed are hereby vested in the said Gregory and Havner, their heirs and assigns, so long as they shall have a legal right to the before mentioned lot."

Sec. 2, enacted that they should make "in the mill dam aforesaid a good and sufficient lock, or apron, constructed in such manner that the free navigation of the river shall not be obstructed."

Sec. 3, required them to pilot and assist all persons or craft passing up or down the stream over said lock or apron without fee or reward.

Sec. 4, required them to complete the dam within five years, and to keep the same in good repair; and Sec. 6, imposed a fine of five dollars for refusing to assist or pilot any person or craft passing up or down the stream over the dam, or for receiving any fee or reward therefor.

Under this act a dam was constructed and mill built in 1805 and 1806, the latter known as Gregory's mill, east of town where D. B. Stewart's mill now stands. In 1832, Messrs. J. B. and R. W. Miles built a large flouring mill at this site, which has been occupied by a mill continuously since 1806. From 1843 till 1853 this mill was in the hands of Mr. Andrew Kessinger, well remembered here as an upright man of business; he was the father of Mr. Joseph L. Kessinger now an active citizen of Athens. The Herrold mill as it is now called, was built by Capt. Silas Bingham in 1816. Previous to his death (which occurred in 1840) Capt. Bingham rented the mill to his step-son, Joseph Herrold, who in 1844 became and still continues the owner of the property. Judge Pruden established his business of carding wool, cloth-dressing, etc., at this mill about 1826 and continued it for several years, when he removed to a new point about two miles below Athens on the river and built up the mills, salt works and other improvements now called Harmony, in Canaan township.

In early times, and for many years after the organization of the county, the passage of the river was made by ferry boats—little scows which were poled and rowed across. In 1800 there was a ferry kept by old Arthur Coates (called Coates's ferry) a few rods below where the south bridge now stands, and another one called Harper's ferry, kept by Wm. Harper, about 100 yards above where the Marietta and Cincinnati railroad crosses the Hockhocking, west of Athens—just where the road turns. Mr. Harper lived a short distance the other side of the river, and Isaac Barker, at that time, in a log house situated on this side and about where the road now turns southward. It was at that time expected that a town would grow up at this ferry, and it was named rather prematurely, Elizabethtown, after a woman who accompanied Mrs. Margaret Snowden to the settlement—her surname is forgotten.

The rates of ferriage for man and beast, loaded teams, etc., were fixed yearly by the county commissioners. There are now several excellent bridges in the township. The East bridge, as it is called, was built about 1834, by Joseph B. and R. W. Miles, and their associates. Isaac Jackson was the principal mechanic, assisted by Oliver Childs. This bridge was modeled after the bridges at Zanesville, Ohio, then recently built by the Buckinghams. The West bridge was built in 1836, and by the same mechanic, Isaac Jackson. The South bridge was built in 1839; Samuel Miller was the principal mechanic, assisted by Francis Beardsley. All three of these bridges were built under acts of incorporation, making them *toll* bridges, but have since been made free by voluntary contributions of the citizens, aided by appropriations of the county. There are two other good bridges in the township, across Margaret's creek, one at its mouth, near the Bingham mills, and the other about a mile above, at the old Goodrich saw mill. Both of these were mainly built by Joseph Herrold, on subscriptions of the neighboring citizens, and appropriations by the county.

The town of Athens had been "confirmed and established," by a legislative act of December 6, 1800; it was regularly incorporated by an act, passed January 28, 1811, entitled "an act to incorporate the town of Athens, and for other purposes." This act enacted that "so much of the township of Athens, county of Athens, as is contained in the plat of the town of

Athens, as recorded in the recorder's office in the county of Washington, be and the same is hereby erected into a town corporate, to be known and distinguished by the name of the town of Athens." It provided for an annual election of a town council and other officers. It also authorized and directed "the trustees of the Ohio university to lease to the county commissioners, on a nominal rent, for ninety-nine years, renewable forever, in-lots Nos. 35 and 37, on which the court house and jail now stand, and also in-lot No. 18, reserved for the purpose of building a school and meeting house;" also, to lease, on the same terms, the grounds reserved for a burying ground.

This act of incorporation was amended February 15, 1812, when the trustees of the Ohio university were authorized and directed to lease to the Methodist society in the town of Athens, on the foregoing terms, "a piece of the public commons which adjoins out-lot No. 61, beginning at the S. E. corner of said lot, thence E. four chains, thence N. eight chains, thence W. four chains, thence S. to the place of beginning—for the use of the said Methodist society, and to build a meeting house thereon for the purposes of worship."

During the next half century, the population of the town and township increased but slowly. The extreme inaccessibility of the town during a long period, from the absence of railroad or other good communications, prevented a large immigration, while the superior agricultural advantages of states lying further west, have drawn away, from time to time, numbers of the citizens. In 1820, the population of the township was 1,114; in 1830, it was 1,703; in 1840, it was 2,282; in 1850, it was 2,360; and in 1860, it was 2,852. The present population of the town of Athens is about two thousand. It is handsomely situated, and, for a town of its class, well built. With a healthful location, in the midst of a region abounding in natural beauties of an uncommonly attractive and picturesque order, and with a quiet and intelligent population, Athens may justly be regarded as a pleasant place of residence. There is good reason also to believe that the future growth of the town will exceed the past. It is now accessible by one railroad, and will soon be the terminus of another. We have, elsewhere in these pages, adverted to the great mineral wealth of the county, and it can not be doubted that these attractions will eventually draw a large and valuable immigration to this point.

A recent triumph of the liberality and active enterprise of the citizens of Athens merits a conspicuous mention—we refer to the securing of the new lunatic asylum. January 17, 1866, Dr. W. P. Johnson, representative from Athens county in the state legislature, caused a resolution to be offered, through Mr. Lockwood, of Licking county, instructing "the committee on benevolent institutions to inquire what action is necessary by the general assembly, to do justice to the incurable insane, and report, by bill or otherwise," which passed the house. February 21, 1866, Dr. Johnson, chairman of the committee aforesaid, reported, by direction of the committee, a "bill to provide for the erection of an additional lunatic asylum, and for the enlargement of the northern and southern lunatic asylums." Meanwhile a flood of light was thrown on the condition of the incurable insane, within the state, by a committee of the state medical society, whose thorough and exhaustive reports on the subject, Dr. Johnson brought before the legislature, contributing much to the success of his measure. His bill, entitled "an act to provide for the erection of an additional lunatic asylum," became a law, April 13, 1867. It provided for the appointment, by the governor, of three trustees, to select and purchase, or receive by gift or donation, a lot of land, not less than fifty nor more than one hundred acres, suitably located for the erection of an asylum, to contain four hundred patients. Mr. W. E. Davis, of Cincinnati, Mr. D. E. Gardner, of Toledo, and Dr. C. McDermont, of Dayton, were appointed trustees; a vacancy occurring in this committee, through the death of Dr. McDermont, Mr. E. H. Moore, of Athens, was appointed in his place. There were various competing points, and for some time the contest was sharp and close; but through the superiority of her claims, the sagacity of her representative, and the liberality of her citizens, Athens finally eclipsed all rivals and secured the asylum. To carry the point, the citizens purchased and made a gift to the state of one hundred and fifty acres of land, lying south of the town, known as the Coates farm. The site is faultless. The land lies beautifully, overlooking the valley of the Hockhocking, with its encircling hills, and commanding on every side a picturesque and varied view. The location was fixed by the trustees in August, 1867. Contracts for the excavation have been let to Messrs. Maris & McAboy; for the brick (about 12,000,000) to Messrs. D. W. H. Day and James W. Sands; and for the masonry to William McAboy. The entire length of the building will be about eight hundred feet, and its cost about four hundred thousand dollars. It will be an elegant and important feature of the place, and can not fail to attract public attention to the town and county.

Officers of the Town of Athens.

The town records from 1811, the date of incorporation, to 1825, are lost. In 1825, James Gillmore was president of the town council, and Joseph B. Miles recorder.

At an election held in the town of Athens, March 6, 1826, the number of votes cast was forty-three, and the following persons were elected members of the town council, viz.: Thomas Brice, by thirty-four votes; Columbus Bierce, by thirty-four votes; Ebenezer Currier, by thirty-one votes; John Brown 2d, by forty-three votes; and Joseph B. Miles, by twenty-three votes. The following town officers were elected: Samuel Knowles, marshal; Eben Foster, supervisor; A. G. Brown, treasurer; Calvary Morris, collector; John Gillmore, assessor. The council elected Ebenezer Currier, president, and Joseph B. Miles, recorder.

March 5, 1827.—Charles Shipman, Columbus Bierce, John Brown 2d, Thomas Brice, and Isaac Taylor, were elected councilmen; William W. Bierce, marshal; John Gillmore, assessor; James J. Fuller, collector; A. G. Brown, treasurer; Eben Foster, supervisor. The council elected Columbus Bierce, president, and John Brown 2d, recorder, for the ensuing year.

March 10, 1828, an election was held, pursuant to an act of the legislature, passed January 24, 1828, entitled "an act to incorporate the town of Athens, in the county of Athens." Nine councilmen were chosen, whose term of office was afterward decided by lot, as follows, viz: Joseph Dana, Thomas Brice, and Jeremiah Olney, to serve three years; Isaac Barker, John Gillmore, and Amos Crippen, to serve two years; and Ebenezer Currier, Eliphaz Perkins, and Norman Root, to serve one year. The council elected, of their own number, Joseph Dana, mayor, and Norman Root, recorder; and they appointed, from the citizens, A. G. Brown, treasurer, John McGill, marshal, John Porter, surveyor of wood and lumber, and William Golden, clerk of the market.

March 9, 1829.—Joseph Dana was elected mayor; Ebenezer Currier, Calvary Morris, and Norman Root, councilmen; and John McGill marshal. Norman Root was chosen recorder for the ensuing year, A. G. Brown, treasurer, and John Porter, surveyor of wood and lumber. The mode of electing the mayor and marshal had been changed by an act of the legislature, passed February 9, 1829, which made these officers elective by the people, instead of by the town council.

March 8, 1830.—John Gillmore, Amos Crippen, and Isaac Barker, were elected to the town council, for three years, and John Perkins for one year; Joseph Dana was elected mayor, and John Sampson, marshal. Norman Root was appointed recorder, John Porter, surveyor of wood and lumber, and Dr. A. V. Medbury, treasurer.

March 14, 1831.—Joseph Dana, Thomas Brice, and John Perkins, were elected councilmen; Joseph Dana was elected mayor, and John Sampson, marshal. The council appointed Norman Root, recorder, Dr. A. V. Medbury, treasurer, and Wm. D. Bartlett, surveyor of wood and lumber for ensuing year.

March 12, 1832.—Hull Foster, Wm. D. Bartlett, and Francis Beardsley, were elected councilmen; John Gillmore, mayor, and Thomas Francis, marshal. The council appointed Thomas Brice recorder, and Dr. Medbury, treasurer.

March 11, 1833.—Samuel Miller, Oliver Childs, and Isaac N. Norton, were elected councilmen; Samuel Miller, mayor, and John Sampson, marshal. Joseph Dana was appointed recorder, and Dr. Medbury, treasurer.

March 10, 1834.—Thomas Francis, A. B. Walker, and Charles Cunningham, were elected councilmen; Samuel Miller, mayor, and John Sampson, marshal. A. B. Walker was appointed recorder, for the ensuing year, and Dr. Medbury, treasurer.

March 9, 1835.—Norman Root, James J. Fuller, and Francis Beardsley, were elected councilmen; Samuel Miller, mayor, and John Sampson, marshal. Edgar P. Jewett was appointed treasurer, and A. B. Walker, recorder, for ensuing year.

March 14, 1836.—I. N. Norton, John Welch, and Leonidas Jewett, were elected councilmen; I. N. Norton, mayor, and

Cyrus Gibson, marshal. John Welch was appointed recorder, and P. S. Baker, treasurer.

March 13, 1837.—Henry Bartlett, John N. Dean, Cephas Carpenter, and Thomas Francis, were elected councilmen; Henry Bartlett, mayor, and Samuel Miller, marshal. Norman Root, appointed recorder, and P. S. Baker, treasurer.

Record of 1838 missing.

March 11, 1839.—John Brown 2d, H. R. Gillmore and Cephas Carpenter were elected councilmen for three years, and Norman Root, Robert McCabe, and Francis Beardsley, for two years. John Brown, elected mayor, and Dr. C. Bierce, marshal. Norman Root appointed recorder, and P. S. Baker, treasurer.

March 9, 1840.—P. S. Baker, John N. Dean, and Cephas Carpenter were elected councilmen; John Brown, mayor, and I. K. Norton, marshal. Norman Root appointed recorder, and A. B. Walker, treasurer.

March 8, 1841.—James J. Fuller, E. Cockerill, and Enos Stimson were elected councilmen; John Brown, mayor, and Benjamin Brown, marshal. Enos Stimson appointed recorder, and A. B. Walker, treasurer.

March 14, 1842.—Leonidas Jewett, Norman Root, and J. L. Currier were elected councilmen; Norman Root, mayor, and John Sampson, marshal. Enos Stimson appointed recorder, and A. B. Walker, treasurer.

March 13, 1843.—John Brown, Ezra Stewart, and Francis Beardsley, were elected councilmen; John Brown, mayor, and Jacob C. McCabe, marshal.

March 11, 1844.—John Ballard, Cephas Carpenter, Sumner Bartlett, and Dr. Wm. Blackstone were elected councilmen; John Brown, mayor, and William Smith, marshal. Leonidas Jewett appointed recorder, and Benjamin Brown, treasurer.

Record of 1845, missing.

March 9, 1846.—Ezra Stewart, Francis Beardsley, and John Brown elected councilmen for three years; Sumner Bartlett, Wm. R. Smith, and J. W. Bayard for two years; John Brown, mayor, and Abel Stedman, marshal. J. W. Bayard appointed recorder, and O. W. Brown, treasurer.

March 8, 1847.—John Ballard, Dr. Wm. Blackstone, and Cephas Carpenter were elected councilmen; John Brown, mayor, and Abel Stedman, marshal. J. W. Bayard appointed recorder, and O. W. Brown, treasurer.

March 13, 1848.—Samuel Miller, Wm. R. Smith, and Joseph Jewett were elected councilmen; Samuel Miller, mayor, and Wm. H. Abbott, marshal. Joseph Jewett appointed recorder, and O. W. Brown, treasurer.

March 12, 1849.—John Brown, Andrew Kessinger and Wm. Walker were elected councilmen; John Brown, mayor, and Abel Stedman, marshal. Joseph Jewett appointed recorder, and O. W. Brown, treasurer.

March 11, 1850.—Joseph M. Dana, Lot L. Smith, and Samuel Pickering were elected councilmen; Samuel Miller, mayor, aud Abel Stedman, marshal. Joseph Jewett appointed recorder, and Leonidas Jewett, treasurer.

March 10, 1851.—John Brown, Joseph M. Dana, Andrew Kessinger, E. P. Talpey, and Wm. Walker, councilmen; Samuel Miller, mayor; Joseph Jewett, recorder L; and . Jewett, treasurer.

March 10, 1852.—Wm. Walker, Norman Root, John B. Paul, Samuel Miller, J. M. Dana, councilmen; John Brown, mayor; Joseph Jewett, recorder; and L. Jewett, treasurer.

April 14, 1853.—John Brown, Samuel Miller, John B. Paul, Joseph Jewett, Wm. Walker, councilmen; Norman Root, mayor; J. M. Dana, recorder; and L. Jewett, treasurer.

April 15, 1854.—John Brown, Wm. Walker, H. K. Blackstone, D. M. Clayton, Henry T. Hoyt, councilmen; Norman Root, mayor; J. M. Dana, recorder; L. Jewett, treasurer.

April, 1855.—Henry T. Hoyt, Jesse Davis, J. Lawrence Currier, J. C. Frost, N. H. Van Vorhes, councilmen; Norman Root, mayor; J. M. Dana, recorder; L. Jewett, treasurer.

April, 1856.—H. K. Blackstone, Wm. P. Kessinger, Oliver

W. Pickering, L. Jewett, E. H. Moore, councilmen; Norman Root, mayor; J. M. Dana, recorder; L. Jewett, treasurer.

April, 1857.—Lot L. Smith, H. K. Blackstone, Wm. P. Kessinger, Geo. W. Baker, O. W. Pickering, councilmen; Norman Root, mayor; J. M. Dana, recorder; H. K. Blackstone, treasurer.

April, 1858.—Henry T. Hoyt, N. H. Van Vorhes, Lot L. Smith, Hiram R. Crippen, Thomas Davis, councilmen; N. Root, mayor; J. M. Dana, recorder; H. T. Hoyt, treasurer.

April, 1859.—H. T. Hoyt, L. L. Smith, Charles H. Grosvenor, Thomas Davis, Hiram R. Crippen, councilmen; N. Root, mayor; J. M. Dana, recorder; H. T. Hoyt, treasurer.

April, 1860.—L. Jewett, W. P. Johnson, H. T. Hoyt, Wm. Golden, Rufus P. Crippen, councilmen; N. Root, mayor; F. H. Stedman, recorder; H. T. Hoyt, treasurer.

April, 1861.—L. Jewett, W. P. Johnson, H. T. Hoyt, Wm. Golden, H. S. Stimson, councilmen; N. Root, mayor; F. H. Stedman, recorder; H. T. Hoyt, treasurer.

April, 1862.—H. T. Hoyt, Wm. Golden, E. H. Moore, Josephus Tucker, E. C. Crippen, councilmen; N. Root. mayor; F. H. Stedman, recorder; H. T. Hoyt, treasurer.

April, 1863.—H. T. Hoyt, E. C. Crippen, Josephus Tucker, Charles P. Ballard, Jesse Davis, councilmen; N. Root, mayor; F. H. Stedman, recorder; H. T. Hoyt, treasurer.

April, 1864.—Abner Cooley, A. D. Brown, H. K. Blackstone, Josephus Tucker, R. P. Crippen, councilmen; Joseph M. Dana, mayor; Simeon W. Pickering, recorder; A. D. Brown, treasurer.

April, 1865.—Jesse Van Law, N. H. Van Vorhes, H. K. Blackstone, Elmer Golden, A. D. Brown, councilmen; J. M. Dana, mayor; S. W. Pickering, recorder; A. D. Brown, treasurer.

April, 1866.—A. D. Brown, H. K. Blackstone, J. W. Harris, N. H. Van Vorhes, Jesse Van Law, councilmen; J. M. Dana, mayor; S. W. Pickering, recorder; A. M. Brown, treasurer.

April, 1867.—H. K. Blackstone, N. H. Van Vorhes, Jesse Van Law, J. H. Falloon, Wm. P. Johnson, councilmen; Geo. W. Baker, mayor; Frederick L. Ballard, recorder; N. H. Van Vorhes, treasurer.

April, 1868.—N. H. Van Vorhes, H. K. Blackstone, C. L. Wilson, H. S. Stimson, Alexander Cochran, councilmen; J. M. Dana, mayor; F. L. Ballard, recorder; N. H. Van Vorhes, treasurer.

Township Officers in Athens Township.

The first election for township officers in Athens township was held at the house of John Havner, on the point of the hill, near where Bing's wagon shop now stands, on the first Monday in April, 1806, when the following persons were elected, viz:

Jehiel Gregory, John Lowry, and William Harper, trustees; John Hewitt, Robert Linzee, Joel Abbot, Daniel Mulford, Canada Lowry, and Uriah Tippee, supervisors; John Corey, clerk; Chauncey Perkins, treasurer; Robert Fulton, lister; Alvan Bingham and Abel Mann, overseers of the poor; Robert Lowry, Philip M. Starr, and William Biggerstaff, constables.

At succeeding elections, the following officers were chosen:

Trustees.

1807	Leonard Jewett,	Jehiel Gregory,	Silas Bingham.
1808	John Havner,	William Harper,	Aaron Young.
1809	Leonard Jewett,	Ebenezer Currier,	John Abbot.
1810	"	Jacob Lindley,	"
1811	Silas Bingham,	Hopson Beebe,	Joseph B. Miles.
1812	Jehiel Gregory,	Martin Mansfield,	William Harper.
1813	Ebenezer Currier,	Joel Abbot,	Stephen Pilcher.
1814	Robert Linzee,	Wm. Whitesides,	"

TRUSTEES.—*Continued.*

1815	Robert Linzee,	Wm. Harper,	Arthur Coates.
1816	"	"	"
1817	Edmund Dorr,	John White,	David Pratt.
1818	"	"	Abel Mann.
1819	"	"	"
1820	"	"	"
1821	"	"	"
1822	"	"	"
1823	"	"	"
1824	"	"	Silas Bingham.
1825	"	"	Columbus Bierce.
1826	"	"	Josiah Coe.
1827	Solomon Goodspeed,	Reuben J. Davis,	"
1828	"	"	"
1829	"	"	"
1830	"	"	"
1831	"	Frederic Abbot,	"
1832	"	"	Samuel Lowry.
1833	John Mintun,	"	"
1834	"	"	Daniel Stewart.
1835	Josiah Coe,	Edmund Dorr,	"
1836	John Brown,	Solomon Goodspeed,	Samuel B. Pruden.
1837	Justus Reynolds,	John White, jr.,	Ebenezer Currier.
1838	"	John Brown,	"
1839	Edmund Dorr,	"	Daniel Stewart.
1840	Robert McCabe,	"	Christopher Sheldon.
1841	"	"	"
1842	Amos Crippen,	Norman Root,	"
1843	John R. McCune,	Justus Reynolds,	"
1844	"	"	"
1845	John Ballard,	Henry Hay,	Wm. T. Dean.
1846	"	"	"
1847	George Connett,	"	Nathan Goodspeed.
1848	"	Andrew Kessinger,	J. R. McCune.
1849	"	John Brown,	"
1850	Leonidas Jewett,	"	Joseph Morrison.
1851	Oliver W. Pickering,	"	"
1852	"	"	"
1853	"	James W. Bayard,	"
1854	Peter W. Boyles,	Richard Dobson,	"
1855	"	"	L. R. Jarvis.
1856	Thomas Davis,	"	Thomas Laughlin.
1857	"	Charles Goodspeed,	"
1858	"	"	Richard Dobson.
1859	"	"	Thomas Laughlin.
1860	"	Ezra Goodspeed,	"
1861	C. R. Sheldon,	"	"
1862	"	"	Alfred Morrison.
1863	"	Jesse Davis,	Jefferson Reynolds.
1864	"	"	A. J. Reynolds.
1865	Ezra Goodspeed,	B. F. Finney,	"
1866	"	"	"
1867	"	"	"
1868	"	Parker Carpenter,	"

Township Treasurers and Clerks since 1807.

	Treasurers.	Clerks.
1807	Chauncey Perkins,	John Corey.
1808	Alexander Stedman,	"
1809	"	"
1810	"	"
1811	"	"
1812	"	"
1813	Eliphaz Perkins,	Nehemiah Gregory.
1814	William Weir,	Alexander Proudfit.
1815	Charles Shipman,	Alvan Bingham.
1816	"	James Gillmore.
1817	Ebenezer Blackstone,	"
1818	John Gillmore,	"
1819	"	"
1820	"	"
1821	"	"
1822	"	"
1823	"	"
1824	James Gillmore,	John Gillmore.
1825	"	"
1826	"	"
1827	"	"
1828	"	"
1829	Charles Shipman,	"
1830	Allan V. Medbury,	"
1831	"	David Pratt.
1832	"	"
1833	Isaac Barker,	Robert E. Constable.
1834	"	A. B. Walker.
1835	A. G. Brown,	"
1836	"	N. B. Purington.
1837	Elias Hibbard,	D. W. Cunningham.
1838	Joseph H. Moore,	"
1839	"	"
1840	"	"
1841	"	"
1842	"	"
1843	"	David M. Clayton.
1844	"	"
1845	E. H. Moore,	"
1846	Samuel Pickering,	Wm. Loring Brown.
1847	"	Wm. H. Bartlett.
1848	Lot L. Smith,	"
1849	Joseph L. Kessinger,	"
1850	"	H. K. Blackstone.
1851	"	Daniel S. Dana.
1852	John B. Paul,	"
1853	"	Samuel S. Knowles.
1854	"	Daniel S. Dana.

TOWNSHIP TREASURERS AND CLERKS.—*Continued.*

	Treasurers.	Clerks.
1855	Wm. P. Kessinger,	Daniel S. Dana.
1856	"	George H. Stewart.
1857	"	"
1858	"	"
1859	Elias Tedrow,	"
1860	"	"
	Elias Tedrow resigned in December, 1860, and A. D. Brown appointed.	
1861	A. D. Brown,	Norman Root.
1862	"	"
1863	"	"
1864	"	"
1865	"	"
1866	"	"
1867	E. H. Moore,	"
1868	"	C. R. Sheldon.

Justices of the Peace.

1814—John L. Lewis, Abel Miller, Henry Bartlett.
1817—Henry Bartlett, Stephen Pilcher.
1829—Reuben J. Davis, A. G. Brown.
1835—A. G. Brown.
1836—Henry Bartlett.
1838—Abram Van Vorhes.
1842—Henry Bartlett.
1844—Norman Root.
1847—A. G. Brown.
1848—Sumner Bartlett.
1850—H. K. Blackstone, Enoch Cabeen.
1851—Daniel S. Dana.
1852—Norman Root.
1853—Daniel S. Dana, Jacob T. Stanley.
1855—Oscar W. Brown.
1856—Norman Root, Deloro Culley.
1858—William Golden, Wm. Loring Brown.
1859—Norman Root.
1861—William Golden, Wm. Loring Brown.
1862—Norman Root.

Justices of the Peace.—*Continued*.

    1864—C. R. Sheldon, Wm. A. Thomas, Wm. L. Brown.
    1865—Norman Root.
    1867—G. W. Baker, O. W. Brown, H. C. Martin.
    1868—W. A. Thomas.

Schools.

The first school established in Athens was in 1801, and was taught by John Goldthwaite. The school house (a log one) was situated on Joseph Higgins's place, about three miles south of Athens. Henry Bartlett taught in this house several quarters, between 1802 and 1806. Michael Higgins, now seventy-four years old, attended Esquire Bartlett's school, and relates that, on one occasion, when the scholars undertook, according to a custom then prevalent, to bar the master out, on a certain day, and had made all very fast, Mr. Bartlett procured a roll of brimstone from the nearest house, climbed to the top of the school house, and dropped the brimstone down the open chimney into the fire; then placing something over the chimney, he soon smoked the boys into an unconditional surrender.

The first school house on the town plat was a small brick building, which stood about where Grosvenor & Dana's law office now is—just east of the Presbyterian church. This has long since disappeared. It was built about 1806 or '7. Capt. David Pratt taught here for several years. Some of the best remembered among his successors are Mrs. Sarah Foster ("Grandma Foster"), Miss Sallie Jewett, the Rev. James McAboy, the Rev. Mr. McDill, Mrs. Burton, Prof. Andrews, L. D. Shepherd, Mr. Sears, Mr. Blake, the Rev. Joseph Marvin, the Rev. Charles Townsend, Samuel Marsh, Miss Haft, and James D. Johnson. About twelve years ago, the union school system, so successful every where, was adopted in Athens, since when the public school has taken a respectable rank. About eight thousand dollars was raised by taxation, and a convenient and spacious school building erected. The site is a commanding one; the building, of brick, is sixty-five feet front by seventy-one deep, and three stories in hight; the first and second stories each thirteen feet high, and the third story eighteen feet. The ground and second floor are each divided into four class rooms, two twenty-two by twenty-eight feet, and two twenty-seven by twenty-eight feet, and the third floor furnishes a hall sixty-two by fifty-six feet. Mr. L. R. Jarvis superintended the stone work, Mr. J. B. Paul, the brick work, and Mr. William Shaffer, the wood work. Mr. Cyrus Grant was the first superintendent of this school, and was succeeded by Mr. J. K. Mower, and Miss Eunice Rice. The Rev. Mr. Travis followed, then Mr. Doan, the Rev. John Pratt, the Rev. W. H. Scott, Captain Charles Barker, and Mr. Goodspeed, the present superintendent. The institution is well sustained and growing in usefulness.

The Methodist Church.

The establishment of the Methodist church, here, antedates that of any other religious society. Three quarters of a century ago, this denomination had already developed that spirit of energy and religious enterprise, which has not only made it the pioneer church, and forerunner of other denominations, but has caused it to become the most powerful church organization in America. We have quoted elsewhere, from the Rev. Mr. Quinn, an account of a missionary tour, which he made up the Hockhocking valley in 1800, when he preached at Athens. The Methodists have had a society here from that time, and during the early as well as later years of their church history here, have numbered among their preachers some very able, earnest, and useful men. In 1805, the Rev. Jacob Young preached on this circuit. The Rev. Geo. C. Light preached here about the same time. In 1806, Peter Cartwright, who afterward became celebrated in the church, visited Athens and Alexander townships, preaching and forming societies. About 1815, the Rev. Thomas Morris (now Bishop Morris), was on this circuit, and preached statedly at Athens. Among the early Methodist preachers here were the Rev. Cornelius Springer, the Rev. Daniel Limerick, the Rev. Curtis Goddard, the Rev. Abraham Lippett, the Rev.

John Ferree, the Rev. Abraham Baker, the Rev. Henry S. Fernandez, the Rev. Absalom Fox, the Rev. Asa Stroud, and the Rev. Robert O. Spencer—some of them being on the Muskingum and some on the Athens circuit.

During the early years of this century, the Methodists held their meetings at different houses, but in 1812 or '13, they built a brick church on the lot now owned and occupied by Prof. W. H. Young, and in 1825, they erected a brick parsonage adjoining. The church building, having been used as such nearly thirty years, fell into decay, and was then used for some years as a foundery; it has now disappeared. The parsonage forms a part of Prof. Young's present house. The present Methodist church was built in 1837. It is to be regretted that a continuous sketch of the Methodist society at Athens can not be furnished; its early establishment and long career of usefulness entitle it to a more extended history than we are able to offer.

The Presbyterian Church.

The First Presbyterian Society of Athens was organized in the autumn of 1809 by the Rev. Jacob Lindley. The original members of the organization were but nine in number, viz: Joshua Wyatt and wife, Josiah Coe, Arthur Coates, Dr. Eliphaz Perkins, Alvan Bingham, Mrs. Sally Foster and the Rev. Jacob

Lindley and wife. Public service was held for a time in the little brick school house which stood just east of the present site of the Presbyterian church, and afterward in the court house until the year 1828, when the present brick church was built. In 1815, the church numbered forty-seven members, and a revival that year added forty-three. In the year 1820, there were fifty-six added to the church, and the whole number of church members at that time was 177.

In 1827, steps were taken for the full organization and incorporation of the society. The following document, though incomplete and without date, possesses some interest as illustrating one step in the history of the church. The original paper, in the hand-writing of Joseph B. Miles, is yellow, time-worn, and mutilated —the last page with the signatures being lost.

"ARTICLES OF ASSOCIATION.

" We, the undersigned, taking into consideration the great importance of religious and moral instruction, and believing that the regular and stated preaching of the gospel is necessary for the promotion of these virtues; and as it is ordained of God that they who preach the gospel, shall live by the gospel, and 'the laboror is worthy of his hire,' and in order to obtain the same, we who receive spiritual food ought to contribute of our earthly substance, as God shall enable us, to those who dispense to us the bread of life, and in order the more effectually to promote these objects, do enter into the following articles of association.

I.

This society shall be known by the name of the First Presbyterian Society of Athens.

II.

There shall be a meeting of this society on the first Monday of May, annually, for the purpose of electing the officers of the society, amending or adding to the articles of association and doing such other business as may be necessary for the society to transact.

III.

The officers of this society, shall consist of three trustees, a clerk, and collector, who shall also be treasurer, to hold their offices for one year, and until others are chosen in their places, to be chosen by a majority of voters present.

IV.

It shall be the duty of the trustees to hire preaching, either by the week, month, or year, as they may think best, to be paid in the kind, and to the amount of subscriptions, to settle with the persons employed; also, to solicit subscriptions, receive donations or contributions, for the purposes of defraying the expenses of preaching, and to give public notice of the annual meetings of the society. Said trustees shall meet on their own adjournment, from time to time, as they may think best for the benefit of the society.

V.

It shall be the duty of the clerk to keep a fair record of the doings of the society, and a fair list of the subscribers' names, with the amount subscribed, and the time of subscribing, and to make out a list of subscriptions to the collector.

VI.

It shall be the duty of the collector to collect and receive all moneys or other property due the society by subscription or otherwise, and to pay out the same by order of the trustees, which order shall be signed by the chairman of the trustees.

VII.

No person shall have a vote to control the funds of this society after it is organized, unless they shall subscribe something towards the support of preaching, and no member shall be eligible to office until after he shall have subscribed.

VIII.

On the death, removal, or resignation of any of the officers of the society, it shall be the duty of the trustees to appoint a person or persons to fill the place, until the next annual election.

IX.

It shall be in the power of any three subscribers to call a meeting of the society at any time when they may think necessary by giving written notice in three public places in the town of Athens, setting forth the objects of said meeting, and having it proclaimed on the Sabbath before said meeting in the congregation.

X.

Should the funds of the society be deemed sufficient at any time to settle a regular preacher of the gospel, by themselves, or with the joint subscriptions of the adjoining settlements, and the society should deem it necessary, it shall be the duty of the trustees in such case, to invite preachers as candidates, but no preacher shall be regularly settled without the consent of two-thirds of the members present at a meeting of the society for the purpose of giving a call.

XI.

The society shall have power to dismiss any officer of the society for misconduct, by a vote of a majority of the members present, at a meeting of the society.

XII.

Owing to the scarcity of money, any of the kinds of country produce are to be received in payment of subscriptions, named in the thirteenth article of this association, the prices of such articles to be fixed by the trustees of the society, on or before the first of November, annually, and any payment made by the subscribers to the person employed to preach, and his receipt produced to the collector, shall be a sufficient voucher for the amount on his subscription.

XIII.

All subscriptions shall be specified in dollars and cents, and we do hereby agree to pay the several amounts annexed to our names for the above purpose, in cash, or wheat, flour, rye, oats, corn, beef, pork, flax, wool, or country linen, at the prices affixed."

Though among the earliest religious societies organized in the state, this church was not incorporated till 1828. The act, passed February 7th of that year, names as the incorporators, Columbus Bierce, Isaac Taylor, Joseph B. Miles, Charles Shipman, Francis Beardsley, Samuel Miller, Eben Foster, John Perkins, Hull Foster, John Gillmore, and Cephas Carpenter, and Messrs. Miles, Bierce, Taylor, Beardsley, and

Carpenter, were constituted trustees of the church, to act as such till the first annual meeting. The Rev. Jacob Lindley acted as moderator of the session and pastor until about 1828, since when, fifteen ministers have served the church either as stated supply or as pastors, among whom will be recognized the names of some very devout and able men. The entire list in the order of time is as follows:

Rev. Jacob Lindley, contemporary; Rev. Samuel Davies Hoge, contemporary; Rev. Robert G. Wilson, Rev. John Spaulding (now of New York city), Rev. William Burton, Rev. Timothy Stearns, Rev. N. B. Purington, Rev. Wm. H. McGuffey, Rev. Wells Andrews, Rev. Aaron Williams, Rev. Moses A. Hoge, Rev. Addison Ballard, Rev. Alfred Ryors, Rev. S. Dieffendorf, Rev. John H. Pratt, Rev. James F. Holcomb.

The Rev. John H. Pratt began his labors here in 1854, laboring one year as "stated supply," after which he received a call as pastor. During the period of his pastorate (fourteen years), two hundred members were added to the church. The deaths and removals of members during the same period were, however, numerous —the latter especially so—so that the present active membership is only about one hundred and twenty-five. During the past few years the church has been rebuilt, and a lecture-room added. The old-fashioned, lofty pulpit (looking up toward which, twenty-five years ago, little children of the writer's age, used to strain their necks till they ached), has given place to a modern platform. In those days, the pulpit being at the front end of the church, the congregation faced about on taking their seats. Thus, facing toward the preacher and the pulpit, they looked also toward the front doors, out of which, as they stood open in fine summer weather, the juveniles could gaze longingly and hear the lowing of the cattle, and watch the entrance of the sabbath-breaking bees, "forever going and coming;" or curiously speculate about the wicked, solitary horseback traveler who, with dusty portmanteau, pursuing his journey through the village, just then passed the church. But "*tempora mutantur et nos mutamur cum illis.*" The times are changed, and we with them. The old pastors are gone; the gray heads of twenty-five years ago have many of them been laid in their last sleep, and the active men of the church then, are the gray heads now. The little boys, whose will then was "the wind's will," and whose thoughts were "long, long thoughts," are in turn, become the active men of the present day. It is *their* children now who are looking at the green hills, listening to the humming bees and thinking strange, mysterious thoughts. Happy children if their childhood be as serene as their fathers' was—if their sabbaths be as quiet and their surroundings as healthful as were those of the old village church.

Cemeteries.

For considerably more than half a century after Athens was settled, the dead were buried in the old grave yard northwest of town, which was set apart for that use by the trustees of the university in 1806. The place never was ornamented to any extent, and for many years past only a few forest trees have given it their grateful shade. Here, a little apart from their surviving friends, rest the fathers of the village.

> "The breezy call of incense-breathing morn,
>   The swallow twittering from the straw-built shed,
> The cock's shrill clarion or the echoing horn
>   No more shall rouse them from their lowly bed."

In January, 1864, the citizens of Athens feeling the need of a more beautiful burying ground, organized the Athens Cemetery Association, with a capital stock of $4,000, divided into shares of $100, which was incorporated under a general law of the state. An eligible site was selected west of the town, and a purchase made of twelve acres, which has since been tastefully laid off into winding walks and drives, and handsomely ornamented with shrubbery. Some appropriate and costly monuments already adorn the new cemetery, which is a place of pleasant resort for the residents of Athens, and is a credit to the town. The organization is officered as follows: Calvary Morris, president, H. J. Topky, secretary, A. B. Walker, treasurer, and Calvary Morris, J. W. Harris, J. H. Pratt, W. P. Johnson, and Jesse Van Law, trustees.

The citizens of Alexander township have recently begun a similar improvement by the addition of several acres to their former burying ground at the Cumberland Presbyterian church, near Hebbardsville. The addition is neatly laid off into lots with avenues and walks, and ornamented with shrubbery. It is to be hoped these examples will be followed by other towns and townships in the county. The appropriate burial of the dead and proper care for their resting place by the living, is a mark of christian civilization, and the universal attention now given to the subject in this country, indicates a pleasing change in public sentiment. Beautiful cemeteries are scattered over the country, some of them very celebrated, and soon no enterprising town will be without one. Lucretius says of the earth—

"*Omniparens, eadem rerum est commune sepulchrum.*"

The parent of all, she is also the common sepulchre. Let our burial places, therefore, be beautified with the "greenery of nature," and let the adornments of art be added to please the senses and soothe the feelings of the living.

Newspapers.

The first newspaper published in Athens, was *The Athens Mirror and Literary Register*, commenced in

1825, by A. G. Brown. The *Mirror* was political and literary in its character, printed once a week on paper of super-royal size (sixteen pages about nine by five inches to each number), and continued through five years. It was printed on a wooden press with a stone bed, and required four *pulls* to each sheet.

Several copies of the old *Mirror*, running from January to May, 1829, are before us, and furnish some interesting bits of local history. Each number contains the advertisements of Joseph B. Miles, Ebenezer Currier, and Thomas Brice, offering their "complete and extensive assortments of goods for sale low for cash, or in exchange for wheat, rye, corn, pork, butter, feathers, rags, calf and deer skins, fur skins, buck horns, ginseng, bees wax, etc."

In February, 1829, the publisher announces that "all who wish to see a fifth volume of the *Mirror* published, are desired to send in their names before the 1st day of May, next;" and earnestly solicits increased patronage. In the issue of February 21, 1829, the editor apologizes for being delayed beyond the usual time for publication, by stating that "a young man in our employ unluckily received a severe hurt while skating on the ice." Probably that young man was John Brough, afterwards governor of Ohio, etc., who was then employed in the office.

About this time the temperance question was considerably discussed in the town. A sermon delivered on the subject, January 22, 1829, by the Rev. Robt. G. Wilson, is published in full in the *Mirror*. A society was formed, of which Dr. Wilson was president, the Rev. John Spaulding vice president, and Professor Joseph Dana secretary, and a pledge was kept at the *Mirror* office for signatures. The constitution of the society, printed in the *Mirror*, is accompanied by the following note: "It is understood that merchants and others having contracts or quantities of spirits now on hand, shall have reasonable time to close and dispose of the same on becoming members." The movement was pushed with great earnestness and success by the good men who inaugurated it, and doubtless there was sufficient need of reform. Some of the seed sown fell on good ground in Ames township, and blossomed forth into the following unique advertisement, which appeared in the *Mirror* of April 25, 1829:

"A CHALLENGE.

"ATTENTION GROG DRINKERS!!

"SAMUEL L. MOHLER, of Ames township, having been for sixteen years in the constant habit of *drinking*, and getting drunk on an average, as often as once a month, has resolved to refrain entirely from the practice in future; and as a test of his sincerity, he offers to pledge the new wood work to a good wagon, against any property of equal value, that he will refrain from drinking ardent spirits longer than any other man who has been in the habit, an equal, or half the length of time;

provided both live to make the trial. Any person disposed to take him up can give notice to that effect.

"April 10, 1829."

We are not able to state whether this interesting challenge was ever accepted or not; perhaps Mr. Mohler's virtuous resolve went toward improving that nameless place which is said to be "paved with good intentions;" we can not tell.

A committee consisting of Thomas Brice, John Gilmore, Amos Crippen, and Norman Root, appointed to settle the accounts of the town of Athens for the year ending February 18, 1829, publish an itemized report, showing the total receipts to have been one hundred and seventy-three dollars and twenty-three cents, and total expenditures one hundred and twelve dollars and ninety-four cents.

The *Mirror* was succeeded in 1830 by *The Western Spectator*, edited and published by Isaac Maxon, who came from Marietta in 1825, bringing young John Brough as a type-setter. The paper continued under Mr. Maxon's management for six years. In 1836 it was bought by Mr. Abram Van Vorhes, who changed the name to the *Hocking Valley Gazette and Athens Messenger*. Under this name Mr. Van Vorhes edited and published the paper for several years, enlarging it to imperial size, printing it with new press and type, and otherwise greatly improving it.

In January, 1844, the *Gazette* was succeeded by the *Athens Messenger*, edited and published for a time by Mr. Nelson H. Van Vorhes, and afterward by him and his brother, Mr. A. J. Van Vorhes. In the spring of 1854, N. H. Van Vorhes retired from the paper, which continued in the hands of his brother until October 1, 1855, when the establishment was purchased by the late Mr. George Walsh, who only retained control one year, when it was once more sold to N. H. Van Vorhes.

Mr. Van Vorhes edited and published the paper till January, 1861; Mr. T. F. Wildes, from January, 1861, till September, 1862; Mr. Jesse Van Law, from September, 1862, till November, 1865; Mr. J. W. Stinchcomb, from November, 1865, till November, 1866; Mr. J. R. S. Bond, from November, 1866, till March, 1868, and Mr. C. E. M. Jennings, from that till the present time.

The Court House.

For about a year and a half after the organization of the county, the court was held in a room, rented for that purpose, of Leonard Jewett and Silas Bingham. In 1807-8, a hewed log court house was erected, very near the spot where the present one stands, in which the courts were held for about ten years. This temple of justice must have been a pretty substantial structure, if its *chimney*, described in the following extract from the records of the county commissioners may be taken as a "specimen brick:"

"*September* 7, 1807. The commissioners proceeded to adopt the following plan for a chimney in the court house in the town of Athens, to wit: The foundation to be laid with stone, one foot below the surface, the remainder to be of brick, to be well laid in good lime mortar; one fire place below and two above—the fire place below to be four feet clear in the back, twenty-two inches deep, and five feet four inches wide in front, to be secured by a bar of iron the size of a common flat bar, and secured with a sufficient bolt let into the discharging piece—the bolt to be secured by a fore lock and key, the bolt about one foot and five or six inches in length, and the discharging piece six inches thick. The fire places above to be each eighteen inches back, and built proportionably with the rest of the chimney, which is to be raised three feet above the top of the building; the upper fire places to be well coated, and the whole to be completed, including the hearths, in a workmanlike manner, on or before the 20th day of November next; which (contract) being put up at public sale, was struck off at seventy-eight dollars."

The resources of the settlement being very limited, this same building was used also for a school house, and meeting house. In the records of the county commissioners we find the following entry:

"*December* 7, 1811.—*Resolved*, by the commissioners, that from and after this date, the court house in the town of Athens shall not be used as a school house or a meeting house, unless the inhabitants of said town shall agree to furnish, for the use of the court, during the time of its session, a sufficient quantity of fire wood, ready cut, fit for the fire; also to keep the house in as good repair as it now is, and keep the same well swept during the sitting of the court; and that the clerk notify the inhabitants as aforesaid, by advertisement posted on the court house door."

Perhaps the school teacher was careless about shutting the door at night, and probably school boys, in those days, like other boys before and since, were not scrupulous about keeping the floor clean; for the next entry on the subject is as follows:

"*June* 2, 1812.—The board appointed Ebenezer Currier a committee to see, on condition the court house is used as a school house, that the door of said house be kept shut whenever the house is not occupied, every night, and that it be kept clean; also, that a sufficient quantity of fire wood be constantly kept for the court and commissioners, and that the house be left in as good repair as when entered upon."

And, finally, on this head, it was ordered, December 8, 1813:

"That the court house shall be no longer used as a school house, and that Henry Bartlett be a committee to take care of the same, and have said house repaired by the 1st of January next."

"*June* 8, 1814, it was *Ordered*, that the north and east sides of lots Nos. 35 and 37, on which the court house and jail now stand, be fenced with good, sawed, white oak palings, of five feet in length, the posts to be of black locust, four by five inches square, and six and a half feet long, the rails of good white oak, and the panels ten feet long, with a small gate before the present court house door, and a gate of ten feet wide near the north east corner, fronting the east."

Caleb Merrit and Joseph B. Miles were appointed a committee to carry the above resolution into effect.

The old hewed log court house was the one in use

while Thomas Ewing was attending college at Athens, and he was, doubtless, a frequent visitor here. Here he probably gained his first familiarity with judicial proceedings, and acquired his earliest knowledge of the workings of the law. The practitioners at the Athens bar of that day, if they noticed an unsophisticated youth, on a back seat, intently listening to their professional efforts, little imagined that that youth would live to become one of the greatest expounders of the law our country has yet produced, and to ornament some of the highest positions in the land.

Proposals for a new court house (the one now in use) must have been published in the spring or early summer of 1814, for in the proceedings of the meeting of the county commissioners, held August 1, of that year, present, Asahel Cooley, Caleb Merrit, and Robert Linzee, it is entered:

"Proceeded to sell, to the lowest bidder, certain articles, agreeable to advertisement, to be furnished for the erecting of a court house, viz: to Ebenezer Currier, twelve hundred feet of black walnut boards, one and one-fourth inches thick; one hundred feet of poplar boards, one and one-half inches thick, and five hundred feet, ditto, one and one-fourth inches thick—to be delivered on the court house lot, piled up properly for drying, and to be delivered on or before the 1st day of January next. To Edmund Dorr, twenty perch of rough stone, for the foundation—to be laid, according to advertisement, before the 15th day of November next."

The following entries, copied from the old records of the county commissioners, mark the progress and history of the present court house:

"*November* 16, 1814.—*Ordered*, that the wall for the foundation of the court house be six inches thicker than described heretofore, and that the same be laid in mortar of lime and coarse sand, and that such further compensation be allowed to Edmund Dorr, contractor for the same, as masons shall adjudge."

"*December* 5, 1814.—County of Athens, to Joseph B. Miles, Dr.,

To 1,925 feet of boards and scantling,	$19 25
Hauling same from mill,	3 00
Drawing plan of court house,	1 00

"*December* 6, 1814.—*Ordered*, that the clerk notify, by advertisement, set up in three public places in Athens, the furnishing of three ranges of cut stone, two feet wide and nine inches thick, to be well laid in lime mortar; also the furnishing of one hundred thousand good merchantable brick, to be delivered on the court house lot by the 1st day of August next. Proposals will be received by the commissioners, in writing, at their meeting, on the second Monday in January next."

"*February* 1, 1815.—The commissioners met for the purpose of consulting as to the practicability of proceeding in building the court house."

It was decided to proceed, and at their meeting, March 7th, the clerk was directed to

"Advertise in the *American Friend*, for furnishing brick and stone in amounts as aforesaid; proposals to be received by the commissioners, at the court house, on the second Monday of April next, from 10 A. M., to 4 P. M., on said day."

"*April* 10, 1815.—The commissioners met for the purpose of contracting for the furnishing of cut stone for the court house; also of one hundred thousand brick for the same. After having received the proposals of Elijah Hatch, Esq., and Edmund Dorr, for furnishing brick, and of William Dorr, William Alcock, and Jonathan Amlin, for furnishing and laying cut and hewed stone," the board adjourned till next day.

"*Tuesday, April* 11.—Proceeded to receive bonds of William Alcock and Jonathan Amlin for the stone work, and agreed with them for the sum of three hundred dollars, payable October 1st, next. Proceeded also to take bonds from Edmund Dorr, for the furnishing of one hundred thousand brick for the court house; amount of said contract, six hundred dollars, in county orders, on the completion of the contract."

June 7, 1815, the clerk was directed to advertise for materials, and making doors and window frames; also for sleepers, joists, and rafters, and for framing timber for floor, laying the brick, etc.

"*July* 17, 1815.—The commissioners proceeded to contract as follows: with John Havner, for laying up the brick walls of court house, five hundred dollars; with Abel Stedman, furnishing timber, framing cupola, etc., two hundred and seventy-four dollars; and with Elijah Hatch, for shingles, sixty-seven dollars."

"*September* 5, 1815.—Agreed with John Porter, he being the lowest bidder, for the following jobs of work, viz: putting a cornice round the court house, at fifty cents per foot; also boarding the roof of the same, for the sum of twelve dollars; and shingling the same at the rate of one dollar and twenty-five cents per thousand, and at one dollar for each hip."

"*September* 6, 1815.—The board appointed James Gillmore superintendent, to oversee and superintend the building of the court house, and to call on Charles Shipman and J. B. Miles to assist him at any time when required."

"*September* 26.—Resolved by the board, that the sum of four hundred dollars be borrowed from the Bank of Marietta, for the purpose of paying for the stone work on the court house, including window sills, etc., and for the purpose of purchasing nails; and that an order issue for the said amount, payable to Asahel Cooley, and that the same be sent by William Skinner, and deposited in the Bank of Marietta, for the purpose of obtaining the sum aforesaid."

"*September* 27.—Busy in making arrangements for the building of the court house, and making proposals to the trustees of the Ohio university for the loan of one thousand dollars."

"*Thursday*, 28.—Agreed with the trustees of the Ohio university, for a loan of one thousand dollars, for one year, at six per cent. interest."

"*Friday*, 29.—*Resolved*, That Robert Linzee and James Gillmore be a committee to examine the mason work of the court house, when finished, and receive the same, and also to ascertain the number of brick in said building."

The laying of the brick was finished in October, 1815, and John Havner received his pay in full, viz: $500, as per contract.

"*Wednesday, December* 6, 1815.—*Resolved*, by the commissioners of the county of Athens, That, in consideration of a subscription by sundry individuals, viz: Josiah Coe, Cephas Carpenter, Mary Ann Ackley, Lydia Ackley, James Gillmore, Jacob Dumbaugh, John Johnstone, Enos Thompson, David Pratt, Daniel Stewart, Joseph B. Miles, Henry Bartlett, Robert Linzee, Charles Shipman, Ebenezer Currier, Eliphaz Perkins, Chauncey F. Perkins, Alvan Bingham, Amos Crippen, John

Porter, James J. Fuller, James Session, Silas Bingham, John White, Abel Stedman, Eliphaz Perkins, jun., S. S. Johnstone, John Havner, Thomas Armstrong, Seth Child, Asahel Cooley, Thomas McClelland, and Arthur Coates, amounting to $506, to be paid into the county treasury to assist in building the court house in said county, and this day presented by a committee appointed for that purpose by the subscribers; the commissioners do agree that the subscribers and their associates have the privilege of holding meetings for religious purposes, on the Sabbath and other days, for eight years from the first day of January, 1816, when it shall not interfere with the county business, upon condition that $500 of the above-named subscription be paid to Henry Bartlett on or before the first day of March next; and that each subscriber, on his paying the sum subscribed by him, shall receive a receipt for the same, to be refunded in eight years, without interest; and *provided* further, that if the said sum of $500 is not paid in by the time specified, then it shall be optional with the commissioners to refund the money or continue the privilege, and if they should not continue the privilege, then the money is to be refunded. And it is also understood that the aforesaid sum of $500 be appropriated for finishing the lower room of the court house, if the whole of said sum be necessary. The following form of receipt shall be given by Henry Bartlett, clerk of the commissioners, for the purposes aforesaid: 'Received of A. B. the sum of ———, which is to be refunded to the said A. B., or his heirs or assigns, at the end of eight years from the first day of January, 1816, out of the county treasury, without interest.'

"*January* 6, 1816.—It is agreed by the commissioners and Joseph B. Miles, that the said Miles furnish the glass and oil for the court house, and that, after deducting the amount of said Miles's subscription from the articles, the balance be paid him, on delivery thereof.

Same day.—" Agreed with John Walker for making the sash for the lower and upper rooms of the court house, priming the same, and setting the glass, and fitting the sash in the frames, at ten cents per light—materials to be furnished by the commissioners. Also, agreed with John Walker for laying the lower floor, at $4 50 per square. The above contracts to be completed by May 1, 1816.

"Agreed with John Porter for finishing the upper part of the cupola, from the cornice up (including cornice), putting up rafters, boarding and shingling roof, putting on timber, with a ball agreeable to a plan this day exhibited, to be completed by May 1st, 1817. Also agreed with John Porter, finishing and building the stairs for the sum of $60; the banisters to be mortised into the hand-rails and string board, and completed in a workmanlike manner.

[Time for completing the above contracts extended to the 1st day of September.]"

*　　*　　*　　*　　*　　*　　*　　*

Same date.—" WHEREAS, Robert Linzee and Asahel Cooley, have loaned of the corporation of the Ohio university, the sum of $1,000 for the use and benefit of the county of Athens, in building the court house; therefore, be it *resolved*, that so much of the tax of this present year be appropriated for the benefit of said Linzee and Cooley, as will satisfy said sum and interest."

Same date.—"*Resolved*, That James Gillmore and Henry Bartlett, be a committee to receive bonds of the several contractors on the court house, and that the said Gillmore and Bartlett, be a committee to dispose of the $1,000 borrowed by Asahel Cooley and Robert Linzee, for the use and benefit of Athens county, which sum said committee are directed to apportion among the different contractors who have heretofore filled their contracts on said building in proportion to their claims, after deducting therefrom six per cent."

"*June* 13, 1816.—Agreed with John Walker, for completing the following jobs or parcels of work: finishing the judges' seats in the court house agreeably to the plan, twenty panels in front, with bed moulding and capping for a cornice; five panels on each side of the bar, nine in front; two sheriffs' boxes;

two tables for the bar, and clerk's seat, agreeably to the plan; after finishing thereof, the same to be adjudged by Messrs. Corp and Shipman, and the price determined by them; also agreed with same for making, finishing, and hanging the three outside doors of the court house, and casing the jambs."

"*June* 25, 1817.—*Resolved*, That the superintending committee be authorized to employ John Bowman to paint the roof, cupola, etc., of the court house."

The foregoing extracts from the old county records include nearly every entry relating to the court house, and quite fully present the history of its erection. The building was about completed during the autumn of 1817, and has been in continuous use ever since. It has undergone changes and repairs both inside and outside, but much of the original work still remains—an evidence of the honesty and fidelity with which the mechanics of those days labored. It is an antiquated and most unornamental building, and must ere long give way to a finer structure; but, perhaps, the walls of its successor will never echo the voices of greater men or better lawyers than have plead within the old court house.

The first resident lawyer in Athens was Artemus Sawyer, a young man of high literary and scholastic attainments, who arrived in 1808. In 1810, he was appointed prosecuting attorney, and acted as such for a few years, until he fell an early victim to habits of intemperance. E. B. Merwin, of Lancaster, acted as prosecutor before Sawyer, and was one of the principal practitioners of this period at the Athens court. Gen. Philemon Beecher, and Wm. W. Irwin, of Lancaster, were also regular attendants. William Woodbridge, of Marietta, practiced here until his removal to Michigan, where he became governor, senator, etc. The Hon. Thomas Ewing attended the courts in Athens county very constantly for several years, after his admission to the bar, as did also the late Samuel F. Vinton, who took up his residence in Gallipolis about 1817. Mr. Vinton represented this district in Congress for twenty-two years. Gen. Goddard, of Zanesville, also practiced here for several years, commencing about 1818. The Hon. Henry Stanbery came in a little later, but practiced for several years in the Athens courts, and his maiden speech was delivered in the present court house.* Messrs. Hocking H. Hunter, Brazee, and Nash must also be added to the great lawyers who practiced here. Gen. Dwight Jarvis, who resided and practiced here about five years,

---

* Mr. Stanbery, in response to an inquiry addressed to him by the writer, touching the correctness of the tradition that his "maiden speech" was delivered here, replied:

"The 'tradition' is correct. I was admitted to the bar at Gallipolis, in May, 1824, and made my first jury speech at Athens in the following June. The case was of a character (in bastardy) and the evidence so broad as not to admit of publication. It involved some nice questions as to the period of gestation, etc., with which, of course, I was not at all familiar; so that I can very truly say that this was my ' first great cause least understood.' I did, however, succeed in making one point which had a telling effect on the jury. The defense was mainly placed on an attempt to impeach the veracity of the mother of the children (for they were twins); I appeared for the mother, and she was the only witness to fix the paternity of the boys on the defendant.

from 1825 to 1830, was the second *resident* lawyer, not reckoning Joseph Dana, then a professor in the university, who though never fairly engaged in the practice, attended to a few cases, at intervals, when not occupied with teaching. At a somewhat later period, the late Judge Arius Nye, of Marietta, was among the most constant and faithful attendants, from abroad, at the Athens bar. Since about 1832, there has been no lack of resident lawyers (some of them of marked ability), and the attendance from abroad has been less frequent; in fact, of late years, non-resident lawyers are seldom seen here. The resident lawyers at the present time are Messrs. Grosvenor & Dana, Messrs. de Steiguer & Jewett, Messrs. Browns & Wildes, Messrs. Golden & Townsend, and Robert E. Constable.

Grand Juries from 1805 to 1815.

The first grand jury that ever sat in the county, was drawn in November, 1805, and was composed as follows:

John Dixon, John Hewitt, Samuel Moore, John Corey, Peter Boyles, Jeremiah Riggs, Canaday Lowry, William How-

---

I argued to the jury that our case was sustained by three witnesses. The counsel for the defense promptly contradicted this assertion, appealing to the jury that the mother was our only witness. I replied that it was true that the mother was the only witness who had testified under oath, but that her testimony was fully corroborated by that of the twins themselves—calling the attention of the jury to certain points of resemblance which they bore to the defendant, and quoting the well known line, ' O, holy nature thou dost never plead in vain.' So it turned out in this instance, for the silent testimony of the twins carried the case."

lett, Robert Fulton, Alvan Bingham, Josiah Coe, Philip M. Starr.

March Term, 1806.—Alvan Bingham, Hopson Beebe, John Thompson, Silas Dean, John Lowry, Josiah Coe, Daniel Stewart, Robert Fulton, Baruch Dorr, Edmund Dorr, Peter Boyles, John Corey, Benaziah Simmons.

July Term, 1806.—Alvan Bingham, John Havner, David Pratt, Reuben Hurlbut, Jacob Boyles, Moses Bean, Canaday Lowry, Alexander Fulton, George Wolf, Joseph Brooks, Abraham Shidler, John Corey, Peter Boyles.

November Term, 1806.—Jehiel Gregory, Silas Dean, Samuel Humphreys, Thomas Sharp, William Howlett, Ignatius Thompson, Trueman Hewx, Michael Barker, Amos Thompson, William Weir, Phineas Allen, Benaziah Simmons, Silas Bingham.

March Term, 1807.—Hopson Beebe, Archibald Stewart, William Brooks, Alvan Bingham, Christopher Wolf, John Thompson, Jared Bobo, John Steele, Abram Pugsley, Josiah Waters, John Miller, John Hewitt, Jason Rice, Jehiel Gregory.

December Term, 1807.—Stephen Pilcher, Joseph Seamans, Obadiah Walker, Benjamin Davis, Jason Rice, John Corey, James Crippen, John Thompson, Jesse Halsey, Nathaniel Williams, John Brooks, Aaron Young, Simon Speed, Jehiel Gregory, Roswell Culver.

April Term, 1808.—George Seamans, Samuel Beaumont, Elijah Pilcher, Joshua Wyatt, Eleazar Penrod, Nehemiah Gregory, Uriah Tippee, John Simontown, Samuel Russell, Charles Harper, David Chapman, Baruch Dorr, Azel Johnson, Leonard Jewett.

August Term, 1808.—John Thompson, Moses Bean, Charles Harper, James Pilcher, David Boyles, John Walker, Ebenezer Currier, William Woodward, Caleb Merritt, Edmund Dorr, John Kelso, Jacob Wolf, John Lowry, William Gabill, Elijah Pilcher.

December Term, 1808.—Amos Thompson, Daniel Stewart, Joseph Fuller, Charles Rice, William Howlett, Robert Palmer,

John Brown, Jacob Boyles, Peter Boyles, Wm. Barrows, John Abbot, Simeon Cooley, Josiah Coe, Peter Grow.

April Term, 1809.—Nathan Woodbury, Azel Johnson, Wm. Peane, Thomas Armstrong, Wm. Harper, Isaac Stanley, Robert Linzee, Othniel Tuttle, Daniel Weethee, Jacob Cowdry, Isaac Barker Joshua Wood, Arthur Coates, John Brown 2d.

August Term, 1809.—Leonard Jewett, Martin Mansfield, Reuben Davis, William Rabb, Caleb Merritt, Daniel Stewart, Wm. Howlett, Wm. Weir, Samuel Coleman, Levi Johnson, Thomas Armstrong, Jacob Humphrey, Stephen Buckingham.

December Term, 1809.—Jehiel Gregory, George Walker, Jason Rice, Zebulon Griffin, Jonathan Watkins, Wm. Burch, Elijah Pilcher, Joseph Pugsley, John Armstrong, John Johnstone, Samuel Luckey, Martin Mansfield, Amos Thompson, Wm. Howlett, Eli Reynolds.

April Term, 1810.—John Brown, Benjamin Davis, Abraham Pugsley, Josiah True, Wm. Brown, Seth Fuller, Peter Phillips, Joshua Wyatt, Amos Crippen, Arthur Coates, Wm. Harper, Samuel Moore, John McKee, Eli Reynolds.

August Term, 1810.—John Corey, Arthur Coates, Daniel Weethee, Eli Reynolds, Abel Mann, James Crippen, Solomon Munroe, Charles Harper, Jarret Bobo, Joel Lowther, Jacob Cowdry, John Thompson, Jarret Jones, Joshua Wood, Elijah Pilcher.

December Term, 1810.—Jehiel Gregory, Joseph Guthrie, Charles Harper, Levi Stedman, James Armstrong, Isaac Wood, Wm. Burch, Joseph Fuller, Nathan Woodbury, Baruch Dorr, Samuel Luckey, Jabez Cooley, Silvanus Ames, Bernardus B. Lottridge, George Barrows.

April Term, 1811.—John Brown, Isaac Stephens, Caleb Merritt, Wm. Brown, Robert McKinstry, Henry Barrows, John Bowman, Abram Pugsley, Nicholas Phillips, Samuel Coleman, John Phillips, Moses Bean, John White.

August Term, 1811.—David Simontown, John Wright, Elisha Alderman, Robert Palmer, Christopher Herrold, George Ewing,

Jonathan Watkins, Isaac Havner, Isaac Wood, Edmund Dorr, Elijah Pilcher, John Abbot, Aaron Young, Moses Kay.

December Term, 1811.—John Phillips, Josiah Coe, Jeremiah Shumway, Thomas Armstrong, Arthur Coates, Thomas Sharp, John White, Nehemiah Davis, Othniel Tuttle, Job Phillips, Wm. Burch, Augusting Webster, John Irwin, John McKee, Robert Lowther.

April Term, 1812.—Silas Bingham, Henry Barrows, Frederick Tubbs, Ebenezer Barrows, Martin Mansfield, John Symmes, Christopher Herrold, Jacob Cowdry, Abel Mann, Wm. McKinstry, Joel Cowdry, Enos Thompson, John Corey, Levi Johnson, Edmund Dorr.

December Term, 1812.—Christopher Wolf, John White, Daniel Weethee, Nathaniel Williams, Hopson Beebe, John Corey, David Pratt, Edmund Dorr, Reuben J. Davis, Jeremiah Riggs, Joseph Guthrie, Arthur Coates, Martin Mansfield, Stephen Pilcher, Charles Harper.

April Term, 1813.—Alvan Bingham, Hopson Beebe, Charles Harper, Edmund Dorr, Arthur Coates, John Connor, Alexander Stedman, Barnet Brice, Eliphalet Case, Eliphalet Wheeler, George Barrows, Daniel Muncie, Alvan Bingham, jr.

August Term, 1813.—Stephen Pilcher, Charles Harper, Peter Grow, Joshua Selby, Ezra Green, B. B. Lottridge, Jacob Barker, Samuel Dailey, Abel Miller, David Pratt, Robert McKinstry, Seth Fuller, Abel Glazer, Jason Rice, Caleb Merritt.

December Term, 1813.—Alvan Bingham, Robert McKinstry, Thomas McClellan, John Brown, John Holmes, John Brooks, Conklin Buckley, Enos Thompson, Seth Fuller, Jehiel Gregory, Peter Boyles, Elisha Hulburt, Henry O'Neil.

September Term, 1814.—Stephen Pilcher, John Bowman, Samuel Luckey, Wm. Dorr, Joseph McMahon, George Walker, Elihu Francis, S. P. Standiff, Elijah Pilcher, John McKee, Arthur Coates, Abel Mann, Luther Danielson, Jonas Smith, Wm. McKinstry.

January Term, 1815.—George Ackley, Justus Reynolds, Jonathan Watkins, Robert McKinstry, Wm. Johnson, Wm. Buffington, Wm. McKinstry, George Barrows, Azel Johnson, Joseph Fuller, Obadiah Walker, Nathan Nye, Jacob Kimes, Josiah Coe.

June Term, 1815.—Josiah Coe, George Reeves, Ezekiel Worthing, David Ducher, John Brooks, Jacob Humphrey, Cephas Carpenter, Isaac Pierce, Charles Devol, John Walker, Asahel Cooley, James Gillmore, John Abbot, John Bowman, Elijah Pilcher.

Personal and Biographical.

A history of Athens county would be very incomplete without a biographical notice of the father and projector of the Ohio university—an institution that has done so much to shape and influence the history of this community. Though never a resident of the county, perhaps no one person has exerted a more deep and lasting influence on its welfare than *Dr. Manasseh Cutler.* He was the son of Hezekiah Cutler, who came from a thorough Puritan stock, and was born at Killingly, Connecticut, May 3, 1742. He graduated at Yale college, at the age of twenty-three, studied theology at Dedham, with the Rev. Thomas Balch, and having settled in the ministry at Ipswich, Massachusetts, in 1771, soon became known for ability and learning. A minister by profession, he was also an ardent votary of science, in some of whose walks he became very eminent. In 1766, he married Mary Balch, daughter of his preceptor in theology, and to them were born seven children, viz: Ephraim, Jervis,

Mary, Charles, Lavinia, Elizabeth, and Temple. Of these only three, Ephraim, Jervis, and Charles ever came to Ohio. Dr. Cutler was elected a member of the American Academy of Arts and Sciences in 1781, of the Philosophical Society of Philadelphia, in 1783; an honorary member of the Massachusetts Medical Society in 1784; received the degree of LL. D. from Yale college in 1789; was elected a member of the Massachusetts Historical Society in 1792, and was a representative in congress in 1800 and 1802. He was also active as president of a bible society in Massachusetts, and was a member of various other scientific bodies than those above named. He was a chaplain in the American army during the revolutionary war, and in one engagement took such an active and gallant part, that the colonel of his regiment presented him with a fine horse captured from the enemy.

On the formation of the Ohio Company in 1787, Dr. Cutler soon became a controlling spirit in that enterprise. In an original memorandum of his, now before us, referring to the origin of the company, etc., he says:

"At this meeting* by ye desire of Major Sargent, I attended. I had suffered exceedingly in ye war, and after it was over, by paper money and ye high price of articles of living. My salary small and family large, for several years I thought ye people had

---

*The meeting of March 1st, 1787.

not done me justice, and I meditated leaving them. Purchasing lands in a new country appeared to be ye only thing I could do to secure a living to myself, and family in that unsettled state of public affairs. I had long before entertained an high opinion of ye lands in ye western country, which was a particular inducement to attend this meeting. The representations and plans of ye country gave me a still more favorable idea, and I determined to join ye association, but without ye most distant thought of taking an active part."

A few days later, he was chosen a director, and appointed as their agent to proceed to New York and negotiate with the congress then sitting there, for a purchase of western lands. From the very interesting journal kept by Dr. Cutler during this trip, we have quoted at some length. He conducted this negotiation with great skill and entire success. *He insisted that there should be an appropriation of land in the company's purchase for the endowment of a university*, and this feature was part of the contract with congress. Thus, the Ohio university is undoubtedly indebted to Dr. Cutler for its existence, and he was in later years very active in furthering its sound organization. He also originated the idea of a donation of land in each township, for educational and religious purposes, and made it a part of the contract with congress that two sections in each township should be reserved as school and ministerial lands.

In the summer of 1788, in order to attend a meeting of the directors of the Ohio Company, and to examine into the condition and prospects of the colony, Dr.

Cutler made a trip to Marietta, where he spent a short time, and became thoroughly acquainted with the nature of the country and wants of the settlers. His versatile talents and unusual business qualifications made his services to the company of great value, and for many years he continued to exercise a controlling influence in this great enterprise. During all this time he did not cease his labors as a minister of the gospel, nor his scientific investigations, particularly his botanical pursuits, in which branch of science he was very eminent.

The latter years of his life were spent peacefully in Massachusetts. He officiated as pastor of one church at Hamilton in that state, for nearly fifty years, and died in 1820.

Eliphaz Perkins, son of John Perkins, a leading citizen of Norwich, Connecticut, was born at that place, August 25, 1753. Deprived of his father at an early age, he was nevertheless enabled, through the exertions of his mother, to obtain a liberal education. Soon after leaving college, Mr. Perkins married Lydia Fitch, daughter of Dr. Jabez Fitch, of Canterbury, Connecticut, and engaged for a time in the mercantile business in that town. Subsequently he engaged in the same business in New Haven; having, however, an inclination to professional pursuits, he finally entered on the study of medicine with his father-in-law, and this was his vocation during the rest of his life. The times being hard, and his family increasing, Dr. Perkins decided to remove to a new country, and, in the spring of 1789, leaving his family in Connecticut, he started for Marietta. On his arrival here he found a number of ·persons from Clarksburg, Virginia, engaged in laying out a road between that place and Marietta. At their urgent solicitation he returned with them to Clarksburg, where he practiced medicine for nearly two years. The Indian war began about this time, and Dr. Perkins witnessed some terrible scenes of border warfare. In one instance the savages killed and scalped a family near where the Doctor was passing the night. One member of the family, a girl about fourteen years old, was scalped and left for dead in the fence corner. Dr. Perkins found her the next morning, still alive, took her under his care, and with good treatment and an elastic constitution, she was finally restored to health.

In the autumn of 1790, Dr. Perkins returned to Connecticut and rejoined his family, whom he had not heard from, nor they from him, for nearly two years. During the next few years, he lived part of the time in Connecticut, and part of the time in Vermont, and practiced his profession. He finally decided to remove his family to the northwest, and they set out for Marietta on the third of June, 1799. He had at this time seven children, the eldest of whom, then a young lady of fifteen (afterwards Mrs. David Pratt, of Athens), kept a journal of their trip to Marietta, which is now before us. She says:

"Mother had a pleasant, easy-going horse, so that she could, whenever she choose, relieve herself from the tiresome motion of the wagon by riding on horseback. The first Sabbath was spent at Brandon, Vermont. It being a rainy day, we did not attend church, but spent the day within doors. The second Sabbath was passed at Williamstown, Massachusetts, where we heard an excellent sermon from mother's brother, the Rev. Ebenezer Fitch. The third Sabbath, we were at Salisbury, Connecticut, where we were hospitably and kindly entertained by friends of the name of Chittenden. Here we also spent Monday in order to recruit our provision chest, which we did abundantly with bread, pies, cakes, etc., through the kind assistance of our friends. The next week brought us into Pennsylvania. At sunset on Saturday evening, we passed through Reading, intending to go a little into the country where we could find pasture for the team. About eleven o'clock we came to a large stone house with a sign for entertainment, where we were admitted. The next day was the Sabbath, and before evening, mother gave birth to twin daughters. We remained here three weeks, when, the babes being healthy, and mother's health better than before, we resumed our journey. But now sickness began to prevail among the rest of the family, probably owing to the hot weather, bad water, and the abundance of fruit which was then ripe and very inviting to children, and doubtless, indulged in too freely by them. The people, at that time, along the mountains, were not very friendly to strangers, especially if they had sickness among them, fearing some contagious disease. Many of them were Dutch, and either did not, or pretended not to understand English, so that it was often with difficulty we found a place to lodge in. Several of the children were obliged to be placed on beds in the wagon, the motion of which, soon became so painful to them, as to make it necessary to suspend traveling for a time. A shelter was necessary. At last, with great difficulty, we found a hut that had been a blacksmith's shop, with a blacksmith's fire-place in it. There was no floor, but the shelter was better than nothing.

Here we remained ten days before the sick were so far recovered as to be able to bear the jolting of the wagon. We then traveled slowly, about six or seven miles a day, till we reached McKeesport on the Monongahela river. Here we were going to take a flat-boat and pursue our journey immediately by water, but some of the children who had been sick took a relapse, and we were detained several weeks. By this time the river was so low as to make navigation dangerous, yet, as we were all so anxious to reach Marietta before cold weather, it was determined to try it. Father procured a flat-boat of the largest and strongest sort, took in two men for rowers, and having placed the family and effects on board, with provisions for the voyage, we set out on the first of November, 1799. Owing to the extreme lowness of the water, we were three days in reaching Pittsburg—only about twelve miles. When we got into the Ohio river, it was very little better. At the end of the first day's travel, about three miles below Pittsburg, our boat fastened on the rocks, swung round, and seemed in imminent danger of being broken in pieces. At length, by great exertions, it was freed from the rocks and got to shore. The children were now so frightened they could not be persuaded to enter the boat again, nor were our parents much less alarmed. A consultation was held, but what could they do? On both sides of the river stretched an unbroken wilderness. The team had previously been sent on by land in charge of the two oldest boys. There were two horses on the boat belonging to the rowers; these father agreed to take and endeavor, without road or compass, to cross the country by land with the family and meet the boat at Wheeling. Taking all of us and the two horses out would somewhat lighten the load, and the men thought they could get on with the boat. Mother was placed on one horse and I on the other, each of us with one child in her lap and one on the horse behind her. Father took one of the babes in his arms, which he carried walking all the way to Wheeling, and the rest of the children walked beside him. In this way we traveled about a week through the forest, sometimes finding little paths, and sometimes no trace at all. There were a few settlers through this region, and we were so fortunate as to find some sort of shelter every night. At last we reached Wheeling. The boat had not yet arrived, but reached there two days later. We all entered the boat once more, and having now more water, we floated along somewhat more easily. After another week of tedious travel, we landed at Marietta on the 18th of November, 1799. But our troubles were not ended. It was impossible to get a comfortable house, and for nearly two months we occupied one not at all fit for winter. One of the children was taken with bilious colic, and his life was despaired of for several weeks. About the last of December we got into a more comfortable house, and just then mother was seized with a nervous fever. Father doctored her and was assisted by other good physicians, but without avail. After a few days of painful sickness, her toils and trials were ended by death. Father was very much crushed by this affliction, and could hardly bear up. In the spring of 1800 father was invited by some gentlemen from the Athens settlement, on the Hockhocking, to settle there. He accepted the invitation and spent the summer practicing over a large extent of sparsely populated country. Having decided to locate at Athens, he procured a house, the best the place could afford, a log cabin with one room, one window, and one door. There was a spring of excellent water near the house, and a shed for horse and cow. Being unable to go for the family himself, he employed a trusty person to escort us through the wilderness from Marietta to Athens. Our goods were sent in a small boat down the Ohio, and up the Hockhocking. Only five of us went over at this time, the other four children being left temporarily with friends in Marietta. I rode on one horse with the babe in my lap, and one of the little girls behind me, and two of the boys rode another horse, the guide walked before and led the way.   *   *   *   *   *   *   *

At last we reached Athens in safety. We were well pleased with our new home, and rejoiced to be with father again, who was not less glad to see us once more. Here we enjoyed peace and happiness. The first settlers here were generally poor, and father found it easier to earn money than to collect it. If the people had not money to pay with, he never distressed them. We suffered many privations; most of our bread had to be prepared from grain ground on hand mills, or horse mills, or pounded in a mortar, dug out of a large stump, with a spring pole fastened to an iron wedge for a pestle. A hand mill was something like a large coffee mill fastened to the side of the house or to a tree close by.

In 1803, father married Miss Catherine Greene, a sister of Mr. Griffin Greene, a prominent citizen of Marietta. Her mother, an aged and pious lady, became an inmate of our family at this time. She died in 1807, in her ninetieth year, and was the first person buried in the old grave-yard north of town."

Dr. Perkins was a man of much culture and refined manners, and, being a skillful physician, his arrival in the community was hailed with general joy. His professional skill, gentle manners, and quiet christian deportment gained him immediate popularity and influence which he was prompt to exert in every good cause. He labored to establish and sustain common schools in the county, and was an ardent friend of and liberal contributor to the Ohio university, of which institution he was one of the first trustees, and for many years treasurer. He was post master at Athens for about seventeen years, and county treasurer for many years. His descendants are widely scattered. His sons, Chauncey and Jabez, studied medicine with their father at Athens. Jabez died January 12th, 1843, having never married. Dr. Chauncey Perkins lives in Erie county, Pennsylvania. Eliphaz was a mechanic in early life, but studied for the ministry and preached for several years before his death; his descendants are in Kansas. John, another son of Dr. Perkins, is well known in Athens, where he has lived nearly seventy years. Henry, another son, graduated at the Ohio university, and in theology at Princeton, New Jersey. He has been pastor of a Presbyterian church at Allentown, New Jersey, over thirty years. One of Dr. Perkins' daughters was married to Captain David Pratt, of Athens; another to Mr. Isaac Taylor, long known as a hotel keeper in this town; another to Dr. Medbury, formerly a physician here; another to Dr. Wm. Thompson, of Richmond, Ohio. Seven of Dr. Perkins' descendants have been ministers of the gospel, and six the wives of ministers; he died at Athens, April 29th, 1828.

The *Rev. Jacob Lindley*, seventh son of Demas Lindley, one of the early settlers of Washington county, Pennsylvania, was born in that county, June 13, 1774. At the age of eighteen he was sent to Jefferson college, Pennsylvania, and from there went to Princeton, New Jersey, where he graduated in 1798. After a course of theological study he was licensed to preach by the "Washington Presbytery," and in 1803, he removed to Ohio, settling first at Beverly, on the Muskingum. Having been selected by the first board of trustees of the Ohio university to organize and conduct that institution, he removed to Athens in 1808, and opened the academy there. For several years he had entire charge of the infant college, which he conducted with distinguished ability and success. He was the prime mover in securing the erection of the college buildings, and also in founding the Presbyterian church at Athens. He labored assiduously here for about twenty years, during part of which time he was the only Presbyterian minister in this portion of the state. He returned in 1829 to Pennsylvania, where he spent the rest of his life, and died at the residence of his son, Dr. Lieutellus Lindley, in Connellsville, Pennsylvania, January 29th, 1857.

Dr. Lindley was no common man, but an earnest thinker and conscientious worker. The leading trait in his character was an inflexible and unswerving devotion to moral principle. His whole life was a continuous effort to promote the moral welfare of others. He was of an amiable disposition, possessed an eminent degree of sound common sense, and an unerring judgment of men. His kindness of heart and known purity of life and conduct gave him great influence with all classes during his long residence at Athens. One who knew him well says: "I have seen him go into a crowd of rough backwoodsmen and hunters, who used to meet at the village tavern every Saturday, and settle and control them in their quarrels and fights, as no other man in that community could." His control of the students under his charge was equally extraordinary, and was always marked not less by gentleness of manner than by firmness of purpose. He led a laborious life at Athens, and his works live after him.

John Brown, well known in southern Ohio as "General Brown," son of Captain Benjamin Brown, one of the pioneers of Ames, was born in Rowe, Massachusetts, December 1, 1785. In 1787, his father's family moved to Hartford, Washington county, New York, and in 1796, with several other families seeking homes in the west, came to the Forks of Yoh, on the Monongahela, three miles above Williamsport, Pennsylvania. Here they remained till February, 1797, building a boat during the winter, in which they completed their journey and arrived at Marietta, February 11, 1797. Of the twenty-three persons of various ages who descended the river in this boat, there are but four now living, viz: Samuel and John Brown, Mrs. Aphia Hamilton, and Mrs. Phebe Sprague. As elsewhere stated, Captain Brown's family came out to Ames township in the spring of 1799, moving their household effects by canoes down the Ohio, and up the Hockhocking and Federal creek—the members of the family not required to work the canoes, coming across the country.

In 1811, Mr. Brown married Sophia Walker, daughter of Dr. Ezra Walker, and continued to live in Ames township till 1817, when he removed to the town of Athens, where he still resides. On coming to Athens,

GEN. JOHN BROWN.

OHIO VALLEY HISTORICAL SERIES.

Robert Clarke & Co. Publishers, Cincinnati O.

he kept a public house one year at the Zadoc Foster house (on the south end of the lot now owned and occupied by Judge Barker), when he bought the corner property in front of the university, and built and kept the " Brown House," so long known to the public, and so kindly remembered by his hosts of friends. He kept this house till December, 1865, a period of forty-seven years.

In 1808, Mr. Brown was elected captain in the militia, and was subsequently made major and colonel, and in 1817 was elected brigadier general. He was county auditor from 1822 to 1827, and has been treasurer of the Ohio university from 1824 to the present time. He was also mayor of Athens for several years, and coroner for two terms. He is, in every good sense, one of the village fathers who has "come down to us from a former generation." Possessed of sound judgment, a kind heart, sterling integrity, and unfailing humor, General Brown has for fifty years had the respect and affectionate regard of this community. His genial wit still oft enlivens the social circle, and his venerable form is recognized with pleasure by all, on the streets of the town where he has lived so long and where, without an enemy in the world, he is cheerfully approaching the end of his journey. He reared here a family of six sons and two daughters; four of the sons graduated at the Ohio university, and three survive, viz: Oscar W., Wm. Loring, and Archibald Douglas;

the latter is cashier of a bank in Pomeroy, Ohio. One of the daughters, Mrs. Hannah Pratt, lives in Illinois, and the other, Mrs. Lucy Hey, in Cincinnati, Ohio.

A. G. Brown, son of Captain Benjamin Brown, was born April 16th, 1798, near Waterford, in Washington county, Ohio, and has lived in Athens county since he was one year old. His youth was passed in working on his father's farm (in Ames township), and in assiduous study and preparation for college. In due time he became a student at the Ohio university, and graduated there in 1822. From 1824 to 1825, he was preceptor in the academical department of the university. In 1825 he began the publication of the *Athens Mirror*, the first paper printed in the county, and continued as its editor and publisher for five years. From 1827 to 1833, he was county recorder, which office he again filled from 1836 to 1841, when he began the practice of law in Athens. In 1841 he became a member of the board of trustees of the university, which position he still holds. He was a delegate to the convention which formed the present constitution of Ohio, and was for two years president judge of the Athens district. For many years past he has practiced law in Athens. Judge Brown came to Athens county when nearly the whole of its area was an unbroken forest and to the town of Athens when it was a mere cluster of log cabins. The personal friend and associate of the leading men of the community who assisted in building up society here, most of whom have passed away, he has witnessed the steady development of the county during considerably more than half a century. Looking back over its whole history to a period before it was organized, he may very truthfully say:

> — " *Quæ ipse vidi,*
> *Et quorum pars magna fui.*"

Judge Brown's sons, Henry T. Brown, an active lawyer and business man, and Louis W. Brown, for many years clerk of the county, are natives of Athens, and well known in the community.

John Perkins, son of Dr. Eliphaz Perkins, was born in Leicester, Vermont, in 1791, and came to the town of Athens with his father's family in the year 1800. His father located at Athens on account of the prospective establishment of the Ohio university here, and since that time two of his sons, five grandsons and two great-grandsons have graduated at this institution. Mr. Perkins has lived in Athens nearly seventy years, and was post master here for about twenty-two years. He has been engaged in mercantile pursuits during a large part of his life, and is known in the county as a most upright man and a good citizen. Though nearly eighty years old, his firm step and clear mind bespeak a temperate life and approving conscience.

Henry Bartlett, the son of Captain William Bartlett, was born at Beverly, Massachusetts, February 3, 1771. His father was a seafaring man, and received, it is believed, the first commission that was issued to engage in privateering, during the revolutionary struggle, in which he rendered conspicuous service. In 1785, Captain Bartlett removed with his family to Westmoreland county, Pennsylvania, and settled near the Forks of Yoh, where he lived till his death in 1794. While living in Westmoreland county, Henry Bartlett married Miss Betsey Corey, and in 1796, brought his young family to the northwestern territory and settled the next year at Athens. During his youth, Mr. Bartlett enjoyed pretty good educational advantages, and after his arrival at Athens was soon recognized as one of the readiest and most accurate clerks and business men in the community. Previous to the organization of the county, he taught school several quarters in the surrounding neighborhoods. Soon after the organization of the county in 1805, he was appointed by the county commissioners as clerk of the board and of the county courts, which position he held, discharging the duties with great fidelity for thirty years. He ceased to be clerk in 1836, and from that time till his death, acted as a justice of the peace in Athens. He was also for many years secretary and auditor of the Ohio university. He died September 9th, 1850. Esquire Bartlett was a man of great purity of character, thoroughly judicial mind and excellent capacity for business. During his early residence here, he adapted himself with admirable facility to pioneer life, and to the changing circumstances of the times, and was for many years almost indispensable in the management of county affairs. He possessed a fine quality of wit and humor, which he was fond of exercising, though always without offense to others, and which made him one of the most popular as he was one of the most highly respected men in the county. His family consisted of two sons and ten daughters, of whom nine daughters are living.

Robert Linzee, a native of western Pennsylvania, came to this county in 1801, and settled on a farm two miles below the town of Athens, on the "River road," where he lived nearly thirty years. Mr. Linzee was a leading man in the early history of the county. He was the first sheriff of the county and held the office several years; was a member of the state legislature several terms, a trustee of the Ohio university and associate judge of the court of common pleas. In 1830 he removed to Mercer county, Ohio, where he died in 1850.

Mr. Linzee occupied a prominent place in county affairs during his residence here, and in private life was an amiable and interesting man. His name is still kindly remembered by those who were acquainted with him, among whom he had many admirers and warm friends.

John Johnson, settled in Athens with his family as early as 1805. One of his daughters was married in 1807 to Robert Linzee, and another, about the same time, to Jacob Dombaugh, who was an active man, and at an early day kept public house where the Brown House is now situated. A son of John Johnson's, Samuel, married a daughter of Abel Glazier, of Ames. In 1815 Mr. Johnson and Mr. Glazier carried the mail, as sub-contractors, between Marietta and Chillicothe, when there were but two post offices on the route, viz., at Athens and Adelphi, Ross county.

Capt. Philip M. Starr, a native of Middletown, Connecticut, came to the town of Athens in 1801, where for several years he followed the mercantile business. Later he located on a rich and valuable farm on the river three miles below Athens where he died in 1857. Capt. Starr was a very active business man, and of more than average mental culture. He had considerable means when he came to the county, and though never in public life he was a man of influence among the early settlers. He devoted the latter part of his life to horticulture and fruit growing, in which he was notably successful.

Joseph B. Miles, for many years a merchant and

leading citizen of Athens, was born in Rutland, Massachusetts, June 21, 1781. In 1791 he removed to the northwestern territory with his parents, who settled at Belpre, in Washington county. Here he lived till he was twenty-seven years old. In 1808 Mr. Miles came to Athens and began business as a merchant. In January, 1809, he married Miss Elizabeth Buckingham, of Carthage township. He lived in Athens for thirty-five years, during which period he was prominent in all social, religious and business movements here. He engaged extensively in the mercantile and milling business, and was universally respected as an upright man and exemplary christian. In 1843 he removed with his family to Washington, Tazewell county, Illinois, where he died September 18th, 1860. His first wife died in Athens in 1821. By his first marriage Mr. Miles had six children— Catherine B., who married Mr. C. Dart and died in Houston, Texas, in February 1866; Lucy W., who married Mr. L. A. Alderson and died in Greenbriar county, Virginia, in 1832; Belinda C., who married Mr. Jared Sperry and now lives in Mt. Vernon, Ohio; Pamelia B., who died before marriage at Havana, Cuba; Elizabeth B., who was married in Natchez and died there of yellow fever in September, 1837; and Benjamin E., who now resides in Washington, Illinois. Mr. Miles married for his second wife Miss Elizabeth Fulton. Their children were Martha M., James H.,

Daniel L., Joseph B., Mary F., William R., and Sarah J. Mary, Martha and Joseph live in Washington, Illinois, James in Chicago, and Sarah J. (Mrs. Robert Wilson) in Farmington, Iowa. William R. died young; and Daniel L., who was lieutenant-colonel of the Forty-seventh Illinois Volunteers, during the war of the rebellion, was killed in a skirmish near Farmington, Tennessee, in May, 1862. Mr. Miles's second wife died in 1862.

Jonathan Wilkins, one of the earliest inhabitants of Athens, was a man of very considerable learning, and for some time taught a pioneer school. Of his son, Timothy Wilkins, the following reminiscence is furnished by Dr. C. F. Perkins; it is hardly less strange than the history immortalized by Tennyson in " Enoch Arden."

Mr. Wilkins was skillful and enterprising in business, but, through no fault of his own, became embarrassed, was hard pressed by creditors, and pursued by writs. In those days, when a man could be imprisoned for a debt of ten dollars, to fail in business was an awful thing. Wilkins was not dishonest, but had a heart to pay if he could. He battled bravely with his misfortunes for a considerable period, but with poor success. One day in the year 1829, full of despair, he came from his home west of town, across the Hockhocking, and having transacted some business with the county clerk, went out, and was supposed to have returned home. The next morning it became known that he was not at his house. Inquiry and search being made, the boat in which he usually crossed the river was seen floating bottom upward, and his hat was also found swimming down the stream. Mr. Wilkins was a popular man in the community; news of his loss soon spread, the people gathered from every quarter and measures were taken to recover the body. The river was dragged, a cannon was fired over the water, and other means resorted to, but to no purpose; the body was not found. The excellent Mrs. Wilkins put on mourning, and friends remembered the departed for a time with affectionate regret. As time sped, the sad incident was forgotten, and Timothy Wilkins passed out of mind. His wife, faithful for a time to his memory, had for years been the wedded partner of another, and a little family was growing up around the remarried woman and her second husband, Mr. Goodrich, himself a well known and worthy citizen.

In 1834, a vague rumor—an undefined whisper from the distant southwest—circulated through the settlement that Mr. Wilkins yet survived. Soon more positive assertions were made, and finally it was said that the missing man was alive and on his way home. At last a neighbor received a letter from Wilkins, announcing his approach; fearing to shock his wife by a sudden appearance, he had himself originated the rumors of safety, and now announced that he would soon be in Athens. He knew of his wife's second marriage, and in friendly spirit proposed to meet her and Mr. Goodrich. Much excitement and distress ensued. Mr. Wilkins arrived; there was a cordial meeting and strange interview among the parties most concerned. The conference was friendly and satisfactory. Messrs. Wilkins and Goodrich honestly left to the wife of their rivalship the final choice of her companion, and she selected her first love, to the great grief, but with the full acquiescence of her second. The reunited pair bade adieu to their friends, and together set out for the distant south.

Mr. Wilkins' disappearance was a ruse to escape his creditors. He went to New Orleans, engaged successfully in boating, accumulated money enough to pay off all his debts, which he honorably did, and returned to claim his beloved.

John Gillmore, was born in Washington county, New York, December 25, 1786. Soon afterward his father's family removed to Rutland, Vermont, whence they emigrated in 1813 to Ohio. They were accompanied by Cephas Carpenter, a relative by marriage, and all settled in Athens. The father, James Gillmore, was the first elder in the Presbyterian church formed here about the time of his arrival, and was an excellent man; he died July 25, 1827. John Gillmore held several minor local offices, and served with credit two terms in the state legislature. In 1836 he removed with his family to Illinois, and finally settled at Rock Island, where he died, July 9th, 1859. The Gillmores are remembered as one of the most substantial families of the town during their long residence here. One of the daughters of Mr. James Gillmore, Ann Eliza, married the Rev. S. S. Miles (brother of Mr. Joseph B. Miles), who now lives in Geneseo, Illinois.

Archibald B. Walker, son of Dr. Ezra Walker, was born in East Poultney, Vermont, October 15th, 1800, and came to Ames township with his father's family when ten years old. In 1825 he married Lucy W., daughter of Judge Silvanus Ames, and in 1826 they removed to the town of Athens, where they have since resided continuously, and reared a family of two sons and four daughters. Soon after coming to Athens, Mr. Walker, having formed a partnership with his brother-in-law, James J. Fuller, engaged for a few years in the cattle-driving and pork-packing business. In 1839 they commenced the manufacture of salt at the old furnace, opposite Chauncey, afterward owned by Judge Pruden, and soon after they bored the wells and erected the furnaces now owned by M. M. Greene & Co., at Salina. For a period of twenty years the firm name of Fuller & Walker was well and favorably known in the valley. The partnership was dissolved in 1853. Since that time, Mr. Walker has not engaged in active business on his own account. During his long residence in the county, he has always been one of the most prompt to embrace, and ardent in the support of every useful local enterprise. At home and abroad, in personal intercourse and through the press, he has ever been ready and efficient in advocating the development of the county, and presenting her claims. He was one of the original friends, and for several years a director of the Marietta & Cincinnati railroad, and an early and strenuous advocate for the construction of the Hockhocking Valley railroad, which is now building under the energetic control of younger men, and which he is likely to live to see finished.

Having been through his whole life scrupulously faithful and exact in the discharge of every duty, public and private, Mr. Walker is peacefully completing the last stage of a long and worthy career in the very spot where he began it. If his part has been acted on a comparatively narrow stage, it has nevertheless, been well acted—"there all the honor lies." Happy in the respect of his neighbors and the affection of children and grand-children, he possesses, in the words of Shakspeare:

"That which should accompany old age,
As honor, love, obedience, troops of friends."

Dr. Leonard Jewett, one of the pioneer physicians of the county, was born September 6, 1770, in Littleton county, Massachusetts. He studied medicine and surgery at the Boston Medical college, and received a diploma from that institution in 1792. In 1796 he married Miss Mary Porter, of Rutledge, Massachusetts. After this he served four years as assistant surgeon in the New York hospital. In 1802 he removed from New York to Washington county, Ohio, and in 1804 or '5 to the town of Athens, and occupied a house built by Captain Silas Bingham, on the lot now owned and occupied by Mr. George W. Norris. In 1806 he was elected to the state senate, which position he held till 1811. When hostilities began in 1812, he was commissioned as surgeon in the army of the northwest, under Harrison, and was assigned to duty on the staff of General Tupper. At the close of the war he returned to Athens and resumed the practice of medicine with success. In 1816, while performing a surgical operation, he received poisonous matter into a small wound on his hand, the absorption of which produced violent inflammation and sudden death; he died May 13, 1816. Dr. Jewett was a gentleman of fine intelligence and professional ability, and there are those living who still cherish his memory as one of the leaders among the early citizens of the county.

Four of his sons survive; three of them, Joseph, Leonard, and Leonidas Jewett, live in the vicinity of Athens, and one resides in Oregon. Leonidas was county auditor from 1839 to 1843, and was for many years a successful lawyer of Athens.

Leonidas Jewett, jr., son of the last named, a lawyer of promise, is settled at Athens, where he was born. During the late war of the rebellion, he served three years with credit as adjutant of the Sixty-first Ohio regiment.

Calvary Morris, was born near Charleston, West Virginia, in 1798, and spent his youth in the Kanawha valley, laboring on a farm, and battling with the hardships of pioneer life. In 1818 he married the eldest daughter of Dr. Leonard Jewett, of Athens, and in the spring of 1819, located permanently in that town. "Finding myself," says Mr. Morris, "a stranger in a strange land, and obliged to make provision for the support of my family, my first step was to rent five acres of ground, upon which to raise a crop of corn. While cultivating that ground, during the summer of 1819, the Rev. Jacob Lindley (then acting president of the Ohio university) came to me and said that a school teacher was much needed in our town, and proposed that I undertake it. I informed him that I was not at all qualified—that reading, writing, spelling, and a limited knowledge of arithmetic was the extent of my education. He said that the wants of the community required that arithmetic, geography, and English grammar be taught in the school, and, 'now,' said he, 'I will tell you what to do. I have the books and you have brains; take my books, go to studying, and recite to me every day for three weeks, and by that time I will have a school made up for you; you will then find no difficulty in keeping ahead of your scholars so as to give satisfaction in teaching, and no one will ever suspect your present lack of qualifications.' I consented, went to work, and at the end of three weeks went into the school. I taught and studied during the day, and cultivated my corn-field part of the time by moonlight, and if there was ever any complaint of my lack of qualifications as a teacher, it never came to my knowledge."

In 1823, Mr. Morris was elected sheriff of Athens county, and re-elected by an almost unanimous vote in 1825. In 1827, at the close of his term as sheriff, he was elected to the lower branch of the state legislature, and re-elected in 1828. In 1829, he was elected to the state senate, and re-elected in 1833. In 1835, when the project of the Hocking canal was being warmly agitated, Mr. Morris was elected again to the popular branch of the assembly from Athens and Hocking counties as the avowed friend of that measure, and in the belief that he was the best man to engineer it through. To his adroit management and indefatigable efforts, the measure was mainly indebted for success, as he had to overcome the almost unanimous opposition of both branches of the legislature and the whole board of canal commissioners.

He had the pleasure of seeing the bill triumphantly passed a few days before the close of the session, and on his return home his constituents tendered him a public dinner.

In 1836 Mr. Morris was elected to congress, and re-elected in 1838 and '40.

In 1843 he retired from public life and engaged, to some extent, in wool growing and in the introduction of fine-wooled sheep into the county, in which business he rendered great service to the farming community.

In 1847 he removed to Cincinnati and engaged in mercantile pursuits, which finally proving unfortunate, he returned to Athens in 1854, and in 1855 was elected probate judge of the county, which office he still holds.

Few men, if any, now living in the county, have filled a larger part in its official history than Judge Morris, and, during his varied services, he has discharged every trust with honor and fidelity. His public life lay chiefly in the better days of the republic, and of our politics, and, from his present standpoint, secure in the confidence and respect of all his neighbors, he has the rare and happy fortune of being able to review his whole career without shame and without remorse.

Judge Morris is a brother of the Reverend Bishop Morris of the M. E. church. William D. Morris, of Illinois, and Levi Morris, of Louisiana, are the other surviving brothers.

Capt. Isaac Barker, came from New Bedford, Massachusetts, to the northwestern territory in the autumn of 1788. For several years he lived in the Belpre settlement on the Ohio river, about fifteen miles from Marietta, and his name is preserved as one of the heads of families who, in the year 1792, took refuge in the block house called "Farmers' Castle," where he and his family remained till the violence of the Indian war was spent. In 1798 he removed with his family of five sons and three daughters to Athens township, and settled near the village of Athens, where he passed the remainder of his life. Capt. Barker was a sea-faring man in early life, being supercargo and captain of an East India vessel, and, during the revolutionary war, took an active part in the privateering service. His sons were Michael, Isaac, Joseph, William, and Timothy.

Michael Barker, son of Capt. Isaac Barker, born in 1776 at New Bedford, Massachusetts, came with his father's family to Marietta in the autumn of 1788. During the Indian war, from 1792 to 1795, while they lived in Farmers' Castle at Belpre, Michael served as a scout or spy against the Indians in a company raised under the authority of the Ohio Company. He came to Athens county and settled near the town of Athens in April, 1798, where he spent the rest of his life. He married a daughter of Wm. Harper, who was county treasurer from 1809 to 1811. Mr. Barker was for many years a constable in Athens township, and held other local offices. He was a man of scrupulous exactness in his dealings, and of much firmness and decision of character. He died June 10th, 1857.

Isaac Barker, jr. (son of Capt. Isaac Barker), long known in Athens county as Judge Barker, was born in Massachusetts, February 17th, 1779. He remembers his father setting out with his family for the northwestern territory, from New Bedford, Massachusetts, in 1788. They had one wagon drawn by two oxen and a horse, and were accompanied on the journey by Capt. Dana and his family, also emigrating to the west. Their journey was not marked by any special incidents. At one stage Capt. Barker's oxen having become footsore, he exchanged them with a Dutch tavern keeper where they stopped for a fresh yoke. The next morning the boys started on early with the team, the father remaining behind a little while. They had not gone far before they came to a very bad place in the road, over which the oxen refused to go. After working with them for some time the boys suddenly thought it was because the Dutch oxen could not understand English that they were so stubborn; one of them accordingly went back for the Dutchman, who soon arrived, and, by dint of considerable hard swearing at the oxen, in good Dutch, got the team over. The emigrants traveled by land to Sum-

JUDGE ISAAC PARKER.

rill's ferry on the Youghiogheny, where they procured keel boats and continued their journey by water to Marietta. Captain Barker's family spent several months in the family of Paul Fearing, at Marietta, and removed thence early in 1790 to Belpre, where he settled on a one-hundred-acre donation lot. They had hard work to get along here, especially for the first year or two. Mr. Barker says corn was four dollars a bushel and none to be had at that. They lived for one year almost solely on corn bread and wild meat. "One quart of cracked corn," he says, "was the daily allowance for our family of eleven. The children used to stand by looking wistfully while their mother baked the daily loaf, and, having received their share, would hoard it carefully, nibbling it like mice during the day." They lived in a block house, or garrison, some four or five years, during the Indian war. At this time, says Mr. Barker, "I was a pretty smart boy and able to handle a gun, and while father and my older brother worked in the field I stood guard with the rifle. Every evening we barred up the door before sundown. In the morning we would open it an hour or so after sunrise, look carefully about, and, if no signs of Indians appeared, brother Michael would go out (the door being instantly barred behind him), and scout around a little." Several men and one or two whole families were killed in that neighborhood by the Indians during these years. Mr. Barker recollects the massacre of the

Armstrong family just across the river from where they lived, the killing of Benoni Hurlbut, the chase of Waldo Putnam and a man by the name of Bradford, by the Indians, and the killing of Jonas Davis. This Mr. Davis was engaged to be married to one of Mr. Barker's sisters. One cold day during the war, seeing an old skiff lodged on the ice some distance up the river, he ventured out to get some nails out of her—they being very scarce. He never returned. Being missed, after several hours, and search made, he was found dead, stripped, and scalped on the ice. Though a mere boy during the war, Judge Barker received at its close one hundred acres of land as a bounty from the Ohio Company—Gen. Putnam saying that he had done a man's work and was entitled to a man's pay. He used frequently to stand guard at the garrison. Capt. Barker's family came to Athens in 1798, poling their goods up the Hockhocking in a light flat boat. These boats were built with a "running board" along each side; a man on each side, furnished with a long pole with a pointed iron socket at the end, would plant it firmly in the bottom at the bow, and then with the upper end against his shoulder would run to the other end of the boat, propelling her by that means. After coming to Athens they lived a year at the point close by Harper's Ferry. Judge Barker tended this ferry for a while, and married Christiana, a daughter of Mr. Harper. At this time they got their milling from

Capt. Devol's floating mill, some five miles up the Muskingum. It took four days to go and come, and Mr. Barker has himself more than once made this long trip to mill, going down the Hocking and up the Ohio in a pirogue and back by the same means, camping out over night.

Moses Hewitt and his family lived a short distance up Margaret's creek. In the year 1800 some thirty or forty Indians came in on Factory run, and three of them came over to Mr. Hewitt's house. They were somewhat in liquor, and Mrs. Hewitt in alarm sent hastily for her husband, who was a short distance from the house. When Mr. Hewitt came he ordered them in their own language (he had been a captive among them several years before), to "go away." They refused and were insulting, whereupon, Mr. Hewitt flew at the drunken ones and knocked one into the fireplace and another headlong out of the door. Mr. Barker was in the house and saw all this. A large athletic Indian, who seemed entirely sober, then grappled with Mr. Hewitt, and, after a violent struggle, threw him on the floor. Mrs. Hewitt and Mr. Barker, excited and alarmed, were about to pull the Indian off, when Hewitt, who was a noted fighter, told them to stand off and let him alone. The fight continued, and Hewitt very soon managed to get his thumb into the Indian's eye, and the Indian's thumb into his mouth, when the latter screamed lustily and begged till Mr.

Hewitt released him. The moment he was on his feet, the Indian ran to the door, and, putting his hand to his mouth, gave a regular war whoop, loud and long continued, and then ran away. Mr. Hewitt himself was now alarmed, thinking that the Indians would come over in the night and kill his family. Accordingly he requested Garner Bobo, a man named Cutter, and Mr. Barker, to stay in the house over night while he took his wife and the children some distance across the river. Mr. Barker says, "We had but one gun among us— Bobo had that. I was armed with a heavy clothes-pounder, and Cutter had a conchshell which he was to blow for help in case of great danger. Thus accoutered we barred the door and prepared to pass the night. We took turns sleeping and watching, and the night passed without any alarm. About daylight I, being on watch, saw some three or four figures gliding about the house and thought the redskins were after us now, sure enough. I woke Bobo who had his gun ready in a minute, and we were preparing for a fight or a siege when we heard a loud laugh outside, and looking out saw Hewitt and two or three others coming up to the house. They had come over to scare us. We saw nothing more of the Indians, and I think this was the last considerable party of them seen in this part of the country."

About this time Mr. Barker and Martin Mansfield, both vigorous and athletic young men, boated a man by the name of King, with his family, from the mouth of the Hockhocking river to the falls near Logan, and then dragging their boat around the falls, continued to within eight miles of Lancaster, the place of destination.

The town plat of Athens was very heavily timbered at that time, and the few cabins that stood here were widely separated. Mr. Barker, though not a great hunter, killed great numbers of deer and turkeys hereabouts. He remembers the following incident:

Chris. Stevens, who lived back of the college green, and a German named Heck, were hunting one day and treed a bear in a large poplar not far from Stevens' house. The bear climbed nearly to the top of the tree, which was very tall. They had but one gun between them and Stevens was to shoot. He had leveled his gun, taken aim, and sighted a long time; Heck stood a little off waiting for him to fire, when, his patience exhausted, he asked, "Why don't you shoot?" Stevens, who was a kind-hearted man, deliberately lowered his gun and said, "I can't bear to see the poor thing *fall so far!*"

"Gott im himmels," cried the German, "gif me de gun den—I shoots him if he falls mit de ground till a a tousand feet," and bruin soon came tumbling down.

Old Capt. Barker's first cabin stood about where Joseph Herrold's house now stands. He afterward built a log house near the river, south of John White's present residence. Judge Barker's first cabin was about one hundred yards west of his father's first house, and he afterward built a two story hewed log house on the river bank just at the turn of the road, which was standing a few years since and occupied by the Beveridge family. In 1815 Judge Barker moved to the town plat and took the "Dunbaugh House," which stood where the "Brown House" now stands, and which had been kept for a few years by one Jacob Dunbaugh. Mr. Barker kept tavern here till 1818, when he bought the lot where he now resides. There was a hewed log house on this lot, and he kept tavern in this while his brick house was building, and till it was finished in 1823, and then in his present dwelling till about 1830.

During his residence here, Mr. Barker has held the offices of county sheriff, county treasurer, collector of rents for the university, and was judge of the court of common pleas for about ten years. He has lived for nearly three score years and ten in the town of Athens, where he is passing the evening of his days in quiet serenity. Though now eighty-nine years old, he devoted a part of every day during this season (1868), to working in his garden—his favorite employment—and is in possession of all his faculties.

Abel Stedman, son of Judge Alexander Stedman, was born at Newbridge, Vermont, February 26, 1785, and came to the town of Athens in 1802. In 1811 he married Miss Sally Foster. In 1812 he enlisted in the

United States service, and on the march from Sandusky to Chillicothe he marched next in the ranks to Thomas Corwin. Returning to Athens he engaged in his trade of house carpenter, and passed the rest of his days here. He was a man of active temperament and untiring industry, a professing christian and full of good works. He died December 20, 1859.

Zadoc Foster, a native of Massachusetts, moved with his family to the northwestern territory in 1796. He came, like many others of that time, with an *ox team* as far as Olean point, on the Allegheny river, and thence proceeded by *raft* down the Ohio to Marietta, in the autumn of 1796. Remaining that winter in the stockade, he made a settlement in the spring at Belpre, and remained there till he came to Athens in 1809. During his residence at the Belpre settlement Indians were frequently seen, but had ceased to be considered dangerous, while the game was so abundant that deers and turkeys were sometimes shot, from the door of the cabin in which he lived.

Mr. Foster kept public house in Athens till his death, by the "cold plague," in 1814, first in the McNichol house, on the lot now occupied by Mr. E. C. Crippen, and afterwards across the street, on the lot now occupied by Judge Barker. His widow, Mrs. Sarah Foster, continued to keep the tavern a few years after his death. She then began to teach a school for young children, in which vocation she was eminently useful and beloved during the remainder of her life. She continued to teach within four days of her death, which occurred in 1849.

Hull Foster, only surviving son of Zadoc Foster, was born in Sudbury, Rutland county, Vermont, January 23, 1796, and came to the northwestern territory, with his father's family, when a few months old. His first visit to Athens was in 1804 or 1805. He came to visit Dr. Leonard Jewett's family, and traveled on horseback from Belpre, there being no visible road, but only a horse path which crossed the river at the present site of Coolville. There was a sort of ferry at this point. At that time one Strickland kept public house in a log building, on the lot now occupied by Judge Barker, and Joseph B. Miles had a small lot of goods in a room of the same house. Timothy Wilkins had a cabin near where General John Brown now lives, and ran a little distillery in the hollow close by. Esquire Henry Bartlett lived in a cabin back of the college green, near the present site of Mr. J. L. Kessinger's house. There was a horse mill on the point of the hill, a short distance northeast of town, on the Bingham farm. Mr. Foster, when a boy, drove the horse at this mill; the usual terms of grinding were, that parties should bring their own horse and pay one-fourth of the corn as toll. In 1809 his father removed with his family to Athens. In the interval a few brick houses had been built; Dr. Eliphaz Perkins had built on the Ballard corner, and Esquire Henry Bartlett on Congress street, nearly opposite Dr. Wilson's present residence; these, with Abbott's tavern, the academy building, near Nelson Van Vorhes' present residence, and a school house just east of where the Presbyterian church now stands, were, it is thought, all the brick buildings here in 1809. When about seventeen, Mr. Foster took up the trade of shoemaking—to use his own expression, "just as a cow does kicking—in her own head." Between 1816 and 1820 he traveled with his kit on his back, through the west and southwest, visiting the present states of Indiana, Kentucky, Tennessee, etc. In 1821 he returned to Athens, resumed his trade, and built the house where Mr. Abner Cooley now lives. Soon after he married his first wife, a daughter of Mr. Ira Carpenter. Since then he has steadily adhered to his trade, at which he has worked for more than fifty years, and still works some, though under no necessity to do so. There is one family in the county for whom he has made shoes for five generations. He has been twice married—his second wife was a daughter of Mr. William Brown, of Lee township— and is now a widower. A man of strong sense, strict integrity, and marked force of character, his life and virtues are known and read of all his neighbors.

Ebenezer Currier, born at Hempstead, Rockingham county, New Hampshire, December 15, 1772, came to Ohio in 1804, and to the town of Athens in 1806, where he lived nearly fifty years. He was one of the pioneer merchants of Athens. In 1811, having to transport a small supply of goods from Baltimore, he hired Archelaus Stewart to fetch them. The latter made the trip to and from Baltimore, all the way in a light wagon, and delivered the goods safely in Athens, after a journey of about two months. During Mr. Currier's long residence here he filled several town and township offices, was justice of the peace, county commissioner, and county treasurer; was four times a member of the state legislature as senator and representative, and for about twenty-one years was associate judge of the court of common pleas. For more than forty years he engaged here in mercantile pursuits, in which he was quite successful, amassing a considerable fortune. Judge Currier died March 2, 1851. Many of his descendants live in the county.

Conrad Hawk was born in Chester county, Pennsylvania. While a young man he removed to Harrison county, Virginia, where he married Miss Nancy Read in 1805, and whence he moved to Athens county in 1810. He settled as a farmer in Athens township, where he died, October 1, 1841. Mr. Hawk's family, formerly well and favorably known in this community, are now scattered. William, the oldest son, died in 1864, while commanding a steamer in General Banks' expedition up the Red river. John lives in Texas; James and Columbus in Clarke county, Ohio, and Geo. W. in Mt. Vernon, Ohio. One of the daughters, now Mrs. Dr. Huxford, lives in Fort Wayne, Indiana, and the other, Mrs. Durbin, in Mt. Vernon, Ohio.

Nicholas Baker, senior, born in England in 1760, was brought to this country at seven years of age, for forty-four years followed the sea, as cabin boy and sailor, and in 1814, with his only son Isaiah Baker, came to Athens county where he lived in his son's family, in the vicinity of Athens, till his death in 1829.

Isaiah Baker, son of the foregoing, born in Barnstable, Massachusetts, in the year 1780, came to this county with his family in 1814, and settled three miles west of Athens, where he followed farming the rest of his life. He died in 1825, leaving seven sons and three daughters, all of whom are living, except one son, Matthias, who was killed by the kick of a horse in 1837. Mr. Baker was a worthy member of the Methodist church.

Nicholas Baker, son of Isaiah, born in Massachusetts in 1799, has lived in Athens (town and township) fifty-four years. Social and genial in his daily intercourse with friends, few men lead a more placid life than

"Uncle Nick." With a heart corresponding in capacity to his ponderous frame, with a healthy and happy temperament, he is one of those kind-hearted men whom dumb animals like and children make friends with. He fondly cherishes the remembrance of his once having lived in Judge Silvanus Ames' family, in Ames township, in the summer of 1817. Edward R. Ames (Rev. Bishop Ames) at that time was eleven years old, and Mr. Baker, partial to him in boyhood, refers to their early acquaintance with lively pleasure. He relates with much gusto and laughter how "the bishop," being naturally rather lazy, would lie on the grass in the shade and amuse young Baker with his talk, while the latter cheerfully performed an extra amount of work for his dreaming companion. Mr. Baker, formerly a farmer, has resided for many years past in the town of Athens. His son, George W. Baker, is now treasurer of Athens county.

Jacob L. Baker, another of the sons of Isaiah Baker, is an extensive farmer in Athens township. He has a family of seven sons and one daughter, most of whom are well settled on good farms in the neighborhood of their father, who manages to buy an additional farm as often as needed, for some of his family.

The five other sons of Isaiah Baker removed to the west and are there settled—most of them in Illinois.

Capt. David Pratt, born at Colchester, Connecticut, in 1780, came with his father's family to Marietta in

1798, and removed to Athens in 1812. Here he was for many years a successful teacher, and there are old men living who well remember his thorough instruction and his stern discipline. In 1814 he married Miss Julia Perkins, eldest daughter of Dr. Eliphaz Perkins, whose christian graces and excellence of character were long known and admired in Athens. To them were born three sons and three daughters, all of whom are now living. The sons are all graduates of the Ohio university; two of them, the Rev. Eliphaz Perkins Pratt and the Rev. John H. Pratt being well-known ministers of the Presbyterian church, and the third, Dr. Robert Pratt, a successful physician in Illinois.

David Pratt died in 1861, and his wife in 1867, aged eighty-three. They were both members of the Presbyterian church in Athens for more than half a century.

Joseph Dana, born at Ipswich, Massachusetts, in 1768, was educated at Dartmouth college and graduated in 1788. He intended to pursue the ministry, but owing to delicate health did not carry out this purpose; he subsequently studied and qualified himself for the practice of the law. He served some time in the Massachusetts legislature, but his health continuing frail, he resolved to leave New England. In 1817 he removed west and settled at Athens, where he at first engaged in the practice of law. Though never a ready speaker, Mr. Dana was a thorough lawyer and fine special pleader—a branch of the practice necessarily more cultivated in those days than now. About two years after coming here he was elected professor of languages in the university—a position for which he was admirably qualified by his fine scholarship and intellectual habits. His connection with the university continued till 1835 when the infirmities of age led him to resign his position.

Professor Dana was an accomplished scholar and cultivated gentleman. He was, for many years, an elder in the Presbyterian church here, and a lofty intellectuality pervaded his religion and all his modes of thought. He died November 18th, 1849. His sons, Joseph M. Dana, Daniel S. Dana, Capt. William Henry Dana, U. S. N., and others of his descendants are well known in this community.

James Brice was born in Maryland in the year 1750, and, removing to western Pennsylvania, settled near Fort Pitt (Pittsburg) in 1787. While living here he held various public stations, such as member of the state legislature, county commissioner, collector of internal revenue, trustee of Washington college, etc. In 1821 he removed further west, and settled in the town of Athens, where he passed the latter years of his life, living in the family of his son. He was a man of high character, and during his long life was an active and exemplary christian. He died in Athens, December 22, 1832.

Barnet Brice, his son, and a native of Pennsylvania, preceded his father to Athens, having settled here in 1807. He kept public house many years (he built the Union hotel now occupied by O. B. Potter), and was extensively acquainted through the country. He died about 1853.

Thomas Brice, another son of James, came to Athens in 1818. He was a successful merchant here for many years, and a large dealer in cattle from 1820 to 1830. He built the brick dwelling house on Court street, now owned and occupied by Dr. W. P. Johnson.

In 1815 *Nathan Dean*, with his family, mostly grown, of six sons and three daughters, came to this county from Norton, Bristol county, Massachusetts. The young people all settled here, and raised respectable families in subsequent life. Three of them, William, Gulliver, and John N. Dean, made the brick, in the summer of 1816, for the central building of the Ohio university in Athens, and later, in 1835, one of them, John N. Dean, made the brick for the two additional or wing buildings of the university. The eldest of the family, afterward Colonel Nathan Dean, settled near Amesville, in the eastern part of the county, and died much respected in the year 1839.

At the time this family left Massachusetts, in 1815,

the manufactures of the country were only so far advanced, that, in making *nails*, their heads were made *singly* by hand, and these brothers had worked considerably at *heading nails by hand* before coming to Ohio. One of their ancestors, James Leonard, is believed to have been the first man that manufactured *iron* in America, and a son of his, Jonathan Leonard, the first to manufacture *steel*. Jonathan went to England and feigned to be *simple*, in order to get work in an establishment manufacturing steel, and thus gained the knowledge which the English were studiously endeavoring to conceal from the artisans of other countries. Upon his return the firm of "Leonard & Kinsley" successfully engaged in the production of steel in this country.

Charles Shipman, for more than twenty years an active and leading citizen of Athens, was born in Saybrook, Connecticut, August 28, 1787. He came to Marietta, with his father's family, in 1790, and they remained in the "stockade" during the Indian war. Colonel Shipman came to the town of Athens in 1813, and engaged in merchandising, in which line his business talent and popular manners soon gave him decided prominence, and ultimately large success. In early times he visited Philadelphia for the purchase of goods, once every year, and sometimes twice a year, always on horseback. Some of the old citizens of Athens still remember the fine sorrel horse, long owned by Colonel Shipman, on which he thus made nineteen trips from Athens to Philadelphia and back.

Colonel Shipman was a man of fine social qualities, genial manners, and benevolent heart. He was the first, or one of the first, merchants in this part of the state to discard the sale of intoxicating drinks, to stop the practice of "treating" customers, and to engage actively in the temperance cause. He was, during the most of his life, a professor of religion, and for many years a ruling elder of the Presbyterian church of Athens.

Colonel Shipman (he was elected colonel of a militia regiment during his residence at Athens) married Frances White Dana, of Belpre, in 1811. She died in 1813. The only issue of this marriage was a son, William C. Shipman, for many years past a citizen of New Albany, Indiana. In 1815 he married Joanna, the eldest daughter of Esquire Henry Bartlett, who is still living in Marietta. Colonel Shipman left Athens in 1836 to reside at Marietta, where he died July 7, 1860.

Silas Pruden, born in Norristown, New Jersey, in 1773, came to Athens county in 1815, and purchased the mills and farm east of Athens, then owned by Col. Jehiel Gregory, who soon after removed to Fayette county, Ohio. Mr. Pruden rebuilt and improved the mills, which were known as the "Pruden mills," till about 1836, when Mr. Pruden sold them with the adjoining farm, etc., to J. B. & R. W. Miles. Mr. Pruden was a man of considerable means, and raised a highly respectable family of six sons and seven daughters. In November, 1832, one of his daughters, Achsah, was married to John Brough, late governor of Ohio. Mr. Pruden was a member of the Presbyterian church during his residence in the county, and a most worthy man. In 1837 he removed to Hocking county, where he died, November 30, 1856.

Samuel B. Pruden, son of Silas Pruden, was born at Norristown, New Jersey, January 17, 1798, and came to Athens county with his father's family in 1815. On arriving at manhood he developed unusual capacity for business, and, during his long residence in the county, was one of her prominent and leading citizens. In 1826 he began the milling and wool-carding business at the "Bingham mills," west of Athens, which he continued about ten years. In 1836 he established himself permanently about two miles below Athens, on the Hockhocking, where he erected an oil mill, a grist and saw mill, and in 1840 a salt boiling establishment. The settlement that he here founded has long been known as Harmony. For many years Mr. Pruden carried on the manufacture of salt at this point, and also at Chauncey, in Dover township, where he owned another furnace. He was associate judge for one term, trustee of the Ohio university for several years, and represented the county in the state legislature in 1854-5. He also held the office of county surveyor for many years. As a member of the Masonic fraternity he advanced from one degree to another in that body, till he became commander of the Athens Encampment of Knights Templar. He died December 10, 1863.

Neil Courtney was an Englishman by birth, and was, for a time, in the British navy during the revolutionary war. Near the close of the war, while the vessel on which he was serving lay off Long Island, he deserted the service into which he had been impressed, swam half a mile to shore, and assumed allegiance to the new government. He came to Athens county in 1806, and settled one mile north of Athens, on what was afterward known as the "Courtney farm." The following entries appear in the old records of the county commissioners:

"*April* 8, 1809. The petitions of William Dorr and Neil Courtney, praying for an alteration in the road leading from the Horse mill to the mouth of Sunday creek, and from Athens to Coe's mill, read the first time. Petition granted. Jehiel Gregory, Samuel Moore, and Robert Linzee appointed viewers, to meet at Neil Courtney's on Monday, the 12th instant, at 9 o'clock A. M."

"*December* 6, 1810. The commissioners agreed, on condition that Neil Courtney produce to them satisfactory proof that he has worked, or expended on the alteration in the road leading from the Horse mill, near Esquire Bingham's, to the mouth of Sunday creek, the sum of five dollars, that then said road shall be established. Proof filed in office of commissioners, February —, 1811."

Mr. Courtney died January 22, 1826, in his sixty-eighth year. Numerous descendants of his are living in this county.

Joseph Goodspeed, born in Barnstable, Massachusetts, in June, 1774, came to this county, with his family of five sons and three daughters, in 1818, and settled on a farm about two miles west of Athens, where he died February 12, 1857. His two sons, David and Ezra Goodspeed, well known in the county as successful farmers, were born in Barnstable, Massachusetts, and came to Athens, with their father, in 1818. Many of their descendants still live in the county, and are highly respected. Major Arza Goodspeed, son of David, was killed before Vicksburg, while bravely doing his duty as a soldier of the Union, and J. McKinly Goodspeed, son of Ezra, and a graduate of the Ohio university, is at present superintendent of the Athens union schools.

Francis Beardsley, born at Stratford, Hartford county, Connecticut, December 28, 1792, came to Athens in 1814, where he has lived ever since. Soon after coming here he married Miss Culver, sister of John Gillmore's wife, who died in ———. For his second wife he married Rebecca, daughter of Esquire Henry Bartlett. Of a retiring disposition and unobtrusive manners, Mr. Beardsley has led a quiet and useful life. A model of christian rectitude under all circumstances, he is respected and esteemed by all who know him.

Norman Root, born in Canaan, Litchfield county, Connecticut, January 22, 1798, removed to Ohio in 1816, and to the town of Athens about the year 1820. In 1824 he married Jane Brice, sister of Thomas Brice, long known as a leading citizen of Athens. In 1827 Mr. Root was elected county auditor, and served till 1839, being re-elected five times. He was also, for many years, recorder of Athens, and held other positions of trust in the community, in all of which he discharged his duty with scrupulous fidelity. He was a man of great modesty and reticence, but of sound judgment and excellent business capacity. He was, for a long time, prominent as a Free Mason, and, for forty years, was a devoted and consistent member of the Methodist church. He died September 21, 1867.

E. Hastings Moore, born in Worcester county, Massachusetts, in 1812, came to Athens county with the family of his father, David Moore, in 1817. For about ten years the youth lived on a farm in Dover township, and then for several years on a farm in this township, about two miles from Athens, whence he finally removed to the town itself, where he has ever since resided. Mr. Moore had a good common school education (he taught some when a young man), and a taste for practical mathematics. In 1836 he became deputy county surveyor, and in 1838 was elected by the people to that office, then a difficult and laborious one. He held this position till 1846, discharging its duties with uncommon accuracy and entire acceptance to the public. In 1846 he was elected county auditor, which office he held, under re-elections, fourteen years. In 1862 he was appointed collector of internal revenue for the fifteenth Ohio district, and held the office till 1866. In 1868 he was elected to the forty-first congress from the fifteenth Ohio district as a republican. He is also president of the First National Bank at Athens.

Mr. Moore is a man of great practical sense and strict integrity, and is esteemed by all as a valuable citizen.

William Golden, born in Mifflin county, Pennsylvania, October 5th, 1799, came to Athens county in 1824, and settled at first in Athens, but later, in Alexander township, as a farmer. Here he was elected justice of the peace for many successive years. He was county sheriff from 1843 to 1847, and county treasurer from 1848 to 1854. In 1843 he removed to the town of Athens, where he has since resided, and is now post master. Three of his sons are living, viz: John C., a farmer and stock dealer in Meigs county, Elmer, a merchant in Jackson, Ohio, and William R.

William Reed Golden, son of the last named, was born in Athens, April 11th, 1827, and passed his early years on his father's farm in Alexander. He was educated at the Ohio university, studied law at Athens with Lot L. Smith, and attended lectures at the National Law School at Ballston Spa, New York, where he graduated in 1851. Returning to Athens, he entered on the practice of his profession here in 1852. In 1865 he was elected, as a democrat, to the state senate, and re-elected in October, 1867, to represent the counties of Athens, Hocking, and Fairfield, composing the ninth senatorial district. He has recently removed to Columbus, Ohio, where he is now engaged in the practice of law.

John Welch, born in 1805, in Harrison county, Ohio, came to Athens county about 1828, and settled in Rome township. Here he and his brother Thomas Welch bought the "Beebe mill," at that time owned by their father, and for some years he pursued the milling business. While performing his duties as miller, Mr. Welch studied law with Professor Joseph

Dana of Athens, going some fourteen miles to recite once in a week or two. Having finished his studies and prepared to change his vocation, he removed to Athens, where he was admitted to the bar in 1833 by the supreme court of Ohio, sitting in Athens county. In this field his success was assured from the start. His eminent abilities, indefatigable industry and devotion to his profession soon placed him at the head of the Athens bar, and finally among the ablest lawyers of the state. He was prosecuting attorney of Athens county for several years; a member of the state senate in 1846–7; a representative in congress in 1851–2; and judge of the common pleas court from 1862 to 1865. February 23d, 1865, he was appointed by the governor, judge of the supreme court of Ohio, in place of Rufus P. Ranney, resigned, and in October, 1865, was elected for Judge Ranney's unexpired term. In October, 1867, he was elected for the fall term, and occupies the position at the present time.

Judge Welch's career, which has been attended with honorable and solid success, is a sufficient eulogy upon his character as a man and citizen, and his ability as a lawyer.

Dr. *Eben G. Carpenter* was born at Alstead, New Hampshire, in 1808. His father was a physician, and, of eight brothers, five studied medicine. Dr. C. graduated at the Berkshire Medical college at Pittsfield,

Massachusetts, in 1831, practiced in New Hampshire a year or so, came to Ohio in 1833 and settled at Chester, Meigs county (then the county seat). In 1836 he came to Athens, where he has lived ever since, engaging very actively in the practice of his profession. Dr. C. has been notably successful as an operative surgeon.

Dr. William Blackstone was born in Bottetourt county, Virginia, in 1796, and came with his father's family to Ohio in 1802, settling first in Pickaway and afterward in Ross county. He studied medicine at Circleville, Ohio, and Lexington, Kentucky, and graduated at the Cincinnati Medical college in 1833, having engaged actively in the practice during several years before this. Dr. B. came to Athens in 1838, and has practiced here continuously since. He and Dr. Carpenter have both partially retired from active practice.

Dr. Perkins, Dr. Jewett, Dr. Bierce (who left here about 1840), Dr. Carpenter, and Dr. Blackstone are the only resident physicians who remained for any length of time in the place during the first half of this century. There are now three practicing physicians here, viz: Dr. W. P. Johnson, Dr. C. L. Wilson, and Dr. George Carpenter.

Nelson H. Van Vorhes, son of Abraham Van Vorhes, himself for many years a leading citizen of the county, was born in Washington county, Pennsylvania, January 23d, 1822. In 1832 his father removed with his family to Athens county, and settled in Alexander township. In 1836, his father having bought the *Western Spectator* and removed to Athens, Nelson entered the printing office as an apprentice. He worked diligently here for some years, part of the time having sole conduct of the paper, as his father was elected to the state legislature, and was absent for several winters. In 1844 he purchased the paper, which he continued to publish (a portion of the time in connection with his brother A. J. Van Vorhes), till 1861 as the *Athens Messenger*. During this time he took an active part in the political contests of the day and in furthering the home and local interests of the county. He served from 1850 to 1853 in the state legislature; in 1853 was whig candidate for secretary of state, but, with the rest of the ticket, failed of election; in 1854 was elected probate judge of the county, but resigned to become a candidate again for the legislature. He was elected, and became speaker of the house, which position he held during two sessions. In 1857 he was re-elected to the legislature. In 1858 he was republican candidate for congress in the 11th district, but was not able to overcome the democratic majority. He was a delegate to the Chicago convention in 1860, and took an active part in the presidential campaign which followed. At the breaking out of the war in 1861,

Mr. Van Vorhes enlisted as a private in the first company of infantry raised at Athens, and on the election of officers was chosen first lieutenant. In 1862, he was appointed colonel of the 92d Ohio regiment of infantry, which command he retained, serving in Western Virginia, till the summer of 1863, when, his health completely failing, he was forced to resign. Col. Van Vorhes has never fully recovered his health. He has held various local offices during the past few years, and possesses, in as high degree as ever, the confidence and respect of the community.

Charles H. Grosvenor, born in Pomfret, Connecticut, September 20, 1833, came to Athens county with his father's family when five years old, and lived in Rome during his youth and early manhood. While clerking in the store of Daniel Stewart he obtained books from Lot L. Smith, of Athens, and read law assiduously. He practiced with success in Athens for a few years prior to the breaking out of the rebellion, and entered the service in July, 1861, as major of the 18th Ohio infantry. He was promoted to lieutenant colonel March 16, 1863. March 14, 1865, Maj. Gen. J. B. Steedman recommended Col. Grosvenor to the secretary of war for promotion "for faithful, distinguished and gallant services." The recommendation was thus indorsed by Maj. Gen. George H. Thomas: "Respectfully forwarded and earnestly recommended.

Lieut. Col. Grosvenor has served under my command since November, 1862, and has, on all occasions, performed his duties with intelligence and zeal." Gen. Grosvenor was promoted to colonel April 8, 1865, and served till the close of the war. He was breveted brigadier general to date from March 13, 1865, and was mustered out October 28th in that year. He is now practicing law in Athens.

Samuel Knowles, a native of Connecticut, and, during early life, a sea-faring man, came to Athens county in 1808 and settled at Hockingport. In 1812 he married Miss Clarissa Curtis, sister of Judge Walter Curtis of Washington county, and in 1820 removed to the town of Athens where he resided for many years. He was elected marshal of the town in 1825 and 1826. He removed to the west many years since and is now living in Knoxville, Iowa.

Samuel S. Knowles, son of the last named, was born at Athens, August 25, 1825, received his early education at the village schools, learned the carpenter trade when seventeen years old and followed it for a few years, entered the academy at Athens at the age of twenty-one, and pursued his studies there and in the university about four years, read law with Lot L. Smith, was admitted to the bar in 1851, elected prosecuting attorney of Athens county the same year, and held the office two terms. He practiced law at Athens till 1862, when he removed to Marietta. In October, 1865, he was elected state senator from the 14th district, comprising Washington, Morgan, and Noble counties, serving two years. In April, 1864, he was elected mayor of Marietta, and re-elected in 1866, serving four years. He is now engaged in the practice of law at Marietta.

John Ballard was born in Charlemont, Massachusetts, October 1st, 1790, and came to Athens in February, 1839. During the greater part of his residence here he engaged successfully in the mercantile business; was also for several years president of the Athens branch of the State Bank, and a leading man in the local enterprises of the place. He has now retired from business. Four of his sons are living, viz: Otis, a banker in Circleville, Ohio; Charles, manufacturer of farm implements in Springfield, O.; James, merchant in Athens, and the Rev. Addison Ballard at Detroit, Michigan.

Thomas F. Wildes was born at Racine, in the dominion of Canada, June 1, 1834, came to Ohio with his father's family in 1839, and to Athens in 1861 as the editor of the *Athens Messenger*. Mr. Wildes was an ardent republican, and in August, 1862, exchanging the pen for the sword, he entered the military service as lieutenant colonel of the 116th Ohio infantry. He was in active service with this regiment during the next two and a half years, in the army of West Virginia, part of the time commanding a brigade. In February, 1865, he was promoted to the colonelcy of the 186th Ohio volunteer infantry, and assigned to duty in the Army of the Cumberland. March 11th, 1865, he was breveted brigadier general and commanded a brigade in the army last named till he was mustered out in September, 1865. He graduated at the law school in Cincinnati in 1866, and has since practiced his profession at Athens.

CHAPTER VII.

The Ohio University.

THE Ohio University was the first one established in all the territory northwest of the river Ohio; it will be interesting, therefore, to trace its history somewhat minutely from the beginning.

In authorizing the Board of Treasury to contract for a sale of lands to the Ohio Company, congress agreed that "two complete townships should be given perpetually to the uses of a university, to be laid off by the purchaser or purchasers as near the centre (of the purchase) as the case may be, so that the same shall be good land; to be applied to the intended object by the legislature of the state."*

There is no doubt that this feature was incorporated in the contract at the instance and by the earnest effort of Dr. Manasseh Cutler. Himself a man of liberal education, thoroughly appreciating the value and pleasures of learning, he regarded the diffusion of knowledge

---

* Appendix *A.*

not merely as a source of individual happiness, but as a chief element of political liberty and a necessary part of the policy of a free state. On the organization of the company he had urged the immediate employment of a competent instructor for the youth of the proposed settlement, and himself was authorized to secure a proper person. After the settlement at Marietta was begun, he was most active in organizing plans of education. Common schools were taught there from the first year of the settlement, and were kept up even during the period of the Indian war.* An academy was established at an early day. These persistent efforts to advance the cause of education are traceable to the energy of Dr. Cutler, who thus gave an impress to the society of the infant colony which has never disappeared. Nor have the beneficent results been confined to Ohio alone. The Ohio university for which he secured so liberal a land endowment (as was then thought), was the first ever thus endowed by congress; but the policy then begun was continued and we now see the universities of Indiana, Illinois, Michigan, Alabama, Mississippi and other states all endowed by congress. It may fairly be asserted that these noble results are the legitimate fruits of Dr. Cutler's early efforts in fixing the policy of congress on the subject.

---

* One of the schools kept during part of that time, was taught in the block house by Dr. Jabez True, an ancestor of the Trues in Dover township.

In his case, surely, the good that he did was not "interred with his bones."

In his reply to the order of congress, Dr. Cutler urged that the location of the lands assigned for the establishment of a university, should be, as nearly as practicable in the center of the first million and a half of acres that the company *should pay for;* for, he said, "to fix it in the center of the *proposed purchase*, might too long defer the establishment.* But this country, it must be remembered, was a wilderness then, and some years of delay necessarily occurred in carrying Dr. Cutler's plans into effect. The college townships were not located and surveyed till 1795.† For some years after that the dense forests that covered the whole region were but slightly invaded by settlers and it was not until the town of Athens had been laid out and "confirmed and established" by the territorial legislature, that any action was taken by that body toward carrying into effect the compact for the establishment of the university. The following is a copy of the first legislative

---

*Appendix *B*.

†From the records of the Ohio Company:

December 16th, 1795.

"The reconnoitering committee having reported that townships number eight and nine in the fourteenth range are most central in the Ohio Company's purchase, and it being fully ascertained that the lands are of an excellent quality.

Resolved, unanimously, that the aforesaid townships number eight and nine in the fourteenth range be reserved for the benefit of an university, as expressed in the original contract with the Board of Treasury.

act passed west of the Allegheny mountains looking to the establishment of a college or seminary of learning.

" *An act establishing an university in the town of Athens.*

WHEREAS, Institutions for the liberal education of youth are essential to the progress of arts and sciences, important to morality, virtue and religion; friendly to the peace, order and prosperity of society, and honorable to the government that encourages and patronizes them; and *whereas,* the congress of the United States did make a grant of two townships of land, within the purchase made by the Ohio Company of Associates, for the encouragement and support of an university therein; and *whereas,* the interference of the legislature is rendered necessary, to point out and direct the mode in which the same shall be brought into operation, that the benefits of the grant may be applied to the purposes designed: Therefore,

SECTION 1. *Be it enacted by the Legislative Council and House of Representatives in General Assembly, and it is hereby enacted by the authority of the same,* That there shall be an university instituted and established in the town of Athens, in the ninth township of the fourteenth range of townships, within the limits of the tract of land purchased by the Ohio Company of Associates, by the name and style of the ' American Western University,' for the instruction of youth in all the various branches of the liberal arts and sciences, for the promotion of good education, virtue, religion and morality, and for conferring all the degrees and literary honors granted in similar institutions.

SEC. 2. *And be it further enacted,* That there shall be and forever remain in the said university, a body politic and corporate by the name and style of ' The President and Trustees of the American Western University,' which body politic and corporate shall consist of the president *ex-officio,* and not more than seventeen nor less than eleven trustees, to be appointed as hereinafter is provided.

SEC. 3. *And be it further enacted*, That the Hon. Rufus Putnam, Joseph Gilman, Return Jonathan Meigs, Jun., and Paul Fearing, Esquires, the Rev. Daniel Story, Griffin Greene, Robert Oliver, Ebenezer Sproat, Dudley Woodbridge and Isaac Pierce, Esquires, together with the president of the said university, for the time being, to be chosen as hereinafter directed, be and hereby are created a body politic and corporate, by the name of 'The President and Trustees of the American Western University,' and that they and their successors, and such others as shall be duly elected members of the said corporation, shall be and remain a body politic and corporate, in law, by that name forever.

SEC. 4. *And be it further enacted*, That the said trustees shall have power and authority to elect a president, who shall preside in the university, and also to appoint a secretary, treasurer, professors, tutors, instructors, and all such officers and servants in the university as they shall deem necessary for carrying into effect the designs of the institution, and shall have authority from time to time, to determine and establish the name, numbers and duties of all the officers and servants to be employed in the university, except wherein provision is otherwise made by this act; and may empower the president, or some other member of the corporation, to administer such oaths as they shall appoint and determine, for the well ordering and good government of the university: *Provided, nevertheless*, That no corporation business shall be transacted at any meeting, unless seven of the trustees, at least, be present.

SEC. 5. *And be it further enacted*, That the said corporation shall have power and authority, from time to time, to make and ordain reasonable rules, orders and by-laws for the government of the corporation, not incompatible with the constitution, laws and ordinances of the United States, the acts of the territory, or the laws of the state in which the university is or may be founded, and the same to repeal as occasion may require, and also to determine the salaries, emoluments and tenures of the several officers.

Sec. 6. *And be it further enacted,* That the said corporation shall have power and authority to suspend, dismiss and disfranchise the president or any member of the said corporation, who shall by his misconduct render himself unworthy of the official station or place he sustains, or who from age or other infirmity, is rendered incapable to perform the duties of his office. And the said corporation shall have power and authority to suspend, dismiss, disfranchise and remove from the university, any professor, instructor, or resident student or servant, whenever the corporation shall deem it expedient for the interest and honor of the university.

Sec. 7. *And be it further enacted,* That whenever the president or any member of the corporation shall be removed by death, resignation, or otherwise, during the recess of the legislature the corporation shall hold a meeting (due notice of the design of which meeting shall be given to the several members) for the supplying such vacancy, who shall continue in office until the end of the next session of the legislature and no longer, by virtue of such appointment; and in order to choose a president or member of the corporation, there shall be, at least, two-thirds of the whole number of said trustees present, and the said election shall be by ballot.

Sec. 8. *And be it further enacted,* That when any member of the corporation shall be removed by death, resignation, or otherwise, such vacancy shall be supplied at the next meeting of the legislature of the territory or state.

Sec. 9. *And be it further enacted,* That the president and such professors, tutors and instructors as the corporation shall appoint for that purpose, shall be styled 'The Faculty of the University,' and shall have power and authority, from time to time, to ordain, regulate and establish the mode and course of education and instruction to be pursued in the university, and also to make public and execute such code of rules, regulations and by-laws as they shall deem necessary for the well ordering and good government of the university, and to repeal or amend any part thereof, which rules, regulations and by-laws shall continue in force till altered or disapproved of by the corporation. And it shall be the duty of the faculty, to lay before the corporation, from time to time, accurate statements of all their proceedings; and the faculty shall direct and cause to be holden in the said university, quarterly in every year, a public examination, at which time the faculty shall attend, when each class of students shall be examined, relative to the proficiency they shall have made in the particular arts and sciences, or branches of education in which they shall have been instructed.

SEC. 10. *And be it further enacted*, That the said corporation may have and keep one common seal, which they may change, break or renew at pleasure; and that all deeds and instruments of writing signed and delivered by the trustees, and sealed with the corporation seal by order of the president and treasurer, shall, when made in their corporate name, be considered in law as the deed and act of the corporation. And the said corporation shall be capable of suing and being sued, pleading and being impleaded, in any action, real, personal or mixed, and the same to prosecute and defend to final judgment and execution, by the name of ' The President and Trustees of the American Western University.' *Provided*, That whenever any suit shall be commenced against the said corporation, the process shall be summons, and the service made by the officer leaving an attested copy of such process with the treasurer of the said corporation, at least twenty days before the return of such process. And the said corporation shall be capable of having and holding and taking in fee simple or by any less estate, by gift, grant, devise or otherwise, any lands or other estate, real or personal.

SEC. 11. Whereas the congress of the United States have given, perpetually, for the use and benefit of an university, the two townships numbered eight and nine, in the fourteenth range of townships, in the grant of land made by congress to the Ohio Company of Associates: Therefore,

Be it further enacted, that the said two townships numbered eight and nine, in the said fourteenth range of townships, be, and the same are hereby vested in the said corporation, which by this act is erected, and in their successors forever, for the sole use, benefit and support of the said university, to be holden by the said corporation, in their corporate capacity, with full powers and authority to divide, subdivide, settle and manage the same, by leasing the said lands for such time or such times and in such way and manner as the said corporation shall judge will best promote the interest and welfare of the said university. *Provided,* That no lease shall be made for a longer term of time than twenty-one years ; and the tenants or lessees of the said university land, appropriated and vested as aforesaid, shall enjoy and exercise all the rights and privileges of citizens which they would be entitled to and enjoy, did they hold the same lands in fee simple, any law to the contrary notwithstanding.

SEC. 12. *And be it further enacted,* That the clear annual rents, issues and profits, of all the estate, real and personal, of which the said corporation shall be seized or possessed of, in their corporate capacity, shall be appropriated to the endowment of the said university, in such manner as shall most effectively promote virtue, morality, piety and the knowledge of such of the languages and of the liberal arts and sciences, as shall hereafter be directed, from time to time, by the said corporation. *Provided, nevertheless,* That in case any donation shall hereafter be made for particular purposes, relative to the design of this institution, and the corporation shall accept and receive the same, every such donation shall be applied in conformity to the intention and direction of the donor or donors.

SEC. 13. *And be it further enacted,* That the treasurer of the said university shall, before he enters upon the execution of the duties of his office, give bonds to the said corporation in such sums and with such sureties, as they shall approve of, conditioned for the faithful discharge of the duties of the said office, and for rendering a just and true account of his doings therein, when all moneys, securities and other property that shall belong to the required ; and also for delivering over to his successor in office, president and trustees of the said university, together with all the books and papers in which his proceedings as treasurer shall be entered and kept, that shall be in his hands at the expiration of his office; and all money that shall be recovered by virtue of any suit at law, upon such bond, shall be paid over to the president and trustees aforesaid, and be subjected to the appropriations above directed in this act.

SEC. 14. *And be it further enacted*, That the lands in the two townships, appropriated and vested as aforesaid, with the buildings which may be erected thereon, for the accommodation of the president, professors and other officers, students and servants of the university, and any buildings appertaining thereto, and also the dwelling houses and out houses, or other buildings of the tenants or lessees, now erected and built, or which may hereafter be built and erected, on the lands within the said township, shall forever be exempted from all territorial and state taxes. *Provided, nevertheless*, That such exemption shall not exclude them from enjoying and exercising all the rights and privileges which otherwise they would be entitled to, under the eleventh section of this act. *Provided, also*, That nothing in this section contained shall be construed as an exemption of the land, houses and other property which now is or hereafter may be found or built within the said townships, from the payment of county taxes, rates and levies; but the said land, houses and other property, now or hereafter to be found in said townships, are hereby declared subject to the payment of county taxes, rates and levies, in the county in which the said townships are or shall be situated, anything in this section to the contrary thereof, notwithstanding. *And provided, also*, That the polls and personal estates of such persons as may and shall live within the said townships, shall be and remain subject to taxation in common with those of other citizens within the territory or state in which the same may be.

SEC. 15. *And be it further enacted*, That it shall be lawful for the aforesaid corporation, or for the trustees acting under this act as hereinafter mentioned, to lease for a small annual rent, on condition of a capital sum being paid in hand or secured to be paid, the whole or any part of the house-lots, and out-lots, of five acres in the town of Athens, laid out agreeably to a resolution of the general assembly of the territory, made and approved December the eighteenth, one thousand seven hundred and ninety-nine, by Rufus Putnam, Benjamin Ives Gilman and Jonathan Stone, Esquires, a committee in the said resolution named and appointed for that purpose; and the capital sum or sums of money, which shall be so received or as much thereof as the corporation shall judge expedient, shall be applied by the trustees to the purpose of erecting buildings for the accommodation of the president, officers and students of the university.

Sec. 16. *And be it further enacted*, That the before named trustees and their successors, and such others as shall be duly elected members of the said corporation, be, and they are hereby empowered to elect a president of the said university, whenever they shall judge it expedient.

Sec. 17. *And be it further enacted*, That until a president of the said university shall be elected, and shall have entered upon the duties of his office, and also in all cases of a vacancy or the absence of the president, the said trustees shall appoint one of their members to preside in their meetings, and all the doings and acts of the trustees, while acting under such circumstances, shall be considered in law as the doings and acts of the corporation, as fully and completely as when the president of the university shall be in office and preside.

Sec. 18. *And be it further enacted*, That the legislature of the territory or the legislature of the state within which the said university is or may be founded, may grant any further or greater powers to, or alter, limit or restrain any of the powers by this act vested in the said corporation, as shall be judged necessary to promote the best interest and prosperity of the said university, with all necessary powers and authority for the better aid, preservation and government thereof.

Sec. 19. *And be it further enacted*, That the Honorable Rufus Putnam, Esquire, shall be, and he is hereby authorized and empowered, to fix the time and place for holding the first meeting of the said corporation, of which he shall give notice in writing to each member, at least fourteen days previous to such meeting.

EDWARD TIFFIN,
Speaker of the House of Representatives.
ROBERT OLIVER,
President of the Council.

Approved—the ninth day of January, 1802.

AR. ST. CLAIR,
*Governor of the Territory of the United States,
Northwest of the Ohio.*

This act was drafted by Dr. Cutler. The original manuscript, differing, however, from the act as passed by the legislature, both in the order of its sections, and in some of its material provisions, is now in the possession of the president of the university. It was sent by Dr. Cutler to Rufus Putnam in July, 1800, accompanied by the following letter, which is so illustrative of Dr. Cutler's ability and sagacity, that we insert it at length:

"HAMILTON, MASS., *June* 30, 1800.
DEAR SIR:
"Such has been my situation that I could not find leisure to copy a rough draft I had made, many months ago, of an incorporating act, until this day. Whether any part of it will be agreeable, I think is very doubtful. I had long been contemplating a very different kind of constitution. Knowing that the colleges at Cambridge and New Haven had derived essential advantages from having the principal civilians in the states concerned in the government, I had thought of a constitution, in

which one portion of the corporate body should be the first characters in civil life, another portion clergymen, and a third wealthy land holders. I had also wished to have two branches in the government of the university, as checks, in some respects on each other, somewhat like the overseers and board of corporation at Cambridge. But so numerous and insurmountable were the difficulties that rose before me when I regarded the situation of your country, that I was obliged to abandon every idea of a government I had long been contemplating. It may be necessary to make a few remarks upon the enclosed draft:

SECTION 1. As the American congress made the grant which is the foundation of the university, no name appeared to me more natural than *American University*. The sound is natural, easy, and agreeable, and no name can be more respectable. There is a Columbian college and a Washington college, etc., already in the country, but no *American college*. I hope the name will not be altered.

SEC. 2. The number of the board of trustees may be thought small; but small numbers feel greater responsibility, do business with more dispatch and generally better, and are less expensive than larger numbers. Dartmouth college has an excellent government, which consists only of the president and ten trustees. The college at New Haven had only ten until connected with civilians. It will be best, on many accounts, to have a vice president. It creates no expense, as he will have no compensation only as a trustee, unless when he acts as president. New Jersey college has found much advantage in having a vice president. The trustees ought to live near the college, and by no means outside of our purchase. There will be many advantages in having the president and vice president members of the board, but I can not now enumerate them—they will readily occur to you.

SEC. 3. The board is the proper body for appointing all officers, and prescribing the duties of such as steward, treasurer, etc., but the duties of all concerned in the immediate government and instruction, should be established by the laws of the university.

SEC. 4. The board must have the power of preserving and of purifying itself. The presidents and vice presidents, I believe, of all colleges hold their offices during good behavior. Other instructors hold their offices during the pleasure of the government, unless special provision is made by the laws of the college. The power of dismissing, rusticating, and expelling students is generally in the hands of the immediate government of colleges, and regulated by college laws. I thought, in this instance, for some special reasons, it would be best to give this power by act of incorporation, to the board in the first instance, but in such a manner that the board can transfer it to the immediate government of the university, and regulate it by college laws.

There has been found advantage in giving the president the right of nomination; no considerable evil can follow. In many colleges the president has the right of appointing his successor; but this I should determinedly oppose.

The incorporating act ought to require public commencements. These ought to be held, and, though there are some inconveniences, there are many and important advantages. The colleges in New York and Philadelphia have suffered much for want of them; in the country they are of the greatest importance. There has often happened, however, absolute necessity for altering the time and place; I have, therefore, so framed this article as to admit of alteration.

SEC. 5. The immediate governors and instructors of the university, it is to be presumed, will always be the best judges of the mode and course of education, and of laws best adapted to the circumstances of the college. I have so constructed this section as to create, in a sense, two branches to the government with a kind of check on each other.

With respect to every part of the incorporating act, I have aimed, as much as possible, at plain general principles, without descending to particular regulations. But, especially in the course of study, and laws and rules for the immediate government of the university, the incorporating act ought to do no more than place the whole power in the hands of the board and instructors. For there must be continual variation as experience and circumstances shall dictate, and to be fettered by an incorporating act might prove extremely injurious to the college. It is safe in their hands, for the board and instructors must always feel the highest inducements to establish the best possible regulations; and they will ever be better judges than a legislature.

But the importance of quarterly examinations is, in my view, so great, and is a regulation so absolutely essential, so apt to be neglected by the government of the university, and so often opposed and resisted by the students, that I would, by all means, insure the practice by making it an article of incorporation.

Sec. 7. To have the two townships as well secured as possible to the board—and as claims to land are liable to so many contests—I thought it would be best to be very particular in describing the title by which the university claims the improvement, and that the disposition of all the funds of the university should be unconditionally within the control of the board, and left wholly to their discretion in applying them. Many colleges have suffered much from having their hands tied, in disposing of the funds to the best advantage, and most for the interest of the institution.

Sec. 8. In all the incorporations granted by the general court of this commonwealth, the amount of the income of real and personal property estate have been, each of them, limited—but to sums far beyond any probability of their ever arising. Whether other states do the same I know not. If your assembly would not be likely to make any limitation, it might be best to say nothing about it. But, if they will do it, then forty and fifty thousand dollars can not be too high, as it must be applied to one of the most useful and important purposes to society and to government. The sums sound large, but no one can say to what amount the income of the endowments of this university may arrive in time. The income of Oxford and Cambridge, in England, is much greater.

SEC. 9. This will be the bugbear. You suggested the idea, though I had often thought of it before. I am in doubt whether the section is clearly and properly expressed, or sufficiently guarded to answer the purpose. But I am in much greater doubt whether it is possible to get any article of this kind inserted in the act. Sure I am it is an object worthy of great exertion to obtain. If those lots and their income were under the direction of the board, it could not fail of rendering them of incomparably more benefit than if they should be placed in the hands of the people. The board will only be the committee for each township, and infinitely better than any committee they can choose. They will have better instructors in their schools, and under better regulations, and the income probably of higher amount than if the people managed the lots themselves. And the ministerial lots may be rendered incomparably more useful. It will tend to prevent sectaries, secure the people from continual contentions among themselves, become a great inducement to entice respectable characters to engage in the ministry, and, in a much greater degree, alleviate the taxes of the people. The lands will also much sooner become productive.

With regard to erecting public buildings for the university, I can not so fully express my mind to you as I would wish. At present, I should think it not best to erect any considerable public building. It will be necessary, in the first instance, to open a Latin school, for I conceive it improbable that any youth can now be found in the country qualified for admission as the students of a college; or, if a freshman class can be formed, it must be small. A building of two stories, pretty large on the ground, in form of a school house, may answer every purpose for some years. I feel an aversion to large buildings for the residence of students, where there are regular families in which they can reside. Chambers in colleges are too often made the secret nurseries of every vice, and the cages of unclean birds.

It must require time to mature plans for large buildings. I will endeavor to attend to the matter, and give you my ideas of public buildings. In the meantime, be assured that I am, with great respect,

Your friend and humble servant,

MANASSEH CUTLER.

RUFUS PUTNAM, Esq., Marietta."

It will be noted that additions to, and material alterations in, the draft as submitted by Dr. Cutler, were made before the incorporating act was passed. Section nine of his draft, referred to by him as the "bugbear," gave the board of trustees full and separate control of the school and ministerial lots, Nos. sixteen and twenty-nine, with authority to lease or improve the same, the rents and income always to go to the respective townships, etc. The charter as passed contains no similar provision.

It does not appear that any effective action was taken under this law of 1802. It is probable that the widely separated residences of the trustees, the difficulty of communication, and the extreme badness of the few roads that existed, operated to prevent action. Doubtless, too, the political excitement of the day had its influence, as the contest relative to the formation of a state government and admission to the Union, was, at that time, absorbing every other interest.

The next legislation on the subject was the following joint resolution passed by the first legislature of the state:

Resolved, That Samuel Carpenter, James Wells, and Henry Abrams, be appointed commissioners to appraise the land included within the two college townships, in the county of Washington, at its real value in its original and unimproved state; to divide and value said land into four different qualities or rates and make return of the quantity contained in each division, as near as may be, and the value thereof, to the next general assembly on oath. And that the said commissioners also value the land in its present situation, mentioning the number of houses and quantity of cleared land contained within the two townships.

Resolved, That the trustees appointed by the act entitled an act establishing an university in the town of Athens, be and they are hereby required to report to the next general assembly of this state, what measures they have taken to carry the said act into operation.

NATHANIEL MASSIE,
Speaker of the Senate.
MICHAEL BALDWIN,

April 16, 1803. *Speaker of the House.*

The land was appraised during the summer and autumn of 1803, and on the 27th of January, 1804, the legislature passed the following:

" *An act allowing compensation to the commissioners for appraising the college lands in the county of Washington.*

SECTION 1. *Be it enacted by the General Assembly, etc.,* That the commissioners appointed to appraise the two college townships in the county of Washington, by a resolution of the first legislature of the state, viz: Samuel Carpenter, James Wells and Henry Abrams, for eighteen days' service each, in accomplishing said business, be, and they are hereby entitled to receive each for said services, the sum of thirty dollars, to be paid out of the contingent fund, to be audited by the auditor and paid out of any monies in the treasury of the state.

NATHANIEL MASSIE,
Speaker of the Senate.
ELIAS LANGHAM,
Speaker of the House.

January 27, 1804."

On the 18th of February, 1804, the legislature passed another act "establishing an university in the town of Athens," differing in some respects from the original act of 1802. We give a synopsis of this act:

SECTION 1. Establishes the university by the name of the "Ohio University;" remainder of the section same as in first act.

SEC. 2. Same as in the first act, except change of name and making the governor of the state, president of the board of trustees, *ex-officio*, and fixing the number of trustees at not less than ten nor more than fifteen.

SEC. 3. Names as the trustees, Elijah Backus, Rufus Putnam, Dudley Woodbridge, Benjamin Tappan, Bazaliel Wells, Nathaniel Massie, Daniel Symmes, Daniel Story, Samuel Carpenter, Rev. James Kilbourne, Griffin Green, Sen., and Joseph Darlinton.

SECS. 4, 5, 6, 7, 8, 9, and 10, same as in the original act.

SEC. 11. *And be it further enacted,* That one or more of the aforesaid trustees (to be appointed by the board for this purpose) shall within six months from the passage of this act, proceed (by the oath of three disinterested and judicious freeholders,) to lay off the lands in said townships (those included in the town of Athens excepted), or such part thereof as they may deem expedient, into tracts of not less than eighty, nor more than two hundred and forty acres, and to estimate and value the same as in their original and unimproved state—for which service such compensation shall be allowed as the treasurer shall think reasonable, to be paid out of the funds of the university; and having thus laid off and estimated said lands, the trustees, after giving four weeks' notice in the newspaper printed at Marietta, shall proceed to make out leases of the said tracts to such of the present occupants as shall apply for the same within three months after such notice given, and to all persons that shall apply hereafter, for the term of ninety years, renewable forever, on a yearly rent of six per centum on the amount of the valuation so made by the said freeholders; and the land so leased shall be subject to a re-valuation at the expiration of thirty-five years, and to another re-valuation at the expiration of sixty years from the commencement of the term of each lease, which re-valuation shall be conducted and made on the principles of the first valuation; and the lessee shall pay a yearly rent of six per centum on the amount of the re-valuation so to be made, and forever thereafter a yearly rent equal to and not exceeding six per centum of the amount of a valuation to be made as aforesaid, at the expiration of the term of ninety years aforesaid (which valuation the trustees and their successors are hereby authorized and directed to make): *Provided*, however, that such last mentioned rent shall be subject to the following regulations, to wit, at the expiration of the aforesaid period of ninety years, three referees shall be appointed, the first by the corporation of the university, the second by the lessees under the provisions of this section of this act, and the third by the two referees thus chosen; or in case either or both of the parties shall neglect to choose such referee or referees, or said referees shall neglect to choose an umpire, the general assembly at its next session shall appoint such number of referees, not exceeding three, as the case may require, which referees shall meet within a reasonable time, to be agreed on between them, at the town of Athens, and there and then determine on and declare the medium price per bushel of the article of wheat, which determination shall be grounded on a calculation of the average price of said article at the town of Marietta for the five preceding years, which declaration shall be made in writing and entered of record on the books of the corporation; and at the commencement of each and every period of twenty years thereafter the amount of rent of such period shall be fixed on and determined, by referees to be chosen upon the principles herein before directed, from a comparison of the aforesaid recorded price of wheat with its average price at Marietta for the five years which shall have been then last past; in which leases shall be reserved a right of distress and of re-entry for non-payment of rent at any time after it shall have been due two months, provided, always that the said corporation shall have power to demand a further yearly rent on the said lands and tenements not exceeding the amount of the tax imposed on property of like description by the state, which rent shall be paid at such time and place, to such person, and collected in such manner, as the corporation shall direct."

SEC. 12. *And be it further enacted*, That the trustees shall lay off the aforesaid town of Athens, conformably to a plan made out by Rufus Putnam and others, in pursuance of a resolution of the territorial legislature of the eighteenth of December, 1799, with such variations, however, as they may find it expedient to make; and the same being thus laid off and a plat of the same, with a designation of the uses of the general parts, recorded in the office of the recorder of the proper county, and six weeks' previous notice given in at least two of the newspapers of this state, may proceed to sell, from time to time, at public auction, such of the house and out-lots as they may think proper, for which lots on payment being made or satisfactory security given, according to the conditions of such sale, they shall execute to the purchasers, respectively, leases for the term of ninety years, renewable forever, on an annual rent equal to and not exceeding six per centum of the amount of the purchase money; which lots with the improvements which may be made on the same shall be subject to such further yearly rent, as may be equal to the tax imposed from time to time, on property of like value and description, by the state; and they are likewise authorized to deliver a reasonable compensation for the improvements which have made on lands within the town of Athens, to be paid out of the funds of the university."

Sec. 13. Trustees to lay off the town of Athens, agreeably to Putnam's plan, &c.

Sec. 14. Provides that the rent and profits of the land shall be appropriated to the endowment of the university.

Sec. 15. Requires the treasurer to give bond.

Sec. 16. *Be it further enacted*, That the said corporation shall have full power from time to time to contract for and cause to be erected such buildings as they shall deem necessary, for the accommodation of the president, professors, tutors, pupils and servants of said university, as also to procure the necessary books and apparatus for the use of said university, and shall cause payment therefor to be made out of the funds of the university, and shall reserve such lot or lots in said town of Athens as they may deem necessary for the purpose aforesaid and for the erection of buildings for the use of the town and county.

Sec. 17. Provides that all the college lands and buildings erected thereon shall forever be exempted from all state taxes.

Sec. 18. Provides that in the absence, &c., of the president &c., one of the trustees may be appointed to preside at their meetings and act in certain cases.

Sec. 19. Provides that the governor of the state shall fix the time for holding the first meeting of the board of trustees.

Sec. 20. Repeals all previous acts and parts of acts inconsistent with this act.

Under this law early steps were taken toward an organization. We quote from the records of the first meeting of trustees:

" At a meeting of the trustees of the Ohio University, convened at the house of Dr. Eliphaz Perkins, in the town of Athens, on the first Monday of June, 1804, the day ordered by His Excellency Edward Tiffin, Esq., governor of the state of Ohio, for the first meeting. The following trustees present, viz :

His Excellency Edward Tiffin, Elijah Backus, Rufus Putnam, Dudley Woodbridge, Daniel Story, Samuel Carpenter, James Kilbourne."

The board elected Governor Tiffin president, Dudley Woodbridge secretary, Eliphaz Perkins treasurer, and adjourned till next day, June 5th. This first session of the board lasted three days, and was principally spent in arranging for the appraisal and leasing of the college lands. Rufus Putnam and Samuel Carpenter were appointed to lay off and appraise such lands in the two townships as were claimed and occupied. Since the surveying of these townships in 1795, numbers of new settlers had come in and occupied the lands. Some of these were rough and determined characters, and were bent on maintaining possession. To adjust these cases, settle disputed titles, etc., required patience, tact, and wisdom. The parties had either to be mollified and induced to come to terms, or be ejected from the lands. The first business of the board was to adjust the claims of conflicting parties, secure titles and protect the corporation in its rights. These matters, together with the surveying and laying out of lots, classifying lands, etc., employed the trustees during this session.

We can not refrain from remarking that the meeting of these men, under the circumstances, afforded a high proof of their character—of their appreciation of the value of education, and their honest devotion to the welfare of the new country. They had traveled fifty, seventy-five or a hundred miles, by blind paths or Indian trails through dense forests, inhabited only by wild animals, to this embryo village, for the purpose of establishing an institution of learning. It is gratifying, after the lapse of nearly three-quarters of a century, to be able to record that, notwithstanding the immense difficulties of the case, their labors, and those of their coadjutors, were ultimately rewarded with complete success.

A vast amount of preliminary labor, however, was yet to be performed before the actual educational work could be begun.

In his message, at the opening of the third session of the general assembly, December 4, 1804, Governor Tiffin gave proper prominence to the topic of schools and education. After general remarks on the subject he then refers to the Ohio university:

"These observations will naturally lead you to inquire whether any, and if any, what improvements are necessary to the act entitled 'an act establishing an university in the town of Athens.' Under this act a quorum of the trustees met in June last, and, so far as their powers extended, carried it into effect; a committee of two members of the board was appointed to superintend the surveying of such part of the two townships of land, which were appropriated for the university, as might be applied for by those willing to become lessees; also to superintend the sales of a small part of the town and out-lots, which were designated by the board to be sold as an experiment; and in exhibit No. 1, I lay before you a communication from

General Putnam*, one of the committee, which shows that the prospects are flattering. But it is necessary to observe, from actual observation, when there, and from information derived from intelligent characters since, that the settlers on these lands were induced to apply for leases, under an impression that the legislature would review the law, and be governed by a more liberal policy. Should it be thought that these lands ought to be valued at a generous price, once for all, and leases be authorized to issue, upon the payment of the legal interest yearly, there can be no doubt but that they would soon be all occupied, and from the sales of the town and out-lots, a sufficient sum would be raised to erect such public buildings as may be immediately wanted; and that the rents of the lands and lots would be sufficient to support the university, answer every purpose for which the donation was originally made, and the state be immediately benefited by the institution.

"It is further thought, that it would greatly increase the demand for those lands and town lots, as well as prepare the way for the accommodation and comfort of the youths who may be sent to the university, if a new county were erected and its seat established at Athens. This may conveniently be done without injury to the counties adjacent, and, in my opinion, the convenience of that part of the country imperiously demands it."

At this session the following act was passed, viz:

---

* General Putnam and Colonel Samuel Carpenter were the committee referred to. The former wrote to Governor Tiffin, November 6, 1804, that the sales of the house and out-lots of the town of Athens amounted to $2,223.50; average of house-lots $43.33½; of the out-lots $39. In the south township (Alexander), seventy-five tracts, or 11,000 acres, were applied for. As to the north township (Athens), under the superintendence of Colonel Carpenter, General Putnam was not fully informed; but in August previous, seventy-five applications for leases, covering 8,760 acres, had been made.

"*An act to amend an act entitled 'an act establishing an university in the town of Athens.'*

"SECTION I. *Be it enacted by the General Assembly of the State of Ohio*, That James Denny, Emanuel Carpenter, Jun., Isaac Dawson, Pelatiah White, and Ezekiel Deming, residents of this state, are appointed appraisers of the two college townships numbered eight and nine, in the fourteenth range of townships within the grant of land made to the Ohio company of associates; and the said appraisers, or any three of them, on oath or affirmation, are hereby required to appraise the townships aforesaid, within nine months, at the present real value, as also in its original and uncultivated state, and make report thereof to the board of trustees of the said university; and the said trustees shall lease the same to any persons who have applied, or may apply, agreeable to law, for the term of ninety-nine years, renewable for ever, with a fixed annual rent of six per centum on the appraised valuation: *provided*, that no lands shall be leased at a less valuation than at the rate of one dollar and seventy-five cents per acre.

SEC. II. *Be it further enacted*, That the commissioners aforesaid shall meet on the first day of April next, at the town of Athens, and shall then proceed to discharge the duties imposed on them by this act, and the act to which this act is an amendment, and shall perform the same within the time mentioned in this act.

SEC. III. *Be it further enacted*, That the trustees of the corporation of the said university lands are hereby authorized and empowered to remove, by due course of law, all persons living on said lands, in case such persons refuse or neglect to take leases within six months after the valuation of the lands as aforesaid.

SEC. IV. *Be it further enacted*, That the secretary of this state shall cause notice to be given, as soon as convenience will permit, to each of the commissioners aforesaid, of their appointment under this act; and the commissioners, respectively, on receiving the notice aforesaid, shall, within a reasonable time thereafter, forward to the governor of this state, their acceptance or declination of the appointment under this act made.

Sec. V. *Be it further enacted,* That so much of the aforesaid act, passed the 18th day of February, 1804, as is contrary to this act, be and the same is hereby repealed. This act shall be in force from and after its passage.

MICHAEL BALDWIN,
Speaker of the House.

DANIEL SYMMES,
Speaker of the Senate.

February 21st, 1805."

The next year was consumed in settling titles, appraising the lands, and accumulating a small fund with which to begin the actual educational work. The second meeting of the board of trustees was called for November 20th, 1805, but no quorum was present and they adjourned. The third meeting was held April 2d, 1806, when the committee for selling town lots reported,* and other business was transacted relative to titles and leases. At this session it was

Resolved, That Jacob Lindley, Rufus Putnam, and William Skinner, be a committee to contract with some person or persons for building a house in the town of Athens for the purpose of an academy, on the credit of the rents that will hereafter become due.

---

* Ante, p. 201.

At the next meeting, December 25, 1806, the committee reported a plan, and were empowered to contract for a building. The academy building was begun very soon after this, and nearly completed in 1807. It was built of brick and stood almost directly east of the present college buildings and just outside of the present enclosure. It has long since disappeared.

March 2d, 1808, the Rev. Jacob Lindley, Eliphaz Perkins, and Rufus Putnam were appointed a committee to report a system " for opening the academy, providing for a preceptor, and conducting that branch of the Ohio university," and they reported a plan of study and certain regulations at that meeting. A few days later Mr. Lindley was chosen preceptor, and entered on his duties in the spring of 1808.

The difficulties of appraising and leasing the lands were still a source of great vexation and labor. The following act of the legislature belongs to this period:

" *An act to amend the several acts establishing an university for the town of Athens.*

SECTION I. *Be it enacted, etc.*, That the trustees of the Ohio university be and they are hereby authorized to lease the appraised lots of land lying in the two college townships, numbers 8 and 9, in the 14th range of townships, of the Ohio Company's purchase, that have been appraised at a less value than one dollar and seventy-five cents per acre, at six per cent. on the appraised value.

SEC. II. *Be it further enacted*, That the said trustees be and they are hereby authorized to appoint appraisers to appraise such parts of the aforesaid townships, as have not been heretofore appraised, whenever they may deem it expedient.

SEC. III. *Be it further enacted*, That so much of the act entitled ' an act establishing an university in the town of Athens,' passed the 21st day of February, 1805, as is contrary to the provisions of this act, be and the same is hereby repealed.

This act to take effect and be in force from and after its passage.

ABRAHAM SHEPHERD,
Speaker of the House.
THOS. KIRKER,
Speaker of the Senate.

January 23*d*, 1807."

The infant college struggled along, and its friends were most persevering in their efforts.

Further legislation becoming necessary, the next winter the legislature passed

"*An act altering several acts establishing an university in the town of Athens.*

SECTION I. *Be it enacted, etc.*, That all persons residing in either of the two college townships, numbered eight and nine, in the fourteenth range in the Ohio Company's purchase, and holding leases, shall be considered as freeholders.

SEC. II. *Be it further enacted*, That the second section of the act entitled ' an act supplementary to, etc.,' passed January 17, 1806, which allows a compensation to the trustees for their services, be and the same is hereby repealed.

SEC. III. *Be it further enacted*, That it shall be the duty of the treasurer of the corporation of the Ohio university, in all cases where the rent of any person or persons has been due for two months, immediately to transmit a certified copy, under his hand and the seal of said corporation, to the collector of the said corporation, of an accurate list of all such delinquents, which list, certified as aforesaid, shall be sufficient power for the said collector to distrain on the goods and chattels of each and every delinquent, and the same to advertise in three public places in the township in which such goods and chattels are distrained, ten days previous to the sale; and the said collector shall then proceed to sell the same at public vendue, and the rent and costs forthwith to pay to the treasurer of said Ohio university, and the overplus, if any, to refund to the delinquent; and for want of goods and chattels, to re-enter and take possession of the premises for the use of the trustees of the said university as provided by law: and the said collector shall receive the same compensation for his services as sheriffs do in similar cases. *Provided*, however, that if any delinquent shall think himself aggrieved, he shall have his action against the said treasurer or collector (as the case may be), or both, and shall recover all damages he may unjustly sustain.

SEC. IV. *Be it further enacted*, That Eliphaz Perkins, Silvanus Ames, Jehiel Gregory, Abel Miller, Leonard Jewett, and Moses Hewitt, be appointed in addition to the present number of trustees of said Ohio university.

SEC. V. *Be it further enacted*, That the said corporation shall have power and authority to adjourn to any period they may think proper; and the number of trustees of said university shall never exceed nineteen, nor be less than eleven, any five of whom shall be a quorum to transact any business of said corporation.

SEC. VI. *Be it further enacted*, That all laws and parts of laws contrary to the provisions of this act be and the same are hereby repealed.

This act to be in force from and after its passage.

PHILEMON BEECHER,
Speaker House of Reps.
THOS. KIRKER,
February 20th, 1808." *Speaker Senate.*

Great difficulty was still experienced, owing to reasons before mentioned, in getting the board together, and also in collecting the rents on the university lands, in money and promptly. The next year further changes were made in the board, and the following act was passed :

"*An act amendatory to the several acts appointing trustees to the Ohio university, and for other purposes.*

SECTION I. *Be it enacted, etc.,* That Robert G. Wilson, Jesup N. Couch, John P. R. Bureau, Elijah Hatch, Jun., and Henry Abrams, be and they are hereby appointed trustees of the Ohio university.

SEC. II. *Be it further enacted,* That the trustees shall have power and authority, until the year one thousand eight hundred and eleven, to receive of any of the lessees in payment of rent, such article or articles of produce as may by them be agreed on at any regular meeting of said trustees; *provided* it shall not exceed two-thirds of the annual rents.

SEC. III. *Be it further enacted,* That nine of the trustees of the said university shall hereafter be necessary to form a quorum to transact the business of said corporation, any law to the contrary notwithstanding.

SEC. IV. *Be it further enacted,* That the trustees shall have authority to resurvey, or cause to be resurveyed, any large tract of land (at the expense and request of the lessee), and the same to lay off in such lots as they shall think will best promote the interests of said institution.

SEC. V. *Be it further enacted,* That when a tract of land has been surveyed and leased to one or more persons, and by him or them sold to one or more persons, the parties shall be entitled to receive from the treasurer of said institution, separate leases

in their own names, by paying a reasonable compensation therefor, to be agreed on by the trustees at a regular meeting.
This act to take effect from and after its passage.
                    ALEXANDER CAMPBELL,
                              Speaker House of Reps.
                    THOS. KIRKER,
                              Speaker of Senate.
February 15th, 1809."

By an act of January 29, 1811, the second section of the foregoing act, relative to receiving produce for rents, was revived and declared to be in force until repealed by future legislation.

By an act passed February 15, 1812, entitled " an act to authorize the trustees of the Ohio university to issue orders in certain cases and for other purposes," the trustees were authorized to lend any surplus moneys of the university at the rate of six per cent. yearly interest to such persons, on such security and under such conditions as the trustees should determine.

Meanwhile Dr. Lindley constituted the whole faculty, and was laboring faithfully with the grammar school which was now in successful operation. In 1812, Mr. Artemas Sawyer, a graduate of Harvard university, an accomplished linguist and fine general scholar, was appointed an assistant instructor in the academy. In the year 1815, the first degree of bachelor of arts awarded in Ohio was conferred by the Ohio university on *Thomas Ewing*. He had entered the institution three years previously and pursued his studies with great energy, spending his later vacations in laying out country roads, surveying, etc., to raise means to carry him through.

In 1815, the success of the university was thought to be so far assured, and the necessity for increased facilities was so apparent, that the trustees resolved to erect a new college building. June 4th, 1816, a committee, consisting of Jacob Lindley, Eliphaz Perkins, and J. Lawrence Lewis, appointed in September previous, reported to the board that, after due advertisement and consultation with an architect, they had contracted with William T. Dean for 370,000 bricks at $4.50 a thousand; with Christopher and Daniel Herrold for 27,964 feet of lumber, to be delivered and piled up during the summer, at $1.12 per hundred feet; with Messrs. Bingham & White for stone; with Pilcher & Francis for laying the foundation of the rough stone and making the window and door sills, and with Wm. and James Wier for digging the cellar—which last was already completed. The corner stone of the building, now known as the center college, was laid in the summer of this year. The work was pushed forward as rapidly as the condition of the treasury would permit, and the building was completed in 1817. The two wing buildings were built in 1836.

About this time a singular expedient was adopted to raise funds. June 16th, 1814, the board of trustees had

Resolved, That a committee of three be appointed to draft a petition to the legislature praying for a grant of a lottery to assist in building a college house for the university. Messrs. Putnam, Hildreth, and Perkins appointed.

The result of their petition and labors in this behalf appear in the following act.

" *An act to authorize the drawing of a lottery for the benefit of the Ohio university.*

WHEREAS, the diffusion of science and literature has ever been found to be auspicious to the interests of liberty and the purity and permanence of republican institutions.

SECTION I. *Be it enacted by the General Assembly of the State of Ohio,* That Eliphaz Perkins, Dudley Woodbridge, Jun., William R. Putnam, John P. R. Bureau, Joseph B. Miles, William Skinner, and Edward W. Tupper, any four of whom shall form a board for transacting business, be and they are hereby appointed commissioners, with full power and authority to raise by lottery, a sum of money not exceeding twenty thousand dollars, to be appropriated to defray the expense of completing the college edifice lately erected at Athens, and to purchase a library and suitable mathematical and philosophical apparatus for the use of the Ohio university.

SEC. II. *Be it further enacted,* That the said commissioners, before they shall proceed to the sale and disposal of the tickets in said lottery, shall enter into sufficient bonds, in the sum of one hundred and fifty thousand dollars, to the treasurer of the state of Ohio and his successors in office, with condition that they will well and truly apply the moneys to the payment of the prizes that shall be drawn in said lottery : *provided* the payment thereof shall be requested within one year after the drawing of said lottery ; also that they will faithfully pay over to the treasurer of the Ohio university the surplus of said moneys, to be by the trustees of said university applied to the purposes specified in the first section of this act; and that in case of failure to draw said lottery within the time limited in this act, the said commissioners shall cause to be refunded to the purchasers, severally, all moneys which they shall have received for tickets in said lottery. And the said bond shall be lodged in the office of the clerk of the court of common pleas, in the county of Athens, and on such bond or office copy thereof, suit or suits may be instituted by any person or persons interested for any breach thereof.

SEC. III. *Be it further enacted,* That the said commissioners are hereby authorized and required to take bond and security from all persons to whom they may deposit for sale, the tickets in said lottery, conditioned that such persons shall justly account for the value of the tickets by him or them received, or return the same; and such bond shall be made payable to the said commissioners by name, and the survivors of them, and if the conditions of any such bond shall be broken, the obligees therein named, or their survivors, may sustain an action thereon, to recover the value of the tickets not accounted for.

SEC. IV. *Be it further enacted,* That the said commissioners, when they shall have sold and disposed of such a proportion of tickets as shall, in their opinion, render expedient the drawing of said lottery, shall proceed to draw the same publicly, having given due notice thereof, by publication in one or more newspapers printed at Marietta, Cincinnati, Pittsburg, Philadelphia, Washington City, and Chillicothe, setting forth the time and place of said drawing.

SEC. V. *Be it further enacted,* That the said commissioners, when about to proceed to the drawing of said lottery, shall be duly sworn by some judge of the supreme court, or of the court of common pleas, to the faithful discharge of the several duties appertaining thereto, and shall also appoint a clerk who shall be sworn to keep a true and impartial account of the drawing.

SEC. VI. *Be it further enacted,* That the trustees of the said

Ohio university are hereby authorized to allow to said commissioners and clerk, a reasonable compensation for their respective services in the management and drawing of said lottery.

SEC. VII. *Be it further enacted*, That the drawing of the said lottery shall be completed by the commissioners aforesaid, within three years from the passage of this act.

DUNCAN McARTHUR,
Speaker of the House.
ABRAHAM SHEPHERD,
Speaker of the Senate.
December 29th, 1817."

This scheme was never carried out. In fact, the commissioners never, so far as can be learned, took any action under the law, and it became a dead letter. It is, however, illustrative of the views which obtained in the state at that day on the subject of lotteries. About this period, and during a few years prior, they were authorized by the legislature for various purposes, such as educational movements, road or river improvements, etc., but shortly after this they were prohibited by law, and public sentiment in Ohio has been, since that time, wholly against them.

In 1819 (Mr. Sawyer having ceased his connection with the institution some time before this), Professor Joseph Dana was brought in as teacher of languages. Mr. Dana was a fine classical scholar, and his fitness for the chair of languages was pre-eminent.

In 1820, the following act was passed by the legislature, viz:

"*An act further to amend the several acts establishing an university in the town of Athens.*

SECTION I. *Be it enacted, etc.*, That it shall be the duty of the president and trustees of the Ohio university, at their first meeting after the taking effect of this act, to appoint three disinterested freeholders as appraisers, whose duty it shall be (after taking an oath faithfully to perform the duties of their appointment), to appraise all such tracts of land, belonging to said institution, as have reverted back to said board, either by re-entry or otherwise, which appraisal shall be made according to the present value of said tracts of land, in money, and the said appraisers shall make out a list of all such tracts of land by them so appraised, together with the appraised value of each tract, which list they shall return to the office of the secretary of the board of trustees.

SEC. II. *Be it further enacted*, That it shall be the duty of the president and trustees to lease all or any part of said tracts of land agreeably to the provisions of the acts of February 21st, 1805, and of January 23d, 1807, and it shall be the duty of the president and trustees, whenever hereafter any tract of land, which has been appraised and leased, shall revert back to the board, either by re-entry or otherwise, to have them appraised and leased as directed in this act.

JOSEPH RICHARDSON,
Speaker of the House.
ALLEN TRIMBLE,
Speaker of the Senate.

February 18*th*, 1820."

The pecuniary embarrassments of the university were so far overcome that its complete organization was accomplished in 1820, and in 1822, the faculty was constituted as follows: Rev. James Irvine, president and professor of mathematics; Joseph Dana, professor of languages; Rev. Jacob Lindley, professor of rhetoric and moral philosophy; Rev. Samuel D. Hoge, professor of natural sciences, and Henry D. Ward, academical preceptor.

From this period may be dated the complete working system and large usefulness of the university. Literary societies had been organized some years before; the nuclei of three respectable libraries—a college library, a library of the Athenian, and one of the Philomathean literary society—had been formed, philosophical apparatus secured, and a fine cabinet of minerals begun.

The institution has had its times of prosperity and depression, but, during the last half century, it has, in the aggregate, accomplished noble results, and sent forth from its halls a large number of able and active men.

At the present time the university is with difficulty sustained, and its condition is no credit to the state. It has an able and faithful corps of instructors, who, in spite of difficulties, are laboring, not without success. But the institution should have state aid. It was the design of the Ohio Company, and the purpose of congress to make it a richly endowed university—the most richly endowed at that time of any in the United States. But, by mismanagement and trickery, it has been, through a series of years, cheated of its revenues. It should have a large income from its original endowment, and that without, in the least degree, burdening the lessees of these lands. The state owes it to the fathers of the university who founded it with prayers and amid difficulties, such as we little comprehend, that it shall not be permanently kept out of its rights by legal technicalities; and we can not doubt that the people and the legislature of Ohio will eventually come to this conclusion. It will be a disgrace to them if the first university founded west of the mountains and around which "memories cluster thick as flowers," shall be allowed to fall into decay and disappear from the land for the want of aid which it has a right to expect and demand.

Trustees of the University from its Organization to the present time.

Elijah Backus,	of Marietta,	from	1804	till	1806.
Gen. Rufus Putnam,	" "	"	"	"	1824.
Dudley Woodbridge,	" "	"	"	"	1823.
Benjamin Tappan,	" Steubenville,	"	"	"	1808.
Bazaleel Wells,	" "	"	"	"	1808.
Gen. Nathaniel Massie,	" Chillicothe,	"	"	"	1808.
Daniel Symmes,	" Cincinnati,	"	"	"	1808.
Rev. Daniel Story,	" Marietta,	"	"	"	1804.
Samuel Carpenter,	" Lancaster,	"	"	"	1821.
Rev. James Kilbourne,	" Worthington,	"	"	"	1820.
Griffin Greene,	" Marietta,	"	"	"	1808.
Joseph Darlington,	" West Union,	"	"	"	1815.
William Creighton,	" Chillicothe,	"	1805	"	1808.
Gen. Joseph Buell,	" Marietta,	"	"	"	1812.
Benjamin Tupper,	" Zanesville,	"	"	"	1814.
Rev. Jacob Lindley,	" Waterford,	"	"	"	1838.
Michael Baldwin,	" Chillicothe,	"	"	"	1809.

Rev. Stephen Lindsley,	of Marietta,	from 1806	till	1826.
William Skinner,	" "	"	"	1840.
Dr. Eliphaz Perkins,	" Athens,	"	"	1819.
Silvanus Ames,	" "	" 1808	"	1823.
Jehiel Gregory,	" "	"	"	1812.
Abel Miller,	" "	"	"	1825.
Dr. Leonard Jewett,	" "	"	"	1813.
Moses Hewitt,	" "	"	"	1814.
Rev. Robert G. Wilson,	" Chillicothe,	" 1809	"	1819.
Jesup N. Couch,	" "	"	"	1821.
J. P. R. Bureau,	" Gallipolis,	"	"	1812.
Elijah Hatch,	" Athens county,	"	"	1849.
Henry Abrams,	" Lancaster,	"	"	1814.
S. P. Hildreth,	" Marietta,	" 1812	"	1819.
Seth Adams,	" Zanesville,	"	"	1838.
William Wilson,	" Newark,	" 1813	"	1819.
John L. Lewis,	" Marietta,	" 1815	"	1819.
Joseph Wood,	" "	"	"	1838.
Rev. James Culbertson,	" Zanesville,	"	"	1847.
Charles R. Sherman,	" Lancaster,	"	"	1833.
Edwin Putnam,	" Putnam,	" 1820	"	1839.
Ephraim Cutler,	" Marietta,	"	"	1849.
Thomas Scott,	" Chillicothe,	"	"	1838.
Robert Linzee,	" Athens,	"	"	1839.
Alexander Harper,	" Zanesville,	" 1821	"	1839.
Return J. Meigs,	" Marietta,	" 1822	"	1825.
Levi Barber,	" "	"	"	1833.
William Rufus Putnam,	" "	" 1823	"	1843.
Rev. James Hoge,	" Columbus,	"	"	1852.
Thomas Ewing,	" Lancaster,	" 1824	"	1832.
Rev. David Young,	" Zanesville,	" 1825	"	1849.
Dudley Woodbridge, Jr.,	" Marietta,	"	"	1843.
Calvary Morris,	" Athens,	"	"	1848.
Lewis Summers,	" Virginia,	" 1819	"	1843.
John L. Frye,	" "	"	"	1839.
James T. Worthington,	" Chillicothe,	" 1830	"	1846.
Rev. James McAboy,		" 1831	"	1833.
Amos Miller,*	" Athens county,	" 1832		
Dr. A. V. Woodbury,	" Athens,	" 1834	"	1839.
William B. Hubbard,	" St. Clairsville,	"		
Gen. S. F. McCracken,	" Lancaster,	"	"	1857.
Nathaniel C. Reid,	" Cincinnati,	" 1840	"	1845.
John Brough,	" Columbus,	"	"	1843.
William Medill,	" Lancaster,	"	"	1847.
A. G. Brown,*	" Athens,	" 1841.		
Rev. James M. Brown,	" Virginia,	" 1842.		

John H. Keith,*	of Chillicothe,	from	1844	till	
V. B. Horton,*	" Pomeroy,	"	"	"	
Joseph Olds,		"	"	"	1846
Rev. William Aiken,	" McConnellsville,	"	1846	"	—
Rev. William Cox,	" Lancaster,	"	"	"	1856
William H. Trimble,	" Hillsborough,	"	"	"	1849
Benjamin F. Hickman,	" Somerset,	"	1847	"	1849
Samuel F. Vinton,	" Gallipolis,	"	1848	"	1862
John Welch,*	" Athens,	"	"		
William P. Cutler,	" Chillicothe,	"	1849	"	1853
Leonidas Jewett,*	" Athens,	"	"		
Joseph M. Dana,*	" "	"	1851.		
S. B. Pruden,	" "	"	"	"	1863.
M. Z. Kreider,	" Lancaster,	"	"	"	1855.
Robert Wright,*	" Logan,	"	1852.		
Horace Wilson,*	" Athens,	"	1853.		
John E. Hanna,*	" McConnellsville,	"	1854.		
Rev. William T. Hand,	" Marietta,	"	"	"	—
John McLean,	" Cincinnati,	"	1856	"	1861.
Geo. M. Woodbridge,*	" Marietta,	"	1857.		
Calvary Morris,*	" Athens,	"	1859.		
Rev. J. M. Trimble,*	" Columbus,	"	1860.		
Rev. B. N. Spahr,*	" Harmar,	"	1861.		
Rev. John M. Leavitt,	" Cincinnati,	"	"	"	—
E. H. Moore,*	" Athens,	"	"		
Dr. William Waddle,*	" Chillicothe,	"	1864.		
H. S. Bundy,*	" Jackson,	"	"		
Dr. W. P. Johnson,*	" Athens,	"	1866.		
Bellamy Storer,*	" Cincinnati,	"	"		

Treasurers.

Dr. Eliphaz Perkins, from 1804 to 1807; Dr. Leonard Jewett, from 1807 to 1808; Joseph B. Miles, from 1808 to 1814; Ebenezer Currier, from 1814 to 1824; General John Brown, from 1824 to present time.

Secretaries.

Dudley Woodbridge, from 1804 to 1808; Henry Bartlett, from 1808 to 1841; A. G. Brown, from 1841 to present time.

---

*Those thus marked constitute the Board of Trustees in 1868.

The following is a list of the presidents and professors of the university from the date of its complete organization.

Presidents.

Rev. Jacob Lindley, from 1808 till 1822; Rev. James Irvine, from 1822 till 1824; Rev. Robert G. Wilson, from 1824 till 1839; Rev. William H. McGuffey, 1839 till 1843; organization suspended from 1843 till 1848; Rev. Alfred Ryors, from 1848 till 1852; Rev. Solomon Howard, from 1852 till present time.

Professors of Ancient Languages.

Joseph Dana, from 1818 to 1819; Rev. J. B. Whittlesey, from 1819 to 1821; Joseph Dana, from 1822 to 1835; Daniel Read, from 1836 to 1838; Rev. Elisha Ballantyne, Greek, from 1838 to 1840; Rev. John M. Stephenson, Greek, from 1840 to 1842; Daniel Read, Latin, from 1838 to 1843; Rev. Wells Andrews, from 1843 to 1848; James Irwin Kuhn, Greek, from 1842 to 1844; Rev. Aaron Williams, from 1844 to 1853; Rev. Addison Ballard, Latin, from 1848 to 1852; Rev. E. E. Bragdon, Latin, from 1853 to 1854; Rev. Clinton W. Sears, from 1854 to 1855; Rev. John M. Leavitt, from 1855 to 1857; Rev. William H. Young, from 1859 to present time.

Professors of Mathematics.

Rev. James Irvine, from 1821 to 1824; Rev. Jacob Lindley, from 1824 to 1826; William Wall, from 1827 to 1836; Rev. L. D. McCabe, from 1844 to 1845; Rev. Wm. J. Hoge, from 1848 to 1851; Rev. Addison Ballard, from 1852 to 1854; Rev. John M. Leavitt, from 1854 to 1855; William H. Young, from 1855 to 1859; Rev. Richard Arthur, from 1859 to 1864; Eli T. Tappan, from 1864 to present time.

Professors of Moral Science and Belles Lettres.

Rev. Jacob Lindley, from 1822 to 1824; Rev. Robert G. Wilson, from 1824 to 1839; Rev. William H. McGuffey, from 1839 to 1843;

Rev. Alfred Ryors, from 1848 to 1852; Rev. Solomon Howard, from 1852 to present time.

Professors of Natural Science.

Rev. Samuel D. Hoge, from 1823 to 1826; Thos. M. Drake, from 1827 to 1834; Rev. Frederic Merrick, from 1838 to 1842; William W. Mather, from 1842 to 1850; Rev. Joseph S. Tomlinson, from 1851 to 1852; Rev. James G. Blair, from 1852 to 1864; Rev. Alex. S. Gibbons, from 1864 to present time.

The present faculty of the university is composed as follows:

President.
REV. SOLOMON HOWARD,
Professor of Intellectual and Moral Philosophy.

WILLIAM H. YOUNG,*
Professor of Greek and Latin Languages.

ELI T. TAPPAN,
Professor of Mathematics.

REV. ALEXANDER S. GIBBONS,
Professor of Mineralogy, Chemistry, and Geology.

W. H. G. ADNEY,
Principal of Preparatory Department.

---

*Professor Young has held this chair from 1859, but was absent from 1861 till 1864, in the military service.

CHAPTER VIII.

Alexander Township.

ALEXANDER, one of the four townships into which the county was divided on its organization, originally included the territory which now forms eleven townships, viz: Bedford, Scipio and Columbia townships of Meigs county; Vinton, Clinton, Madison, Elk and Knox of Vinton county; and Lee, Lodi and Alexander of Athens county. Its territorial extent was the same as that of Ames and just twice that of Athens. The township was located and surveyed in 1795. Athens and Alexander being the "college townships," were generally spoken of in connection, and, as Alexander lay south of Athens, it was for a long time familiarly designated as "Southtown." Among the residents of Alexander as early as 1805 were Robert Ross, William Gabriel, Amos Thompson, Enos Thompson, Edward Martin, Isaac Stanley, John, Jonathan, Joseph, Thomas and Isaac Brooks, Matthew Haning, Thomas and John Armstrong, Jared, Israel and Martin Bobo,

Caleb Merritt, Joel Lowther, Michael Bowers, William Strond, Esquire Bowman, Abner Smith, Charles and Isaiah Shepherd, Thomas Sharp, and Richard and William Reeves. The population of the township in 1820 was 854; in 1830 it was 882; in 1840 it was 1,451; in 1850 it was 1,735; in 1860 it was 1,675. Hebbardsville,* pleasantly situated in the western part of the township, is the principal center of population.

Jeremiah Clements and Israel Bobo, noted as hunters in the early settlement of the county, killed in one season sixty-five bears in one neighborhood, included in the site of the present town of Hebbardsville. The same men were fond of whisky, and, to get a supply, took a horse-load of bear skins to the Ohio river and traded for a barrel of the desired article. The next difficulty was how to get it home. They finally cut two poles from the forest and formed a sort of drag to be drawn by the horse, the largest ends of the poles resting on the ground. The barrel of whisky was then secured between the poles and thus dragged through the woods to Alexander township, where they lived. This was the first barrel of whisky ever brought into Alexander. In after years the use of it became common and greatly the fashion, but at the present time it is not kept for sale at any place in the township.

In Alexander the Methodists were, as usual, the pio-

---

*Hebbardsville is the spelling adopted by the Post office Department at Washington, and used in the official records.

neer church. At a very early day they built a meeting house at "Centre Stake," and the Presbyterians not long after built one near the site of the present Cumberland Presbyterian church. There are now in the township three Methodist churches, three Free Will Baptist, one Old School Presbyterian and one Cumberland Presbyterian. Near the latter church is located the principal cemetery in the township, which is being tastefully improved. Pleasanton, situated in the eastern part of the township, on the road between Athens and Pomeroy, is a thrifty settlement, containing about twenty-five families. Simon Pierce built the first house here about 1817. Other settlers located here from time to time, and in 1851 a post office was established and the place called Pleasanton.

The early records of the township were destroyed by fire in the house of John McKee in 1827 or 1828, but as nearly as can be ascertained the first trustees were Caleb Merritt, John Brooks, and Thomas Sharp, and Caleb Merritt the first justice of the peace.

Trustees since 1829.

 1829 Ziba Lindley, Sen., Samuel McKee, Nicholas Misner.
 1830 Ziba Lindley, Sen., Samuel McKee, Elias N. Nichols.
 1831 Ziba Lindley, Jun., Samuel McKee, Elias N. Nichols.
 1832 Samuel Earhart, Asa Stearns, Benjamin Parks, Jun.
 1833 Samuel Earhart, John V. Brown, Benjamin Parks, Jun.
 1834 Ziba Lindley, Jun., Jesse M. Mahon, Benjamin Parks, Jun.
 1835 Ziba Lindley, Jun., John Brooks, Samuel Earhart.

Alexander Township.

1836 Daniel Dudley, Ami Conde, Archelaus T. Clark.
1837 Samuel Earhart, John Brooks, Jun., Archelaus Stanley.
1838 Wm. B. Reynolds, John Brooks, Jun., Franklin Burnham.
1839 Wm. B. Reynolds, John Brooks, Jun., Franklin Burnham.
1840 John Rickey, Peter Morse, John W. Drake.
1841 Franklin Burnham, John Grey, A. Love.
1842 Franklin Burnham, J. H. Brooks, A. Love.
1843 J. W. Drake, Ziba Lindley, Jun., A. Love.
1844 J. W. Drake, Ziba Lindley, Jun., A. Burtnett.
1845 J. W. Drake, Moses Patterson, A. Burtnett.
1846 George Bean, Daniel Teters, A. Burtnett.
1847 George Bean, John H. Brooks, Abram McVey.
1848 Archelaus Stanley, John H. Brooks, Abram McVey.
1849 James S. Hawk, A. G. Henderson, William Wood.
1850 John Rickey, Joseph W. Blackwood, John W. Drake.
1851 John Rickey, George Bean, William Wood.
1852 John Rickey, Franklin Burnham, William Wood.
1853 Daniel Teters, Peter Long, William Wood.
1854 Missing.
1855 Alexander Love, James H. Martin, Abram Coe.
1856 Alexander Love, James H. Martin, William Campbell.
1857 Moses Patterson, William Wood, William Campbell.
1858 Moses Patterson, Isaac Stanley, George W. Sams.
1859 E. N. Blake, John Rickey, George W. Sams.
1860 E. N. Nichols, John Rickey, George W. Sams.
1861 E. N. Blake, John Rickey, George W. Sams.
1862 E. N. Blake, John Rickey, George W. Sams.
1863 E. N, Blake, Isaiah Bean, Isaac Brooks, Jun.
1864 E. N. Blake, Isaiah Bean, Isaac Stanley, Jun.
1865 B. Rickey, Isaiah Bean, Peter Long.
1866 B. Rickey, Isaiah Bean, Homer Chase.
1867 S. B. Blake, Isaiah Bean, P. G. Hibbard.
1868 Samuel Blake, Isaiah Bean, William Bean.

Justices of the Peace.

   1829 Ami Conde, J. M. Gorsline.
   1831 Samuel McKee.
   1832 J. M. Gorsline, Alfred Dunlap, Samuel Earhart.
   1834 Josiah Wilson.
   1835 William Golden.
   1837 Josiah Wilson.
   1838 William Golden.
   1849 Franklin Burnham.
   1850 John Camp, Joseph W. Blackwood.
   1852 Franklin Burnham.
   1853 John Camp, Joseph W. Blackwood.
   1854 Joseph McPherson, George Adair.
   1855 Daniel Drake.
   1857 Joseph McPherson, A. S. Coe.
   1858 Daniel Drake.
   1860 James Strite, L. Oliver.
   1861 L. C. Crouch, Wm. B. Dickerson, A. S. Coe, A. C. Murphy, S. H. Kinney.
   1863 Leven Oliver.
   1864 Wm. Watson, Amos C. Murphy.
   1866 Leven Oliver.
   1867 Wm. Watson, Amos C. Murphy.
   1868 Peter Vorhes.

Personal and Biographical.

Thomas Armstrong, born April 2, 1777, in Greene county, Pennsylvania, came to Athens county in 1799, and settled in Alexander township, where his son, Elmer Armstrong, now lives. Mrs. Alice Armstrong, wife of Thomas, was also a native of Greene county, Pennsylvania, and daughter of Col. Wm. Crawford, who served creditably in the revolutionary and Indian wars.

In March, 1799, Mr. Armstrong and wife, with their first child, then three months old, accompanied by Charles Harper, wife and child, put their movable goods, consisting in part of furniture, live stock, etc., and forty young apple trees, into a flatboat at the mouth of Muddy creek, on the Monongahela river, and set out for the northwestern territory. Landing at the mouth of the Hockhocking, in April 1799, the women and children, and live stock, were sent forward from this point by land to Athens, while the goods, provisions, etc., were *poled* up the river by Messrs. Armstrong and Harper in a pirogue. There was no road from Athens to Alexander (their destination), but the woods being tolerably open, they made "a rig" from poles, to which a horse was hitched, and thus their goods were hauled out. Provisions were scarce, and the new settlers depended mainly on hunting for meat, and on the skins of the wild animals, which the men very generally used, for clothes. Mr. Armstrong himself was never much of a hunter, but frequently received a share of the meat and skins for packing the game home for the hunters on his horse. The manner of packing bears and deer was to take the entrails out, skin the nose of the animal for a crupper for the horse, place the skin on the back of the horse, tying the skin of the fore-legs around his breast; then put on a second one, with the two flesh sides together. Buffalo skins were cut in strips and used for bed cords, and for harness "tugs" in hauling. On one occasion, Mrs. Armstrong saw the dogs pursue a deer on to the ice in the creek, near the house, when, there being no man at hand, she hastened down with an ax and butcher's knife, and, the deer being helpless on the ice, killed it with the ax and cut its throat with the knife. The skin of this deer was dressed, made into *gloves* by Mrs. A., and sent to her friends in Pennsylvania.

In her youth, Mrs. Armstrong spent some time in a fort, which was on her father's farm, near Carmichaeltown, Pennsylvania. During that period the Indians were peaceable, and, for a time, committed no hostilities. But, one Sabbath morning, the Reverend John Corbley, a Baptist minister, started to church, a short distance from the fort, and, when returning to the house for something which had been forgotten, he and the family were furiously set upon by Indians. The savages instantly killed the wife and babe, and scalped the two daughters. Mr. Corbley and two boys made their escape into the fort. Col. Crawford immediately went with a party in pursuit. He did not overtake the Indians, but found the woman and child dead, and the two girls yet alive. They were carried into the fort, their wounds dressed, and both recovered, married, and raised families, and a daughter of one of them is now living in St. Mary's, Ohio.

In the summer of 1799, Mr. Armstrong prepared to erect a substantial log house on his place. On such occasions, the settlers from far and near were expected to assemble and aid in the labor. It was also an occasion of much mirth and good feeling; the slender news of the settlement was discussed, and there was a general interchange of neighborly offices. Among others who came to assist Mr. Armstrong at his "raising" were John Thompson, then a prominent citizen of the township, but long since dead, and Wm. Gabriel, Matthew Haning, and Thomas Jones, who settled in Alexander in 1798 and 1799.

Mr. Armstrong was for several years lister of taxes in Alexander, and collector of college rents. He was also sheriff of the county, and held other positions of trust in the community. He died October 22, 1853.

Elmer Armstrong, youngest son of the preceding, was born in Alexander township, January 17, 1812, and now lives on the farm which his father settled upon in 1799. One of the apple trees, brought from Pennsylvania by his father in 1799, and planted on the place that year, is still living—measures seven feet seven and a half inches in circumference, and rarely fails to bear a good annual crop of apples. Mr. Armstrong married the daughter of Levi Booth, formerly of Alexander, and has one son and two daughters. He has for many years been well known as a prosperous farmer and successful dealer in live stock.

Samuel L. Blake, born in Middletown, Middlesex county, Connecticut, in 1779, removed in 1816 to Alexander township, where he lived the rest of his life. He was a thorough farmer, a man of excellent character and sound judgment, and assisted largely in molding the society of the township. He died March 16, 1859, leaving a large number of descendants, some of whom are well known in the county.

A large family of *Hibbards*, originally from Vermont, came to Athens county at an early day. Elisha and John in 1816, Alanson and Elias and their sister Pamela (afterwards Mrs. Sabinus Rice), in 1817, and Dr. James S. Hibbard in 1823. The Rev. Ebenezer Hibbard, eldest brother of this family, who was pastor of a church in Vermont forty years, came to Alexander township in 1831, and settled at Hebbardsville, giving his name, slightly altered, to the village. He preached in this neighborhood some time, and then removed to Amesville and preached there till his death in 1835.

Capt. Amos Northrop, born in Litchfield county, Connecticut, December 19, 1796, came to this county in the autumn of 1814, and ultimately settled in Alexander township, where he still resides in the town of Hebbardsville. In early life Capt. Northrop developed some military taste. He served in the war of 1812, and, after coming to this county, was captain of the militia for several years. He is now deputy sheriff of the county, and also coroner, which last position he has held for a number of years. Though in his seventy-third year he is an active and efficient man.

William Sickles, born in Pennsylvania, May 1st, 1802, came to Athens county in 1805, with his father's family, and settled on the Thomas Grim farm in Waterloo. After two years they removed to Alexander and settled on the Peter Long farm, where they lived about twenty-three years, and afterwards several years again in Waterloo. When a young man Mr. Sickles has killed as many as five deer in one day. In one autumn he killed in the aggregate forty-nine deer. Joseph Bobo, of Lodi, and Abram Gabriel each killed in that season the same number—forty-nine. He remembers when there was but one house on the road between Alexander and the present town of Jackson, then called Scioto Salt Works. He has ground a great many bushels of corn in a hand mill made of two stones; the upper one revolved on the lower by means of a short handle let into the edge.

In the year 1817 *John M. Chase*, a native of Danville, Maine, moved to the county, and settled as a farmer in Alexander township, where he resided till his death in 1860. Of his family two sons and four daughters are now living in this and the adjoining county of Meigs.

Gardiner F. Chase, his son, born in Danville, Maine, in 1811, came to Alexander in 1817, and now lives on the farm on which his father settled in that year.

William Gorsline, born on Long Island, New York, in 1755, came to Athens county and settled in Alexander township in 1817. He brought with him a family of three sons and three daughters, of whom only one (Mr. J. M. Gorsline, of Lee township) survives. Mr. Gorsline was a man of fine intelligence. He died July 7th, 1825.

Abram and *Jacob McVey*, brothers, came to Athens from Washington county, Pennsylvania, in 1832, and settled in Alexander township. Some of their descendants are still living in the county. About the same time a large emigration from Washington and Greene counties, Pennsylvania, came to Athens and settled mostly in Alexander. Among them were Joseph Post, Moses, William and John Patterson and their families, Jacob and David Cook, Dennis Drake, Peter Vorhes and family, of whom five sons are living in the county, John Gray, Elijah Brown and his sons Henry and Jerry, Lawrence Blakeway, Cephas and Zenas DeCamp, John Winget, Joseph Barmore, William Russell, David Pierce, John Cowan, John Brownlee, Ziba Lindley, Sen., and family, Elisha Jolly, William E. Bane, Absalom Conkey, John Clutter, Daniel Espy, Solomon Leighty, Amzi Axtell, Edward Fletcher, Samuel Lively, William Hoaglan, Abram Enlow, Joseph Parker, Ludlow Squires, Hezekiah Topping, and Henry Carey. They formed a valuable class of citizens, distinguished for thrift and taste in the management of farms, stock, etc.

CHAPTER IX.

Ames Township.

THIS was one of the four original townships into which the county was divided on its organization in 1805. The county included then more than twice its present area, and Ames comprised the territory which now forms the townships of Marion and Homer in Morgan county; Ward, Green, and Starr in Hocking county, and Trimble, York, Dover, Bern, and Ames in Athens county. The settlement of Ames was begun about a year after that of Athens, and the first settlers were Judge Ephraim Cutler and George Ewing, with their families. In the summer of 1797 Ephraim Cutler, one of the original associates of the Ohio Company, finding that a considerable portion of his lands lay on the waters of Federal creek, in the sixth township, of the thirteenth range, and being desirous to visit them and fix their location, explored a way and cut a horse path through the wilderness from Waterford on the Muskingum, to what is now Ames township. He was accompanied and assisted by Mr. George Ewing, who, with his little family, had come from western Virginia to the Ohio Company's purchase in 1794, and had lived till the close of the Indian war in one of the block houses of the Waterford settlement. In the autumn of 1797 they made a second visit to and more thorough exploration of Mr. Cutler's lands. This time they were accompanied by Captain Benjamin Brown who had recently arrived in the colony from Massachusetts. Mr. Ewing and Capt. Brown each owned one hundred acres of land in the company's "donation" tract on the Muskingum, which they exchanged with Mr. Cutler for land on Federal creek, agreeing to assist him in forming a settlement. They found a fertile region, heavily timbered, well watered, and abounding in game. Traces of the buffalo and elk showed that they were not yet exterminated, and deer, bears, wild turkeys, and smaller game were found in great abundance. Wolves and panthers were very numerous, and continued for many years to be a source of annoyance and danger.

The result of their second visit to the valley of Federal creek was a determination to locate there. Mr. Ewing brought his family out in March, 1798, and settled on what is now known as the Thomas Gardner farm. It was nearly a year later that Judge Cutler and Capt. Brown brought their families over from Waterford. The domestic effects and portable property of the two families were loaded into large canoes and sent, in charge of Capt. Brown, down the Muskingum and Ohio rivers to the mouth of the Hockhocking, and up that stream to Federal creek, a distance of about eighty miles. The women and children, on horse back, were escorted by Mr. Cutler through the pathless woods and over the hills to their new home. In a narrative written a few years later Mr. Cutler thus refers to this journey:

"I, with four horses, took Mrs. Brown and Mrs. Cutler and all our children to go twenty miles through an entire wilderness to our new home. Night overtook us before we were able to cross Sharp's fork of Federal creek, and we were obliged to encamp. We experienced a very rainy night. The creek in the morning was rapidly rising. I hurried, got Mrs. Brown and Mrs. Cutler and the children, with the baggage and horses, over the creek, all except A. G. Brown,* then a child three or four years old, whom I took in my arms, and as I stepped on a drift of flood-wood, which reached across the creek, it broke away from the bank. We were in danger, but a gracious Providence preserved us and we got safely across. We arrived at our camp, near where we built our cabin, May 7th, 1799."

Mr. Cutler settled on lands now owned by his son, Mr. William P. Cutler, and Capt. Brown on the farm where Daniel Fleming now lives. In May, 1800, Silvanus Ames, afterward known as Judge Ames, came from Belpre with his family and settled near Mr. Cutler on the farm which he occupied till his death in 1823.

---

* Judge Brown of Athens.

Deacon Joshua Wyatt came with his family about the same time and settled on the farm in section 1 now owned by the heirs of George Wyatt. All of these men bore a large part in the early history of Amesville. Their wives, too, were persons of solid minds and superior culture. The writer remembers to have heard Mrs. Ames, who had been tenderly reared in the family of a New England clergyman, but whose energy and character were equal to any occasion, describe the hardships of her tedious journey from Massachusetts to Ohio, in the year 1799, which she made all the way on horseback, carrying an infant in her arms. Mrs. Cutler and Mrs. Wyatt were also women of great excellence; the former died in 1809, and the latter a few years later.

A pioneer settlement is fortunate if its founders cultivate at the beginning a respect for law and order, due regard for the ordinances of religion, and a healthy desire for literary culture. These early influences seem to be permanent, and the character of a community for generations is often fixed for good or evil by the forces dominant at its birth. Amesville, not less than the sister settlement at Athens, was favored in this regard.

"Schools of an elevated character," says Ephraim Cutler, "were soon established. Two gentlemen, graduates of Harvard college—Mr. Moses Everett, son of the Rev. Moses Everett, of Dorchester, Massachusetts, and Mr. Charles Cutler—taught successively several years.

For some time the youth enjoyed no other means of acquiring knowledge. Mr. Cutler took the *United States Gazette*, at that time the only newspaper taken in the settlement; and that, except by fortunate accident, did not arrive much oftener than once in three months." Steps were taken, at an early day, to form a circulating library. In 1803 the inhabitants of Ames assembled in public meeting to consider the subject of roads, which, having been disposed of, the intellectual wants of the settlement became a topic of discussion. They were entirely isolated and remote from established schools and libraries, and felt keenly the necessity of providing some means for their own and their children's mental improvement. The establishment of a library was suggested, and all agreed that this was the readiest way to meet the case, provided funds could be raised and the books obtained. The scarcity of money seemed an almost insuperable obstacle. We can form little idea at this day of the almost total dearth of any medium of exchange which existed in our pioneer settlements. The little transactions of the colony were carried on almost wholly by barter and exchange in kind. Very little more produce was raised than each family needed, and, indeed, there was no market for any surplus. Judge A. G. Brown says that, soon after they settled in Ames, his older brother raised a little crop of hemp, which they took in a canoe down Federal creek and the Hockhocking, and up to Marietta, where they succeeded in disposing of it for a small sum; and adds: "So scarce was money that I can hardly remember ever seeing a piece of coin till I was a well-grown boy. It was with difficulty we obtained enough to pay our taxes with and buy tea for mother—as for clothes and other things, we either depended on the forests for them, or bartered for them, or did without." In this great scarcity of money the purchase of books for a library seemed like an impossibility; but the subject was canvassed by the meeting, and it was resolved to attempt it. Before the end of the year, by dint of economy, and using every ingenious device to procure necessary funds, a sum of money was raised. Some of the settlers were good hunters, and, there being a ready cash market for furs and skins, which were bought by the agents of John Jacob Astor and others, these easily paid their subscriptions. At all events, the movement was successful, and the money was paid in. Esquire Samuel Brown was just ready to make a business trip to New England. He was going in a light wagon, and took with him a quantity of bear-skins and other furs, which he designed exchanging in Boston for such goods as were needed in the settlement. The money was placed in his hands, and he was deputed to make the first purchase of books for the embryo library—the first in Ohio. He was furnished with letters to the Rev. Thaddeus M. Harris (a gentleman of education and note, who had visited the western country a short time before), and the Rev. Dr. Cutler, who accompanied Mr. Brown to Boston and selected a valuable collection of books. *This was the first public library formed in the northwestern territory*, though not, as some have supposed, the first incorporated. The "Dayton library society" was incorporated February 21, 1805; a library "at Granville, in the county of Fairfield," January 26, 1807; one at Newtown, Hamilton county, February 10, 1808, and the "Coon-skin library," as it has been familiarly called of late years, was incorporated, under the name of the "Western library association," by an act passed February 19, 1810. But, that to Athens county belongs the honor of having given birth to the first library created in the territory of the northwest, does not admit of any doubt. The original record of the association is before us, entitled "Laws and regulations of the Western library association, founded at Ames, February 2, 1804." The preamble to the articles sets forth that, "considering the many beneficial effects which social libraries are calculated to produce in societies where they are established, as a source both of rational entertainment and instruction, we, the subscribers, wishing to participate in those blessings, agree to form ourselves into a society for this purpose, under the title of the Western library association, in the town of Ames. Furthermore, at a meeting of the said association, at the house of Christopher Herrold, on Thursday, the 2d of February,

1804, agreed that the following articles be adopted as the rules of the society." The shares were $2.50 each, and each share paid a tax of twenty-five cents a year. Among the founders and original stockholders, whose names are subscribed to the articles, were the following, viz.: Ephraim Cutler, four shares; Jason Rice, two; Silvanus Ames, two; Benjamin L. Brown, one; Martin Boyles, one; Ezra Green, one; George Ewing, one; John Brown, Jun., one; Josiah True, one; George Ewing, Jun., one; Daniel Weethee, two; Timothy Wilkins, two; Benjamin Brown, one; Samuel Brown, 2d, one; Samuel Brown, Sen., one; Simon Converse, one; Christopher Herrold, one; Edmund Dorr, one; George Wolf, one; Nathan Woodbury, one; Joshua Wyatt, one; George Walker, one; Elijah Hatch, one; Zebulon Griffin, one; Jehiel Gregory, one; George Castle, one; Samuel Brown, one, etc. Among the subscribers in later years appear the names of Dr. Ezra Walker, Othniel Nye, Sally Rice, Nehemiah Gregory, Thomas Ewing, Jason Rice, Lucy Ames, John M. Hibbard, Seth Child, Ebenezer Champlin, Elisha Lattimer, Cyrus Tuttle, Pearly Brown, Robert Fulton, R. S. Lovell, Michael Tippie, James Pugsley, and others among the early residents of Ames.

December 17th, 1804, a meeting of the shareholders was held at the house of Silvanus Ames, and Ephraim Cutler was elected librarian. It was also "voted to accept fifty-one books, purchased by Samuel Brown."

At the annual meeting held at the house of Ephraim Cutler, January 7th, 1805, the committee reported that they "have received pay for thirty-two shares, amounting to $82.50, of which they have laid out $73.50 for books." For this year Benjamin Brown, Ephraim Cutler and Daniel Weethee were elected the committee of managers, and Ephraim Cutler librarian. "Voted that the thanks of this association be transmitted, post paid, to the Rev. Thaddeus M. Harris, for his assistance rendered in the selection and purchase of the books which constitute our library." The list of this first purchase of books is before us. It contains "Robertson's North America;" "Harris' Encyclopedia," 4 volumes; "Morse's Geography," 2 volumes; "Adams' Truth of Religion;" "Goldsmith's Works," 4 volumes; "Evelina," 2 volumes; "Children of the Abbey," 2 volumes; "Blair's Lectures;" "Clark's Discourses;" "Ramsey's American Revolution," 2 volumes; "Goldsmith's Animated Nature," 4 volumes; "Playfair's History of Jacobinism," 2 volumes; "George Barnwell;" "Camilla," 3 volumes; "Beggar Girl," 3 volumes, &c. Later purchases included "Shakspeare;" "Don Quixote;" "Locke's Essays," "Scottish Chiefs," "Josephus," "Smith's Wealth of Nations," "Spectator," "Plutarch's Lives," "Arabian Nights," "Life of Washington," &c. In 1807 John Brown was elected librarian, and William Green, Thos. M. Hamilton and John Brown managers for one year.

In 1808 George Walker, Benjamin Brown and Samuel Beaumont were elected managers, and George Walker librarian. In 1809 John Brown, Benjamin Brown and Seth Fuller were elected managers, and John Brown librarian. In 1811 (under the incorporating act) Silvanus Ames, Ezra Green and George Ewing were chosen directors, Seth Fuller, treasurer, and Benjamin Brown, librarian. In 1812, '13 and '14 the same officers were re-elected. In 1815 Seth Fuller, Geo. Walker and Ezra Green were chosen directors, John Brown, 2d, treasurer, and Benjamin Brown, librarian. From 1816 to 1820 the directors were Seth Fuller, Josiah True and Ezra Green. Benjamin Brown was librarian during 1816 and 1817, and Dr. Ezra Walker during 1818 and 1819.*

We have given considerable space to an account of

---

*A somewhat fanciful account of the formation of this library has heretofore appeared in print styling it the "Coon-skin library," and stating that the first purchase of books was made wholly with the furs and skins of wild animals. Some hunting adventures supposed to have occurred in the pursuit of skins are given, and the founders of the library appear rather in the light of literary Nimrods, with whom the chase was an intellectual pastime, and every crack of whose rifles brought down a volume of poems or history. The account we have given is the correct one, our facts having been obtained from one of the surviving founders, and from the records. Certainly some coon skins were sold to raise money by some of the subscribers; and doubtless some hemp, grain, deer or bear-skins, and whatever else would fetch a price; but the sobriquet of "Coon-skin library" was only invented comparatively a few years since. The literal truth about this event is sufficiently interesting, and that we have given.

the formation and early history of this, the first public library formed in the state of Ohio, because of the interesting nature of the event, and because nearly all of the founders of the library have descendants still living in the county, who will read with pride of the part their ancestors took in establishing an institution which worked such great and lasting good. The library received additions from time to time, until there were finally accumulated several hundred volumes—a considerable library for the place and period. Many years later it was divided, and part taken to Dover township (where some of the original stockholders lived), where it formed the nucleus of another library, which was incorporated by an act of the legislature, passed December 21, 1830. The portion retained in Ames township was sold by the shareholders in the year 1860 or 1861 to Messrs. J. H. Glazier, A. W. Glazier and E. H. Brawley, and they afterwards sold it to Mr. William P. Cutler, of Washington county (son of Judge Ephraim Cutler), who still has it in his possession.

In the year 1798 Samuel, John and Thos. McCune, three brothers, and David, Jacob and Peter Boyles, came from Pennsylvania and settled temporarily on the Hockhocking, on what is now N. O. Warren's farm, where they remained till 1802, when they removed to the township of Ames and settled within half a mile of the present village of Amesville. George Ewing, Jun., brother of Thomas Ewing, married a daughter of this David Boyles. The three McCune brothers, as also two of the Boyles brothers, were strong, athletic men, and great hunters, sometimes killing, it is said, twelve or fourteen deer and three or four bears in a day. John McCune was something of a mechanic, and used to repair the guns of his neighbors. On one occasion a man brought his gun to be mended and borrowed McCune's gun to use in the meantime. Before repairing the gun McCune went out with it to kill some game. Coming unexpectedly on a bear, he tried to shoot it, but the gun failed to go off, when the bear, as if seeing his advantage, made for the hunter. McCune, unlike his gun, went off. He ran as fast as he could for some distance, the bear closely pursuing, and McCune trying every few rods to fire his gun, which, however seemed to like the situation, and refused to be discharged. After running about half a mile, a neighbor's dogs came to his assistance, and Bruin was driven off but not killed. Wolves were, of course, very abundant at that time, and killing a wolf was a common occurrence. The wife of John McCune seeing something pass the door of their cabin one evening which she took for a dog, set their own dog upon it, and, at the same time stepping out of the door, found it was a large black wolf. Arming herself with a pitchfork that stood within reach, she and the dog kept up a running fight of several rods and finally killed the wolf.

John Boyles and John McCune, while hunting one day, came upon a mother bear and two cubs. Boyles fired at and wounded the old bear, and then, wishing to see his dog kill one of the cubs, laid down his gun and hissed his dog on to attack the cub—the old bear and other cub beating a retreat. Boyles, becoming interested in the fight between his dog and the cub, had approached near them, when he was disagreeably startled by seeing the old bear return, brought by the cries of the cub, and place herself between *him and his gun*. He was preparing to make the best battle he could with his hunting knife, when McCune, hearing his call for help, hastened to the spot and dispatched the bear by a bullet from his rifle. The sons of the McCune brothers still live in the county, and, like their fathers before them, have been famous hunters and contributed much toward ridding the settlement and eastern part of the county of the wild game and "vermin" that so annoyed the early settlers. Jacob McCune, one of the sons of John McCune, a few years since, on the occasion of a squirrel hunt, killed in one day one hundred and three grey squirrels, and Samuel McCune, his brother, killed eighty-three.

The year 1805 was a year of unexampled drought, and a scarcity almost amounting to a famine prevailed through all the settlements of this region. The inhabitants of Ames and Athens townships lived almost exclusively during the winter of 1805-6 on the meat of deer, bears, &c., and were compelled to go to Lancaster and Marietta for breadstuff.

In 1806 or 1807 Joab Hoisington settled in the township, and in 1807 Azor Nash, an eccentric character, well known here in early times. Elijah Latimer and Obediah Clark came about the same time. The latter, who married a sister of Thomas Ewing, had been a fifer in the army, and used to play the violin at the country dances in Ames.

The first school taught in the township was in a cabin on the old Cutler place, in 1802, by Charles Cutler, a graduate of Harvard college, and eminently qualified for teaching. At an exhibition given at the close of the term, when the children recited dialogues or other pieces committed for the occasion, Thomas Ewing and John Brown, two of the pupils, spoke the dialogue of Brutus and Cassius, from Shakspeare. In 1804 a log school house was built on Silas Dean's place, near the present village of Amesville, and close by the site of the late George Walker's store. Moses Everett, a graduate of Harvard, taught the first quarter in this house. General John Brown taught here in 1807. The next school house was built in 1811, on Silvanus Ames' farm, and for several years served as a meeting house and school house for the settlement. Sophia Walker, then recently from Vermont, taught the first quarter in this house, and Dr. Ezra Walker, her father, taught here in the winter of 1811–12.

An incident connected with early preaching among the pioneer settlements may be mentioned. A neighborhood in the lower settlement in Ames township, in which 'Squire John Brown lived, secured the services of Elder Asa Stearns, a Free Will Baptist, to preach for them once a month during the year, to be paid with *three barrels of whisky*. Mr. Stearns had an arrangement with Ebenezer Currier, at Athens, to take the whisky and allow him therefor twenty-four dollars, to be credited to him toward the farm he had bought of Judge Currier. The contract was faithfully carried out on all hands, Elder Stearns visiting his little congregation every third Saturday of each month during the year, at the end of which he received his salary in whisky and made the transfer of it as agreed to Judge Currier.

The Rev. J. H. Hopkins, an early resident of Ames, says: "Among the pioneers of Methodism here were Gulliver Dean and wife, Mr. Haight, Judge Walker's family, the McCunes, &c. The class formed at Ames, early in this century, was ministered to at first by Mr. Austin Thompson and Mr. Dickson, local preachers, and the Rev. Messrs. Ferree, Baker, R. O. Spencer, Henry Fernandez, and Abraham Lippett, Athens circuit, preached to them. A great many years ago, when William Miller first published his lectures on the prophecies concerning the second coming of Christ, some of our people became very much alarmed to think the end of all things was so near. There was one old sister, quite a good woman too, no doubt, but possessed of a large share of credulousness, and consequently ready to gulp down almost anything that came from the mouth of Mr. Miller touching the signs of Christ's coming and the end of the world. She awoke one winter night, the weather extremely cold; quite a deep snow had fallen, and the roads and sledding were fine. The wind was blowing hard, and a lot of old clap-boards that had been loosely thrown down near the house, were flapping and making quite a noise. She shook the old man and told him to arise, for the day of judgment had come, or at least that Gabriel and his angels were at hand. The old man raised himself up a little and said: 'Old woman, what put this into your head? you are always anticipating some wonderful event.' 'It must be so,' was the reply, 'for I have been listening for some time to the rumbling of Gabriel's chariot wheels.' The old man told her just to lie down and be quiet, for said he, 'Gabriel is too wise a creature ever to come to our world on wheels, while the sledding continues as good as it is now.'"

In early times much attention was given to militia organizations. The first organization in the eastern part of the county was made at the house of Judge Ames, in 1803, when Silvanus Ames was elected captain, Josiah True, of Dover township, lieutenant, and Samuel Brown, of Ames, ensign. The first company muster in the same neighborhood was in 1804. At the next election of officers, in 1808, John Brown was made captain and George Ewing lieutenant. John Brown was subsequently advanced to major, colonel and brigadier general, to which last position he was elected in 1817, the brigade being composed of Athens, Morgan, Washington, Meigs, Gallia, and Vinton counties. The first battalion muster was held at Athens in 1805. Another was held a short time afterward on Esquire Daniel Stewart's place in Rome township, and a third on Wm. Henry's place in Canaan. Regimental musters were held annually for many years at Athens, and Colonel Jehiel Gregory, of Athens, was the first colonel; after him came Silvanus Ames, Edmund Dorr, John Brown, Charles Shipman, Calvary Morris, Absalom Boyles, Nathan Dean, Ziba Lindley, Jun., Charles Cutler, Jonas Rice, and Amos Thompson.

General John Brown was lister of lands for Ames township in 1807, in connection with which he recalls the following anecdote. As his quaint style can not be improved, we give his own words: "In 1807 I was elected lister (an office somewhat like the present assessor) of Ames township, which at that time was about thirty miles east and west, and twelve or fourteen miles north and south, while the inhabitants were few and far between. In discharging that duty I learned how hard it is to levy taxes so as to give satisfaction to all. At that time the tax on all horses three years old, *in April preceding*, was forty cents per head; on all cattle three years old ten cents. The great difficulty was to settle as to age. Some would not tell, some would prevaricate, sometimes the man of the family was not at home, and the woman did not know, &c. One old lady I found fully posted. I had looked about the place and found they did work with two yoke of cattle; but the woman said these were 'late calves'—would be three years old during the summer. There were several cows evidently giving milk, but, somehow, none but the bell cow was old enough for me. Out of a lot of three or four horses only one was three years old. I quizzed the old lady about the singularity of nearly all the colts and calves in the settlement coming *after* April. 'Ah,' said she, 'you are a single man and young yet, but you *will* learn that Providence arranges these things.' That was a clincher, and I left."

The same year the county commissioners appointed him collector of the resident land tax, and the following is a copy of the land tax duplicate as levied by him that year for the whole township:

Residents' Lands, Ames Township, 1807.

Proprietors.	Acres.	Range.	Township.	Section.	County.	Original Proprietors.	Dollars.	Cents.
Silvanus Ames............108	13	6	4, 9	Athens.	Manasseh Cutler.......		43
John Brown................132	13	6	14	"	Winsor...................		87
Benjamin Brown..........200	13	6	4	"	Man. Cutler..........		80
William Brown 140	13	6	4	"	" "		56
Joseph Bullard............ 60	16	...	...	"	Elisha Whitney........		24
Samuel Beaumont........320	13	6	18	"	John Meigs 1		28
Jacob Boyles...............100	13	6	2	"	Israel Thorndike......		40
David Case.................100	14	...	...	"	Amos Porter............		65
Silas Dean 600	13	6	3	"	Israel Thorndike......2		40
" 340	13	6	24	"	George Wilson.........1		36
" 123	13	6	9	"	Wm. Bartlett...........		49
" 252	13	6	9	"	I. Thorndike............1		05
Reuben Davis............. 80	14	10	7	"	Jno. Alden.............		32
Nehemiah Davis.......... 80	14	10	...	"	" "		32
Benjamin Davis..........100	14	10	...	"	Andrew Peters.........		65
George Ewing, jun.......320	13	6	5	"	Benj. Converse.........1		28
Upton Farmer............. 90	16	...	...	"	Elisha Whitney.........		58
Seth Fuller.................113	13	6	12	Gallia.	William Bartlett........		45
" " 100	12	2	...	Washing.	Matt. Manchester......		80
" " 8	8	...	...	Athens.	" "		4
Joseph Fuller..............195	14	10	...	"	John Dodge.............		78
" " 262	14	10	...	"	Enoch Wing.............1		05
" " 50	14	10	...	"	" "		20
Zebulon Griffin...........320	13	6	18	"	John Meigs.............1		28
" " 262	13	6	18	"	" " 1		05
Abel Glazier..............100	13	6	4	"	Man. Cutler.............		40
Ezra Green................200	13	6	2	"	Israel Thorndike........		80
" " 131	13	6	20	"	Nathan Proctor.........		52
Joab Hoisington......... 66	13	6	14	"	Winsor...................		43
Thomas M. Hamilton..131	13	6	20	"	Nathan Proctor.........		52
Christopher Harold......200	13	6	36	"	Haffield White..........		80
Reuben Hurlbut......... 50	Lot No. 649			"	Jno. Reed...............		20
" " 100	Lot No. 648			"	Jno. Matthews...........		40
Azel Johnson.............215	14	10	18	"	Aug. Blanchard..........		86
Moses Kay................ 50	16	...	...	"	Elisha Whitney.........		20
Noah Linscott............100	13	6	36	"	Haffield Whitney.......		40
Isaac Linscott............ 60	13	6	5	"	Benjamin Converse.....		24
Joseph Linscott.......... 50	13	6	5	"	" "		20
Israel Linscott............ 50	13	6	5	"	" "		20

Ames Township.

RESIDENTS' LANDS—*Continued.*

Proprietors.	Acres.	Range.	Township.	Section.	County.	Original Proprietors.	Dollars.	Cents.
Daniel Lewis	200	...	...	...	Athens.			80
Samuel Mansfield	100	14	10	...	"			40
James McClure	100	9	3	27	Washing.	Samuel Brown		40
Samuel McCune	100	13	6	2	Athens.	Israel Thorndike		40
John McCune	100	13	6	2	"	" "		40
Hosea Neal	46	14	10	17	"	Samuel Hildreth		16
Cyrus Paulk	4	14	10	17	"	" "		2
Joseph Pugsley	100	14	10	17	"	" "		40
Abram Pugsley	390	14	10	17	"	" "	1	56
Robert Palmer	66	13	6	14	"	Winsor		43
Isaac Peterson	50	Lot No. 649			"	Jno. Reed	1	20
Horace Parsons	100	11	9	9	Washing.	Reuben Cooley		40
Jason Rice	112	13	6	4	Athens.	Man'h Cutler	1	44
Isaac Stephens	100	14	10	...	"	Haffield White		40
John Swett	100	13	6	30	"	" "		40
Jonathan Swett	100	(donation).			Washing.	Jonathan Swett		40
Jonathan Swett, sen	100	(donation).			"	" "		40
Elisha Tuttle	100	14	11	11	Athens.	Andrew Peters		40
Solomon Tuttle	130	14	11	11	"	" "		52
Othniel Tuttle	80	14	10	19	"	Nathan Proctor		52
Josiah True	137	14	10	18	"	A. Blanchard		55
" "	100	(donation).			Washing.	Josiah True		40
William Woodward	640	13	7	2	Athens.	R. Underwood	2	56
Nathan Woodbury	902	14	10	6	"	Nathan Woodbury	3	60
" "	100	11	9	...	"	" "		40
" "	8	...	...	...	"	" "		4
" "	160	9	2	23	Washing.	" "		64
" "	100	11	9	9	"	" "		40
" "	City lot, Marietta.				"	" "		...
Daniel Weethee	175	14	10	18	Athens.	A. Blanchard		70
John Wilson	150	14	10	...	"	Jno. Dodge		98
George Walker	100	13	6	7	"	Jno. Friend		40
George Wolf	100	13	6	36	"	H. White		40
Jonathan Watkins	100	13	6	36	"	" "		40
Joshua Wyatt	640	13	6	1	"	Peter Shaw	2	56

Total amount of duplicate..................$47 41

The first election for township officers in Ames was held June 1, 1802 (nearly three years before the organization of the county), at the house of Silvanus Ames, and resulted as follows:

Nathan Woodbury, George Ewing and Samuel Brown, trustees; Daniel Weethee, clerk; Josiah True and Samuel Brown, overseers of the poor; Nathan Woodbury, Joseph Pugsley and John Swett, fence viewers; George Wolf and Christopher Herrold, house appraisers; Daniel Converse, lister; Samuel Brown and Benjamin Brown, supervisors; Daniel Converse and Silvanus Ames, constables.

In 1803 the following were elected:

Benjamin Brown, Silvanus Ames and Daniel Weethee, trustees; George Ewing, clerk; Nathan Woodbury and Joshua Wyatt, overseers of the poor; Benjamin Brown, John Brown and Samuel Brown, fence viewers; Jacob Boyles and Edmund Dorr, house appraisers; Josiah True, lister; William Brown, John Brown and Josiah True, supervisors; William Brown and Josiah True, constables.

Township Trustees since 1804.

1804	David Boyles,	Azel Johnson,	Nathan Woodbury.
1805	Benjamin Brown,	Josiah True,	Daniel Weethee.
1806	Ephraim Cutler,	John Brown,	"
1807	Abel Glazier,	Benjamin Davis,	Zebulon Griffin.
1808	Robert Palmer,	Reuben J. Davis,	George Walker.
1809–10	Seth Fuller,	Josiah True,	George Wolf.
1811	Silvanus Ames,	George Ewing,	Daniel Weethee.
1812	Joshua Wyatt,	Seth Fuller,	John Brown, 2d.
1813–15	Ezra Green,	"	"
1816	Jason Rice,	Russell S. Lovell,	Daniel Phillips.
1817	Silvanus Ames,	"	Jonas Rice.
1818	Jacob Boarman,	"	Ezra Green.
1819	"	John Brown,	"
1820	Seth Fuller,	James Cable,	James Mitchell.
1821	"	"	Ezra Walker.

Ames Township.

Trustees—*Continued.*

1822–23	John Wyatt,	Charles Cutler,	Alanson Hibbard.
1824	"	Jacob Boarman,	David Trowbridge.
1825	John Columbia,	John Boyles,	John M. Hibbard.
1826	Charles Cutler,	Elisha McEvers,	Morris Bryson.
1827–28	Sabinus Rice,	L. G. Brown,	"
1829	Absalom Boyles,	Jacob Boarman,	John B. Brown.
1830	James Brawley,	"	Gulliver Dean.
1831	Daniel Cable,	George Black,	"
1832	Silvanus Howe,	"	Jonathan Buzzard.
1833	John Carter,	Sabinus Rice,	"
1834	"	Absalom Boyles,	Silvanus Howe.
1835	L. G. Brown,	John B. Miller,	"
1836	"	Lewis Rathburn,	Daniel S. McDougal.
1837	R. G. Carter,	"	"
1838	"	Charles Cutler,	"
1839	Daniel Rose,	William Robinson,	"
1840–45	John T. Glazier,	John Carter,	James G. Owen.
1846–49	"	D. S. McDougal,	Solomon Koons.
1850	George Linscott,	"	"
1851–52	James Patterson,	"	"
1853	"	G. M. McDougal,	"
1854–55	"	"	George Linscott.
1856–57	Almon Henry,	"	"
1858	John E. Vore,	"	"
1859–60	"	F. L. Junod,	"
1861	Moses Curtis,	Solomon Koons,	E. P. Henry.
1862	F. L. Junod,	C. J. Brown,	G. W. Wright.
1863	"	"	C. H. Wyatt.
1864–65	N. P. Hoisington,	"	Daniel Fleming.
1866	"	Almon Henry,	"
1867	"	Edmund Wheeler,	O. N. Owen.
1868	"	Daniel Fleming,	Ezra Wolfe.

Township Clerks since 1804.

1804, Benjamin Brown; 1805, Harris Parsons; 1806, Geo. Walker; 1807, Benj. Davis; 1808, Martin Boyles; 1809–18, George Walker; 1819–22, Benjamin Davis; 1823–24, Sabinus Rice; 1825–26, David Trowbridge; 1827–28, Geo. Walker, Jun.; 1829–30, Wm. R. Walker; 1831, Hiram Cable; 1832–44, R. A. Fulton; 1845 to present time, J. H. Glazier.

Justices of the Peace.

1803—Ephraim Cutler, Samuel Brown.
1805—John Brown.
1806—Daniel Weethee.

JUSTICES OF THE PEACE—*Continued.*

1807—George Walker.
1808—John Brown, Jonathan Watkins.
1810—George Walker, Benjamin Davis.
1811—Thos. M. Hamilton.
1813—George Walker—served till 1830.
1819—Martin Boyles—served till about 1828.
1828—John Brown.
1831—Wm. R. Walker, John B. Brown.
1834—Sabinus Rice, Charles Carter.
1837—R. A. Fulton.
1840—H. B. Brawley, R. A. Fulton.
1843—R. A. Fulton.
1845—James Bryson.
1846—Henry Clark, Lewis Rathburn.
1847—Henry Clark, James Bryson.
1849—J. M. Mitchell.
1850—Henry Clark, James Bryson.
1852—J. M. Mitchell, J. G. Owen.
1853—James Bryson.
1855—R. A. Fulton, Jas. G. Owen.
1857—Gilbert M. McDougal.
1858—Robert A. Fulton, James G. Owen.
1860—Gilbert M. McDougal.
1861—Robert A. Fulton, William Mason.
1862—James G. Owen.
1863—F. L. Junod, R. R. Ellis.
1864—Lewis Carpenter.
1865—Frederick P. Kasler, James M. Mitchell.
1866—N. P. Hoisington.
1868—Lorenzo Fulton, David L. Rathburn.

H. B. Brawley served one term about 1840; Lewis Rathburn a term, elected about 1845, and William

Mason a term, about 1846; but the records do not furnish exact dates.

The original township of Ames contained three hundred and sixty square miles—more than one fourth of the territorial area of Rhode Island. By the formation of new townships and counties at intervals during forty years, her extensive domain has been reduced to six miles square—the limits of a regular surveyed township. Ames has not kept pace with some other parts of the county in population, being now ninth in that regard; but in respect of the *character* of her population, business enterprise, moral and educational movements, etc., she is second to none.

Amesville, handsomely located and well built, is a thriving and interesting village. One of the best academies in the county is located here. It originated in a meeting of the citizens held in November, 1852, to consider their educational wants, when George Wyatt, Robert Henry, J. T. Glazier, James Patterson, and A. S. Dickey, were appointed a committee to report a plan for organizing a seminary. They reported on the 25th of that month, and this action was followed in due time by the incorporation of "The Amesville Academy."

The school has been exceedingly well sustained, and is one of marked usefulness. Its teachers have been Mr. J. P. Weethee, from 1854 to 1856; P. B. Davis, from 1856 to 1857; A. C. Kelly, from 1857 to 1858; Mr. McGonagle, from 1858 to 1860; E. P. Henry, from 1860 to 1861; J. H. Doan, from 1861 to 1862; J. M. Goodspeed, from 1862 to 1864; Miss L. M. Dowling, from 1864 to 1866. The present teachers are the Rev. H. C. Cheadle, principal, and Miss M. G. Keyes, assistant, under whose management the school is growing in popularity and usefulness.

The population of Ames in 1820 was 721; in 1830 it was 857; in 1840 it was 1,431; in 1850 it was 1,482; in 1860 it was 1,335.

Personal and Biographical.

Ephraim Cutler, known in the early history of Athens county as Judge Cutler, was the oldest son of Dr. Manasseh Cutler, and was born at Edgartown, Duke's county, Massachusetts, April 12th, 1767. He did not receive a collegiate education, but, being an industrious reader, he acquired during youth considerable mental culture, and a large store of useful knowledge. From the age of three years he lived with his grandparents, at Killingly, Connecticut, both of whom he was wont to mention in after life with great respect and affection. His grandfather was a pure and pious man, and an ardent patriot. In a sketch written long afterward, Judge Cutler says:

"I well remember that the express with the news of the battle of Lexington, which was the commencement of the revolutionary struggle, came directly to my grandfather's house in the night after the battle. He was in bed, and I slept with him. He arose immediately and fired his gun three times, which was, doubtless, the agreed signal, as it was universally expected that there would be an attack from the British. Before sunrise he, with fifteen others, had started for the battlefield. Before leaving he gave a particular charge to his housekeeper to provide carefully for the wants of any soldier who might call during his absence."

In 1787 Mr. Cutler married Miss Leah Atwood, of Killingly, a lady whose great worth and excellence of character were for many years well known in Athens county. After his marriage he engaged for a few years in mercantile pursuits at Killingly. In 1795 he accepted the agency of the Ohio Company, in which he had been a shareholder from the beginning, and, on the 15th of June in that year, set out with his wife and four children for the company's purchase in the northwestern territory. The journey was made in the usual way of that time—in wagons across the mountains to the headwaters of the Ohio, and thence down the river in a small flat boat. While descending the river they lost two of their children, Hezekiah, the youngest, and Mary, the eldest, whose remains were buried in the forest on the banks of the beautiful river. They arrived at Marietta, September 18, 1795, having been more than three months on the way, and thirty-one days on the river. At Marietta Mr. Cutler lay sick for several weeks in the block house. As soon as he was able they proceeded to the garrison at Waterford, where they remained till the spring of 1799. The circumstances of his removal to and settlement in Ames, in 1799, are narrated elsewhere. Mr. and Mrs. Cutler brought with them to their new home four children—Nancy and Charles, born in New England, and Mary and Daniel, born in Waterford. All of these, except Charles, are still living. Nancy, now Mrs. Carter, lives in Franklin county, Ohio. Mary, Mrs. Gulliver Dean, lives in Ames township, near the old Cutler homestead. Daniel lives in Kansas and is an intelligent and prosperous farmer.

For the next few years Mr. Cutler devoted himself with great energy to developing the interests of the Ohio Company, and of the Amesville settlement in particular, taking a leading part in all the social, political and educational movements of the day. During the first year of his residence in the territory he had been commissioned by Governor St. Clair captain of the militia, justice of the peace, judge of the court of quarter sessions and of the court of common pleas. He was appointed by the territorial legislature, at its first session, one of the seven commissioners to lease the school and ministerial lands in each township of the Ohio Company's purchase. In September, 1801, while living in Ames, Judge Cutler was elected to represent Washington county in the territorial legislature. At this legislature, which sat at Chillicothe, the question of the formation of a state government came up, and Judge Cutler and his colleague, William R. Putnam, were the only two who voted against the measure. In doing this they represented the wishes of their constituents, who were opposed to forming a state government so soon. This vote made them for a short time very unpopular in Chillicothe, and for two nights a mob threatened to attack the house where they boarded. In September, 1802, still living in Ames, Judge Cutler was chosen as one of the four delegates from Washington county to the convention to form a state constitution. In this convention, and in the framing of the first constitution of Ohio, he exercised a large influence. Article III, establishing the judicial system of the state, was almost wholly shaped and drafted by him. But the greatest service rendered by Judge Cutler in this convention was his determined opposition to the introduction of slavery into the state of Ohio; for, strange as it may seem, a strong effort was made to fasten this system on the state, notwithstanding the positive language and the solemn compact of the ordinance of 1787. There were delegates in the convention who, representing the sentiments of settlers from slave-holding states, claimed that the ordinance was in the nature of a contract, and was not binding till its terms had been accepted by the new state; and, consequently, that if she chose to reject any portion of the proposed terms, it was competent for her to do so, while adopting her fundamental law and becoming a state. We have not space to describe the contest in detail. A determined effort was made by the party referred to to plant slavery on the soil of Ohio, and the great name and influence of Thomas Jefferson were used to further the attempt.* Judge Cutler stood in the breach, and with all his power and great persistency battled against this movement. His friends rallied around him; he was finally successful, and to Ephraim Cutler more than to any other man posterity is indebted for shutting and barring the doors against the introduction into Ohio of the monstrous system of African slavery.

Mr. Cutler also took a leading part in framing and securing the passage of secs. 3, 25 and 26 of article VIII of the constitution, relating to religion and education.

In December, 1806, Judge Cutler removed from Athens to Washington county, settling on the Ohio river about six miles below Marietta. Here his first wife died in 1807. In 1808 he married Sarah Parker, a native of Newburyport, Massachusetts. Four of the children by this marriage are still living, the only son, William P. Cutler, being esteemed among the first men in the state.†

---

*It was then a theory of Jefferson's that the extension of slavery diluted and weakened it. He desired, or at least professed to desire, its extinction.

†He was born near Marietta, July 12, 1813; was a member of the Ohio legislature from 1844 to 1846, officiating as speaker of the house during his last term; was a member of the constitutional convention of 1850; afterwards was for some years president of the Marietta & Cincinnati Railroad Company; was elected in 1860 a representative to the 37th congress, and has been for a few years past again officially connected with the above mentioned railroad.

In 1818 Judge Cutler again appeared in public life as a member of the Ohio legislature from Washington county. We regret that we can not exhibit in detail his noble services at this period of his life; we can only state the results. He succeeded in changing the land tax system from a direct tax to an *ad valorem* basis. Prior to 1824 the whole burden of state taxes was laid on the lands as a direct tax, levied by the acre and without reference to value. Consequently thinly populated counties like Athens and Washington actually paid more into the treasury than wealthy and populous counties like Hamilton and Butler. The system was grossly unequal and oppressive. Judge Cutler's clear vision enabled him to perceive this, and he labored long and successfully to change it, so that taxes should be assessed on the whole property of the people according to value.

His other great achievement at this time was the establishment of an excellent common school system. The first public allusion to education in Ohio is found in an oration by Solomon Drown, delivered at Marietta, April 7th, 1789. The first memorial on behalf of the general interest of public schools read in the Ohio legislature was offered in 1816, by the Rev. Samuel P. Robbins, of Marietta, but prior to 1820 there was no organized sentiment in the state on the subject of common schools, and no general legislation. In 1821 the legislature passed an act for the regulation

Eng‡ by A H Ritchie

JUDGE EPHRAIM CUTLER.

OHIO VALLEY HISTORICAL SERIES.

Robert Clarke & Co. Publishers, Cincinnati, O.

and support of common schools, but it did not provide any adequate revenue for their maintenance, and was by no means an efficient system. The common school question was an issue in the elections of 1824. Several ardent advocates of a thorough system were elected, among them Judge Cutler, as senator from Washington county. We do not aver that he alone deserves the credit for the success of the measure in the legislature of 1824–5, but he was the acknowledged leader of the friends of common schools, and his experience in public affairs and as a legislator rendered his services of the greatest value. On the 5th of February, 1825, an excellent school bill, providing a thorough system and liberal support therefor by taxation, was passed by the legislature. When the vote in the senate was taken, Judge Cutler and Mr. Nathan Guilford (senator from Cincinnati, who was an ardent and able friend of the cause, and who drafted the bill), were standing side by side. When the result was announced, a majority for the bill of twenty-two votes, Judge Cutler turned to Mr. Guilford, and, with great solemnity and earnestness, said: "Now, Lord, lettest thou thy servant depart in peace, according to thy word, for mine eyes have seen thy salvation."

The latter years of Judge Cutler's life were spent quietly at his place in Washington county, amid the enjoyments of home and the affectionate attention of relatives and friends. He died July 8th, 1853.

George Ewing, commonly called during his residence in the county Lieut. Ewing, was, it is believed, the first white settler within the bounds of what is now Ames township. A native of Salem, New Jersey, he entered the continental army at the beginning of the revolutionary war, and served with credit during its whole course. For his bravery and good conduct he received, soon after entering the service, a commission as first lieutenant of the Jersey Line, which position he held till the return of peace. Shortly after the conclusion of the war he emigrated to what is now Ohio county, West Virginia, which then constituted the very frontier of civilization, and was, with the surrounding region, the scene of many a bloody conflict between the "Long-Knives" and the red men. After a few years' residence here he removed with his wife and young family, in 1793, to the Waterford settlement, on the Muskingum river, where he passed a year or two in the block house, until the danger from Indian attacks, then imminent, had passed. In the spring of 1798, Lieutenant Ewing, encouraged and assisted by Judge Cutler, removed his family to a place seventeen miles northwest of the frontier settlements, in what is now Ames township, and became the pioneer of that section of country. He settled on what is now known as the Thomas Gardiner farm. During the period of his residence here he was an active supporter of schools and every means of developing and improving the community. He was chosen township trustee at the first election, in 1802, and in after years filled that position and the office of township clerk. He was fond of reading, possessed a bright and active mind, and a fund of sterling sense, combined with lively wit and good humor. In 1818 he removed to Perry county, Indiana, where he died about the year 1830.

Thomas Ewing, son of the last named, was born in Ohio county, West Virginia, December 28th, 1789. The following autobiographical sketch, kindly furnished for these pages by this now great and venerable man, will be read with especial interest:

My father settled in what is now Ames township, Athens county, early in April, 1798. He removed from the mouth of Olive Green creek, on the Muskingum river, and the nearest neighbor with whom he had association, was, in that direction, distant about eighteen miles. There were a few families settled, about the same time, on or near the present site of the town of Athens, but no road or even pathway led to them; the distance was about twelve miles. There was also an old pioneer hunter encamped at the mouth of Federal creek, distant about ten miles. This, as far as I know, comprised the population statistics of what is now Athens county. I do not know the date of the settlement in what was called No. 5—Cooley's settlement—it was early.

At the time of my father's removal, I was with my aunt, Mrs. Morgan, near West Liberty, Virginia, going to school. I was a few months in my ninth year. Early in the year 1798, I think in May, my uncle brought me home. We descended the Ohio river in a flat boat to the mouth of Little Hocking, and crossed a bottom and a pine hill along a dim foot path, some ten or fifteen miles, and took quarters for the night at Dailey's camp. I was tired and slept well on the bear-skin bed which the rough old dame spread for me, and in the morning my uncle engaged a son of our host, a boy of eighteen, who had seen my father's cabin, to pilot us.

I was now at home, and fairly an inceptive citizen of the future Athens county. The young savage, our pilot, was much struck with some of the rude implements of civilization which he saw my brother using, especially the auger, and expressed the opinion that with an axe and an auger a man could make everything he wanted except a gun and bullet molds. My brother was engaged in making some bedsteads. He had already finished a table, in the manufacture of which he had used also an adze to smooth the plank, which he split in good width from straight grained trees. Transportation was exceedingly difficult, and our furniture, of the rudest kind, composed of articles of the first necessity. Our kitchen utensils were "the big kettle," "the little kettle," the bake oven, frying pan, and pot; the latter had a small hole in the bottom which was mended with a button, keyed with a nail through the eye on the outside of the pot. We had no table furniture that would break—little of any kind. Our meat—bear meat, or raccoon, with venison or turkey, cooked together and seasoned to the taste (a most savory dish)—was cut up in morsels and placed in the centre of the table, and the younger members of the family, armed with sharpened sticks, helped themselves about as well as with four-tined forks; great care was taken in selecting wholesome sticks, as sassafras, spice-bush, hazel, or hickory. Sometimes the children were allowed, by way of pic-nic, to cut with the butcher-knife from the fresh bear meat and venison their slices and stick them, alternately, on a sharpened spit and roast before a fine hickory fire; this made a most royal dish. Bears, deer, and raccoons remained in abundance, until replaced by herds of swine. The great west would have settled slowly without *corn* and *hogs*. A bushel of seed wheat will produce, at the end of ten months, fifteen or twenty bushels; a bushel of corn, at the end of five months, four hundred bushels, and it is used to much advantage for the last two months. Our horned cattle do not double in a year; hogs, in the same time, increase twenty fold. It was deemed almost sacrilege to kill a sheep, and I remember well the first beef I tasted. I thought it coarse and stringy compared with venison. We had wild fruits of several varieties, very abundant, and some of them exceedingly fine. There was a sharp ridge quite near my father's house, on which I had selected four or five service or juneberry bushes, that I could easily climb, and kept an eye on them till they should get fully ripe. At the proper time, I went with one of my sisters to gather them, but a bear had been in advance of me. The limbs of all the bushes were brought down to the trunk like a folded umbrella, and the berries all gone; there were plenty still in the woods for children and bears, but few so choice or easy of access as these. We had a great variety of wild plums, some exceedingly fine—better, to my taste, than the best tame varieties. I have not seen any of the choice varieties within the last thirty years.

We, of course, had no mills. The nearest was on Wolf creek, about fourteen miles distant; from this we brought our first summer's supply of breadstuffs. After we gathered our first crop of corn my father instituted a hand mill which, as a kind of common property, supplied the neighborhood, after we had neighbors, for several years, until Christopher Herrold set up a horse mill on the ridge, and Henry Barrows a water mill near the mouth of Federal creek.

For the first year I was a lonely boy. My brother George, eleven years older than I, was too much a man to be my companion, and my sisters could not be with me, generally, in the woods and among the rocks and caves; but a small spaniel dog, almost as intelligent as a boy, was always with me. I was the reader of the family, but we had few books. I remember but but one beside "Watts' Psalms and Hymns" that a child could read—" The Vicar of Wakefield," which was almost committed to memory—the poetry which it contained, entirely.

Our first neighbor was Capt. Benjamin Brown, who had been an officer in the Revolutionary war. He was a man of strong intellect, without much culture. He told me many anecdotes of the war which interested me, and, among other things that I remember, gave me an account of Doctor Jenner's then recent discovery of the kine pox as a preventive of the small pox, better than I have ever yet read in any written treatise, and I remember it better than any account which I have since read. He lent me a book—one number of a periodical called the " Athenian Oracle"—something like our modern " Notes and Queries," from which, however, I learned but little. I found, too, a companion in his son, John, four years my senior, still enjoying sound health in his ripe old age.

In 1801, some one of my father's family being ill, Dr. Baker, who lived at Waterford, eighteen miles distant, was called in. He took notice of me as a reading boy, and told me he had a book he would lend me if I would come for it. I got leave of my father and went, the little spaniel being my traveling companion. The book was a translation of Virgil, the Bucolics and Georgics torn out, but the Æneid perfect. I have not happened to meet with the translation since, and do not know whose it was. The opening lines, as I remember them, were—

> " Arms and the man I sing who first from Troy,
> Came to the Italian and Lavinian shores,
> Exiled by fate, much tossed by land and sea,
> By power divine and cruel Juno's rage;
> Much, too, in war, he suffered, till he reared
> A city, and to Latium brought his gods—
> Hence sprung his Latin progeny, the kings
> Of Alba, and the walls of towering Rome."

When I returned home with my book, and for some weeks after, my father had hands employed in clearing a new field. On Sundays, and at leisure hours I read to them, and never had a more attentive audience. At that point in the narrative, where

Æneas discloses to Dido his purpose of leaving her, and tells her of the vision of Mercury bearing the mandate of Jove, one of the men sprang to his feet, declared he did not believe a word of that—he had got tired of her, and it was all a made up story as an excuse to be off—and it was a d——d shame after what she had done for him. So the reputation of Æneas suffered by that day's reading.

Our next neighbors were Ephraim Cutler, Silvanus Ames, William Brown, a married son of the Captain; and, four or five miles distant, Nathan Woodbury, George Wolf, and Christopher Herrold—and about the same time, or a little later, Silas Dean, a rich old bachelor, Martin Boyles, and John and Samuel McCune. Mr. Cutler and my father purchased "Morse's Geography," the first edition, about 1800, for his oldest son, Charles, and myself—it in effect became my book, as Charles never used it, and I studied it most intently. By this, with such explanations as my father gave me, I acquired quite a competent knowledge of geography, and something of general history.

About this time the neighbors in our and the surrounding settlements, met and agreed to purchase books and to make a common library. They were all poor, and subscriptions small, but they raised in all about one hundred dollars. All my accumulated wealth, ten coon-skins, went into the fund, and Squire Sam. Brown, of Sunday creek, who was going to Boston, was charged with the purchase. After an absence of many weeks, he brought the books to Capt. Ben. Brown's in a sack on a pack horse. I was present at the untying of the sack and pouring out of the treasure. There were about sixty volumes, I think, and well selected; the library of the Vatican was nothing to it, and there never was a library better read. This, with occasional additions, furnished me with reading while I remained at home.

We were quite fortunate in our schools. Moses Everett, a graduate of Yale, but an intemperate young man, who had been banished by his friends, was our first teacher; after him,

Charles Cutler, a brother of Ephraim, and also a graduate of Yale. They were learned young men and faithful to their vocation. They boarded alternate weeks with their scholars, and made the winter evenings pleasant and instructive. After Barrows' mill was built at the mouth of Federal creek, I being the mill boy, used to take my two-horse loads of grain in the evening, have my grist ground, and take it home in the morning. There was an eccentric person living near the mill whose name was Jones (we called him Doctor); he was always dressed in deer-skin, his principal vocation being hunting, and I always found him in the evening, in cool weather, lying with his feet to the fire. He was a scholar, banished no doubt for intemperance; he had books, and finding my fancy for them, had me read to him, while he lay drying his feet. He was fond of poetry, and did something to correct my pronunciation and prosody. Thus, the excessive use of alcohol was the indirect means of furnishing me with school teachers.

My father entertained the impression that I would one day be a scholar, though quite unable to lend me any pecuniary aid. I grew up with the same impression until, in my nineteenth year, I almost abandoned hope. On reflection, however, I determined to make one effort to earn the means to procure an education. Having got the summer's work well disposed of, I asked of my father leave to go for a few months and try my fortune. He consented, and I set out on foot next morning, made my way through the woods to the Ohio river, got on a keel boat as a hand at small wages, and in about a week landed at Kanawha salines. I engaged and went to work at once, and in three months satisfied myself that I could earn money slowly but surely, and on my return home in December, 1809, I went to Athens and spent three months there as a student, by way of testing my capacity. I left the academy in the spring with a sufficiently high opinion of myself, and returned to Kanawha to earn money to complete my education. This year I was successful, paid off some debts which troubled my father, and returned home and spent the winter with the new books which had accumulated in the library, which, with my father's aid, I read to much advantage. I went to Kanawha the third year, and after a severe summer's labor I returned home with about six hundred dollars in money, but sick and exhausted. Instead, however, of sending for a physician, I got Don Quixote, a recent purchase, from the library, and laughed myself well in about ten days. I then went to Athens, entered as a regular student, and continued my studies there till the spring of 1815, when I left, a pretty good though an irregular scholar. During my academic term I went to Gallipolis and taught school a quarter and studied French.* I found my funds likely to fall short,

---

*While pursuing his studies, Mr. Ewing was also occasionally employed by the commissioners of Athens county as a surveyor, to run country roads, and such entries as the following appear in the records of that period:

"*March 7th*, 1814. A petition signed by George Ewing and others, praying for a road, beginning at the Thirty-One mile tree in Ames township, on the state road; thence passing through the west part of Amos Linscott's improvement, to the mouth of Ewing's run; thence to intersect the Lancaster road near Abel Glazier's. Read in open meeting. Order issued."

"*March 8th*. The commissioners appoint Thomas Ewing surveyor, and Jehiel Gregory, Jr., John White, and Stephen Pilcher viewers of said road, to meet at the house of Jno. Brown, Esq., in Ames township, on Monday, March 21, at 10 o'clock, A. M."

"*June 8th*, 1814. County of Athens to Thomas Ewing, Dr. To surveying, protracting, etc., the above road, 1½ days, at $1 50 per day. (Paid.) - - - - - $2 25"

* * * * * *

"*June 6th*, 1815. The Board appointed George Walker, John Brown 2d, and Ezra Green viewers, and Thomas Ewing surveyor of the road petitioned for by Elisha Alderman and others, in Ames township."

and went a fourth time to Kanawha, where, in six weeks, I earned one hundred and fifty dollars, which I thought would suffice, and returned to my studies; after two years' rest the severe labor in the salines this time went hard with me.

After finishing my studies at Athens, I read Blackstone's Commentaries at home, and in July, 1815, went to Lancaster to study law. A. B. Walker, then a boy of about fifteen years, accompanied me to Lancaster to bring back my horse, and I remained and studied law with Gen. Beecher. I was admitted to the bar in August, 1816, after fourteen months' very diligent study—the first six months about sixteen hours a day.

"*July* 17*th*, 1815. County of Athens to Thomas Ewing, Dr. To surveying and protracting the above road, including chain carriers, axemen, &c.   -   -   -   -   -   -   - $4 10"

Mr. Ewing says he was, on leaving college, "a pretty good, though an irregular scholar." The extent of his education is somewhat shown by the following extract from the records of the Ohio university :

"*May* 3*d*, 1815. The committee appointed by the board of trustees to examine Thomas Ewing and John Hunter, condidates for a degree of bachelor of arts and sciences, beg leave to report :

That they have examined the applicants aforesaid in the different branches of literature, viz: in grammar, rhetoric, the languages, natural and moral philosophy, logic, astronomy, geography, and the various branches of mathematics, and that they have witnessed with much gratification the proficiency made by the before named students. They therefore report the following resolutions :

1. *Resolved*, That the said Thomas Ewing and John Hunter merit the approbation of the board of trustees, and that they are each entitled to a degree of bachelor of arts and sciences.

2. That the president be authorized and required to inform the said Thomas Ewing and John Hunter that they are each so entitled to such degree in this seminary, and your committee recommend that the same be conferred.

3. That the secretary of the board deliver to the said Thomas Ewing and John Hunter each a copy of these resolutions.

JESSUP N. COUCH,
CHARLES R. SHERMAN,
STEPHEN LINDLEY,
J. LAWRENCE LEWIS,

} *Committee.*

Report accepted."

I made my first speech at Circleville, the November following. Gen. Beecher first gave me slander case to study and prepare. I spent much time with it, but time wasted, as the cause was continued the first day of the court. He then gave me a case of contract, chiefly in depositions, which I studied diligently, but that also was continued; a few minutes afterward a case was called, and Gen. Beecher told me *that* was ready—the jury was sworn, witnesses called, and the cause went on. In the examination of one of the witnesses, I thought I discovered an important fact not noticed by either counsel, and I asked leave to cross-examine further. I elicited the fact which was decisive of the case. This gave me confidence. I argued the cause closely and well, and was abundantly congratulated by the members of the bar who were present.

My next attempt was in Lancaster. Mr. Sherman, father of the general, asked me to argue a cause of his, which gave room for some discussion. I had short notice, but was quite successful, and, the cause being appealed, Mr. Sherman sent his client to employ me with him. I had as yet got no fees, and my funds were very low. This November I attended the Athens court. I had nothing to do there, but met an old neighbor, Elisha Alderman, who wanted me to go to Marietta, to defend his brother, a boy, who was to be tried for larceny. It was out of my intended beat, but I wanted business and fees, and agreed to go for $25, of which I received $10 in hand. I have had several fees since of $10,000 and upwards, but never one of which I felt the value, or in truth as valuable to me as this. I went, tried my boy, and he was convicted, but the court granted a new trial. On my way to Marietta at the next term I thought of a ground of excluding the evidence, which had escaped me on the first trial. It was not obvious, but sound. I took it, excluded the evidence and acquitted my client. This caused a sensation. I was employed at once in twelve penitentiary cases, under indictment at that term, for making and passing counterfeit money, horse stealing and perjury. As a professional man my fortune was thus briefly made.

Mr. Ewing's professional career thus begun, was destined to be one of uninterrupted success. In 1816 he was appointed by the commissioners prosecutor for Athens county, and continued for many years to attend the courts of Athens regularly. His eminent abilities soon gave him a commanding position among the lawyers of Ohio, and in 1830 he was elected to the United States senate, where he remained till 1837. He was a member of President Harrison's cabinet, as secretary of the treasury, in 1841. On the accession of President Taylor, in 1849, he was invited into the cabinet, and became secretary of the interior. In 1850 he was appointed United States senator from Ohio, holding the position till 1851, when he retired from public life and resumed the practice of law. As a lawyer, orator, publicist and statesman, Thomas Ewing ranks among the greatest the United States has produced, and Athens county may well be proud to have nourished, during his childhood and youth, so noble a citizen.

Capt. Benjamin Brown, father of General John, and of Judge A. G. Brown, and one of the most prominent among the early settlers of Ames, was born October 17, 1745, at Leicester, Massachusetts. His grandfather, William Brown, came from England to America while a youth, was the first settler in the town of Hatfield, on the Connecticut river, and was often engaged in the Indian wars of that period. Capt. John Brown, father of Benjamin, served with credit in the colonial army during the French war, and represented the town of Leicester in the Massachusetts legislature during, and for many years after, the revolutionary war. In February, 1775, Benjamin Brown, then thirty years old, joined a regiment of minute men, and two months later was engaged in active hostilities. In May he was commissioned a lieutenant in Colonel Prescott's regiment of the Massachusetts line, and in June participated in the battle of Bunker's Hill. Two of his brothers, Pearly and John Brown, were also engaged in this battle, the latter being dangerously wounded in two places, and borne off the field during the engagement. This brother Pearly was subsequently killed at the battle of White Plains, and another brother, William, died in hospital. In January, 1777, Lieut. Brown was commissioned a captain in the eighth regiment Massachusetts line. His regiment took a very active part in the operations directed against Burgoyne during the summer of 1777, and Capt. Brown was engaged in nearly all of the battles that preceded Burgoyne's surrender, in some of which he particularly distinguished himself by his gallantry and daring. A short time after this he was offered the position of aide-de-camp on Baron Steuben's staff, but declined it, fearing that his military knowledge was inadequate. In 1779, compelled by the necessities of his family and other personal reasons, he resigned his commission and returned home to provide for their support. About the year 1789 he removed with his family to Hartford, Washington county, New York, then a new settlement, whence he again migrated in the fall of 1796, and sought a home in the northwestern territory. He reached Marietta in the spring of 1797, and in 1799 came to Ames township, in company with Judge Cutler, as elsewhere stated. He was one of the prominent citizens during the time he resided in Ames, holding various township offices, and contributing largely to the advancement of the settlement. In 1817, his health becoming feeble, he went to live with his son, Gen. John Brown, in Athens, and here he died in October, 1821.

His wife, whom he married in Massachusetts in 1772, and who bore him a large family of children, died at Athens in 1840, aged eighty-six years.

John Brown (nephew of Capt. Brown), born February 10, 1774, at Leicester, Massachusetts, married Miss Polly Green, of Spencer, Massachusetts, in 1797, and set out for the Ohio Company's purchase in the autumn of 1801. He brought his young family and few effects over the mountains, with one horse, in a little wagon, and, when descending difficult places in the road, attached a small tree to the rear end of his wagon, to act as a break, or lock. When he reached Wheeling, on the Ohio river, after a most toilsome journey, he "swapped" his wagon for a canoe and two heifers, and proceeded down the river toward his destination. His second son, Lemuel Green Brown, was born the day after their landing, near Marietta, and the head of the family found himself in these rather difficult circumstances, with but fifty cents in his pocket. As soon as practicable he resumed travel, and reached Ames township in March, 1802. He first settled on the farm now owned and occupied by the heirs of Stephen Green, where he lived for a short time, and thence moved to where John D. Brown now lives. He was soon elected a justice of the peace, and was frequently re-elected, holding the position, altogether, twenty-seven years. He was also at one time one of the appraisers of the college lands in this county, and of the same in Miami county. In 1811 he built a brick house on his farm in Ames (one of the first brick houses, if not the first, erected in this part of the county), where for many years he kept public house. Being situated on the principal thoroughfare from Marietta westward, it was, during fifteen or twenty years, much resorted to by travelers. The building was standing till within a few years. Of excellent business capacity, and of a kind and genial nature, Mr. Brown was always able and willing to relieve the poor and help the distressed. His house was at all times open for religious services, and a list was made of seventy-two preachers, who, at different times, had held meetings there. He was twice married, and his second wife is still living in the county, nearly eighty years old. He died July 23, 1833.

Pearly Brown, oldest son of the preceding, was born in Massachusetts, July 24, 1798, and was four years old when brought to this county. In the year 1819 he married Eliza Hulbert (who is still living), and settled in Ames township, on a new farm, given him by his father. A hard-working and energetic man, he soon improved his circumstances, and laid the foundation for a competence. To afford some idea of the prices that prevailed when he was a young man, Mr. Brown states that he worked a week for Judge Currier, in Athens, in 1823, at 31¼ cents a day, and at Saturday night was paid in two tin cups at 25 cents each; a quarter of a pound of tea, 50 cents; one pound of coffee, 50 cents, and 37½ cents in money—making $1.87½—with which valuables he walked home—ten miles. While yet living with his father, in 1814 or 1815, he was hired to carry the mail, with two other riders, between Marietta and Chillicothe, the distance being about one hundred miles, and to make three trips a week, or two hundred miles a week for each rider; for which service he received $6 a month. He cultivated his farm in Ames till 1829 or 1830, when he removed to McArthurstown (then in Athens county), and engaged for many years in selling goods and dealing in live stock. In 1839 he and his partners drove across the mountains to the eastern markets 2,100 cattle, 1,300 hogs, 1,800 sheep and 20 horses. He was at the same time quite extensively engaged in the mercantile business with his brother, Samuel H. Brown, well known in the county for many years, and till his death in 1854, as an untiring business man. Pearly Brown has held the positions of county commissioner and justice of the peace, and is widely known in this and adjoining counties as a man of unswerving integrity. He has reared a family of three sons and six daughters. His oldest son, Pinckney Brown, is an extensive dealer in live stock.

John B. Brown, another son of John, was born in the year 1803, in Ames township, where he has lived ever since. He has been successful in life, and is respected as one of the solid men of the community.

Samuel H. Brown, youngest son of John, was born in Ames township, October 8th, 1807. He became an active business man, and well known in southern Ohio and in the eastern markets as an extensive and successful cattle dealer, in which business he engaged, with little intermission, for over twenty-two years. He served as justice of the peace and associate judge in this county. He removed to Meigs county about 1850, and died there October 2d, 1854. He was an honest and capable man.

Samuel Brown, brother of John and nephew of Capt. Benjamin Brown, a native of Massachusetts, came to the northwestern territory in 1797, and settled with his family on "Round Bottom," on the Muskingum river. In the year 1800 he bought a piece of land on Sunday creek, within the limits of Ames township as soon after defined, but in the present township of Dover. In 1805 he returned to Washington county (having sold his farm on Sunday creek), and opened a new farm about eight miles west of Marietta. He lived here till 1835, when he took up his residence with his son-in-law, Mr. James Dickey, at whose house he died January 15, 1841.

William Brown, son of Capt. Benjamin Brown, settled in Ames township in the year 1800, and lived here till about 1817, when he removed to the Moses Hewitt farm, in Waterloo. In 1820 he moved to Lee township, where he lived until a short time before his death, which took place at his son, Leonard Brown's, in Athens. His son, Austin, still lives in Lee township, on a part of the old homestead. Another son, Leonard, who served one term as sheriff and two terms as treasurer of the county, now lives in the town of Albany. He is engaged in the mercantile business, and is a leading citizen.

John Brown, son of Samuel, was born in Ames township, December 23, 1801, but lived the greater part of the time, until 1840, in Washington county, about eight miles from Marietta. In that year he bought property in Albany, Athens county, where he located and engaged successfully for many years in the mercantile business. In 1867 he associated with him his son, J. D. Brown, and engaged in the banking business. During the present year they have removed from Albany to Athens, which is Mr. Brown's present residence. He is a gentleman of fine business capacity, and a public spirited citizen.

Silvanus Ames, long known in this county as Judge Ames, was born at Bridgewater, Massachusetts, March 26, 1771. His father, whose ancestor, William Ames, came from England in 1643, was a graduate of Harvard college, and an Episcopalian clergyman. He preached several years at Trinity church, in Taunton, Massachusetts, was afterwards a chaplain in the revolutionary army, and died in the camp at Valley Forge, during the hard winter of 1777–78. Silvanus Ames married Nabby Lee Johnson in 1795, and moved to the northwestern territory in 1798. They settled temporarily in Belpre, whence they removed to Ames township, in May, 1800, and settled on the farm now owned by the Henrys, and still familiarly called the "Ames farm." Mr. Ames' strong sense and solid judgment gave him a commanding influence among the early settlers, and he was soon brought into the public life of that day. He was the second sheriff of the county, colonel of militia, trustee of the Ohio university for many years, and associate judge from 1813 to 1823. He was also several times elected representative to the state legislature, and in all of these positions evinced a capacity for public affairs, and gained the approbation of the community. Intimately connected, as he was, with the political movements of the day, Judge Ames' house became the resort of the political leaders in southern Ohio, and a favorite stopping place of public men, when making their long trips between the east and west. He was an active and liberal supporter of all educational and religious movements, and an acknowledged leader in the community for several years. He died September 23, 1823. At the time of his death his family consisted of five sons and four daughters, of whom four sons and two daughters are now living, viz: the Rev. Bishop E. R. Ames, John, in Kansas, Charles B., in the state of Mississippi, and George W., at Greencastle, Indiana. One of the daughters, Mrs. Eliza Dawes, lives at Ripon, Wisconsin, and the other, Mrs. A. B. Walker, at Athens. Another daughter, Mrs. de Steiguer, died at Athens, July 29, 1851; a son of her's, Rodolph de Steiguer, a native of the county, is a leading lawyer at Athens.

Capt. *Sabinus Rice*, son of Jason and Sarah Hibbard Rice, was born in Poultney, Vermont, December 18, 1795, and came with his father's family to Ohio in the year 1800. The journey from New England was made in the usual way at that time—by wagon to Pittsburg, and thence down the Ohio river by flat boat. His parents lived for about three years at the White Oak settlement, on the Muskingum river, a few miles north of Marietta, whence, in 1803, they removed to Ames township, where they bought and settled on an eighty acre farm. By hard work and good management they acquired a comfortable competency, and the later years of the old people were passed in ease. The Rice family will long be remembered in the community where they lived, for their hospitality, refinement and intelligence.

Jason Rice died in 1843, in his eighty-eighth year. His wife died in 1824, aged sixty-two years. Their children were Reuben, Ambrose, Jonas, Sabinus, Sally, Jason and Melona, of whom the two last only are living. Jason is a farmer in Ames township and highly respected, and the sister, now Mrs. William Corner, lives in Malta, Ohio. Jonas Rice died on the Mississippi river, near Natchez, in 1829, of yellow fever. A grandson of his, Thomas H. Sheldon, is now cashier of the National Bank at Athens. Ambrose, who possessed great mathematical talent, removed to the northern part of Ohio, where he became very wealthy, and died many years since. Sabinus Rice, a man of excellent judgment and most amiable character, was one of the leading citizens of Ames. He died July 23, 1852. His only son, Sabinus Jason Rice, died in Ames township, in April, 1857, leaving a wife and two children. Of the daughters of Capt. Rice, Mrs. Esther Richardson lives in Spring Hill, Ohio; Mrs. Rebecca R. Hibbard in Wauseon, Fulton county, Ohio, and Mrs. Eunice M. Mower in Springfield, Ohio.

Isaac Linscott, a native of Maine, and of English extraction, came to Ames township in the year 1800, and settled with his large family on the farm now owned by George Linscott, Jun., where he lived till 1824. His descendants, mostly farmers, are very numerous, being scattered through Ames, Bern and Dover townships, and inherit the energy, thrift and strict honesty of their ancestor. The children of Isaac Linscott were Noah, Lydia, Joseph, Isaac, Miriam, Eleanor, Olive, Israel, Amos, John, Mary and Jonathan. Linscott's run, a branch of Ewing's run, received its name from this family.

Joshua Wyatt, known during his residence in Athens county as "Deacon Wyatt," was a native of Beverly, Massachusetts, whence he came out as far west as Uniontown, Pennsylvania, in 1790, and from thence to Marietta, in 1799. He settled with his family in Ames township in 1801, having the year before opened a few acres of land, and got a house under way, which was finished after the family moved in. His family and goods came up the Hockhocking, in a boat, to Warren's station, in Canaan township, whence they were taken in teams across to his place in Ames. His effects made seventeen wagon loads, and were mostly hauled by Peter Mansfield, through the woods, without as yet any road. From the date of his settlement in the township till his death, in 1822, he was a leading citizen. He was a man of distinguished piety, and his life, both in public and in private, was singularly devout. Upon the organization of the first Presbyterian church in Athens he was chosen one of the elders, and, with Deacon Ackley and Judge Alvan Bingham, continued to act as such for several years. Soon after settling in Ames, as early as 1805, he appointed and himself conducted religious reading and prayer meetings at the school house. These meetings were kept up as long as he lived. His eldest daughter, Betsy Wyatt, married William Parker, May 13, 1802. This was the first wedding in Ames township, and supposed to be the second marriage in the county.

John McDougal, born in Schenectady county, New York, August 26, 1776, came to Athens county in July, 1817, and settled in Ames township, on the creek which now bears his name, where he continued to live till his death in 1854.

Gilbert McDougal, his youngest son, was born in Ames township, June 30, 1819, and now resides on the old place owned by his late father. He is a successful farmer, has taught the district school in his vicinity seventeen quarters, held the office of justice of the peace six years, and county commissioner seven years.

Col. Absalom Boyles, born in Franklin county, Pennsylvania, in 1797, came with his father's family to the northwestern territory in 1799, and to Ames township in 1801. He grew up with the community, and was largely identified with the development of the township and county during a long and active life. With fine intelligence, high sense of honor and ardent desire to benefit others, he was always one of the first and most active supporters of social reform, and of every movement that tended to the common welfare. He held various civil positions in the township and county, and, in connection with the early militia organization of the county, was commissioned, by Governor Ethan A. Brown, ensign in 1819; lieutenant in 1820; captain in 1821; by Governor Trimble, lieutenant colonel in 1822, and by Governor Morrow, colonel in 1823.

He lived an honorable and useful life, and died May 3, 1863, on the farm near Amesville, where he had resided for sixty-two years.

Abel Glazier was born in Massachusetts, in 1769. During early life he lived for a time in Washington county, New York, whence he removed to Athens county, and settled in Ames township in 1804. He bought of Capt. Benj. Brown the farm on which Daniel Fleming now lives, and afterward married a daughter of Capt. Brown. He lived in the township over thirty years, during which time he was one of its most prominent and useful citizens. He died in January, 1837. Numerous descendants of his are living in the county, and are highly and justly esteemed in the communities where they dwell, for their intelligence, energy, and sterling qualities. Two of his grandsons, J. H. Glazier and A. W. Glazier, are among the first citizens of Ames township.

George Walker (known during his residence in the county as Judge Walker) was born in Boston, Massachusetts, in 1774. His father, John Walker, came of an old family in Leicestershire, England, was a graduate of the university of Edinburgh, and a barrister at law, removed to America in 1753, married in Boston, and settled in Hartford, Connecticut. George received a good business education, and engaged in mercantile business in Cooperstown, New York. For several years he was highly successful, but, through the dishonesty of a partner, he became deeply involved, and was compelled to close business at a great sacrifice. Disheartened by his losses, and soured by the meanness and dishonesty of his late associates, he determined to seek his fortune in a newer country, and came to Athens county in 1804. Here he purchased and settled on a farm near the present town of Amesville, where he remained all his life. The country was almost a wilderness, and the farm uncultivated, nor had the owner any practical knowledge of the work before him. Mrs. L. W. Ryors, to whom we are indebted for the substance of this sketch, says: "I have heard my mother say that, had it not been for the aid of the man who accompanied them in their long journey as a driver of a wagon, they would have suffered. His name was William Hassey, and he continued to live with the family, a faithful friend and helper, for nearly fifty years. In this wild pioneer life this man was invaluable in every respect, assisting my mother in her new and trying duties, and instructing my father in the art of felling trees and removing brush—not greatly to the credit of his pupil, as the family tradition testifies that he never learned to perform, with skill, that first and necessary part of pioneer life."

Soon after his arrival in the township, Mr. Walker was elected a justice of the peace, which position he

REV. E. R. AMES, D. D.

ONE OF THE BISHOPS OF THE METHODIST EPISCOPAL CHURCH

held, continuously, for about twenty-four years. He also acted as county commissioner for sixteen years, and was elected by the legislature, an associate judge of the court of common pleas, which office he held for fourteen years. He was one of the founders and principal supporters of the Western library association, of which Mrs. Ryors recalls some reminiscences. She says: "As long as I can remember this library was kept at my father's house, and it was most highly prized by the whole family. Books, now a necessity, were then, in that isolated place, a rare luxury. The books were selected with good judgment, and comprised a little of everything—poetry, history, romance, law, medicine, and some scientific and religious works. Poems and novels were the first attraction, I am sorry to say, for the female portion of the family, but they were soon exhausted, and we were glad to turn to more substantial reading. It was no uncommon thing to find a child reading eagerly from the heavy volumes of Rollin or Hume. I was not more than ten or eleven years old, when, in the absence of any 'juvenile books,' I read, with delight, Milton's 'Paradise Lost' and the translation of Homer's 'Iliad.'"

An active supporter of schools and of every movement calculated to promote the welfare of the community, Judge Walker exercised during his whole life a large and healthful influence. He died in 1856. His wife, who is still remembered by some of her contemporaries as a most amiable christian lady, died in 1850, aged seventy-one years.

Judge Walker had one son—George Walker, Jun., who was, for many years, a successful business man in Amesville. He is deceased. Of his seven daughters, the eldest was married to Col. Charles Cutler; the second to Edgar Jewett, of Athens; two of the others married physicians; one a banker, and one a merchant. Another daughter, Mrs. Ryors, relict of the Rev. Alfred Ryors, minister of the Presbyterian church, is well known in Athens. Her accomplished husband, for many years connected with the Ohio university, and subsequently president of the Indiana state university, was one of the choicest among the many rare and scholarly men, who, during its history, have been associated with the university at Athens. He died at Danville, Kentucky, May 8, 1858.

Edward R. Ames, third son of Silvanus Ames, was born in Ames township, May 20, 1806, on the farm now owned by James and George Henry. His early education, though limited, was healthful and solid, and, while still a youth, having access to the local library in Amesville, he formed a taste for reading that has largely influenced the conduct of his life. At the age of twenty he left his father's farm to attend the Ohio university at Athens, where he remained some two or three years, mainly supporting himself, meanwhile, by teaching and other chance employments. While at college he became a member of the Methodist church.

In the autumn of 1828 the late Bishop Roberts presided over the Ohio conference of the Methodist church, which was held at Chillicothe. To see their manner of doing business, and to obtain some knowledge as to the growth of the church, the young collegian attended the session. Bishop Roberts, who had a rare discernment of men, saw the youth and that there was something more than ordinary in him. The result of their acquaintance was, that, acting on the advice of the bishop to "go west," young Ames accompanied him a few weeks later to the Illinois conference, held that year in Madison, Indiana. Here he made further acquaintance with active Methodists from the western states, and, at their suggestion, he proceeded to Illinois and opened a high school at Lebanon, in the present county of St. Clair. He had fine success as a teacher, and remained here, making friends and influence, till 1830. In the autumn of this year he was licensed to preach by the Illinois conference, and was admitted and appointed to Shoal Creek circuit, embracing an indefinite extent of country.

Thenceforward, for some years, his was the usual history of a Methodist itinerant. He was elected as a delegate from the Indiana conference to the general conference, which met in Baltimore in 1840, and, by that body, was elected corresponding secretary of the missionary society for the south and west. This was before the days of railroads. Traveling was slow and difficult, and the labors of his office were arduous and wide extended. During the four years that he filled it, he traveled some twenty-five thousand miles. In one tour he passed over the entire frontier line, from Lake Superior to Texas, camping out almost the whole route, and one part of the time so destitute of provisions that, for two days, the only nourishment of himself and fellow travelers, was a little moistened maple sugar.

In 1852 he was elected one of the bishops of the Methodist Episcopal church, since when his official labors have been most onerous, responsible, and unremitting. Possessed of extraordinary capacity for business, and of great physical endurance, no task appals, and apparently no amount of labor fatigues him. His character and talents are so well known, both in and out of the church, as to render any analysis or description of them unnecessary in this place.

Bishop Ames is esteemed one of the most eloquent preachers in the Methodist church, as he certainly is one of the most popular. A well known minister and editor of the church says:

"As a conference debater he was always effective. We often met in the conference room, but never did we hear him make a speech ten minutes long. He listened to the discussion till he saw the strong points of a case, and these he would present in a few clear, terse statements, which could not be misunderstood, and which went far toward conviction. As a public speaker he is impressive and commanding, whether on the platform or in the pulpit. His voice is quite peculiar, and while under his management it is quite effective, yet it should never be imitated. He rises calmly, states his subject clearly, introduces it with some striking remark, which at once rivets the attention, and then by an easy, direct manner, moves along the track of thought chosen for the occasion. His sermons, though never written, are evidently carefully thought out. His style is molded by the old English classics. Many of his sentences are pure aphorisms. On he talks, till he talks up into the highest realm of thought. We think perhaps his most effective preaching was when he was presiding elder, and addressed gathered thousands on western camp grounds. Then we have seen his whole soul aroused, and his full tide of impassioned oratory was almost resistless. We forbear sketching some of those scenes, though they pass before us."

During the greater part of his adult life, Bishop Ames has resided in Indiana, though his official duties have required protracted absences from home, and long journeys to the most distant parts of the country. A few years since he removed to Baltimore, Maryland, which is his present place of residence. Of late years he has frequently visited Athens, where he has relatives living, and where he finds great enjoyment in meeting the friends of his youth, and in recalling early memories. He is very fond of familiar converse, and, in his "hours of ease," talks in the most genial manner, of early reminiscences or of more modern and weighty affairs. During an evening recently passed by the writer in his company, when his boyhood and early life were the topic of speech, he gave, with much amusement, the following account of

A WOLF HUNT.

"In 1822 Pitt Putnam, of Marietta, organized a grand wolf hunt, to be held on the head waters of Big run. I suppose Putnam inherited his aversion to wolves from his Massachusetts ancestor, as men sometimes inherit politics or religion; at any rate he seemed to think that he had a call to exterminate wolves. The region fixed on for the hunt lay in Washington county, not far from the borders of Ames, and a great many of the male inhabitants of Ames and Bern took part in it. A space about four miles square was surveyed in the heart of the forest, and marked all the way around by blazing the trees. General notice was given some weeks beforehand through the newspaper printed at Marietta, and I remember that a rude diagram of the country and of the line of battle was published. The plan of proceeding was well organized. The hunters were to be stationed at regular distances from each other, all the way around the tract, some supplied with guns and others with horns. Certain men were appointed captains, lieutenants, etc., and gave orders to those nearest them. On the appointed day the hunters assembled from all directions, and were soon placed. I was then only sixteen years old, and was more highly excited over the affair than I am apt to become over any event now-a-days. When all was ready, the men stationed, armed, etc., a horn was blown by the leader, and the signal in a few minutes passed around the whole circuit; whereupon they all began to march toward a common center, keeping in line. Each man was ordered to make as great a hubbub as possible, those with horns to blow them and the rest to shout and halloo. I was a pretty well grown boy of my age, and was allowed to march with the rest. Furnished with a tin horn nearly as long as myself, I blew such blasts as would, I suppose, have shaken down the walls of Jericho, if they had been there, and blew till I had no strength to blow any more. The object of the noise, hooting, blowing horns and beating bushes was to scare up the wolves, and drive them before us, and, of course, when the poor doomed wolves had been thus driven closer and closer to a common center by the contracting lines, the purpose was to slay them ruthlessly, by the hundreds, that is, if they were *there*. As we drew near the center, where there was a running brook and a cave in the rocks, the excitement increased. Soon wild animals of different sorts were seen darting about. There were deer in considerable numbers, and though in poor condition, as I remember, a great many were killed. In their fright and eagerness to escape, they ran directly at the lines of hunters, and I saw some of them leap clear over the heads of the men. Foxes were numerous too, and a good many were killed, with smaller game of different sorts. But we were after wolves; and after all our marching and hallooing, and beating of bushes, my recollection is that not a single wolf was captured or killed—or, if any, only one or two—and the whole affair was a laughable failure, so far as the wolf part was concerned. I think I have never wasted so much breath to so little profit as I did in blowing that tin horn. I walked home a tired boy, and very skeptical as to Pitt Putnam's having any great inspiration as a wolf hunter."

Doctor Ezra Walker, the first resident physician of Ames township, was born December 9, 1776, at Killingly, Connecticut, in which state he studied his profession, and practiced for some years. Removing from Connecticut he settled in Poultney, Vermont, about the year 1800, and from thence migrated with his family to Marietta, in the autumn of 1810. He remained on the Muskingum till the spring of 1811, when he came with his family, consisting of wife and seven children, into Ames township, and immediately resumed the practice of medicine. He pursued a general practice for more than twenty years, and, in a few families who would never excuse him, he continued to practice for almost forty years, or till near the close of his life. When he began to practice medicine in the county, and for many years later, what with bad roads or no roads at all, absence of bridges, sparse and scattered settlements, etc., his long rides, frequently of fifteen or twenty miles, were always attended with difficulties and sometimes with dangers. In one instance he had to cross the country from where the present town of Plymouth, Washington county, is situated, to another settlement at Barrows' mill, in Rome township, which took him till far in the evening, when he found himself followed by wolves. As their numbers increased the animals were emboldened to contract their circle around him, till he was obliged to climb into a tree for safety; and there he spent the night, keeping a sharp lookout for his horse beneath, and trying to frighten away the wolves, by beating with a club against the body of the tree in which he was perched. When day dawned his hungry enemies gradually drew off, and the doctor proceeded on his journey. When he reached the first cabin, not very far distant, and situated just below the present site of Big Run station, he found the wolves had taken this man's premises in their retreat, and killed a calf near his house for their breakfast.

Doctor Walker taught school in Ames, for one or two quarters in 1811–12, always holding himself ready, however, to attend the sick. By means of his profession, and by farming some, he gained for himself and family a comfortable subsistence, living to see his children all creditably settled in life. He died January 9, 1852.

His eldest daughter was married to John Brown (now General Brown), in 1811, and his second daughter to the late James J. Fuller, of Athens, in 1815. Mrs. Brown died in 1853, and Mrs. Fuller in 1864. His sons, William R. Walker, Archibald B. Walker, Ezra Walker, and Ralph M. Walker, were natives of East Poultney, Vermont, but were reared from boyhood in Athens county. William R., though a man of fine native talent and much refinement of character, was oppressed by self-distrust and timidity. He lived for a short time, during the early portion of his adult life, in Lancaster, Ohio, where he was highly respected for his integrity, business talent, and literary culture. Among those whose friendship he acquired at that time and always retained, was Mr. Hocking H. Hunter, who recently stated to the writer that, he "had never in all his life, seen any person who recited and acted the part of Hamlet so perfectly, in his opinion, as Wm. R. Walker." At that time fine business prospects were opened to him, and for awhile he revolved "enterprises of great pith and moment." But melancholy overcame him. He abandoned active business and the wide fields of usefulness that were opening before him, returned to the paternal farm, and there passed the rest of his life, remote from the society which he was so well calculated to adorn. An amiable christian gentleman, he lived and died respected by the whole community. His death took place in 1855.

Ezra Walker, another son of Dr. Walker, graduated at the Ohio university in 1829, studied law with Judge Summers at Charleston, West Virginia, and settled in that place. He published the *Kanawha Republican* for several years, and afterward was superintendent of the "James River and Kanawha Improvement" more than twenty years, and until his death in March, 1853. He was widely known and universally respected.

Ralph M. Walker, the youngest brother, graduated at the Western Reserve college. The greater part of his life has been passed as a teacher in Otterbein college, Franklin county, Ohio, and in the Grand River institute in Ashtabula county. He now lives in Missouri.

David Rathburn, born in Rhode Island in 1766, removed to the state of New York, where he lived several years, and thence, in 1809, to Ames township in Athens county. Here he rented the Cutler farm for one year, and then moved up into the "hill settlement," some five miles further north, where he tended the horse mill owned by Christopher Herrold, for about four years. This was the first mill erected in this part of the country, and was patronized by the settlers for many miles around. In 1814 he bought a farm on the little creek where Judge Walker lived, and resided there till his death, March 8, 1850. After coming on this farm, Mr. Rathburn got up an excellent hand mill that proved a great convenience to the neighborhood at times. He had great skill in trapping wild animals, and his neighbors, for miles around, would come to him for instruction in preparing bait and setting traps for wolves. He left two sons and four daughters; the sons and one daughter, wife of Judge R. A. Fulton, are still living in the same neighborhood in Ames township.

Capt. Thomas S. Lovell was born in Barnstable county, Massachusetts, January 18, 1785. At the age of fifteen he went to sea as cabin boy, and, during his first cruise of three years, was advanced before the mast. Returning home he went to school for one or two terms, learned something of navigation and a little mathematics, then took to the sea again. He was successful in his calling, became master of a ship before he was twenty-one years old, and before he had reached his twenty-ninth year had crossed the Atlantic forty-two times. Capt. Lovell says:

"In 1812, when war began, I loaded my ship with corn in Philadelphia for a Spanish port, depending on the good sailing of my ship for safety. I went through safely, sold my cargo at a good advance, and lay in the harbor five months, waiting for an opportunity to get out, the bay of Biscay being alive with armed vessels. When I thought it was safe to come out I did so, but myself and crew were captured. My ship was ballasted with sand. The English were very anxious to know what had become of the proceeds of my cargo. I told them I had remitted it to London, but they thought that was a Yankee lie, and they probed the sand through and through to find the money, but to no effect. I was then taken before the admiral (I forget his name), and he finally cleared me and gave me a permit to St. Ubes in Portugal, there to load with salt, and I made a good voyage home."

Finding times dull (in 1814), and commerce languishing, he resolved to quit the sea. We give Capt. Lovell's language again:

"My brother Russell and myself were partners in business, and, as times were so very dull, we decided to emigrate to the west. So we sold our property, rigged what was called a Yankee wagon, and a small wagon and team of five horses, and started for Ohio. We traveled by land to Redstone, Fayette county, Pennsylvania, where we separated. My brother took the teams down by land, while I, with a flat-bottomed boat, a queer kind of craft without mast, jib, or sail, took the families and most of the effects by water to Marietta. From there we came on to Athens county, and settled on Sharp's fork of Federal creek, in what was then Ames township. We reached here November 18, 1814, after a journey of ten weeks. For awhile both families lived in one cabin, not a large one either, belonging to Job Phillips, and we had hard sailing to get along. I was willing to work, but did not know any more about farming than a land-lubber does about working a ship—however, we got along. Wolves were very troublesome; they killed our sheep constantly, and once they killed a yearling steer of mine. Elijah Latimer, who lived near us, was a famous hunter. I sold him thirty acres of land adjoining my farm, and took pay in hunting. He would furnish venison for my family, and also fight off the wolves whenever they invaded my sheep flock. Sugar making was quite an occupation when I came here. When I commenced I tapped trees without regard to kind—smooth-bark hickories, buckeyes, and sugar trees. The first pig I ever owned in Ohio got badly scratched by a bear. The men folks were all away from home, and the bear came into the door yard after some fresh pork, but piggy ran under the house and escaped with a severe cuff or two. My dogs would often tree a bear twenty or thirty rods from the cabin, when I would call Latimer and he would shoot him. They frequently weighed two hundred and fifty and three hundred pounds. Wild turkeys were very plenty. I have often set a square pen made of rails, then scattered a little corn about and into it, and caught eight or ten fine ones at a time. The pen being covered at the top the turkeys could not fly out, and they never thought of ducking their heads to get out by the same passage they came in. We had great difficulty in getting grain ground. We were far from any mill, and I have often ridden on horseback to Lancaster to get a bushel of corn ground. Before coming west I had heard that there was shipbuilding on the Ohio river, and my real object in coming to Ohio was to take out ships. There had been a few built at Marietta before I came out, but I think there was only one built after I came here, and I took that to New Orleans, where I fitted her for sea, then sailed across the gulf to Havana, and from there to Baltimore. There I bought a horse and rode home, and made a good trip."

Touching this vessel and voyage we are able to add a little to Capt. Lovell's reminiscence.

We find the following item in the *Cincinnati Gazette* of April 15, 1816:

" Came to anchor before this place (Cincinnati), on last Saturday evening, the schooner *Maria*, Captain Lovell, of and from Marietta, Ohio, bound to Boston, Mass., full cargo of pork, flour and lard. The *Maria* is 50 tons burthen, has 51 feet straight rabbit, 18 feet beam, and draws six feet of water. She was built, rigged, and loaded at Marietta, and is owned by Messrs. Moses McFarland and Edmund B. Dana—the latter gentleman on board. The *Maria* sailed hence yesterday at 11 o'clock. The present state of the water is favorable to her descent of the river. May prosperous gales waft her to her port of destination."

And in *Niles' Weekly Register*, published at Baltimore, we find the following item in the issue of July 13, 1816:

" *Singular arrival.* A fine schooner arrived at Baltimore last week, in 46 days from Marietta, Ohio, with a cargo of pork. It is well observed that 'the mountains have melted away before the enterprise and indefatigability of our countrymen.'"

The farmers of Athens county have a somewhat better mode now of getting their produce to market than by salt water.

Captain Lovell is living on the farm where he first settled in 1814. At that time it was in Ames township, Athens county, then in Homer township, and finally in Marion township, Morgan county. Thus, living in one spot for fifty-four years, Captain Lovell has been a citizen of three different townships and two counties. He is in his eighty-fifth year and is unusually bright for one of his age.

The Lovell brothers married sisters and lived on adjoining farms for many years. Russell was a painter and was killed by the kick of a horse in the town of Athens—year unknown.

Lewis Columbia, born in France in 1770, came to Ames township is 1815 and settled on the creek above the Owens settlement, whence, after a few years, he moved on to Walker's branch and settled on the farm now owned by Mahlon Kasler. Here he erected a rude tannery, the first established in this part of the country, which served a good purpose to a limited extent in tanning the skins of wild animals, with which the region then abounded. He died in 1825.

Gulliver Dean, born in Norton, Bristol county, Massachusetts, August 9, 1772, came to Athens county with his father's family in the year 1815. In 1818 he married Miss Mary Cutler, second daughter of Judge Ephraim Cutler. He settled in Ames township where he still resides, and where his family are well known and highly respected.

CHAPTER X.

Bern Township.

BERN was originally included in Ames township, and was not separately organized till 1828. Incorporated with Ames for thirty years, much of its early history will be found in connection with that township.

March 3, 1828, the county commissioners resolved "that the original surveyed township No. 7 in range 12 in Athens county, at present a part of Ames township, be set off, and that a township by the name of *Bern* be established as above described." The electors were directed to meet at the house of John Henry on the first Monday of April at 9 o'clock A. M. to elect township officers.

The lands of Bern lie exceedingly well for agricultural purposes, and her farmers compare favorably with any for thrift and enterprise. The township is well watered by the head waters of Federal creek, Sharp's fork of which traverses it from north to south. Its population in 1830 was 223; in 1840 it was 381; in 1850 it was 819; in 1860 it was 1,022. There are but thirty sections in Bern, the eastern tier of sections having been set off to Washington county in 1807. Coal is known to exist here in great abundance, and salt water has been found of good quality and in workable quantity.

Township Trustees.

1828–30	John Henry,	James Dickey,	John Wickham.
1831–33	"	David James,	Jeffrey Buchanan.
1834	Dyar Selby, Sen.,	John Wickham,	James Dickey.
1835	William J. Brown,	"	"
1836	"	David James,	"
1837	Matthew Henry,	"	"
1838	"	"	Wm. J. Brown.
1839	"	James Dickey,	"
1840	J. E. Vore,	"	John Work.
1841	David James,	Thornton Swart,	"
1842	"	James Dickey,	Dyar Selby, Jun.
1843	Joseph McCune,	"	"
1844	"	"	Reuben Hague.
1845	David James,	"	"
1846	Jesse Carr,	Dyar Selby,	John Work.
1847	David Colvin,	Robert Henry,	Wm. Rardin.
1848	"	Levi Ellis,	"
1849	"	Edward Ginn,	Calvin Tracy.
1850	James Henry,	"	J. E. Vore.
1851	Lewis Dille,	Reuben Hague,	Calvin Tracy.
1852	"	Edward Ginn,	"
1853	Andrew Ogg,	Philip W. Lampson,	John E. Vore.
1854	"	J. S. King,	"
1855	H. C. Selby,	"	John Whaley.
1856	"	Philip W. Lampson,	David Gilchrist.
1857	David James,	Edward Ginn,	"
1858	Levi Rardin,	J. M. Smith,	George Wyatt.
1859	Clark Dodds,	Washington Endicott,	"
1860	Dyar Selby,	"	H. T. McCune.
1861	H. C. Selby,	"	Warren W. Wickham.
1862	Dyar Selby,	Thomas Dickson,	"
1863	Elijah Hanson,	"	"
1864	Owen Gifford,	"	Washington Endicott,
1865	Levi Rardin,	"	"
1866	H. C. Selby,	"	"
1867	"	H. L. Driggs,	Elijah Hanson.
1868	S. J. Wells,	Elijah White,	"

Justices of the Peace.

 1828—Thaddeus Crippen and Wm. T. Brown.
 1831—Matthew Henry and W. T. Brown.
 1834—Levi Ellis and Robert Henry.
 1836—David Dille.
 1837—Robert Henry.
 1839—Dyar Selby.
 1840—Robert Work.
 1841—Calvin Tracy.
 1843—John Brawley and P. W. Sampson.
 1844—Dyar Selby, Jun.
 1846—John Brawley.
 1847—Dyar Selby, Jun.
 1850—Dyar Selby, Jun.
 1852—Philip W. Lampson.
 1853—Thomas Bruce.
 1854—Elijah Hanson.
 1855—Philip W. Lampson.
 1857—Elijah Hanson.
 1858—Philip W. Lampson.
 1859—Robert Henry (refused to qualify), and Seaborn Carr.
 1860—Aaron Smith.
 1862—Seaborn Carr.
 1863—Watson Harris.
 1864—W. W. Wickham.
 1866—Watson Harris.
 1867—Edwin F. Glazier.
 1868—Hiram C. Selby.

Personal and Biographical.

James Dickey was born of Irish parents in Carlisle, Pennsylvania, September 3, 1788, came to the northwestern territory with his father's family in 1798 and settled first in Washington county. When a young man Mr. Dickey was employed as a post rider to carry the mail on horseback, between Marietta and Chillicothe, a distance of about one hundred miles. Between 1806 and 1814 he was variously engaged in the mail service, sometimes as a sub contractor, but always doing the riding of one hand himself. At that time the mail service in this section was one of great hardship and frequently of danger, as the numerous streams along the route, all destitute of bridges, were often swollen and had to be crossed at the peril of life. From 1812 to 1814, during the war with Great Britain, the great East and West mail was sent over this route, the bag being sometimes nearly filled with government dispatches alone. The riders (three in number), each made one round trip a week from Marietta to Chillicothe and return, regardless of weather and of all obstacles. Mr. Dickey once swam the creek near Amesville in the night, running great risk and getting the mail thoroughly wet. On reaching John Brown's in Ames, one of his regular stopping places, he spent a short time drying the mail bag before the fire and then went on in the darkness.

During the war the contract required the mail to be carried at the rate of five miles an hour, and the government enforced the condition rigorously. Mr. Dickey became noted for his energy and fidelity in fulfilling his mail contracts, and in this, as in all other respects, established a reputation for strict integrity and rare business capacity. At one of his stations on the route he had a rest of about two hours once a week, and this was usually spent by him in hunting. He often killed one and sometimes two deer, or perhaps several wild turkeys, if they were soonest found, and brought them in for the family with whom he boarded, and received credit for the game on his board account; in this way he paid nearly his whole board and horse keeping at this station.

In 1815 Mr. Dickey married Betsy, daughter of Samuel Brown, and bought a small farm near Mr. Brown's, eight miles west of Marietta, where he lived till he removed to Bern. He came to Bern in 1821 and settled on Sharp's fork where he opened a large farm, and where he lived about thirty-four years and reared a family of three sons and two daughters. His house in Bern became a favorite and noted stopping place for travelers and there are many who still remember his hospitality and good cheer. Mr. Dickey never sought office or notoriety; he however served as county commissioner and township trustee at different times. In 1852 or '3, after his wife's death, he disposed of his farm in Bern among his sons, and a few years later went to live with his son Mr. A. S. Dickey, in McConnellsville, where he died June 12, 1862.

John Henry, a native of Ireland, settled in Bern township in 1817, being then fifty-three years old.

He bought a section of land here and opened up the farm where his son Charles Henry now lives. On this farm he lived till his death in February, 1854. Mr. Henry was twice married. By his first wife he had four sons and five daughters, and by his second four sons and six daughters. He live to see eight sons and ten daughters married and comfortably settled, and left behind him at his death eighteen children, fifty-six grandchildren and a number of great grandchildren. He was a member of the Presbyterian church and a leading and influential citizen during the active years of his life. Several of his descendants have intermarried with the family of Abel Glazier and are well known throughout the county.

John Wickham, son of Joseph Wickham, was born in Vermont, July 1, 1784, and came to Athens county with his father's family in 1805, settling first in Rome township. Later he removed to Bern township where he died March 19, 1863. He served as a volunteer in the war of 1812, and was marching to join Hull's army (his command being yet two days' march distant), when that general surrendered.

Warren W. Wickham, son of John, lives on the farm of his late father at the mouth of Marietta run in Bern township—has been a justice of the peace and township trustee.

William Rardin, born near Pittsburg, April 29, 1797, came here in 1822 and settled on the state road between Marietta and Athens. For many years the wolves were a great scourge, and the secluded valley of the Marietta run, at the head of which he lived, was about their last retreat. Mr. Rardin has been a farmer all his life and his descendants are well known in the township.

Dyar Selby, born in New York in 1784, came to Ohio at an early day, and about 1833 settled in Bern township—has been township trustee and justice of the peace. His descendants live in Bern.

Edmund Perry, David Parkins, and John E. Vore, all settled in Bern at an early day, and were among the most respected citizens. Mr. Vore is known as an extensive stock dealer and was county commissioner for several years.

Thornton Swart, born in Loudoun county, Virginia, in 1793, settled in this township in 1838 on Possum run, adjoining Owen Gifford's place. Mr. S. served in the war of 1812. He now resides with his son.

David and *Daniel James* and Philip W. Lampson, well known citizens, settled here in 1820. The James family still live in Bern. Mr. Lampson went to Kansas in 1864.

CHAPTER XI.

Canaan Township.

IT is difficult to separate the first settlement of Canaan township from that of Athens, of which Canaan was originally a part. It will have been noticed that the pioneer settlements clung pretty closely to the water courses. In the absence of roads or any other means of communication, the navigable streams always decide the movements of emigration. The Hockhocking was, from all accounts, a considerably deeper stream and carried much more water seventy-five years ago than now, and was easily navigable for heavily laden barges. It thus became valuable as a means of communcation and supplies, and the regions accessible by it were the first to be settled in the county. Accordingly, many of the first settlers of Athens township located within the present limits of Canaan, whose rich bottom lands proved very attractive. The township was organized in 1819.

The first election for township officers was held at

the house of Edward Pilcher, on the first Monday of April in that year. The name of *Canaan* was suggested by Judge Walker, of Ames township, one of the county commissioners at this time.

The population of the township in 1820 was 356; in 1830 it was 375; in 1840 it was 800; in 1850 it was 1,142, and in 1860 it was 1,272.

The first election for township trustees was held at the house of Edward Pilcher, April 5, 1819. John C. Carico and Stephen Pilcher were judges, and Joshua Hoskinson and John McGill clerks of the election.

Township Trustees.

1819	Parker Carpenter,	Stephen Pilcher,	George Bean.
1820	Martin Mansfield,	"	"
1821	"	Martin Boyles,	"
1822	Parker Carpenter,	"	Elijah Pilcher.
1823	Martin Mansfield,	Andrew J. Hoskinson,	Samuel Warren.
1824	"	"	Philip M. Starr.
1825	Joshua Hoskinson,	Stephen Pilcher,	John Boyles.
1826	John C. Carico,	George Boyles,	William Hallert.
1827	Stephen Pilcher,	Parker Carpenter,	John Boyles.
1828	No election—old trustees acted.		
1829	Stephen Pilcher,	Parker Carpenter,	Joshua Hoskinson.
1830	Martin Mansfield,	Martin Boyles,	Elijah Pilcher.
1831	"	"	Stephen Pilcher.
1832–33	William Burch,	George Bean,	"
1834	"	Martin Mansfield,	Robert Bean.
1835	Elijah Pilcher,	Joshua Hoskinson,	"
1836	Martin Mansfield,	"	Frederic Wood.
1837	Amos Miller,	John G. Bean,	Parker Carpenter.
1838	Martin Mansfield,	Jacob Tedrow,	"
1839–40	Elijah Pilcher,	John Boyles,	John G. Bean.
1841	E. C. Wright,	Richard Poston,	David Jordan.
1842	D. M. Pruden,	"	"
1843	"	Isaac Long,	"
1844–45	"	G. N. Reade,	"
1846	Clayton Starr,	"	Harrison Halbert.
1847	"	"	D. M. Pruden.
1848	William Henry,	N. O. Warren,	John Druggan.
1849	David Jordan,	"	"
1850	Richard Poston,	Peter Sams,	Peter Stalder.

TRUSTEES—*Continued.*

1851	A. Buckley,	George Mansfield,	Peter Stalder.
1852–53	Peter Davis,	David Jordan,	Nathan S. Pilcher.
1854	"	Peter Stalder,	Peter Finsterwald.
1855	"	"	Peter Finch.
1856	David Jordan,	"	"
1857	"	"	Peter Finsterwald.
1858	Nicholas Stalder,	James Sams,	Peter Davis.
1859	"	Joseph Border,	Thomas Grosvenor.
1860–61	"	Henry Finsterwald,	E. D. Sheridan.
1862	L. D. Bean,	"	S. L. Mohler.
1863	Curtis Bean,	"	William Burch.
1864	S. McLeade,	"	"
1865	C. B. Cunningham,	J. W. Baird,	Joshua Wyatt.
1866	Curtis Bean,	N. Warren,	J. W. Baird.
1867	"	"	Peter Finsterwald.
1868	"	F. C. Wyatt,	"

Successive Justices of the Peace.

1818—Stephen Pilcher.
1819—Martin Mansfield.
1820—William Stewart.
1822—Martin Mansfield.
1823—Stephen Pilcher.
1825—William Thompson.
1827—Stephen Pilcher.
1828—William Thompson.
1830—Joshua Hoskinson.
1831—Martin Mansfield.
1833—John McGill.
1834—George Bean.
1835—John McGill.
1837—George Bean.
1838—Joshua Hoskinson.
1840—George Bean.
1841—George N. Reade.
1843—Robert Bean.
1844—George N. Reade.
1847—D. M. Pruden.

JUSTICES OF THE PEACE—*Continued.*

1848—A. Buckley.
1850—Nathan S. Pilcher and Aaron Hull.
1851—Richard Poston.
1853—Nathan S. Pilcher and Aaron Hull.
1854—Elijah Tucker and Thomas Grosvenor.
1856—Joseph Border, Charles C. Pruden, and Peter Davis.
1859-1865—David Love and J. Warren Baird.

Personal and Biographical.

William Jackson settled in what is now Canaan township in 1799. A native of Ireland, he came to this country with his father's family when nine years old, and lived for twelve or fifteen years in Westmoreland county, Pennsylvania, whence, after his marriage, he removed to the northwestern territory, and settled near the site of the present village of New England in Canaan township. He was a man of fine natural ability, good education, and considerable culture. In 1800 he surveyed the first road through the woods from Marietta to Chillicothe. In January, 1803, he was elected representative from this (then Washington) county to the state legislature, in opposition to Ephraim Cutler, and was an influential member of that body. In the fall of 1803 he was re-elected, and in the session of 1803-4, by a well-timed speech, defeated a bill offered by Philemon Beecher, requiring a property qualification for office holders. In 1804 he declined a renomination, in consequence of having received an appointment from the government to survey a large district of country on the Wabash river. In the discharge of this duty he went to Vincennes, Indiana, and died there soon after his arrival. Mr. John Jackson, of New England village, who died in the winter of 1867, was a son of his.

The Barrows brothers, William, George, and Henry, came to what is now Canaan township in 1797, and settled near where N. O. Warren now resides. During the next year they brought out their father, Ebenezer Barrows, and the rest of the family from the east. The old man had been a soldier in the French and revolutionary wars. His descendants are widely scattered through Indiana, Illinois, Michigan, and Iowa. One of his daughters, Mrs. Ebenezer Culver, is living in Upper Sandusky, Ohio, aged ninety years. Two of his grandsons, Voltaire and Massena, own the old Barrows' mill on Federal creek. Perry Barrows has a farm near the mill tract. These are sons of Henry Barrows. Several of the children of George Barrows survive. Parker, now seventy years old, is a respectable farmer of Canaan township. Orange and George, also farmers, live in Rome township, the latter on the old farm. Between seventy-five and eighty of the descendants of Ebenezer Barrows, are known to have served in the Union army during the late rebellion.

Joseph Simmons was born in Pennsylvania in 1772, and settled in Canaan township in 1797. He says:

"The forests were full of game, and we could kill all the wild meat we wanted, but salt was the great need. However, we had to have it, and used to pack it on horses from the salt licks (over forty miles), at the rate of $4.00 a bushel, bitter water included. We raised corn, and we had a little hand mill to grind our hominy and meal for mush. There was a little *tub* mill on Margaret's creek and one on Duck creek (Washington county), but none on Hockhocking. The number of males within the present limits of the township was six or seven, during the year after I came here."

Martin Mansfield, born in New Jersey in 1779, settled in Canaan township in 1797, died August 7, 1860. His descendants are numerous and highly respected in the county. His brother Peter settled in Canaan on Willow creek about the same time, and was a leading man among the pioneers. Three of his sons, George, William, and Allen, still live in the same neighborhood.

Peter Boyles, a native of Bedford county, Pennsylvania, settled in what is now Canaan township in 1795. He was probably the first white settler within the present county of Athens. This was the year of the treaty of Greenville, and the close of the Indian war. Athens county was the very frontier at that time, and Mr. Boyles, in settling here, took his life in his hand, for this section was by no means safe in that year from Indian outrages. He lived in Canaan township till 1827, when he removed west, and died in Missouri in 1843. The date of his settlement here is accurately fixed by his son, George Boyles, who is still living in Andrew county, Missouri, and who was born in Canaan township June 5, 1795. He was, beyond doubt, the first white child born in Athens county. He says he was born "on the school section between the graveyard and the river." Mr. Hocking H. Hunter, of Lancaster, Ohio, has frequently been accorded the distinction of having been the first white child born in the Hockhocking valley. He was not born till August 23, 1801. It hardly admits of a question that George Boyles, a native of Canaan, was the first white child born on the waters of the Hockhocking.

John Boyles, son of Peter, was born in Pennsylvania in 1791, came to Canaan township with his father's family in 1795, and lived there till his death in 1849. Some of his descendants still reside in the county.

Peter W. Boyles, son of John Boyles, was born in Canaan township, December 20, 1820, and has since passed his life in this county. He now owns and lives on the "Daniel Stewart farm" in Rome township— probably the best farm in the county. Samuel S. Boyles, another son of John, lives in Lodi township. Both he and Peter W. are prosperous and highly respected citizens.

Samuel Gillett was born in Hartford county, Connecticut, September 26, 1785, and came to Athens county in 1818. He first settled in Ames, where in 1819 he established a tannery, which was located near where the old brick church stood in after years. He frequently tanned the skins of wild animals, panthers, bears, etc., which were, even as late as that, sometimes used for clothing or household purposes. In 1823 he removed to Canaan township, and settled on Stroud's run, about four miles east of Athens. He and his present wife were married in 1809.

Abel Miller came to Athens county in 1802 from Middletown, Connecticut. In 1803 he purchased land two miles below the town of Athens in what is now Canaan township, and built a log cabin the same year. In a few years he had opened a fine farm, which is still known as among the best in the valley. Mr. Miller was for a long time county surveyor. He surveyed the two college townships at one time, preparatory to a leasing of the lands. He was appointed a trustee of the Ohio university in 1808, and served in that capacity till 1825 when he resigned. He was several times elected a justice of the peace, and served seven years as an associate judge. He died April 23, 1827, at the age of fifty years. Judge Miller was a man of large acquaintance, and deserved popularity through this and adjoining counties. He was a superior judge, a good citizen, and an excellent man.

Captain Parker Carpenter, a native of Killingly, Connecticut, came to this township in 1817, and settled on a new farm a little north of the present village of New England. He served in the war of 1812, before leaving Connecticut. A few years before his death he removed to Athens township and settled on a fine farm about two miles from Athens, where he died November 6, 1852, aged seventy-three years. He was an excellent citizen. Some of his descendants still live in the county, and are highly respected.

Joshua Hoskinson was born in Maryland in 1791, and settled with his father's family in Canaan township in 1810. Deer, bears, and wolves were quite plenty in this region at that time. In his younger days Mr. Hoskinson was fond of hunting, though he says "Peter Mansfield and William Burch were the best; they caught and killed more wolves than any men we had." Mr. Hoskinson volunteered in the war of 1812, and entered the service under Captain Jehiel Gregory of Athens. He says:

"We went into winter quarters on the head waters of the Scioto, about the time that the British and Indians took possession of the French settlement on the Maumee river. General Tappan called for volunteers from his brigade to go on an expedition against the British on the Maumee, and I volunteered. There were about seven hundred officers and men. We took five days' rations and started, I think, on the 7th of November, 1812. On the 13th, we came to the rapids of the Maumee.

That night our scouts reported that the river was rising. Captain Gregory led the battalion forward, and with great difficulty we waded the river. But we went no further nor met the enemy. The failure of our provisions was, I suppose, the reason of our hasty return. On our march back to camp we were three days without anything to eat except spice-bush and slippery-elm bark. When we were about a day and a half's march from camp, and nearly starved, we were met by pack horses with flour."

Mr. Hoskinson was county commissioner twelve years, justice of the peace six years, and has held other local offices.

William Henry was born in Newport, eight miles above Marietta, October 18, 1804, and came to Athens county with his father's family when sixteen years of age. He married a daughter of Captain Parker Carpenter, and ultimately settled in Canaan township on the farm formerly owned by Colonel William Stewart, on the Hockhocking, about eight miles below Athens. Mr. Henry is an excellent citizen and highly respected.

CHAPTER XII.

Carthage Township.

THIS township, originally a part of Troy, was separately organized in 1819. The following appears in the records of the county commissioners:

"*November 10th,* 1819—*Resolved,* that all that part of the township of Troy included in township No. 5, in the 12th range and the east half of township No. 4, in the 13th range, be a separate township by the name of *Carthage.*"

And at the same session the inhabitants were directed to meet on a specified day and elect township officers.

The first justice of the peace in Carthage was Milton Buckingham. Joseph Guthrie and Francis Caldwell were also among the earliest. Among the early township trustees were Stephen Buckingham, Joseph Guthrie, Francis Caldwell, Alexander Caldwell, Moses Elliott, and B. B. Lottridge.

Joseph Guthrie built the first grist mill in the township about the year 1820, on a small stream on his farm (near the southeast corner of section six), called after himself, and which still retains the name of Guthrie creek. Since that time there have been two or three small grist mills built on a little stream in the northeast corner of the township formerly called Lizzie run but now called Little Jordan. There have also been several saw mills built in the township in later years, but all have fallen into disuse, and at present there is not a mill in the township worth mentioning. There are nine school districts in Carthage, with nine good country school houses and five churches—two Methodist, one Presbyterian, one United Brethren, and one Christian or Campbellite. The Methodists, as usual, were the pioneers, their society having been organized about the year 1812; the Christian church was organized about 1835, the United Brethren about 1840, and the Presbyterian in 1850.

The early records of the township are lost, and there is no list of its officers prior to 1855. The population in 1820 was 320; in 1830 it was 395; in 1840 it was 734; in 1850 it was 1,087; in 1860 it was 1,127.

Township Trustees since 1855.

1855	Hiram Frost,	Vincent Caldwell,	Caleb Wells.
1856–57	Jacob S. Coen,	R. M. Wilson,	Walter Glazier.
1858	"	"	William Mills.
1859	Cyrenus Stout,	Simeon Buck,	Asa P. Jeffers.
1860	Walter Glazier,	James Buck,	"
1861	"	S. H. Lottridge,	Cyrenus Stout.
1862	William Merrill,	"	
1863	Aaron Stort,	William Russel,	John W. Nicholson.
1864	S. H. Lottridge,	Amasa Saunders,	Charles Stout.

TRUSTEES—*Continued.*

1865	William Russell,	Amasa Saunders,	Charles Stout.
1866	"	David G. Frost,	John W. Nicholson.
1867	"	"	E. M. Young.
1868	Avery N. Saunders,	Joseph D. Webster,	Hiram C. Frost.

Township Clerks since 1855.

    1855—Washington Hull.
    1856-60—James Elliott.
    1861-62—David Frost.
    1863—James Elliott, who has been re-elected each year since.

Justices of the Peace since 1852.

    1852—Daniel Tubbs, S. W. Lottridge, and John Elliott.
    1855—Isaac Hull and Richard M. Wilson.
    1857—John Whittington.
    1858—Richard M. Wilson.
    1860—John Whittington.
    1861—Jacob S. Coen.
    1863—John Whittington.
    1864—Jacob S. Coen.
    1865—Curtis Raincer and John Hammond.
    1866—Simon H. Lottridge.

Personal and Biographical.

The first white settler within the limits of what is now Carthage township was *Asahel Cooley, Sen.* He came from near Springfield, Massachusetts, to Belpre in 1797, moved to what is now Athens county in 1799, traversing a dense wilderness between the Muskingum and the Hockhocking, and settled within the present limits of Carthage. With the aid of his grown up sons he had soon cleared a piece of land and prepared a home which was known long afterward for its good cheer and genuine hospitality. Esquire Cooley was a man of well-informed mind, active business habits and gentlemanly manners. He was for many years justice of the peace and county commissioner, and held other offices of trust in the very early history of the county. His oldest son, *Simeon Cooley*, built the Coolville mills in 1815, and, in connection with them, what was then considered a large distillery. He laid out near his mills the now neat and thriving village of Coolville which, with a slight abbreviation, bears his name. The youngest and only surviving son of Esquire Cooley, Heman Cooley, is a respectable farmer living near Coolville in Troy township, and is now seventy-three years of age.

The next year after Asahel Cooley came, his brother-in-law, Mr. Abram Frost, and settled in Carthage with a large family. Many of his descendants have removed to western states. One of his sons, Heman Frost, settled as a farmer in Rome township, where he was highly respected, and, during his long residence there of about forty years, ranked as one of her best citizens. He died June 5, 1868, aged seventy-eight years. His last illness was caused by a severe fall from a scaffold in his barn.

Bernardus B. Lottridge, born in New York in 1779, came to Athens county and settled in Carthage township in 1805 as a farmer. Like most of the pioneers he had but slender means, and depended chiefly on his energy, industry, and muscle. These soon won him a good farm, and placed his family on a comfortable footing. He held different local offices, and was an excellent citizen. He died in 1849. One of his sons, the late Isaac Lottridge, represented Athens county for one session in the state legislature. Another, Simon H. Lottridge, born in Carthage township in 1807, lives on the farm that his father owned. He is now a justice of the peace and highly respected. The widow of Bernardus B. Lottridge still lives, aged eighty-seven years. She thinks that there were not more than ten or twelve persons living within the present bounds of Carthage when she and her husband settled here. The forests were full of game and wild animals. She remembers that one evening a large panther walked into their house and stood before the fire. His rifle not being in the house Mr. Lottridge seized the butcher knife and would have attacked the animal instantly but for the entreaties of his wife. She supposes that her screams frightened the panther, for in a few moments he darted out at the door and made off. Her husband frequently killed panthers and bears—the meat of the latter being a favorite article of diet. She remembers that nearly the last, if not the very last, bear that Mr. Lottridge killed, he attacked and killed with no other weapon but a hickory club.

Ebenezer Buckingham, Sen., settled in what is now Carthage township in 1801, near to Esquire Cooley. He was the father of the late Ebenezer Buckingham of Muskingum county, who was at one time esteemed one of the wealthiest men of southern Ohio. Stephen Buckingham, his brother, settled near him and about the same time.

William Jeffers, born in Chester county, Pennsylvania, in 1786, settled in Carthage township as a farmer in 1807. He has lived in the township continuously for over sixty years, and is a highly respected citizen. His oldest son, A. P. Jeffers, was born in 1810 in Carthage, where he still lives. He was for several years one of the township trustees. Two of the sons of A. P. Jeffers served in the 53d regiment O. V. I.

R. W. Jeffers, another son of William, was born in Carthage township in 1814, and is still living there a respectable farmer.

Alexander Caldwell was born in Ireland in 1791, came to the United States in 1804 and to Carthage township in 1816, where he settled as a farmer and still lives. He served one term as justice of the peace and several years as township trustee. His descendants are numerous and respectable.

Moses Elliott, born February 1, 1784, in the county of Donegal, Ireland, came to the United States in 1819, and settled as a farmer in Carthage township in 1823. He lived on the farm where he first settled, till his death in 1854. He was a justice of the peace for twelve years, and was highly respected as a citizen. His family, two sons and five daughters, are all living.

John Elliott, his oldest son, born in Ireland in 1816, came to Carthage with his father's family in 1823, and lived here till 1859. He was county commissioner several years and much esteemed. In 1859 he removed to southwestern Missouri, where he still resides. During the late war he was driven away from his farm on account of his Union sentiments, and was absent several years, but since the return of peace has resumed his residence there.

James Elliott, youngest son of Moses, was born in Carthage in 1826, and has lived ever since on the farm where he was born. He has been township clerk for many years, and is held in high esteem by the whole community.

James Baker was born in Coshocton county, Ohio, in the year 1805, and came to Carthage in 1826, where he has followed the joint vocation of farmer and miller. Six of his sons and one son-in-law were in the Union army during the late war.

Daniel Boyd was born in Ireland in 1794, emigrated to the United States in 1819, and settled in Carthage township as a farmer in 1838. He was an active member of the Methodist church and an excellent citizen. He died August 20, 1867. His oldest son, Dr. John E. Boyd, died in West Virginia in 1855. His other two sons, Hugh and William F., graduated at the Ohio university in 1860 and 1866, respectively, and have engaged successfully in teaching.

Abraham Norris, born in New York in 1807, came to Ohio and settled in Carthage in 1829, where he now lives a farmer.

Peter Hammond was born in York county, Pennsylvania, in 1794, and settled in Carthage township as a farmer in 1845. His oldest son, John Hammond, is now a justice of the peace. Three of his sons served in the Union army.

Nathaniel Martin was born in Massachusetts in 1789, and came to Carthage in 1836, where he has since lived a farmer. He served as township treasurer for twenty-two years consecutively.

Caleb P. Wells was born in New Hampshire in the year 1800. He married the only daughter of Mr. Martin, and moved to Carthage with his father-in-law in 1836, where he has since lived a farmer.

Walter Glazier was born in Ames township, in this county, in 1807, and removed to Carthage in 1837. He has served as justice of the peace five years, township assessor seven years, and township trustee twelve years. Two of his sons and a step-son served in the Union army.

John Lawrence was born in New Hampshire in 1808, and settled as a farmer in Carthage township in 1837, where he has since lived. His oldest son, John W. Lawrence, an excellent man and citizen, served faithfully in the Union army, and was killed in battle near the close of the war.

Edward Lawrence, born in New Hampshire in 1810, settled in Carthage in 1841. His occupation is farming. He was appointed postmaster at Lottridge, when the office was established, in 1851, and still holds the position.

William Mills was born in Washington county, Pennsylvania, in 1808, removed to Jefferson county, Ohio, in 1812, and to Carthage township in 1839, where he still lives. By occupation he is a farmer. He served one year as township trustee, and one year as assessor.

CHAPTER XIII.

Dover Township.

THE township of Dover originally formed a part of Ames, and as such was settled as early as 1799. It was not, however, separately organized as a township till 1811. On the 4th of April, 1811, the county commissioners ordered:

"That so much of the township of Ames as lies west of the thirteenth range, be erected into a separate township by the name of *Dover*.

"*Ordered*, further, That the clerk of the board notify the inhabitants of the township of Dover to meet at the house of Othniel Tuttle in said township, on Saturday, the 20th of April, instant, for the purpose of electing township officers."

Thus Dover, as originally organized (including all that part of Ames lying west of the thirteenth range), comprised the present townships of Ward, Green, and Starr, in Hocking county, and Trimble, York, and Dover, in Athens. The main settlements were on Sunday creek and near the waters of the Hockhocking, and it was many years before the forests of the remote parts of the township were invaded by any but the solitary hunter and trapper, or the hardy frontiersman who could not brook near neighborhood.

Among the early settlers of Dover were Daniel Weethee, Josiah True, Abraham Pugsley, Azel Johnson, Henry O'Neill, Samuel Tannehill, Barney J. Robinson, Cornelius Shoemaker, Nehemiah Davis, James Pickett, Jeremiah Cass, Jonathan Watkins, the Nye family, Reuben J. Davis, the Fullers, Luther Danielson, George Wilson, Benjamin Davis, Uriah Nash, Eliphalet Wheeler, Reuben Hurlbut, Samuel Stacey, Thomas A. Smith, Uriah Tippee, Abner Connett, and others mentioned elsewhere.

The township is thoroughly well watered by the Hockhocking river, Sunday creek, and their tributaries. A portion of its surface is rather rough, but the hills are of moderate elevation, and admirably adapted to the growth of wheat and fruits, and to sheep raising; while in other parts of the township are broad and fertile plains. The mineral resources of the township are extensive and valuable. In the southern portion are the salt regions, near the junction of Sunday creek with the Hockhocking, about Chauncey and Salina. There are two extensive deposits of coal—a vein four feet thick mined from the surface, and another six feet thick reached by shafting about a hundred feet. There are also excellent limestone and building stone in the township.

There are three villages in Dover, viz: Millfield, on Sunday creek, in the northern part of the township, with a population of about two hundred; Salina, a thriving village on the Hockhocking, where the salt works of M. M. Greene & Co. are situated, and Chauncey, on the opposite side of the river from Salina. Chauncey was laid out in 1839. About 1831 Resolved Fuller bored a salt well on the upper portion of his fine farm (including the present site of Chauncey), obtained good salt water, and prepared to manufacture salt on a small scale. In 1833, however, he sold his works and about four hundred acres of land to Calvary Morris and Norman Root, of Athens, who built an enlarged furnace and so extended the business, that in 1837 they sold it to Messrs. Ewing and Vinton for six thousand five hundred dollars. In 1838 Messrs. Ewing and Vinton, together with Elihu Chauncey and Nicholas Biddle, capitalists of Philadelphia, bought Resolved Fuller's farm, on which Chauncey is located, for twelve thousand five hundred dollars, and the next year laid off the town. They invested largely in surrounding lands, bored other salt wells, built a brick hotel and several houses, and expected to establish a thriving town. But the place has never prospered greatly, and has at present a population of only one hundred and fifty.

The total population of Dover in 1820 was 607; in 1830 it was 550 (its territory having been curtailed); in 1840 it was 1290; in 1850 it was 1232; in 1860 it was 1423.

"Weethee college," at Mt. Auburn in the northern part of the township, is one of the best educational establishments in the county. It was founded in 1861 entirely through the efforts of the Rev. J. P. Weethee, who continues to be its controller and liberal patron. Youth of both sexes are taught here, and the institution has begun a career of assured success and usefulness.

The early settlers of Dover were sterling men and not behind any others in the country in their desire for knowledge and progress. Part of the credit of forming the old "Coonskin library" justly belongs to them. Many shares were taken by persons living in those parts which afterward became Dover, and by the men who were in later years the fathers of the township. In January, 1816, at a meeting of the shareholders of the library it was

"*Resolved*, That one of the directors of the association be hereafter chosen from among the shareholders belonging to the township of Dover, and the said director shall have the care of as many books belonging to the library as the shareholders in Dover are entitled to draw, and shall deliver out, receive in and mark the damages on said books agreeably to the rules and regulations of the society; and once in six months he shall deliver over to the society all the books in his care, and meet the other directors for the purpose of transacting the necessary business of the society."

Eventually a division of the library was made, and by an act of the legislature passed December 21, 1830, the "Dover library association" was incorporated, with Daniel Weethee, Alanson Hibbard, Azariah Pratt, Josiah True, John B. Johnson, William Hyde, and John Pugsley as the original incorporators, and Daniel Weethee, Alanson Hibbard, and Azariah Pratt as directors for the first year.

We have not been able to procure the records of the township previous to 1825; they have been lost or destroyed. The following are the township trustees since that time.

Township Trustees since 1825.

1825	Resolved Fuller,	Daniel Weethee,	Samuel B. Johnson.
1826	Jonathan Allen,	Simon H. Mansfield,	William Bagley.
1827	Jeremiah Morris,	"	Josiah True.
1828	Resolved Fuller,	"	"
1829	Jeremiah Morris,	"	Horace Carter.
1830	Daniel Weethee,	"	Josiah True.
1831	Samuel Stevens,	Jeremiah Morris,	"
1832	"	Robert Conn,	"
1833	"	"	"
1834	John Armstrong,	"	"
1835	Jeremiah Morris,	Jonathan Connett,	"
1836–37	John Armstrong,	S. R. Fox,	"
1838	Record lost.		
1839	John Armstrong,	Matthew McCune,	David Tarrnerd.
1840	Mason B. Brown,	Harry Clark,	Josiah True.
1841	Jeremiah Morris,	Matthew McCune,	"
1842	John Armstrong,	"	"
1843–44	Albert Harper,	"	"
1845	William Hyde,	"	"
1846	Azariah Pratt,	"	"
1847	Henry Brown,	"	"
1848	Azariah Pratt,	"	"
1849	William Edwards,	Austen Fuller,	"

History of Athens County, Ohio.

TRUSTEES—*Continued.*

1850–51	Matthew McCune,	Austen Fuller,	W. S. Hyde.
1852	"	"	James Culver.
1853	Seth Fuller,	"	John Spencer.
1854	"	W. S. Hyde,	"
1855	Samuel Augustin,	"	Woodruff Connett.
1856–57	John Cradlebaugh,	"	Austen Fuller.
1858	"	"	E. D. Harper.
1859–60	"	Austen Fuller,	O. G. Berge.
1861	Alex. Stephenson,	"	"
1862	Ebenezer Pratt,	Joseph Tippy,	W. S. Hyde.
1863	O. G. Birge,	"	"
1864	"	J. W. P. Cook,	"
1865–66	"	"	"
1867	"	R. N. Fuller,	"
1868	George Connett,	Samuel Augustin,	Ebenezer Pratt.

Justices of the Peace since 1825.

    1826—D. Herrold.
    1827–31—Josiah True.
    1832–33—Simon H. Mansfield.
    1834–37—Josiah True.
    1839—Frederick Cradlebaugh.
    1841—John Armstrong.
    1843—Josiah True.
    1845—Charles R. Smith.
    1846—Hiram Fuller.
    1851—Charles R. Smith.
    1852—J. W. P. Cook.
    1853—Hiram Fuller.
    1854—William Edwards.
    1855—E. D. Varner.
    1856—Hiram Fuller and Charles R. Smith.
    1858—Josephus Calvert.
    1859—Hiram Fuller and John Smith.
    1862—J. W. P. Cook, Hiram Fuller, and John Smith.
    1865—Job S. King.
    1868—Hiram Fuller, Charles R. Smith, and John Smith.

Personal and Biographical.

Daniel Weethee was born in New Hampshire in 1779. He was a cooper by trade, and saved money enough, during his youth, to buy a tract of land in what is now Dover township. At the age of nineteen he set out for the northwestern territory, made the tedious journey on foot and alone, and reached Marietta about the middle of December, 1798. The next spring he and another young man, Josiah True, came out to Dover, traveling through the woods by the aid of a compass. Arrived here they built a log cabin for their joint occupancy (they were both unmarried), and lived together about three years. Mr. True managed, by hard work and by selling skins, furs, etc., to secure means enough to purchase a piece of land, and bought part of the farm now owned by his son, Austin True, where he lived during the rest of his life. Thus they lived for about three years in this truly pioneer fashion, with no companions but the forest trees, and no neighbors but the wild game of all sorts which abounded near their cabin.

In 1802 Mr. Weethee married Lucy Wilkins, daughter of John Wilkins, one of the early settlers of Athens township, and the next year Mr. True married Almira, a daughter of Solomon Tuttle, then living on the creek a few miles above, in what is now Trimble township.

In 1804 Abraham Pugsley came in with his family, and settled on the section south of Mr. Weethee and Mr. True. Mr. Pugsley, who was a good citizen and excellent man, reared a large and respectable family here. He was drowned during the winter of the "cold plague" in 1814, while crossing the creek on the ice to visit a sick family. His oldest son, John, died several years since. The youngest son, James, is living, though very old.

One of the daughters of Abraham Pugsley had a singular adventure in early life. She was married, when only thirteen years of age, to a man named Neal. Her husband enlisted in the army in 1812, and, after he had left home with his company, on a keel boat, from the mouth of the Hockhocking (where they then lived), for Newport, Kentucky, the rendezvous, his wife determined to follow him and share his fortunes, whatever they might be. She started down the river alone in a canoe, and passed the first night in the little craft on the water; but the next day overtook her husband, and proceeded with him to St. Louis. Thence his company was ordered to some point further west. While going up the river the boat was landed for some purpose, when Indians fired from an ambush and killed her husband and the infant in her arms, wounding her at the same time. The company, with Mrs. Neal, returned to St. Louis, from whence she rode on a pony all the way back to her father's in Dover township.

In 1817 she was again married to Mr. John Fulton, and died in May, 1866.

In 1800 the Sweat family came to Dover, and settled near the present site of Millfield. In 1802 John Sweat built a rude mill there for grinding corn, which was greatly prized by the settlement. Even persons from Athens made use of this mill till the Gregory mill was built, about four years later.

In 1802 Azel Johnson, with his family, settled in Dover, on the creek and joining the Weethee farm. Many of his descendants are still living in the township. Azel and Benjamin Johnson are sons of his.

The Nye family, consisting of Ebenezer, the father (a native of Tolland, Connecticut, who came to the territory in 1790), and four sons, viz: George, Neal, Nathan, and Theodorus, came out from Marietta in 1814, and settled in Dover about a mile north of Chauncey. The eldest son died in 1825, leaving a widow, Mrs. Lydia Nye, now living at an advanced age with her son, George Nye, on the place first occupied by his father. The other brothers removed to Meigs county, where their descendants are numerous and respectable.

In 1820 the Nyes and some others formed a company to bore a salt well, on the place where Jeremiah Morris now lives, but, after boring to a considerable depth, abandoned the undertaking. Ten or twelve years later it was resumed by John Pugsley, who, after boring a little deeper, struck a vein of good salt water. This was the first successful salt well bored in the Hockhocking valley. About this time (1820) came the Cass, the Chadwell, the Nesmith, and the Pratt families, who have lived in Dover nearly fifty years, and are all excellent people.

Three sons of Daniel Weethee, the pioneer, are now living. Daniel W. Weethee lives on a fine farm in Trimble township; Lorentius Weethee owns and occupies the old homestead in Dover; and Jonathan P. Weethee, who graduated at the Ohio university in 1832, and has been actively engaged during his life in the ministry and in teaching in this and other states, is now the president of Weethee college at Mt. Auburn, in Dover.

Josiah True, the companion and friend of Daniel Weethee, was born in New Hampshire, October 25, 1776, came to Marietta in 1793, and to Dover township in 1800. He held the office of justice of the peace in Dover, from 1815 till 1851, and was respected and popular. He died September 16, 1855. Mr. True was one of the founders of the "Coonskin library," of Ames, and always a leader in pioneer improvements. One of the first spinning wheels introduced into Dover was bought by him in 1803. Having accumulated a few bear and deer skins he carried them on his back to Zanesville, forty miles distant, purchased the wheel with the proceeds of the skins, brought it home on his back (walking all the way), and made the round trip of eighty miles *in two days.*

Most of the early settlers engaged more or less in hunting, depending mainly on the forests for fresh meat. On one occasion Josiah True and Cyrus Tuttle, his brother-in-law, drove a bear into a cave on the farm now owned by Mr. Austin True, in Dover. They succeeded in shooting the animal in a narrow passage of the cave, and, having fastened a hickory withe to his nose, were about to drag it to the open air. Mr. True entered the cave, and got behind the dead bear to assist Tuttle in shoving it out, when another bear, hitherto unobserved, came rushing from the rear end of the cave, directly on and over True's back, crushing him down on his face with great violence, and so made its escape out of the cave.

Mr. True, at a very early day, bought some choice apples at Marietta, and sowed the seed from them, from which he established the first nursery attempted in the county. Most of the old orchards on Sunday and Monday creeks were planted from this nursery, and some of the trees are still bearing.

Nehemiah Davis, "Elder Davis," a native of Maine, came to Marietta in November, 1797, lived in Washington county several years, and removed to Dover township in 1808. While living in Washington county

Elder Davis organized a Baptist church, believed to be the first Baptist church in Ohio. He died August 23, 1823. Some of his descendants are living in the county, and a granddaughter married Colonel James H. Goodman, present state auditor of Ohio.

CHAPTER XIV.

Lee Township.

LEE township, originally a part of Alexander, was separately orgainzed in November, 1819. Among the earliest settlers here were Capt. John Martin, a revolutionary soldier, Philip Smith, Henry Cassel, Ziba McVey, Daniel Knowlton, George Canny, John Holdren, William Brown, William Graham, Jacob Lentner, James McGonnegal, Francis Thomas, Samuel Luckey, Hiram Howlett, and John Doughty.

The population of the township in 1820 was 342; in 1830 it was 418; in 1840 it was 848; in 1850 it was 961; in 1860 it was 1,301. The inhabitants of Lee are principally engaged in agriculture, and her farmers rank among the best. Latterly they have given especial attention to the growing of fine stock.

The center of population in the township is Albany, a neat village and handsomely located. No community in the county has attended more earnestly to the cause of education than the citizens of Albany, and they have several excellent local schools. The "Atwood institute," originally founded, and for a few years conducted, as a "manual labor school," is now controlled by the Free-will Baptists, and, under the management of the Rev. Mr. Chase, is proving a successful and useful school. It has at present three teachers—two male and one female—and about eighty scholars. All the branches usually taught in academies of this class are taught here. The colored people have a good school in Albany, conducted by capable teachers, and attended by young colored persons of both sexes from distant parts of the state. They have a handsome school building, conspicuously located, which has been built mainly by the contributions of colored people, and the good management and complete success, thus far, of their enterprise, are highly creditable. The "district school," divided into an upper and lower department—the former superintended by Mr. J. C. Woodyard, and the latter by Miss Mary L. Kerr—is also a well-managed and useful school. And, finally, there is a good public school for colored children.

Albany also possesses an excellent public library, called the "Wells library." It was founded by Mr. Henry Wells, who, dying in 1860, bequeathed one thousand dollars for that purpose as a perpetual fund, the interest to be expended in books, and the further sum of two hundred and fifty dollars for an immediate purchase. The money was securely invested in 1861, by Mr. E. H. Moore, of Athens, whom Mr. Wells made his trustee for this purpose, and about seven hundred dollars worth of books have already been purchased by Mr. Leonard Brown, the purchasing committee. For some time the library was kept in a room gratuitously furnished by the Free Masons of Albany, but in March, 1868, Mrs. Mary Weethee, mother of the founder of the library, bequeathed a frame building to be used as a library room, provided the town should keep it in repair and pay the taxes. The library, consisting now of about four hundred volumes, is a settled and very creditable institution. By the rules of the library any family, living within the corporation, may, for one dollar a year, draw out two volumes at a time for not more than four weeks, and the library is open two hours every Thursday for members. An interesting instance is thus afforded, of the great and perpetual good that may be accomplished by a very small sum well directed. Possibly the excellent example will incite others to similar action, and so its usefulness be indefinitely multiplied. Mr. Wells was a grandson of Hiram Howlett, one of the early settlers of Lee.

The village of Albany is located on sections two and three, and was laid out into lots by William Graham, in 1832 or 1833. The first house in the village was built by Lucius R. Beckley, on the ground now owned by Atkins & Stanly, and known as the old Brown store. In 1840 John Brown purchased this property and commenced selling goods here. Albany has a population of about six hundred, with the usual complement of business men and mechanics. The Free Masons and Sons of Temperance have each a hall in the village. No liquor is sold within the corporation.

The town was incorporated in 1844. At the first election for town officers John V. Brown was chosen mayor, and J. M. Gorsline recorder. For a number of years afterward there was no election, but since 1855 they have been held regularly.

Town Officers of Albany since 1855.

1855.—Mayor, Albert Vorhes; Recorder, Henry Wells; Treasurer, John Vorhes; Councilmen, John Brown, J. M. Gorsline, Wm. Smith, Peter Morse, and David Sampson.

1856.—Mayor, Albert Vorhes; Recorder, John Brown; Treasurer, John Vorhes; Councilmen, Wm. R. Collins, Peter Morse, W. W. Kurtz, J. M. Gorsline, and P. McCann.

1857.—Mayor, A. Palmer; Recorder, J. E. Rutledge; Treasurer, John Vorhes; Councilmen, H. L. Graham, David Sampson, John Dewing, Wm. C. Lindley, and John Slaughter.

1858.—Mayor, Almus Lindley; Recorder, J. E. Rutledge; Treasurer, H. L. Graham; Councilmen, John Dewing, Wm. C. Lindley, C. D. Lindley, A. Vorhes, and Chandler Rossetter.

1859.—Mayor, W. B. Dicksen; Recorder, J. E. Rutledge; Treasurer, H. L. Graham; Councilmen, W. C. Lindley, John Slaughter, S. M. Preshaw, J. Q. Mitchell, and Almus Lindley.

1860.—Mayor, S. M. Preshaw; Recorder, W. A. Rigg; Treasurer, H. L. Graham; Councilmen, Almus Lindley, John Q. Mitchell, John Brown, John Slaughter, and Albert Vorhes.

1861.—Mayor, John Brown; Recorder, Thomas D. McGrath; Treasurer, Albert Vorhes; Councilmen, A. D. Jaynes, John Vorhes, C. L. Wilson, Wm. C. Lindley, and George Rice.

1862.—Mayor, James M. Gorsline; Recorder, A. Palmer; Treasurer, A. D. Jaynes; Councilmen, John Brown, John Dewing, Almus Lindley, John Vorhes, and Leonard Brown.

1863.—Mayor, James M. Gorsline; Recorder, A. Palmer; Treasurer, A. D. Jaynes; Councilmen, John Vorhes, John Q. Mitchell, John Dewing, W. W. Kurtz, and T. D. Garvin.

1864.—Mayor, James M. Gorsline; Recorder, Ira Graham; Treasurer, T. D. McGrath; Councilmen, Leonard Brown, John Vorhes, T. D. Garvin, John Dewing, and A. D. Jaynes.

1865.—Mayor, James M. Gorsline; Recorder, Ira Graham; Treasurer, T. D. McGrath; Councilmen, Leonard Brown, John Vorhes, A. Palmer, John Dewing, and A. D. Jaynes.

1866.—Mayor, James M. Gorsline; Recorder, Daniel N. Brown; Treasurer, John Brown; Councilmen, John Dewing, A. Vorhes, Wm. C. Lindley, Isaac Stanly, Jun., and A. Palmer.

1867.—Mayor, James M. Gorsline; Recorder, Daniel N. Brown; Treasurer, James D. Brown; Councilmen, Wm. C. Lindley, Isaac Stanley, Jun., A. Vorhes, Leonard Brown, and James McClure.

1868.—Mayor, James M. Gorsline; Recorder, Albert Lawson; Treasurer, James D. Brown; Councilmen, Wm. C. Lindley, James McClure, Leonard Brown, A. Vorhes, and W. W. Blake.

Township Trustees.

1820	Jacob Lentner,	James McGonnegal,	Ephraim Martin.
1821	Francis Thomas,	"	Elisha Chapman.
1822	Ephraim Martin,	"	Daniel Rowell.
1823	Joseph Wallace,	Francis Thomas,	William Brown.
1824–27	Ephraim Martin,	"	James McGonnegal.
1828	Samuel Martin,	"	"
1829–30	James Magee,	George Reeves,	McCowen Bean.
1831	Wm. Graham,	Wm. Thompson,	"
1832	Joseph Martin,	"	John Havener.

TRUSTEES—*Continued.*

1833–35	Wm. Graham,	James McGonnegal,	Joseph Martin.
1836	Joseph Post,	Wm Thompson,	Nimrod Dailey.
1837–40	Wm. Graham,	Michael Canney,	"
1841–42	John T. Winn,	Joseph Post,	Jacob Lentner.
1843–44	Wm. Graham,	Wm. Henderson,	"
1845–46	F. E. Clark,	A. G. Henderson,	James Greathouse.
1847	"	Travis Wilson,	"
1848	"	John Brown,	George Holdren.
1849	Andrew Means,	John Dewing,	"
1850	F. E. Clark,	D. M. Ross,	A. W. Brown.
1851	"	Leonard Brown,	D. M. Ross,
1852	James Holmes,	B. Goodrich,	John T. Winn.
1853–54	"	A. Enlow,	"
1855	"	Samuel Shuster,	"
1856	"	Jacob McVey,	"
1857	"	James Clements,	"
1858	"	"	Benjamin Rickey.
1859	"	"	A. W. Brown.
1860	"	W. W. Kurtz,	"
1861	"	A. Wilson,	"
1862–63	"	A. Jennings,	"
1864	"	A. Wilson,	"
1865	"	Wm. C. Lindley,	Robert Dickson.
1866–67	Lemuel Cline,	Jacob McVey,	"
1868	Albert Vorhes,	"	"

Justices of the Peace.

1820—Isaac Baker.
1822—Abner C. Martin.
1823—Isaac Baker.
1824—Joseph Wallace.
1825—McCowen Bean, Michael Canney, James McGee.
1828—Jacob Lentner.
1831—McCowen Bean and Abner C. Martin.
1832—Jacob Lentner.
1834—Abner C. Martin.
1835—Jacob Lentner.
1837—Abner C. Martin.
1838—John Dickson.
1839—Lucius Beckley.
1840—Abraham Enlow.
1841—A. Warner.
1842—John T. Winn.

JUSTICES OF THE PEACE—*Continued.*

 1843—George Means and Francis E. Clark.
 1844—Edmund Morse.
 1845—A. G. Henderson and Peter Morse.
 1846—Francis E. Clark.
 1847—George Holdren.
 1849—D. M. Ross and Francis E. Clark.
 1850—Joseph Post.
 1852—James Clements and Francis E. Clark.
 1853—Joseph Post.
 1854—George Johnson.
 1855—James Clements, John Brown and Jacob McVey.
 1856—Harvey L. Graham.
 1858—James Clements and Jacob McVey.
 1859—Harvey L. Graham.
 1860—Peter Morse.
 1861—E. R. Cooper.
 1862—James M. Gorsline.
 1864—E. R. Cooper.
 1865—James M. Gorsline.
 1867—John Q. Mitchell and Isaac Friedlein.
 1868—Abraham Enlow.

Biographical and Personal.

 John Holdren, now living in Lee township, was born in Bucks county, Pennsylvania, October 15, 1777, and came to Athens county in 1798 accompanied by another young man named John Konker. Soon after reaching Athens they took up land in the south part of Alexander township and made a temporary settlement on the waters of Margaret's creek. Their neighbors, at intervals of several miles, were the Hanings, the Brooks family, Joseph Long, Esquire Merritt, and Henry

Cassel. Mr. Cassel built a grist mill soon afterward in Lee township on the place now owned by William Minear. Mr. Holdren was engaged during six or seven years working at the Scioto salt works at the site of the present town of Jackson, and "could then cut his six cords of wood in a day and help load it." He went out there the second year after salt was discovered by the whites. Previous to this the Indians had produced scanty supplies of salt by drilling holes into the rocks fifteen or eighteen inches deep, when the cavity would gradually fill up with the brinish water which, evaporated by the heat of the sun, would produce salt. The whites bored wells to some depth, built furnaces, and for many years furnished salt for the surrounding settlements to the distance of seventy-five or eighty miles. Mr. Holdren settled permanently in Lee township in 1820. His nearest neighbors were James McGonnegal, Israel Bobo, and George Canney, and soon afterward came David Doughty, James Luckey, Thomas Jones, John Havner, John and Ephraim Martin, Daniel Knowlton, Jacob Lentner, and the Robinetts. When a young man Mr. Holdren was a successful hunter. He and John Jones (a brother-in-law of Judge Isaac Barker), killed forty-six bears in six weeks' hunting on the head waters of Sunday, Monday, and Rush creeks. They sometimes killed in a fall season forty to fifty deer for their winter's stock of provisions and turkeys beyond count. Mr. Holdren once killed four deer in one day, and he and two of his boys in a hunt of two weeks killed thirty. On one hunting expedition, having shot and wounded a large black bear, his dog ran in to seize the animal, but bruin, though hurt, was full of life, and was making quick work of the dog when Holdren rushed in, knife in hand, to finish him. The bear released the dog and sprang on the man, at the first dash tearing his large blanket entirely from his body; Holdren plunged his knife hilt deep into the animal and then turned to run. He made his escape, but says it was the narrowest he ever had. The bear got away. At that time the skins of bears brought from three to five dollars each, and good hunters often made it profitable. Mr. Holdren served in the war of 1812. Among those who entered the army at that time he remembers Barnet Brice, John Wood, Reuben Reeves, David Vaughn, Ira Foster, Joel Stroud, Jehiel Gregory, Nehemiah Gregory, and William McNichol. Mr. Holdren is the oldest person in the county, being now ninety-one years old. He and his aged wife live with a married daughter on a comfortable farm about two miles from Albany, and the old man, aided by a staff in each hand, sometimes walks to the village.

CHAPTER XV.

Lodi Township.

THIS township was originally a part of Alexander. The eastern half of Lodi was included in Carthage when that township was organized in 1819, and was not detached till 1826. Lodi was separately organized in April of that year, and, according to the records, only fourteen votes were cast at the first township election held in the spring of 1827. The population of the township in 1830 was 276; in 1840 it was 754; in 1850 it was 1,336; in 1860 it was 1,598. Joseph Thompson was one of the earliest settlers in Lodi. He lived on the farm now owned by Cyrus Blazer, and built the first flouring mill about 1815. Some of his descendants still reside here. Before he built his mill (which has long since disappeared), the inhabitants of this region used to get their milling done at Coolville, more than fifteen miles off. The second mill was built in 1825 by Ezra Miller; it was very small and has also disappeared. At present there is an excellent steam flouring mill in the township of ample capacity. The first religious society formed in Lodi was by the Methodists in 1820 under the supervision of the Rev. Goddard Curtis. They worshiped for many years in a small school house on Shade river. At present the Methodists have a flourishing society that worships in "Morse chapel," an excellent frame church building, and another large class meet in what is called "Cremer's" or Wesley Chapel. The Cumberland Presbyterians organized a society here about 1843 and built a good frame church, but it was destroyed by fire soon afterward. About 1840 the Christians (or Campbellites) formed a society and built a church which, soon after its completion, was demolished by a large forest tree falling on it. They have recently erected a good frame building in the township. There is a very creditable school at Pleasant Valley (Shade post office), in the township, called the "Pleasant Valley seminary." The building, a two-story frame forty by thirty feet, with a cupola and bell, was erected in 1867 by the voluntary contributions of the citizens. It cost $2,000—Mr. Joseph Cremer's donation of $500 was the largest individual subscription. The school opened in December, 1867, under the superintendence of Mr. Daniel D. Clark, a graduate of the Ohio university, who is still the teacher. The trustees are Dr. E. M. Bean, Cyrus Blazer, Asbury Cremer, John Buck, William Angell, John Burson, and W. S. Williams. The school promises to be one of permanent usefulness.

Township Trustees.

1827-28	Joseph Thompson,	Elam Frost,	John L. Kelly.
1829	"	Rufus P. Cooley,	"
1830	Francis B. Drake,	Thomas Miles,	Abner Frost.
1831	Joseph Thompson,	Elam Frost,	John L. Kelly.
1832	"	Thomas Miles,	A. M. Williams.
1833	John Bodwell,	Francis B. Drake,	Abner Frost.
1834	Luther Dinsmore,	John L. Kelly,	J. B. Force.
1835	"	"	G. H. Cooley.
1836	Charles Brown,	"	John Carlton,
1837	Samuel Day,	George Eaton,	Cyrus O. McGrath.
1838	Joseph Bobo,	John Carlton,	David Whaley.
1839	Calvin P. Dains,	Ezra H. Miller,	Rufus P. Cooley.
1840	Samuel Day,	Wakeman Hull,	"
1841	"	Julius Stone,	George Blazer.
1842	"	Jehu Acley,	Churchill Creesey.
1843	Wakeman Hull,	"	"
1844	John Cather,	"	"
1845	Joseph Cremer,	John L. Kelly,	John Whittington.
1846	James G. Roberts,	Wakeman Hull,	"
1847	Julius Stone,	"	John L. Kelly.
1848	William Jeffers,	"	"
1849	"	D. H. Miles,	Amos Moore.
1850	"	Joseph Cremer,	William Bart.
1851	Churchill Creesey,	Ebenezer Williams,	"
1852	"	"	D. H. Miles.
1853	Joseph Cremer,	"	"
1854	E. Williams,	David Hart,	Wm. Jeffers.
1855	Wm. Wilson,	D. D. Miller,	"
1856-57	John Kelly,	"	"
1858	"	David Hart,	"
1859	John Kinney,	"	"
1860	John Cowan,	Joseph Creesey,	"
1861-62	"	"	Lewis Dains.
1863	"	"	John Cather.
1864	"	"	James Wilson.
1865	John Buck,	A. J. Howard,	Lewis Dains.
1866	Moses Lawrence,	"	F. J. Cremer.
1867-68	Wm. Jeffers,	Joseph Creesey,	"

Township Clerks.

1827-31—G. D. Drake.
1832—Rufus P. Cooley.
1833—Joseph B. Force.
1834-36—Rufus P. Cooley.
1837-39—John L. Kelly.

TOWNSHIP CLERKS—*Continued.*

    1840-41—John Cather.
    1842—Jonathan Witham.
    1843—John Cather.
    1844—D. H. Miles.
    1845—Stephen Gates.
    1846-47—Joseph Cremer.
    1848—William H. Hull.
    1849—L. D. Evans.
    1850—Matthew Wilson.
    1851—R. P. Cooley.
    1852-64—Isaac Bedell.
    1865-66—R. R. Cooley.
    1867-68—John Crather.

Successive Justices of the Peace.

    1827—Joseph Thompson.
    1829-32—Rufus P. Cooley.
    1833—Joseph Thompson.
    1835—Rufus P. Cooley and Luther Dinsmore.
    1837—Smith C. Allen.
    1838—Churchill Creesey.
    1839—William Lee.
    1840—Richard St. Clair.
    1841—Julius Stone.
    1842—David H. Miles.
    1843—Richard St. Clair.
    1845—David H. Miles.
    1846—Isaac Woodyard.
    1848—John Cather.
    1849—Isaac Woodyard.
    1851—Lorenzo D. Evans.
    1852—Isaac Woodyard.
    1854—Lorenzo D. Evans and David Hart.
    1857-60—Lorenzo D. Evans and Elisha Langhead.

History of Athens County, Ohio. 485

JUSTICES OF THE PEACE—*Continued.*

1861—Benoni R. Pierce.
1863—John Kelly.
1864—Nelson Lord.
1866—Waldron S. Williams.
1867—Nelson Lord.
1868—William J. Shaffer.

NARRATIVE OF JOSEPH BOBO, OF LODI.

My father, Henry Bobo, was born and reared in Prince William county, Virginia, and my mother, whose maiden name was Sarah Black, in Loudoun county, in the same state. They came to Athens county in 1798, and settled on Margaret's creek, two miles from Athens. I was born here October 24, 1802. In 1810 my father removed to what is now Lodi township. I was eight years old, and can remember a little about the removal. Lodi was all wilderness then. I think there was but one man living in the (present) township when we moved in, and that was Joseph Thompson. He lived on the farm now owned by Cyrus Blazer. After I was thirteen years old I used to go to mill at Coolville, about fifteen miles distant, and there was but one house on the road, called the "brick house," about eight miles west of Coolville. I once went to mill more than seventy miles, thus: from Athens to the mouth of Hockhocking (by water), forty miles; then up the Ohio to Marietta, thirty miles; then up the Muskingum to the horse mill, two miles, making altogether about seventy-two miles. Sometimes three or four men would form a party, go down the Hockhocking, and up the Ohio to Belpre, in a canoe. There they would get their grain and go on to the horse mill above Marietta, where they had to give one-fourth for grinding, then home again with the canoe. When they reached Athens (which was called "the point" when I was a little boy), each man would shoulder his sack and pack it home. My father and a few others had hand mills, with which they could grind corn in the fall of the year, when the corn is soft. In this way we got our bread.

So far as meat was concerned we had plenty by killing it in the woods. Deer, bears, and turkeys were very plenty, and I have seen a good many elk when I was a boy, and some buffaloes. My father was considerable of a hunter, and killed a great many deer and bears. I remember an adventure he had with a bear when I was about fifteen years old. In the forepart of winter the fat bears would go into a hollow tree or cave, and stay there till spring. They were always fat when they came out in the spring. Frequently, they went into pretty rough caves or holes in the rocks. Father would go in, with a pine torch in one hand and his gun in the other, and crawl as close as he could, and then shoot. The time I am speaking of, he and George Shidler found a hole in the rocks they had never been in before, so father lighted his torch and started in to explore as usual. He had gone about twenty-five feet, looking all the time to see if there was any thing, when suddenly the bear struck the torch with his paw, and put out the light. Father got out of that as quickly as possible, and told Shidler what had happened, and that the bear was lying in a very difficult place to shoot, for it was around the corner of a rock which he could not pass, and the hole was very small. But father determined to go in again, and told George to stand at the mouth of the hole, and, if the bear came out, to shoot it. He lighted his torch again, and got as near the bear as he could, and fired, but only wounded him. The bear started for the mouth of the hole, right toward father, who just had time to lie down flat on his belly, when the bear rushed over him, tearing his clothes pretty badly, and leaving marks of claws on his back that he carried to his grave. Shidler was ready at the mouth of the hole, and, when the bear came out, gave him an ounce of lead that settled him. They dressed the bear and it weighed three hundred and ninety pounds. My father killed as many as seven deer in one day, and that often. He also killed elk and a few buffaloes after we came here, but the buffaloes left very soon.

I think the last one seen in this region, was in Bedford township, Meigs county, in 1815, where it was wounded. When I was a young man I have stood in one spot, behind a large tree, in Lodi township, and killed three deer as fast as I could load and shoot. My brother, Thomas Bobo, killed twelve deer the year he was twelve years old.

CHAPTER XVI.

Rome Township.

ROME was formed from a portion of the township of Troy in 1811. The first entry on the subject, in the records of the county commissioners, is as follows:

"*Thursday, April 4,* 1811.—*Ordered* by the commissioners, That so much of the township of Troy as is contained in the original surveyed townships, numbered 5 and 6, in the 11th range, and 6 in the 12th range, be erected into a new township by the name of *Rome*. . . . . . .

"*Ordered* by the commissioners, That their clerk notify the inhabitants of the township of Rome to meet at the house of Amos Crippen, in said township, on Saturday the 20th instant, for the purpose of electing township officers."

But no election was held under this order, and, on the 4th of June ensuing, the commissioners

"*Ordered,* That the boundaries of the township of Rome be as follows, to wit: beginning at the southwest corner of township No. 6 in the 12th range, thence east on the township line until it intersects the river Hockhocking, thence up said river until it intersects the range line between the 11th and 12th ranges, thence on said range line (being the line between the counties of Athens and Washington) to the south boundary of Ames township, thence west on said township line to the township of Athens, thence south to the place of beginning, and that the remainder of the township of Rome be and is hereby attached to the township of Troy. [This refers to the previous order of April 4th.]

"*Ordered* by the commissioners, That their clerk notify, by advertisement, the inhabitants of the township of Rome to meet at the house of Daniel Stewart, on Saturday, the 15th instant, for the purpose of electing township officers."

The only change that has since been made in these boundaries, was by an act of the legislature, passed February 10, 1814, which detached sections 31 and 32, township 6, range 11, from Washington county, and added them to Rome, thus taking in the strip east of the Hockhocking, and causing the offset at the southeast corner of the township.

The population of Rome in 1820 was 497; in 1830 it was 522; in 1840 it was 852; in 1850 it was 1,309; in 1860 it was 1581.

The Methodist church was planted in this township at a very early day. Daniel and Archelaus Stewart were the first to move in the matter of forming a society here. They settled here in 1802. About two years later Daniel Stewart rode twenty miles to meet the Rev. Jacob Young, who was then on the Marietta circuit, and engaged him to visit Rome township. Mr. Young came according to promise. In his autobiography, published a few years since, in narrating the events of 1855, Mr. Young speaks of Daniel Stewart:

"Under whose hospitable roof I have spent many a happy night, and from whose hand I had received many a dollar, when I stood in great need of money. I first lodged with this good man in 1804, preached and organized a church in his house. He was then in the vigor of manhood, and was one of most active and enterprising men in Ohio."

William Pilcher, Job Ruter, Eliphalet Case, Elijah Rowell, and their wives, were among the earliest members of the society thus formed by "Father Young." The Methodists now have three neat and substantial church buildings in the township, where services are held regularly. One of the first ministers who preached in the township, was the Rev. Cyrus Paulk, jr., who preached in 1803, and, thereafter, regularly for many years. He was a "Calvinist Baptist." There is one Baptist and one United Brethren church in Rome.

The first school house in the township, a log structure sixteen feet square, was built in 1804, on the east bank of Federal creek, about two hundred yards below the bridge and near the mouth of the creek. Abraham Richards was the first teacher, and Mrs. Polly Driggs, a daughter of Ebenezer Barrows, was the next. The school was supported by subscription, and was the center of a school district about five miles in diameter.

There are now eleven school houses in the township, each with ample accommodations for forty scholars.

The "Miller seminary," owned and managed by the Rev. Amos Miller, is pleasantly located on his farm, about one mile east of Savannah, near the Hockhocking river, and three miles from the Marietta & Cincinnati railroad. When first established, in 1841, Prof. Miller used a large room in his dwelling house as a school room. As the school increased a separate building on his farm was made use of, and, in 1859, Prof. Miller erected a handsome and convenient two-story building, in which the school has since been kept. Neat cottages have been built close at hand, for the use of pupils who desire to board themselves.

The seminary will accommodate one hundred pupils. Some hundreds of youths of both sexes have been taught here, and the institution is a credit to the founder and to the county. Professor Miller has taught in Athens county at intervals, and most of the time for the last forty-two years.

At Savannah is located the "Savannah academy." This school, the management and success of which have been highly creditable to all concerned, was founded in the spring of 1867 through the efforts of some public spirited citizens of the township. Frederic Finsterwald, Peter Boyles, Vincent Caldwell, Harvey Pierce, and John Caldwell were elected the first board of trustees of the academy and have been its steady patrons and supporters. They employed Mr. George W. Boyce as principal teacher, and the school has been well patronized from the beginning. More than one hundred and forty scholars, in the aggregate, attended during the first year. The active interest in education thus manifested, and the liberal support accorded to this enterprise by the leading citizens of the neighborhood, are worthy of the highest commendation.

There is also a good school at Big Run, founded in 1866 through the voluntary contributions of the citizens. A neat and convenient school building has been erected, and the school is useful and prosperous. It is under the management at present of Miss Elizabeth Monahan.

In 1808 the first bridge in the township was built over Federal creek, near its mouth, by Elijah Hatch, and in 1818 a second one was built at the same place. Both were clumsy structures, and neither of them very permanent. In 1842 a greatly superior bridge was erected by Peter Beebe, Isaac Jackson being the architect; it was at first a toll bridge but is now free. About the year 1851 or 1852, a bridge was built over Federal creek near the mouth of Big Run but was soon swept away; another has since been erected on the same site. The bridge at Savannah was built about ten years ago, the funds being supplied partly by the county and partly by subscription. Another has been built over the Hockhocking about two miles below Savannah, the funds being raised in the same manner.

The first grist and saw mill in the township was built in 1802 by George, Henry, and James Barrows on Federal creek, about a mile from its mouth. The mill was a log building with only one run of stones, which were made of the "Laurel hill granite" and run by a large undershot wheel. This enterprise was hailed with delight by some half dozen infant settlements, some of them distant fifteen or twenty miles. Before this the nearest mill, where wheat could be ground, was Devol's, on the Muskingum, at least forty miles distant. Many families, however, possessed that great desideratum of pioneer life, the primitive hand mill and the "hominy block." There were also a few horse mills in the county, but they were only used for grinding or, as it was called, "cracking" corn. In 1818 Reuben Farnsworth built the first mill on the Hockhocking river, within the township limits. This was one of the most solid and substantial mill structures ever erected in the county. Farnsworth failed, and the mill passed into the hands of Peter Beebe, who afterward sold it to Thomas Welch. It was sold by Mr. Welch to Cook, Crippen & Co., who are the present owners.

In 1820 the Savannah mill (grist and saw mill) was built by Ezra Stewart and his brother Charles, sons of Esquire Daniel Stewart. It has three run of stones and does a great amount of custom work. It is situated on the Hockhocking river, in the village of Savannah, about three miles from the west line of Rome township. About 1834 Alexander Stewart and George Warren built the Stewart mill (a saw mill), near Savannah; but it was soon destroyed by fire, and a large three-story grist and saw mill was erected on the site by Daniel B. Stewart. In 1844 Mr. Stewart connected a woolen factory with the establishment, which is now owned by Captain Charles Byron, late of the 3d regiment O. V. I. It runs four hundred and seventy spindles, has four looms, four carding machines, two spinning jacks, and a full set of fulling and dressing machinery. During the season of 1867 the mill manufactured eight thousand pounds of rolls, ten thousand pounds of yarn, and six thousand pounds of wool into cloth. The grist and saw mill are still in active operation. Two miles above Savannah are the Kincade mills built in 1842 by John and Allen Kincade, and now being rebuilt by John Kincade on an enlarged plan and in a more substantial manner. About 1854 Heman Frost—son of Abram Frost, one of the pioneers of Carthage township—built a grist and saw mill three miles below Cook & Crippen's mill; it was subsequently replaced by a saw mill, which was swept off by a high "freshet" in the spring of 1867.

What was called "upper settlement" of Rome township was formed in the year 1808 by Joshua Selby,

John Thompson, Robert Calvert, and Jonathan Simmons, from Virginia, and Richard, George, and James Simmons from Pennsylvania. They were all good citizens. In 1810 or 1811 Christopher Herrold, one of the pioneers of Ames township, settled in Rome. He was a Pennsylvania German and a man of enterprise and thrift. He afterward removed to Dover.

A singular evidence of the enterprising spirit of the early settlers is afforded by the fact that in 1811 a sea-going vessel was built in Rome township, a mile below the mouth of Federal creek on the south bank of the Hockhocking. She was launched and taken to New Orleans in the spring of 1812. The vessel was built by Captain Caleb Barstow, from Providence, Rhode Island, and was called *The Enterprise.*

Elections, musters, and house raisings were in early times events of special interest. Plenty of good cheer abounded on such occasions, and boisterous frolicking, with the roughest sort of practical jokes, was the order of the day. Colonel Wm. Stewart, an early resident of the county, furnishes the following account of a house raising in Rome township:

" As early as the spring of 1804 father built what was then called a double log barn, about eighteen feet high, all of white oak timber. It required nearly all the settlers of Rome, Carthage, Troy, Ames, and Canaan townships to raise it. In those days, however, no one thought of not responding to such a call, and on this occasion they were all present. As early as sunrise there were about fifty men on hand. As was the universal custom in those days father furnished a copious supply of old rye whisky, and by breakfast time—about 7 o'clock—many of the men felt its effects. The building went on, however, with a will, and the heavy logs were rushed up on large skids with a strength and daring that were surprising, the men cheering and laughing all the while. Dinner came on. According to custom three large chicken pies were placed on the table, one in the center and one at each end. A large decanter of whisky stood by the center one. The crowd being seated grace was said by father, and all being hungry were ready to fallto vigorously when James Crippen (he and his brother Amos were the leading spirits of the day), having made an excavation in the center of the chicken pie, seized the decanter and said, 'Gentlemen, it has all got to go one way at last, so here goes,' and with that he poured the whisky, more than a quart, into the smoking pie. It produced a great laugh; some ate heartily of the pie, some cautiously, and some declined the new sauce, yet all in great glee. After dinner all hands went to work again, and by dark the barn was completed—the greatest day's work, I suspect, ever performed in the county. The work over, father thanked them all for their kindness. James Crippen responded, saying, 'No thanks, Daniel, what we've done to-day we owe to every one that makes a like call; but before we part we desire to have a social dance, and especially do we wish to dance with the good old lady Mrs. Wickham and her husband,' and walking up to the old lady he immediately led her out for a jig. In less than a minute they were dancing with all their might, the men singing and beating time. At least twenty of the men danced a jig in turn with Mrs. Wickham till she was tired out, and then they danced with old Mr. Wickham till he was exhausted. But they were not through yet. Mr. Wickham being tired out it was proposed in great glee to bury him. An old ox sled was immediately procured, two boards laid on it, and Mr. Wickham laid on the boards. Numbers of the men seized the sled and prepared to drag it over the ground, while others with cowbells and sleighbells led the procession. The sled was drawn several times around the yard amid great noise and laughter, and then the old man was released. It was nearly midnight before the scene closed and all left. During the whole day and evening there was no profanity nor any hard words used. All was cheerful labor, and innocent, though boisterous, mirth."

Esquire Elmer Rowell, to whom we are indebted for many facts concerning the early settlement of Rome township, says:

" When I first settled here the nearest post office was at Athens, sixteen or seventeen miles distant, and I have frequently gone that distance for a single expected letter; now there are four post offices in the township. Then we went thirty miles to obtain our necessary dry goods, groceries, hardware, etc.; now there are seven or eight good country stores in the township. While musing on the times and people of fifty-five years ago, the whole scene for thirty miles up and down the valley seems photographed on my memory—the men and women, their costumes, the log cabins and the cleared patches. The men all dressed in homespun during summer, and during winter a great part of the clothing consisted of buckskin; the females, both matron and lass, for every day in homespun, except in later years, now and then began to appear in a ' factory dress,' and all had for Sunday and holidays the more costly and gayer calico and cambric dresses. Those were the days of warm friendships and close attachments. Common hardships and labors begot a fellow feeling. If there was a cabin to raise, every man for miles around turned out with alacrity to help raise it and put on the last clapboard. If there was any job too heavy for one man to do, all assisted. When a hunter or any one else was belated, be he a stranger or acquaintance, he found a home and a welcome in any log cabin he might chance to find."

Between 1800 and 1810 the township received a number of good settlers. John Johnson and father on the Hockhocking opposite Federal creek; Job Ruter, with his sons Martin and Calvin, on the river about two miles above Federal creek; and about the same time came Nathan Conner, Rev. Moses Osborn, the Calverts, the Thompsons, the Selbys, and the Mitchells, all of whom settled on the river. Most of these came from Virginia. Also prominent among the early settlers were Abraham Sharp, who gave his name to Sharp's run and Sharp's fork of Federal creek; Francis Munn, a revolutionary soldier, Archibald Dorough, Thomas Richardson, Dr. Seth Driggs, the Hewitts, Jeremiah Conant, Wm. Pilcher, Aaron Orm, Thomas Swan, Aaron Butts, Eli Catlin, Daniel Anderson, a lieutenant in the revolutionary army, David Chapman, and Enos Thompson, a Methodist preacher.

When war was declared in 1812 Athens county was called on for a company of infantry to consist of fifty men. To raise these the militia regiment, then commanded by Colonel Edmund Dorr, was summoned together and volunteers called for. The quota was filled in a few minutes by volunteering, and of the fifty men, nearly one-fifth were from Rome township, and all of these from the school district of which the old school house was the center. Their names were James Crippen, Peter Beebe, Thaddeus Crippen, Ebenezer Hatch, Charles Stewart, William Starr, Andrew Stewart, John

Wickham, and Daniel Muncie. Subsequently, when the company was enlarged to sixty, Rome sent one more volunteer, George Driggs, and he is the only survivor of the whole number. In 1813, when the governor of Ohio called for forty days mounted riflemen, George Barrows, Montgomery Perry, and a young man named Swann, went from Rome.

William T. Hatch, son of Elijah Hatch, was the first male child born in the township, and his sister Harriet, the late Mrs. Hill, is said to have been the first female. Mrs. Elijah Hatch, mother of Judge Hatch, was the first person who died in the township.

Township Trustees since 1811.

1811	Job Ruter,	Elijah Hatch,	James Crippen.
1812	Daniel Stewart,	George Barrows,	John Thompson.
1813	Elijah Rowell,	James Crippen,	"
1814	Daniel Stewart,	"	Joshua Selby.
1815	"	"	William Barrows.
1816	"	Elijah Hatch,	Joshua Selby.
1817	James Crippen,	John Thompson,	Henry Barrows.
1818–19	"	Archelaus Stewart,	"
1820	"	"	Daniel Stewart.
1821	"	John Thompson,	"
1822	Elijah Hatch,	Joshua Selby,	"
1823	James Crippen,	Elmer Rowell,	Archelaus Stewart.
1824	William S. Doan,	Joshua Selby,	Henry Barrows.
1825	Daniel Stewart,	Elijah Dalbey,	Peter Beebe.
1826	"	"	James Crippen.
1827	"	Josephus Butts,	Joshua Selby.
1828	John Thompson,	"	"
1829	John Johnson,	"	"
1830	John Thompson,	"	Daniel D. Cross.
1831	John Johnson,	"	Joseph Mitchell.
1832	William S. Doan,	James E. Hatch,	"
1833–34	Levi Stewart,	"	"
1835	Alexander Stewart,	"	Peter Beebe.
1836	Joseph Mitchell,	"	Samuel Hill.
1837	"	S. T. Richardson,	George Warren.
1838	James E. Hatch,	Joshua Calvert,	"
1839	Peter Beebe,	Wilson Selby,	Wm. P. Doan.
1840–41	"	Joseph Mitchell,	Levi Stewart.

Rome Township.

TOWNSHIP TRUSTEES—*Continued.*

1842	Daniel B. Stewart,	William Mitchell,	Nelson Cook.
1843	William P. Doan,	William Crippen,	B. F. Johnson.
1844	Peter Grosvenor,	William R. Winner,	Joseph Mitchell.
1845	"	Levi Stewart,	"
1846	D. B. Stewart,	William Simmons,	B. F. Johnson.
1847	"	"	Abraham Parrill.
1848	Elmer Rowell,	Artemus S. Crippen,	Levi Stewart.
1849	"	Peter Grosvenor,	"
1850	Nelson Cook,	"	Connell Roberts.
1851	"	"	T. F. Jones.
1852	Levi Stewart,	"	W. R. Winner.
1853–55	Elmer Rowell,	D. B. Stewart,	Wilson Selby.
1856	T. R. Rider,	Perry Barrows,	Harvey Pierce.
1857	"	Voltaire Barrows,	"
1858	Josephus Tucker,	Perry Barrows,	Elmer Rowell.
1859	James Rice,	Heman Frost,	Artemus Buckley.
1860–61	"	Josephus Tucker,	W. L. Petty.
1862	A. S. Crippen,	Artemus Buckley,	G. S. Simpson.
1863	"	P. W. Boyles,	James Cross.
1864	Blanford Cook,	"	"
1865	"	"	J. W. Johnson.
1866	"	Joseph Patterson,	Harvey Pierce.
1867–68	"	Amos Patterson,	Robert Bean.

Township Clerks.

1811—Caleb Barstow.
1812—Amos Crippen.
1813–15—Elijah Hatch.
1816–20—William Stewart.
1821—John Green.
1822—Daniel Stewart.
1823–25—Elijah Hatch.
1826—John Thompson.
1827–28—Samuel Thompson.
1829—Edmund Cook.
1830–31—Guy Barrows.
1832—John Welch.
1833—Elijah Hatch.
1834—Wilson Selby.
1835—Thomas Newcomb.
1836–37—Blanford Cook.
1838–39—Elmer Rowell.

History of Athens County, Ohio.

TOWNSHIP CLERKS—*Continued.*

1840-42—Wilson Selby.
1843—E. B. Parrill.
1844-45—Wilson Selby.
1846-47—Joshua Calvert.
1848—B. F. Johnson.
1849—Sydney S. Beebe.
1850-51—B. F. Johnson.
1852—Joshua Calvert.
1853-55—B. F. Johnson.
1856-57—Charles H. Grosvenor.
1858—Robert Bean.
1859-62—Blanford Cook.
1863—James Moore.
1864-65—Harvey Pierce.
1866—Charles Dean.
1867-68—George M. Ross.

The first township treasurer in Rome was Amos Crippen, elected in 1811. Then followed in succession George Barrows, Daniel Stewart, Hopson Beebe, David Chapman, Charles Beebe, John Johnson, John M. Perry, Peter Beebe, Sydney S. Beebe, Guy Barrows, James Starr, Hiram Stewart, Daniel B. Stewart and B. F. Johnson.

Successive Justices of the Peace.

Elijah Hatch, Daniel Stewart, James Crippen, Elmer Rowell, John Thompson, Thomas Welch, Joseph Mitchell, C. C. Beard, Joshua Calvert, H. S. Butts, D. D. Cross, Timothy F. Jones, Thomas Grosvenor, Abraham Parrill, Heman Frost, Elam Frost, R. A. Fulton, S. S. Beebe.

Personal and Biographical.

The first person who settled in what is now Rome township was *David Dailey,* a veteran soldier of the revolution, and decidedly "a character." Born in Vermont in 1750, he removed to western New York after his discharge from the army, and thence to Cannonsburg, Pennsylvania, whence he migrated in the year 1797 to the northwestern territory. With his family, consisting of two daughters and five sons, of whom Benonah H. Dailey, of Carthage township (the youngest son), is now the sole survivor, he came down the Ohio river in a pirogue to the mouth of the Hockhocking, and up that stream to the mouth of Federal creek, where he at once opened up a farm. The place on which he settled is now known as the Beebe farm.

Around him was an unbroken wilderness. The nearest neighbors were at the settlement at Athens, about twelve miles distant. Parties of Indians were frequently seen on hunting excursions, or on their way to Wheeling to barter their furs. Having lived about three years on the farm first settled by him, he sold it to Judge Elijah Hatch, and, with his family, removed to Carthage township. Dailey was a famous hunter, fond of the exciting sports of pioneer life, and cultivated a sort of contempt for the comforts and conveniences of civilization. With his dogs and hunting equipments, and with a dead bear or deer on his back, homeward bound, he was as happy as a king. The story of his many rencounters with wolves, bears, and panthers, after settling in Athens county, would form an interesting narrative, and graphically illustrate the excitements of pioneer life. Our informant says:

"I exceedingly regret that some of these stories, which I have heard him relate, are so blurred in memory that I find it impossible to reproduce them. And, then, the old man told them with such a peculiar zest that much would unavoidably be lost in a repetition. His imperturbable gravity, the immobility of his countenance, even when uttering a dry joke or relating an amusing anecdote, at which the bystanders were in a perfect roar of laughter, were wonderful. Yet I have often seen his eyes fill with tears at a tale of suffering. Even in relating the death of a favorite dog—Piper—belonging to a fellow huntsman, the tears would start. He assisted in burying the dog with 'military honors,' on the bank of a *branch* now bearing the dog's name."

Captain Chittenden, afterward governor of Vermont, commanded the company in which Dailey served during the revolutionary war. Several years after he came to Ohio to live, Dailey applied for a pension, and walked all the way to Vermont to obtain, from his old captain, the necessary certificate and vouchers. After his return to the west he would often relate, with much gusto, the hearty greetings and warm welcome he received from the governor, and, during his stay of several days, remembered to have particularly relished the governor's "cognac."

The old man was exceedingly severe in his criticisms on St. Clair's disastrous campaign against the Indians, in 1791. It so happened, on one occasion, that St. Clair, while governor of the northwestern territory, in passing across the country, called at Dailey's cabin in Rome, to obtain refreshments for himself and horse. Dailey's larder, however, was exhausted, and, though full of hospitality, he could do little or nothing for the hungry governor, who was compelled to press on to Athens, where he arrived very much exhausted and very angry. The incident worked on his mind to such a degree, vexing him more the more he dwelt upon it, that he threatened to send Dailey out of the territory— declaring that he would not have such a shiftless man within his jurisdiction. This, Dailey pretty soon heard of. Not long afterward the governor met Dailey in "Southtown" (Alexander), and thought it a good opportunity to at least administer a sound reprimand for his delinquency as an agriculturist, and commenced with, "Well, Mr. Dailey, how do you succeed in farming at the mouth of Federal creek?" Dailey, assuming an unusual amount of solemn gravity, replied: "Pretty d——d poorly, as you did fighting the Indians; but I think the difference, if any, is on my side, for, being born without a shirt, I have made out *to hold my own* till the present time, which is an almighty sight better than you did." The governor let Dailey alone after that.

Elijah Hatch (Judge Hatch) migrated from the eastern part of the state of New York to the northwestern territory, and settled in Rome township in the year 1800. In 1801 he went back and removed his father, Elijah Hatch, Sen., and his mother, with their family, to this township—the former being seventy-two, and the latter seventy-one years old at that time. They came in wagons to the Youghiogheny, in Pennsylvania, where, in connection with others, they procured a flat boat, twenty-five feet long by twelve feet wide, which they loaded with seven horses, one wagon, one carriage, a quantity of hardware and farming utensils, and fifteen persons—men, women, and children. Thus they proceeded down the Youghiogheny, Monongahela, and Ohio rivers, to the Ohio Company's purchase. Judge Hatch was the first man who ever drove a team, with a wagon, through the woods, from the mouth of little Hocking to the big Hockhocking. He struck the latter stream two and a half miles below the mouth of Federal creek, about half a mile below where the present ridge road now joins the Hocking road.

Judge Hatch possessed talents above mediocrity, a sound judgment in public affairs, and was an active and influential man in the early settlement of the county. He was appointed judge of the court of common pleas by Governor Tiffin, in 1805, and was afterward appointed or elected several times to that position. He served nine terms in the state legislature, being first elected in 1804, and was appointed by that body one of the first board of trustees of the Ohio university, which position he held for the remainder of his life. He was a man of affable and courteous demeanor, possessing a large fund of anecdote and social qualities, that made him always a welcome guest at pioneer gatherings. He died January 19, 1849, aged eighty-one years.

Roswell Culver and *Joel Spenser* settled, with their families, in Rome about 1801. They were brothers-in-law of Judge Hatch, having married sisters. The "widow Comfort Crippen," another of Judge Hatch's sisters, settled in 1804 on the river, about a mile and a half below the mouth of Federal creek. She brought with her six sons and three daughters. One of the sons was Amos Crippen, long a leading citizen of the county, and the memory of one of the daughters, who was married to A. G. Brown, of Athens, is still fondly cherished by her relatives and friends. Of this large family, brought into Rome in 1804, only one now survives, viz: Mrs. Orinda Branch, of Middleport, Meigs county. One of the sisters, the late Mrs. Olive Currier, relict of Judge Ebenezer Currier, died at her residence in Athens, January 7, 1868, aged eighty-two years.

Elmer Rowell, one of the few surviving pioneers of this period, was born in the county of Middlesex,

Massachusetts, in the year 1793, of excellent parentage, the family on both sides of the house being noted for their sterling honesty, intelligence, and patriotism. In 1811 his father, Elijah Rowell, migrated with his little family to the then "far west," and settled in Rome township, where Mr. Rowell has passed nearly the whole of his peaceful and useful life, and where he continues to reside, respected and beloved by all who know him. In the year 1812 young Rowell, then only nineteen years old, began to teach school, and continued teaching during the winter season for many years. He had eminent fitness for educating the young, and his unwearying fidelity and philosophic methods of instruction gained for him a deserved popularity. In 1815 he married Esther Culver, daughter of Roswell Culver, who is still living. To them were born six children, of which only three survive, viz: Ohiolus, born in Rome township in 1816, now a farmer in the same township, Mrs. Theresa P. Dorr, wife of Edmund Dorr, and William Wirt Rowell. Esquire Rowell has been a farmer during the most of his life. He has always taken a lively interest in the welfare of the community where he dwells, and has filled, at different times, all the township offices and the office of county commissioner.

Eliphalet Case came to Rome township, with his family, in 1808, and brought into cultivation the fine farm on which Professor Miller now lives. Case married a daughter of Job Ruter, and was an influential citizen during the early days of the county.

Joseph Wickham settled in Rome in 1805. He was a native of England, and serving on an English vessel when the revolutionary war broke out. He deserted, joined the American army, and served till the close of hostilities. After the war he lived for a time in Vermont. Having married there he set out, in the winter of 1804, for the new state of Ohio, but the roads getting very bad he disposed of his horses and wagon, bought a yoke of cattle and a *sled*, and came on to "Olean point." Here he procured a white pine raft, and floated down to the mouth of Hockhocking, and thence came up that river to Rome township, where he lived till his death, May 3, 1833, aged seventy-four years. One of his grandsons, Killian V. Whaley, was a member of the 38th and 39th congress from West Virginia. Another of them, William Reed, is known as one of the enterprising business men of the township.

Timothy Jones, a native of Rhode Island, was born of wealthy parents, graduated at Brown university, became a lawyer and also a graduate in medicine, and held a high social position in Providence, Rhode Island, where he lived. In 1805, when near fifty years old, his wife having died, he relinquished the comforts of settled life and removed to Ohio. He arrived in Rome township in that year and buried himself in the forests of Federal creek. He was a man of considerable scientific research. During the revolutionary war he obtained the first premium, offered by the legislature of Massachusetts, for the manufacture of saltpeter. His descendants possess the certificate of his admission to the bar in Providence, in 1786. Dressed in the garb of a pioneer working on his farm on Federal creek, he presented to those who knew his history and character an interesting study. Some time after coming here he married a second wife—the widow Polly Hewitt, a daughter of Ebenezer Barrows. The Rev. T. F. Jones is a son of theirs. An aged citizen of Rome, who knew Dr. Jones, says, "in the forest he was a hunter—in the log cabin parlor a perfect Chesterfield."

Leonard Jewett in 1804 or 1805 settled at the mouth of Federal creek on a fine tract of land which lay chiefly on the south side of the Hockhocking. He sold out very soon to Mr. John Johnson and removed to Athens. Mr. Johnson married Miss Sarah Wyatt, a daughter of Deacon Joshua Wyatt, of Ames, and a woman of rare excellence. By their industry and good management they in a few years opened up one of the best farms in the county. Mr. Johnson was a "close dealer," and so tenacious of his rights as to be thought by some a hard man; but he was benevolent at heart, and would rather give away a dollar than be cheated of a cent. Many a destitute emigrant or needy family has had timely relief at his hands. He was the father of Dr. Wm. P. Johnson, the present representative of the county in the state legislature, and whose character as a man, as a physician and a public officer is too well known in his native county to require comment. Mrs. John Johnson, who was born in Beverly, Massachusetts, in 1786, and came to Athens county with her father's family when she was fourteen years old, died December 26, 1859.

Daniel Stewart was born in Litchfield, Connecticut, November 18, 1762. When fifteen years old he enlisted as a soldier in the revolutionary army, and served till the close of the war. He then removed to Sussex county, New Jersey, where he engaged successfully in business for several years and accumulated some means. In 1801 he exchanged his property in New Jersey for two shares in the Ohio Company's purchase and closed out his business with a view to moving west. Colonel William Stewart, a son who accompanied his father to Ohio, says:

"In October, 1802, father returned to the old farm to rig out a team for emigration to the northwestern territory. The preparations having been completed, a day and hour were set for starting. At the appointed time, 8 o'clock A. M., about a hundred friends and neighbors from all quarters came flocking in to bid us farewell, and I shall never forget the scene that followed. They all thought we were going so far beyond the world's boundary that we should never be heard of again. The hubbub lasted till 5 o'clock in the afternoon before father could say good bye with a strong voice, and then we started. Went three miles and camped for the night. The next morning we moved on. The teams were heavily loaded and the roads tolerable till we approached the Alleghany mountains when they became terribly rough and dangerous. Crossing the mountains the family were afraid to ride in the wagons and, therefore, walked this part of the way. At the very steep descents father would cut saplings, fasten them top foremost to the tail of the wagon and then go down, depending on the saplings as a brake. The journey was a long, wearisome and dangerous one, but we finally reached the Hockhocking in safety."

This was in the winter. Mr. Stewart settled on a fine tract of land on the river about a mile above the mouth of Federal creek. Possessing considerable means, great energy, and uncommon business talent, he soon had the best farm in the county. As early as 1810 he had an orchard of three thousand bearing fruit trees—two thousand peach, and one thousand apple trees—at that time probably the largest orchard in the state. As his means increased so did his benevolence and public spirit. In business he left no points unguarded, and no man could defraud or overreach him with impunity; but if he husbanded closely he gave liberally, and was always accessible to the claims of the really needy, and of educational and religious movements. He was one of the first two justices of the peace in the township (Elijah Hatch being the other), and acted as such, altogether, more than twenty years. He was county commissioner for many years, and was appointed by the legislature one of the early appraisers of the college lands, Captain Joshua Wyatt and John Brown being the other two. Few men have left more decided marks on the history of the county, in its social and business affairs, than Mr. Stewart. An active member of the Methodist church for sixty years of his life he always contributed liberally to the support of its ministers and the erection of churches. He died February 20, 1858.

Mr. Stewart had fourteen children, viz: Andrew, William, Charles, John, Ezra, George, Lois, Sarah, Mary, Lucinda, Harriet, Alexander, Daniel B., and Hiram. One of these, the Rev. John Stewart, has been a traveling preacher in the Methodist church for fifty years. Another, Ezra Stewart, married Harriet, daughter of Esquire Henry Bartlett, in 1826, and spent his life in the mercantile business in Athens. He was a man of wonderful energy and endurance, and his unusual capacity for business is well remembered. He died in Athens, November 28, 1858. William Stewart came to this county with his father's family in 1802, and lived here nearly forty years. When seventeen years old he was elected a lieutenant in the militia, and was captain of a company raised here in 1812, which expected to be but was not called into the service.

Some years later he was appointed a colonel. The contract for erecting the Ohio university building was awarded to him in 1817, and several years later the contract for building the county jail. In 1840 he removed to Lee county, Iowa. In 1847 he was elected superintendent of the common schools in that state, and during that and the next year organized one hundred and five school districts. He has held other public offices in Iowa.

Daniel B. Stewart, son of Daniel, was born on the old Stewart farm in Rome township, September 26, 1812. The first school he remembers and which he attended was kept by Jabez Bowman, on the hill about a quarter of a mile below the old homestead. This school was supported by contributions of its patrons. As he grew up Mr. Stewart developed a great fondness for machinery, and was never happier than when managing or handling it. He finally obtained his father's consent that he should go into the mill at Savannah as manager. Here he succeeded admirably, and without any instruction. After he had run this mill about two years he bought it of his father, run it two years more and then sold it to James E. and William T. Hatch. The next two years he lived in Meigs county, engaging in the mercantile business at Rutland with his brother Alexander. Returning to this county he started a store at Coolville, and also bought the saw mill on the river two miles below Savannah. This was in 1836. In 1837 the mill was burned. Mr. Stewart rebuilt it in 1838, putting in at that time the first patent Parker wheel used on the Hockhocking. In 1842 he added a grist mill, and in 1844 a woolen factory to the property. In 1864 he sold these mills, and in 1867 removed to the town of Athens, where he owns the old Miles or Gregory mill, and has added to it a woolen factory. Though not among the largest this factory is one of the best arranged and most complete in the country, and may challenge comparison with any of its size to be found east or west. It is capable of carding and spinning three hundred pounds of wool daily, and when the looms are all in, can make six hundred yards of cloth a day.

Mr. Stewart has been one of the most energetic and useful business men in the county. At one time he was the owner of four mills on the Hockhocking, and part of the time also cultivated five farms in Rome township, raising as high as four thousand five hundred bushels of wheat in one year. He served as justice of the peace twenty-one years, and in 1860 was chosen presidential elector for this district.

Alexander Stedman, a native of Vermont, and by profession an architect, settled in Rome township in 1804, having previously lived for nearly two years at Athens. In 1805 he was appointed one of the judges of the court of common pleas for Athens county and held the position for several years. Soon after coming here he married the widow Comfort Crippen. One of his sons, Eli Stedman, was a minister and somewhat celebrated as a pulpit orator. Another, Levi Stedman, was for many years a prominent citizen of this county, serving as county commissioner, etc. On the organization of Meigs county, in 1819, he moved thither, and was one the first common pleas judges in that county. Another son, Bial, was an associate judge of Washington county. Judge Stedman was a man of excellent judgment and of commanding influence among the pioneers. Some of his descendants are still living in the county. A grandson, Frederic Stedman, was elected sheriff of the county in 1861, but left his office and entered the Union army as captain of a company of infantry.

Amos Miller, only son of Judge Abel Miller, was born in Athens county, July 27, 1807. The early years of his life were passed on his father's farm in Canaan. At the age of sixteen he entered the Ohio university, and graduated in the class of 1830. In 1831 he was elected sheriff of the county, which office he held for two terms. In 1832 he was elected by the legislature a member of the board of trustees of the Ohio university, which position he has held continuously ever since.

In 1840 he removed to Rome township (having

previously purchased the Case farm), where, in 1841, he established the Miller seminary, which, from a very small beginning, has become one of the most prosperous and useful academies in this section of country. Professor Miller, though not an aged man, may be classed among the pioneers.

Captain Hopson Beebe was born in Connecticut, February 17, 1749, was a soldier of the revolutionary war, and settled in Rome township in 1804, where he resided till his death in 1836. One of his sons, the venerable Mr. Charles Beebe, now in his eighty-third year, resided on the "old farm" until quite recently. He now lives with Mrs. J. W. Johnson in this township. Doctor Wm. Beebe, another son, was an assistant surgeon in General Tupper's brigade in the war of 1812. After the war he settled in Belpre, and practiced medicine there for the rest of his life. *His* son, Dr. Wm. Beebe (grandson of Captain Hopson Beebe), is now a practicing physician in Barlow, Washington county.

The youngest son, Peter Beebe, was an active and successful business man, and for several years one of the township trustees. He died in the prime of life in 1849.

Thomas Welch, removed from the northern part of the state and settled in Rome township in 1826. He remained here several years, living part of the time at the mills and part of the time on the "Case farm," which he bought and cultivated. About 1828 he sold the mills to his two sons, Thomas and John Welch, the latter of whom is further noticed in connection with Athens township.

Peter Grosvenor, born at Pomfret, Windham county, Connecticut, January 25, 1794, removed to Athens county and settled in Rome township in May, 1838. His father, Colonel Thomas Grosvenor, served with distinction through the revolutionary war, part of the time on the staff of General Warren and of General Washington, and was wounded at the battle of Bunker Hill. Peter Grosvenor served in the war of 1812. He was among the first to clear up and make an improvement on the present road from the Canaan line to Federal creek, the northwestern part of Rome, where he settled, being at that time very sparsely populated. He died September 29, 1859, on the farm where he first settled. Mr. Grosvenor was a man of uncompromising integrity and an excellent citizen. Four of his sons served in the Union army during the war of the rebellion. Edward Grosvenor entered as a private, and for good conduct was commissioned a captain in the 92d regiment O. V. I. He died while on the march with Sherman's army "to the sea." Daniel A. Grosvenor served as a private in the 3d Ohio regiment, and John M. served in the quartermaster's department.

Thomas Grosvenor, a brother of Peter, settled near him in 1839. He lived in Rome about twenty years and then removed to Washington county, where he died April 9, 1867, aged eighty-one years. All of his sons, five in number, enlisted in the Union army at the beginning of the war of the rebellion. Of the nine sons of the two Grosvenor families who volunteered only four lived to return.

William S. Doan came from New England to Washington county in 1806, to Athens county in 1813, and settled in Rome about 1820. He was an industrious farmer and a good citizen. Several of his descendants now live in the township. Mr. Charles Doan is a grandson of his.

CHAPTER XVII.

Trimble Township.

TRIMBLE township was originally a part of Ames, from which it was stricken off and separately organized in April, 1827. It lies at the extreme northern limit of the county, on the waters of Sunday creek, the main branch of which runs, somewhat centrally, from north to south, through the township. It was named after Governor Allen Trimble, one of the early governors of Ohio.

The first settlement made in this township was by Solomon Tuttle, Sen., in 1802. He, with his son, Cyrus Tuttle, and his brother, Nial Tuttle, all from Vermont, settled on the main creek. Soon after them came Joseph McDaniel and William Morrow. Mr. Bagley, with several sons, came from Vermont and settled in 1820, on the west fork of the creek, below what is now called Hartleyville. One of his sons, William Bagley, being a clothier by trade, established a pioneer factory for dressing cloth and, in connection with it, a flour mill, the flour being bolted by hand. This was the first mill in the township, and has been kept up, with various improvements, ever since. It is now owned by Mr. Perry Zimmerman. Samuel Bagley, a tanner by trade, established the first tan yard in the township, about the year 1820.

In 1822 a school was taught by Nancy Bagley, a native of Vermont, near the forks of the creek. About 1824 a few families established a school of eight or ten scholars, which was taught by John Morrow, in a log school house without any floor. His compensation was one dollar and fifty cents a week. The school house was located on the creek between Solomon Tuttle's and James Dew's. Among the few scholars in this pioneer school was Mr. E. H. Moore, now president of the First National bank in Athens, who also taught a district school in the same place in 1832.

The Baptists, Methodists, and Christians, were the first religious societies formed in the township, and continue to be the leading organizations.

William Bagley's mill on the west fork of Sunday creek was, as before stated, the first in the township. In 1825 Jonathan Watkins built a mill at the village first known as *Oxford*, but since called *Trimble*. It was at first only a saw mill, but, after two or three years, a grist mill was connected with it. This mill continued to be the principal one in the township till 1865, when it was destroyed by fire.

The people of this township are chiefly engaged in agriculture, and the lands are being rapidly improved. Considerable attention is given to stock growing and to the culture of tobacco. Coal of excellent quality, both bituminous and cannel, exists here in large deposits, which, as soon as it becomes accessible by branch railroads, now projected, will command the attention of capitalists. Iron ore of good quality is also found in various parts of the township, and near to large deposits of good limestone. Salt water of great strength, and thought by competent judges to be equal to any in the Hockhocking valley, has recently been found in abundance in a well bored for oil by Mr. R. J. Arnold. This well is on the Zanesville road near the northern line of the county. It is a little over one thousand feet in depth. About twenty-five years ago the Eggleston salt works on Green's run, near the south line of the township, were operated successfully. At that time this was esteemed a valuable well, but for many years past it has not been used.

The center of population in the township is the village of Trimble, situated on section 8. It has a post office, two stores, three physicians, the requisite number of mechanics, and a population of about two hundred.

The population of the township in 1830 was 190; in 1840 it was 762; in 1850 it was 924; in 1860 it was 1,112.

At the first election for township officers in 1827, which was held at the house of William Bagley, James Price, James Bosworth, and Jeremiah Cass were judges of the election, and Samuel B. Johnson and Cyrus Tuttle, clerks.

Township Trustees.

1827	William Bagley,	James Bosworth,	Solomon Newton.
1828	Jeremiah Cass,	Elijah Alderman,	"
1829	Joseph McDonald,	James Price,	"
1830	David Eggleston,	"	"
1831	Jonathan Watkins,	"	"
1832	Wanting.		
1833	Elijah Alderman,	Thomas Dew,	John Ivers.
1834	"	Luther Mingus,	Enoch Rutter.
1835	Wanting.		
1836	Solomon Newton,	Andrew McKee,	William Shaner.
1837	Jonathan Watkins,	"	"
1838	Solomon Newton,	"	Ebenezer Shaner.
1839	William McKee,	"	John Ivers.
1840	Thos. L. Love,	Andrew Rutter,	Wanting.
1841	James Hage,	W J. Hartley,	"
1842	"	John B. Johnson,	"
1843	"	Isaac N. Joseph,	William J. Hartley.
1844	William McClellan,	"	"
1845	Andrew McKee,	Caleb Carter,	Isaac Blackwood.
1846	Wanting.		
1847	William McClellan,	Andrew Dew,	J. D. Davis.
1848	Andrew McKee,	"	"
1849–50	William McClellan,	"	"
1851	"	William H. Peugh,	S. T. Grow.
1852	Wanting.		
1853	James Hage,	John Ivers,	Wanting.
1854	Andrew Dew,	"	William McClellan.
1855	Wanting.		
1856	Joseph Allen,	B. Worrell,	Andrew Dew.
1857	Benjamin Norris,	J. M. Johnson,	"
1858–59	William H. Peugh,	William McClellan,	S. P. Grow.
1860–61	"	"	L. H. Rinehart.
1862		"	Samuel Woodworth.
1863	Samuel Banks,	John Shaner,	"
1864	"	John Gift,	Dorsey McClellan.
1865–66	Milton Monroe,	"	J. C. Lefever.
1867	William H. Peugh,	Isaac Blackwood,	Lemuel Bethel.
1868	Samuel Banks,	J. M. Amos,	Joseph Allen.

Successive Justices of the Peace.

1827—William Bagley.
1830—James Price and Jeremiah Cass.
1833—Daniel Frazer and Samuel Mills.
1834—Emory Newton.
1836—Seth Pratt and Samuel Mills.
1838—Solomon Newton.
1839—Samuel Mills.
1840—David Allen.
1841—John Ivers.
1842—Morris Bryson.
1844—John Ivers.
1845—Morris Bryson.
1847—Isaac N. Joseph.
1848—George W. Roberts.
1850—Aquilla Norris and Benjamin Norris.
1851—Benjamin Norris and George W. Roberts.
1853—Alexander McClellan.
1854—William Biddison.
1856—Isaac N. Joseph.
1857—John M. Johnson (resigned February 3, 1858).
1858—Morris Bryson.
1859—William H. Peugh.
1861—Morris Bryson.
1862—L. Bethel.
1864—William Biddison.
1865—William Koons.
1867—J. S. Dew.
1868—Samuel Banks.

Personal and Biographical.

Jonathan Watkins, Sen., came from Athens township in 1803, and settled in the lower part of Trimble, and soon after Eliphalet Wheeler settled near him. Mr.

Watkins was a blacksmith, but, like most of the early settlers, occasionally engaged in hunting. He shot a buffalo soon after settling in Trimble, and broke its fore leg. He pursued the animal, thus crippled, from Green's run in Trimble township, across Wolf plains, and over the Hockhocking some distance, but failed to capture it.

Samuel Clark settled here about 1820.

James Bosworth, from Fall River, Massachusetts, came here in 1821, but, after living in the township a few years, went back to New England.

Enos Barnes, from New England, a son-in-law Mr. Bagley, settled here in 1818. He was a blacsmith.

Solomon Newton, a native of Worcester, Massachusetts, came to Athens county in 1821, and settled in Trimble in 1822. His place was on the creek about three miles below James Dew's, and, being situated on the main road between Athens and Zanesville, was formerly very well known. Mr. Newton died in 1849.

About 1814 *James* and *Thomas Dew*, brothers, came to Athens county with their parents, from Maryland, and made permanent settlements. James settled just outside of the present limits of Trimble township. Several of his sons, including Dr. J. S. Dew and Mr. Henry C. Dew, now live in Trimble.

James Price, a native of Rhode Island, settled in Trimble in 1820. One of his sons, Mr. Abel Price, is now living in the township.

John B. Johnson, son of Azel Johnson, one of the early settlers of Dover township, settled in Trimble as a farmer in 1820. He was the father of Mr. J. M. Johnson, recently sheriff of the county.

CHAPTER XVIII.

Troy Township.

THIS township was settled under the auspices of the Ohio Company in the year 1798—about a year after the settlement of Athens and Ames. Some events connected with its history can, however, be traced back to a period nearly twenty-five years prior to that date. We have referred elsewhere to "Dunmore's war" and to the building of a fort at the mouth of the Hockhocking in 1774. When the first settlers came into Troy in 1798, the outlines of Dunmore's camping ground were plainly discernible. Over a tract containing about twenty acres young saplings and underbrush had grown up, and it had the appearance of an old clearing. For many years after this the settlers used to find, in plowing their fields, mementoes of Dunmore's army, such as hatchets, gun barrels, bullets, etc. A rusty, but tolerably well preserved sword is still to be seen (or was recently), in the college museum at Athens, which was found on the west side of the Hockhocking near the roots of a fallen tree. Possibly in that campaign across Athens county, made nearly a century ago, it adorned the person of some young English nobleman whom love of adventure or of fame induced to accompany Lord Dunmore in his arduous march; or, perhaps, it was wielded by the strong arm of some native son of Virginia, who, a few months later, was striking swift and manful blows for his country's independence. Whatever its history, it has long rested in silence and rust. Though it may once have "spoken for itself," it is never likely to find tongue again, and every observer is at liberty to imagine for himself who its owner was and what its history may have been.

From its position at the mouth of one river and on the banks of another, both of which were more or less frequented by the Indians, this section of country must have been very familiar to them. Perhaps for hundreds of years before the white man came hither, the light canoe of the Indian used to glide down the Hockhocking, and from its narrow channel out upon the smooth flowing waters of the Ohio.

In 1798 a company of about forty persons, including men, women and children, started from near Springfield, Massachusetts, for the west. They landed at Belpre, and from thence came in 1799 to what is now Troy township and settled on the Hockhocking about seven miles from its mouth. In this party were

Eleazur Washburn, Noah, Cyrus, and Xerxes Paulk, Horace Parsons, and Ephraim Frost with their families. Xerxes Paulk and Horace Parsons were Baptist preachers; the latter was pastor of the first Baptist church in the township for about thirty years.

Troy, as its boundaries were originally defined by the county commissioners at their first meeting,* comprised the territory which now constitutes the townships of Orange and Olive in Meigs county, and Rome, Carthage, and Troy in Athens county. At that time the Hockhocking river was the dividing line between Athens and Washington counties, but by an act of the legislature passed February 18, 1807, the portion of township No. 5, range 11 (now Troy), lying east of the river, was detached from Washington and added to Athens county. The formation of Carthage township in 1810 and of Rome in 1811, and the erection of Meigs county in 1819, taking off two townships, reduced Troy to its present limits. The population of the township in 1820 was 541; in 1830 it was 459; in 1840 it was 1,056; in 1850 it was 1,421; in 1860 it was 1,747. The first election for township officers was held in 1805 at the house of Ebenezer Buckingham. Stephen Buckingham was township lister for that year. These men were the founders of the Buckingham family which, removing subsequently to Muskingum county, became celebrated for wealth and social influence.

---

*See page 147

Rome township being stricken off from Troy in 1811 took with it many of the prominent early settlers, some of whom are noticed in Chapter XVI, as Asahel Cooley, Levi Stedman, Daniel Stewart, and others. Kingman Dutton, father of Mr. Samuel Dutton, still living in Troy, settled at the mouth of Hockhocking with his family in 1806. At that time there were only two roads in the township—one passed through the center, running from Belpre to Chillicothe, the ferry of which was kept about two and a half miles above the present site of Coolville by Xerxes Paulk; and another from Belpre down the Ohio to the mouth of Hockhocking, thence by the ridge (through Carthage township), to Athens. About 1815 a road was laid out from the mouth of Hockhocking up the eastern bank of the river to Federal creek, where it intersected the Federal creek road from the Ames settlement. At this early period the great majority of the emigrants to Athens county used to come down the Ohio to the mouth of Hockhocking and then ascend that river in pirogues or canoes. Kingman Dutton kept a number of these craft, and he and his son carried on the business of conveying emigrants and their goods up the Hockhocking. Abram Brookhart settled in Troy in 1811, and was township trustee for several years; Jonas Smith, who came in 1810, was township trustee for several terms; Silas Blizzard and Martin Griffin came in 1810. The township records prior to 1837 are lost.

Troy Township.

Township Trustees since 1837.

1837	M. L. Bestow,	Jesse Derry,	Samuel Dutton.
1838	"	"	Ferdinand Paulk.
1839	Nicholas Baker,	Jedediah Fuller,	"
1840	"	"	Wm. Kincade.
1841	"	Samuel Dutton,	Heman Cooley.
1842	Josephus Tucker,	"	Wm. W. Barrows.
1843–44	"	Nicholas Baker,	John Brookhart.
1845	Samuel Dutton,	"	M. L. Bestow.
1846	Josephus Tucker,	"	Ferdinand Paulk.
1847	"	"	Samuel Humphrey.
1848	J. M. Maxwell,	R. M. Wilson,	R. K. Bridges.
1849	Heman Cooley,	Samuel Dutton,	Thomas Richardson.
1850	R. M. Wilson,	Samuel Humphrey,	J. M. Maxwell.
1851	Stephen Warren,	Josephus Tucker,	"
1852–53	M. L. Bestow,	"	Samuel Humphrey.
1854	Samuel Dutton,	"	C. Creesey
1855	Thomas Richardson,	"	"
1856	S. A. Gibbs,	"	"
1857–59	M. L. Bestow,	"	Thomas Richardson.
1860	"	Samuel Humphrey,	James Morrison.
1861	Thomas Richardson,	"	"
1862	R. K. Bridges,	Shephard Humphrey,	"
1863	M. L. Bestow,	"	Thomas Richardson.
1864	John Frame,	E. H. Williams,	"
1865	"	"	F. W. Tipton.
1866	Thomas Smith,	"	Thomas Richardson.
1867–68	R. F. Parrish,	James B. Dutton,	"

Clerks and Treasurers since 1837.

	Clerks.	Treasurers.
1837–38	Isaac A. Dinsmore,	R. B. Blair.
1839	C. F. Devol,	"
1840	Eps Storey,	John Frame.
1841	"	A. C. Wedge.
1842–54	R. H. Lord,	John Frame.
1855	M. L. Bestow,	C. W. Waterman.
1856	"	Jefferson Cole.
1867–68	John Mitchell,	A. J. Frame.

Among the justices of the peace prior to 1837 were Charles Devol, W. S. Cockrell, Luther Hopkins, Aaron Butts, Jacob S. Miller, Nathan Cole, Jedediah Fuller, Marcus L. Bestow, and Ferdinand Paulk.

Justices of the Peace since 1838.

1838—John Pratt.
1839—Roswell Washburn.
1841—Sylvester A. Gibbs.
1842—Roswell Washburn.
1843—Sylvester A. Gibbs.
1845—Roswell Washburn.
1846—Sylvester A. Gibbs.
1847—Wm. F. Pilcher.
1850-52—Sylvester A. Gibbs and Wm. F. Pilcher.
1853—Jonathan Pussey.
1854—Wm. F. Pilcher.
1855—Sylvester A. Gibbs.
1857—Wm. F. Pilcher.
1858—Sylvester A. Gibbs.
1859—Wm. F. Pilcher.
1861—D. P. Scott.
1862—Wm. F. Pilcher.
1864—D. P. Scott.
1865-68—Wm. F. Pilcher and Wm. G. Boyd.

The present population of the township, owing to the losses in war, drainage by emigration and other natural causes, is but slightly greater than it was in 1860. Hockingport, at the mouth of the Hockhocking river, one of the earliest settlements in the county, gives no signs of future growth. Formerly, when the merchants of Athens, Amesville, Coolville, and other places had their goods landed at Hockingport and hauled thence to various parts of the county, the place had some activity. But since the construction of the

Marietta & Cincinnati railroad, Hockingport has been deprived of its principal source of business. A much more interesting and thriving village is Coolville, on the west bank of the Hockhocking five miles from its mouth, the settlement of which was begun in 1814 by Simeon W. Cooley and his son Heman, who built a mill there. The town was laid out in 1818, incorporated in 1855, and its present population is about three hundred. Surrounded with a good agricultural region and an industrious population, Coolville is likely to continue one of the most pleasant villages in the county. It has three churches, two district schools, a prosperous seminary, a town hall, masonic hall, etc.

Personal and Biographical.

Among the earliest settlers in Troy were Benajah Hoyt, Xerxes Paulk, Joseph Guthrie, Daniel Stewart, the Barrows family, William Pilcher, Asahel Cooley, John Torrence, Oliver Rice, Cummins Porter, Stephen Buckingham, Abram Richardson, Truman Hickox, and the Frost family. Some of these are noticed in connection with Rome and Carthage. Benajah Hoyt was probably the first white settler in Troy. He came from Nova Scotia to the mouth of the Hockhocking with his family in 1797. E. H. Williams, a grandson of his, owns and resides on the lot in Hockingport on which Hoyt first built a cabin. One of Mr. Hoyt's daughters, Sarah, married Captain Charles

Devol, of Washington county. They had two sons and two daughters. Frank Devol, the oldest son, is a wealthy farmer in one of the western states. The youngest son, Prescott H. Devol, is noticed elsewhere. The eldest daughter of Mrs. Devol married Benjamin Dana of Washington county (both now deceased) ; and the youngest, Henrietta, is the wife of Mr. Samuel S. Knowles, late member of the state senate, and a well known lawyer of Marietta. Mrs. Devol is still living in Mr. Knowles' family. Among the early settlers at Coolville were the Cooleys, Jacob S. Miller and Alfred Hobby. Mr. John Frame settled here in 1833, and in 1840 commenced merchandizing and dealing in wool, grain, and country produce. Though over sixty years of age he still engages actively in business, having associated his sons with him. Dr. John Pratt, a native of Schuyler county, New York, settled in Coolville in 1835. He is now sixty-eight years of age, hale and healthy, and has practiced his profession in this community for a third of a century.

CHAPTER XIX.

Waterloo Township.

WATERLOO was originally a part of Athens township, and was not separately organized till April, 1826. Joseph Hewitt and William Lowry were principally instrumental in securing the township organization. The name of *Waterloo* was suggested by General John Brown, of Athens. The first election for township officers was held April 3, 1826, at the house of Joseph Hewitt. Joseph Bullard, Abram Fee, and Silas Bingham were judges of the election, and Andrew Glass and Pardon C. Hewitt clerks. The following persons voted, viz: William Lowry, James Lowry, Joseph Hewitt, P. C. Hewitt, Ezekiel Robinett, Lemuel Robinett, Nathan Robinett, Wm. Young, Wm. Young, Jun., Silas Bingham, Andrew Glass, Joseph C. Martin, Horace Martin, Abram Fee, Joseph Bullard, John Bullard, Samuel Lowry, Jun., Abram Gabriel, Elias Gabriel, and Elias Young. The election results were as follows: William Lowry and Joseph Hewitt were elected justices of the peace; Alexander Young, Elias Gabriel, and Silas Bingham trustees; Andrew Glass clerk; Horace Martin treasurer; William Young and Ezekiel Robinett overseers of the poor; Joseph Lowry and Samuel Lowry fence-viewers; William Young, Nathan Robinett, and John Bullard supervisors; William Lowry and Joseph Hewitt constables. At this time William Lowry and Joseph Hewitt were the only two "whigs" in the township, yet they were both elected magistrates, showing that party feeling did not enter greatly into the election.

Township Trustees since 1827.

1827	William Lowry,	Elias Gabriel,	Silas Benjamin.
1828–30	"	Abram Gabriel,	Hezekiah Robinett.
1831–34	"	Daniel Lowry,	Jeremiah Thompson.
1835	"	William Handberry,	Samuel Lowry.
1836	John Mintun,	"	George Hewitt.
1837	"	"	William Lowry.
1838–39	Hugh Laughlin,	William Mills,	Elias Gabriel.
1840	William Handberry,	William Herron,	"
1841–42	"	Elias Gabriel,	Pardon C. Hewitt.
1843	"	"	Simon Elliott.
1844	"	"	Daniel McCoy.
1845	John Mintun,	Simon Elliott,	Pardon C. Hewitt.
1846	"	William Lowry,	"
1847	"	Hugh Boden,	Robert McNeal.
1848	"	"	John Means.
1849	Andrew Herron,	Robert McNeal,	"
1850	Hugh Boden,	Robert H. Cotton,	"
1851	"	"	Robert Spear.
1852	"	"	Joseph McNeal.
1853	"	John Means,	"
1854	John Mintun,	Samuel Spencer,	P. B. Wilson.
1855	William Lowry,	Robert Spear,	"
1856	"	Charles Burr,	Jonathan Mintun.
1857–58	"	"	P. B. Wilson.
1859–60	Robert H. Cotton,	William Swaim,	Samuel Cagg.
1861–62	Moses Gabriel,	"	"
1863	"	"	Peter Beckter.
1864	James Boden,	"	Richard Dowler.
1865	James Bell,	James Mayhugh,	Moses Kennard.

Waterloo Township.

TRUSTEES—*Continued.*

1866	James Bell,	Daniel McCoy,	Joseph McNeal.
1867	T. J. Allison,	Abraham Martin,	"
1868	Samuel Cagg,	E. H. Phillips,	Richard Jams.

Township Clerks and Treasurers.

	Clerks.	Treasurers.
1826–27	Andrew Glass.	Horace Martin.
1828	Elias Gabriel.	Lemuel Robinett.
1829	"	Isaac Pearce.
1830	William Young.	Alexander Young.
1831	Samuel Lowry.	Wilson Phillips.
1832	William Handberry.	"
1833–34	"	Joseph Brooks.
1835	Elijah Lowry.	"
1836	David G. Benjamin.	Daniel Lowry.
1837	"	Elias Gabriel.
1838	William Johnstone.	Wanting.
1839–40	R. H. Cotton.	Alexander Young.
1841	William Young.	"
1842	James Holmes.	Elijah Lowry.
1843–44	"	Alexander Young.
1845–46	W. C. Allen.	"
1847	James Holmes.	"
1848–50	W. C. Allen.	William Herron.
1851–52	David W. Mintun.	"
1853	William C. Allen.	William Herron.
1854–55	George Dixon.	"
1856	Asa Thomas.	"
1857	George Dixon.	"
1858–59	Bingham Goodrich.	Hugh Boden.
1860	S. C. Teeters.	"
1861	A. G. Patterson.	"
1862	John Nichols.	"
1863	"	Thomas Withers.
1864	A. G. Robinett.	"
1865	Marcus L. Griswold.	Nelson Squires.
1866	H. C. Wilson.	A. G. Patterson.
1867	Lafayette Hawk.	"
1868	J. B. Miller.	"

We have not the early records of justices of the peace. The following have served since 1853, viz: Robert McNeal, Pardon C. Hewitt, Hugh Boden, Elijah Lowry, and Lafayette Hawk.

The population of Waterloo has steadily increased since its organization; in 1830 it was 216; in 1840 it was 741; in 1850 it was 1,016; in 1860 it was 1,483. The surface of the township is rough, but the soil is well adapted for agriculture, and the annual yield of cereals and of hay, and increase of live stock, afford sufficient evidence of the enterprise and thrift of the farmers of Waterloo. The township is also very rich in coal, which is already taken out in large quantities, and which will eventually be a great source of wealth. Marshfield, a thriving business station on the Marietta and Cincinnati Railroad, seven miles from Athens, is the center of population. The village has about two hundred and fifty inhabitants, and does quite a business in the shipping of country produce. The Methodists have a good church here. There is the usual proportion of stores, a drug store, an excellent tannery, etc. About 1836 several families settled in Waterloo from Morgan and Muskingum counties and parts contiguous. Among these were the families of James Mayhugh, Samuel Allison, Lewis Davis, Hugh Boden, William and Joseph Johnson, Robert Cotton, Daniel McCoy, and others—all good citizens. Some of these have left the county, but descendants of most of them are still living here.

Personal and Biographical.

Moses Hewitt was the first white settler within the present limits of Waterloo. He settled in this township with his family about 1806, and there was not at that time another family within many miles of him. The second family was Abram Fee's, who settled on the place now owned by Mr. Warren Foster, son of Mr. Hull Foster, of Athens. The third family was that of Ezekiel Robinett, Sen., and the fourth that of Colonel William Lowry. Col. Lowry was born November 15, 1779, in Berkeley county, Virginia, and was taken when an infant with his father's family to Green county, Virginia. He says: "That country was then a dense wilderness, infested with Indians. The settlers had to fight every summer for four years after my father moved there. At one time, my father's was the frontier house but one, and the inmates of that one were all killed by the Indians except one boy twelve years old, who made his escape. When I was eighteen years old (1797) my father removed to the northwestern territory and settled in what is now Athens county, and near the town of Athens. We came down the Ohio river to the mouth of Hockhocking, in flat-boats, and up the Hockhocking in canoes. At that time we had to bring our breadstuff from the Ohio river, the nearest mill being a floating one at Vienna, eight miles above the mouth of

Kanawha river, on the Virginia shore. The second year after we came here, we pounded our corn on a hominy-block, took the finer part for bread and made the coarse into hominy. For meat we depended on the woods and our rifles, and always had plenty of bear, deer, and turkey meat. The first mill that I remember was built by Capt. John Hewitt, on Margaret's creek, within a mile of the mouth. It went into operation in the year 1801. I came to Waterloo, from Athens, in February, 1820. This region was all a wilderness then, there being only three families besides mine in the township. Joseph Brookson started the first grist and saw mill in Waterloo, where Newton Hewitt's saw mill now stands. There were a great many bears and deer here at that time, and wolves and panthers were also pretty numerous and very annoying." Col. Lowry is still living in Waterloo, in his seventy-ninth year.

Prominent among the citizens of Waterloo, are Mr. Jesse Jones, a native of Virginia, who settled on Little Raccoon at an early day; Mr. Hugh Boden, a native of Ireland, who settled here in 1839, and now lives in Marshfield; Mr. James Mayhugh, a native of Maryland, who settled here as a farmer in 1836, and now engaged in business in Marshfield; all of whom have reared respectable families, and are highly esteemed.

Robert H. Cotton settled here in 1836. He was a native of Virginia and a model farmer. He settled on the farm where the village of Marshfield now stands, and sold that land to the railroad company.

Samuel Allison, a native of Maryland, settled here in 1836, as a farmer. He reared a large family, some of whom have been well known in the county. Mr. W. H. Allison, a son of his, now lives in Chillicothe, but owns considerable property in Athens county.

CHAPTER XX.

York Township.

THIS township was a part of Ames until 1811, and then, on the organization of Dover, became a part of the latter township. York was separately organized in June, 1818, and the first election for township officers was held at the house of Ebenezer Blackstone.

The population in 1820 was 341; in 1830 it was 871; in 1840 it was 1,601; in 1850 it was 1,391; in 1860 it was 1,836.

The township is traversed by the Hocking Valley canal, which crosses it from northeast to southwest, and has heretofore furnished an excellent outlet for the coal which is mined at and near Nelsonville in great quantities. In the vast deposits of this mineral which underlie a large part of the township, York possesses an undeveloped wealth that will reward the labor and enterprise of many generations yet to come. An active coal trade has existed at Nelsonville for several years past, which will be greatly increased by the opening of the Hocking Valley railroad, and there can be no doubt that this township will, at some future day, be the seat of great wealth and manufacturing life.

The town of Nelsonville, near the northern limit of the township, is a thrifty village, with a population of 1,700 and steadily increasing. It was laid out in June, 1818, and named after Mr. Daniel Nelson, who owned the land on which the town is situated. The town was incorporated by act of the legislature passed in 1838. The first election for town officers was held April 27, 1839, when Charles Cable was elected mayor; A. J. Bond recorder; John Coe, S. M. Sheppard, John Hull, W. W. Poston, and James Rusk trustees. Luther Burt was appointed marshal of the village, and Robert Miller treasurer. James Rusk declining to serve as trustee, Thomas L. Mintun was appointed in his place. Since then the following persons have been elected mayor.

Mayors.

 1840—William Burlingame.
 1841—Ebenezer Fenimore.
 1842—Solomon Roberts.
 1843-44—James Deaver.
 1845—R. G. McLean.
 1846-47—No record.
 1848-49—Lewis Steenrod.
[Mr. Steenrod having resigned, A. J. Guitteau was appointed for his unexpired term.]

MAYORS—*Continued.*

1850–51—B. A. Lincoln.
1852—Thomas L. Mintun.
1853—L. Hutchins.
1854—H. H. Miers.
1855—A. M. Burgess.
1856–57—C. T. Hydé.
1858—J. E. Price.
1859–60—A. H. Burrell.
1861—J. E. Howe.
1862–63—M. A. Stewart.
1864—James Eddington.
1865—H. H. Miers.
1866—Jacob C. Frost.
1867—R. R. Patterson.
1868—John F. Welch.

The township records from 1818 to 1844 can not be found.

Township Trustees since 1844.

1844	Joshua Sheffield,	T. M. Boyles,	James H. Devore.
1845–48	"	"	W. W. Poston.
1849	Alvin Baker,	L. D. Poston,	Pierson Vore.
1850	"	"	John Dew.
1851	Thomas Dew,	Joseph Brett,	A. H. Cowen.
1852	J. G. Miers,	"	"
1853	Joshua Sheffield,	"	"
1854	"	Aaron Lewis,	J. G. Miers.
1855	"	John Hull,	Thomas L. Mintun.
1856–57	"	"	Aaron Lewis.
1858	"	M. D. Socie,	Ashford Poston.
1859	"	John Miers,	John Hull.
1860–61	"	G. L. Cooley,	Moses Lewis.
1862	Richard Matheny,	"	William Allbright.
1863	"	"	J. G. Miers.
1864–66	"	Ashford Poston,	"
1867	Aaron Lewis,	P. H. Moore,	"
1868	Moses Lewis,	R. R. Patterson,	"

Township Clerks and Treasurers since 1844.

	Clerks.	Treasurers.
1844	Robert Miller.	Cornelius Steenrod.
1845-48	Noah Wilder.	"
1849	Thomas L. Mintun.	"
1850	John Cheshire.	"
1851	J. B. Harper.	J. E. Price.
1852	Cornelius Steenrod.	"
1853	John Cheshire.	"
1854-58	Lewis Steenrod.	Cornelius Steenrod.
1859-61	Ashford Poston.	"
1862-63	Samuel N. Poston.	"
1864-67	John Harrison.	John W. Scott.

Justices of the Peace since 1844.

1844—William E. Brown.
1845—Noah Wilder.
1846—Christian Harmon.
1848—B. F. Harper.
1849—Noah Wilder.
1850—Thomas L. Mintun.
1851—Alvin Baker.
1853—Joseph Britt.
1854-60—Joshua Sheffield and Thomas L. Mintun.
1861—Robert R. Patterson.
1862—Joseph Britt.
1863-66—Ashford Porter and Robert Patterson.
1867—Thomas L. Mintun.

Personal and Biographical.

Prominent among the early citizens of York was Mr. James Knight. He was born in Pulborough, England, and emigrated to the United States when thirty-two years old, came immediately to York township, and settled here in July, 1821. He became at once thoroughly identified with the interests of the township, and especially of Nelsonville, and during his residence here was one of the most active and influential citizens, participating earnestly in the local improvements and social movements of the day, such as the building of bridges, school and meeting houses, the establishment of Sunday and day schools, etc. He kept public house in Nelsonville for many years, and was very assiduous in imparting information about the Hockhocking valley to travelers. He aided largely in the construction of the first bridge over the Hockhocking, at Nelsonville, in 1827, and also in the erection of a second one in 1832, and of the bridge across Monday creek, three miles below Nelsonville, in 1832. These bridges were mainly built on individual subscriptions, paid, in many instances, in *grain* and *labor*, and the original subscription papers, with the plans of the work and the written contracts therefor, were found in complete order among Mr. Knight's papers after his death.

In 1832 he prepared, by request, a circular calling attention to the importance of an immediate improvement of the Hockhocking valley by a canal from Lancaster to the Ohio river, which was sent to leading men throughout southern Ohio, and which contributed much toward the chartering of the "Hocking Valley canal" in the spring of 1839 and its construction soon after. Mr. Knight died August 26, 1836, aged forty-seven years. The following memoranda are in his handwriting:

"Mr. Edward Redman, Mrs. Redman, Harriet Redman, arrived 26th May, 1832.

"Charles Wheeler arrived July 19th.

"Captain Hale, with Samuel Older, wife and eight children; Thomas Older, William Thaire, wife and children; James Smart, wife and two children; William Saunders, wife and four children; Barberry, wife and children; George Tribe and wife; George Hook and Ned Smithers arrived at Nelsonville July 30th, 1832, at 11 o'clock in the forenoon.

"Peter Smithers and wife and children at Pittsburg. Charles Southerton, wife and children at Sunday creek. Howick, ditto. Captain Hale stayed fifteen days at Nelsonville. Graffham and family arrived August 21st, 1832. Miss Courtauld arrived November 20, 1834."

L. D. Poston was born in Hampshire county, Virginia, March 29, 1812, and came to Athens county in September, 1830. For about two years after coming here he worked out by the month, then engaged in buying and selling cattle till October, 1835, when he settled in Nelsonville in the mercantile business. The letter of credit, on which he purchased his first stock of goods, was given him by J. N. and J. H. Norton, and Ezra and William Stewart of Athens. In 1852 Mr. Poston began extensive coal operations which he still continues, owning some of the most valuable coal lands and mines in the township. He is a man of strict integrity, fine business capacity, and an excellent citizen. By his own efforts and attention to business he has become one of the wealthiest men in the county.

Samuel Robbins was one of the early settlers of York. He was born in Massachusetts in 1771, came to Athens county in 1819, and to Nelsonville in 1822, where he lived the rest of his life. He built and carried on the first tannery in this part of the county. He died September 21, 1832. His descendants are mostly living in York.

Solomon Roberts, a native of New York, came to Athens county in 1819 and settled in Nelsonville in March, 1821. He found here less than half a dozen cabins and one frame house. Coal was not known to exist about Nelsonville for several years after this date. Mr. Roberts being a blacksmith got his coal from Minker's run and Monday creek, for some time after he came here. Prior to the opening of the canal, samples of the Nelsonville coal were sent in wagons to Lancaster, Circleville, and other towns for blacksmithing, and its quality fully tested and approved. Mr. Roberts and his son, Mr. W. P. Roberts, are well known in Nelsonville.

Lewis Steenrod was born in a block house at Wheeling, Virginia, in June, 1791, came to Ohio in 1805, and resided in Muskingum county about eight miles east of Zanesville for over forty years. In 1850 he removed with his family to Nelsonville where he died December 10, 1860. "Father" Steenrod, as he was called, was a man of benevolent heart and gentle life. He was a member of the Baptist church, having united with that organization in 1812. Some of his descendants remain in the county.

APPENDIX.

APPENDIX.

A.

Powers to the Board of Treasury to contract for the sale of lands in the Western Territory.

[From Old Journals of Congress, Vol. 4, Appendix, p. 17.]

July 23, 1787.—The report of a committee, consisting of Mr. Carrington, Mr. King, Mr. Dane, Mr. Madison and Mr. Benson, amended to read as follows, viz :

That the Board of Treasury be authorized and empowered to contract with any person or persons for a grant of a tract of land, which shall be bounded by the Ohio, from the mouth of the Scioto to the intersection of the western boundary of the tenth township from the Ohio; thence by a due west line to Scioto; thence by the Scioto to the beginning, upon the following terms, to wit : The tract to be surveyed and its contents ascertained by the geographer, or some other officer of the United States, who shall plainly mark the said east and west line, and shall render one complete plat to the Board of Treasury, and another to the purchaser or purchasers. The purchaser or purchasers, within seven years from the completion of this work, to lay off the whole tract, at their own expense, into townships and fractional parts of townships, and to divide the same into lots, according to the land ordinance of the 20th of May, 1785; complete returns whereof to be made to the Treasury Board. The lot No. 16 in each township, or fractional part of a township, to be given perpetually for the purposes contained in the said ordinance. The lot No. 29 in each township, or fractional part of a township, to be given perpetually for the purposes of religion. The lots Nos. 8, 11 and 26, in each township, or fractional part of a township, to be reserved for the future disposition of congress. Not more than two complete townships to be given perpetually for the purposes of an university, to be laid off by the purchaser or purchasers, as near the centre as may be (so that the same shall be of good land), to be applied to the intended object by the Legislature of the State. The price to be not less than one dollar per acre for the contents of the said tract, excepting the reservations and gifts aforesaid, payable in specie, loan-office certificates reduced to specie value, or certificates of liquidated debts of the U. States, liable to a reduction by an allowance for bad land, and all incidental charges and circumstances whatever; *provided*, that all such allowance shall not exceed, in the whole, one-third of a dollar per acre. And, in making payment, the principal only of the said certificates shall be admitted, and the Board of Treasury, for such interest as may be due on the certificates rendered in payment as aforesaid, prior to January 1, 1786, shall issue indents for interest to the possessors, which shall be receivable in payment as other indents for interest, of the existing requisitions of congress; and for such interest as may be due on the said certificates, between that period and the period of payment, the said Board shall issue indents, the payment of which to be provided for in future requisitions or otherwise. Such of the purchasers as may possess rights for bounties of land to the late army, to be permitted to render the same in discharge of the contract, acre for acre; *provided*, that the aggregate of such rights shall not exceed one-seventh part of the land to be paid for; and *provided further*, that there shall be no future claim against the United States on account of the said rights. Not less than 500,000 dollars of the purchase money to be paid down upon closing the contract, and the remainder upon the completion of the work to be performed by the geographer, or other officer, on the part of the United States. Good and sufficient security to be given by the purchaser or purchasers for the completion of the contract on his or their part. The grant to be made upon the full payment of the consideration money, and a right of entry and occupancy to be acquired immediately, for so much of the tract as shall be agreed upon between the Board of Treasury and the purchasers.

July 23, 1787.—*Ordered*, That the above be referred to the Board of Treasury to take order.

B.

Letter of the Ohio Company to the Board of Treasury.

[From Old Journals of Congress, Vol. 4, Appendix, p. 17.]

" *July* 26, 1787.

" *New York, July* 26*th*, 1787.

" GENTLEMEN :

" We observe, by the act of the 23d instant, that your honorable Board is authorized to enter into a contract for the sale of a tract of land therein described, on certain conditions expressed in the act. As we suppose this measure has been adopted in consequence of proposals made by us, in behalf of ourselves and associates, to a Committee of Congress, we beg leave to inform you that we are ready to enter into a contract for the purchase of the lands described in the act ; *provided*, you can conceive yourselves authorized to admit of the following conditions, which in some degree vary from the report of the committee, viz :

The subordinate surveys shall be completed as mentioned in the act, unless the frequency of Indian irruptions may render the same impracticable without a heavy expense to the company.

The mode of payment we propose is half a million of dollars when the contract is executed; another half million when the tract, as described, is surveyed by the proper officer of the United States; and the remainder in six equal payments, computed from the day of the second payment.

The lands assigned for the establishment of an university to be as nearly as possible in the centre of the first million and a half of acres we shall *pay for;* for to fix it in the centre of the proposed purchase, might too long defer the establishment.

When the second payment is made, the purchasers shall receive a deed for as great a quantity of land as a million of dollars will pay for at the price agreed on; after which we will agree not to receive any further deeds for any of the lands purchased, only at such periods and on such conditions as may be agreed on betwixt the Board and the purchasers.

As to the security, which the act says shall be good and sufficient, we are unable to determine what those terms may mean in the contemplation of Congress, or of your honorable Board; we shall, therefore, only observe that our private fortunes, and that of most of our associates, being embarked in the support of the purchase, it is not possible for us to offer any adequate security but that of the land itself, as is usual in great land purchases.

We will agree so to regulate the contracts that we shall never be entitled to a right of entry or occupancy but on the lands actually paid for, nor receive any deeds till our payments amount to a million of dollars, and then only in proportion to such payment. The advance we shall always be under without any formal deed, together with the improvements made on the lands will, we presume, be ample security, even if it was not the interest as well as the disposition of the company, to lay the foundation of their establishment on a sacred regard to the rights of property.

If these terms are admitted we shall be ready to conclude the contract.

We have the honor to be, with the greatest respect, gentlemen,

Your obedient, humble servants,
MANASSEH CUTLER,
WINTHROP SARGENT."

"The Honorable The Board of Treasury."

"*July* 27, 1787.—*Ordered,* That the above letter, from Manasseh Cutler and Winthrop Sargent, to the Board of Treasury, containing proposals for the purchase of a tract of land, described in the act of Congress of the 23d instant, be referred to the Board of Treasury to take order ; *provided,* that after the date of the second payment therein proposed to be made, the residue shall be paid in six equal and half yearly instalments, until the whole thereof shall be completed, and that the purchasers stipulate to pay interest on the sums due, from the completion of the survey to be performed by the geographer."

[The boundaries contemplated by the letter and order above were allowed and confirmed by the act of 21st April, 1792. See page 561.]

C.

Contract of the Ohio Company with the Board of Treasury.

[Extract from old Records.]

"The contract of the Ohio Company with the Honorable Board of Treasury of the United States of America, made by the Rev. Mr. *Manasseh Cutler* and Major *Winthrop Sargent,* as agents for the Directors of said Company, at New York, October 27, 1787:

"This Indenture, made the 27th day of October, in the year of our Lord one thousand seven hundred and eighty-seven, between *Samuel Osgood*, *Walter Livingston* and *Arthur Lee*, Esquires, (the Board of Treasury for the United States of America), acting by and under the authority of the Honorable, the Congress of the said States of the one part, and *Manasseh Cutler* and *Winthrop Sargent*, both of the Commonwealth of Massachusetts, as Agents for the Directors of the Ohio Company of associates, so called, of the other part: Whereas, the Congress of the United States aforesaid, in and by their several resolutions and votes of the twenty-third and twenty-seventh days of July last past, did authorize and empower the Board of Treasury aforesaid to contract with any person or persons for a grant of the tract of land in the said resolutions mentioned, upon such terms and conditions, for such considerations and under such reservations, as in the said resolutions is expressed. And, whereas, by virtue and in consequence of the said resolutions and votes, the said parties of the first part have contracted and agreed with the parties of the second part, agents as aforesaid, for a grant of the tract of land hereinafter mentioned.

Now, therefore, this indenture witnesseth, That the said parties of the first part, in order to carry their said agreement, as far as possible, into effect, and for and in consideration of the sum of five hundred thousand dollars well and truly paid into the Treasury of the said United States by the said parties of the second part, before the ensealing and delivery of these presents, the receipt whereof the said Board of Treasury do hereby acknowledge, and do hereby, on the behalf of the said United States, acquit, release, exonerate and forever discharge the said parties of the second part, and the said Ohio Company of associates and every of them, their and every of their heirs, executors, administrators and assigns forever, by these presents; and also in consideration of the further sum of five hundred thousand dollars, secured to be paid as hereinafter is mentioned, have, in behalf of the said United States and the Congress thereof, covenanted and agreed, and do hereby covenant and agree, to and with the said parties of the second part, their heirs and assigns, that within one month of the payment of the said last-mentioned sum of five hundred thousand dollars, in the manner hereinafter prescribed, a full and ample grant and conveyance shall be executed, in due form of law, under the seal of the said United States, whereby the people of the said United States or the Congress thereof, or such officer or officers as shall be duly authorized for that purpose, shall grant, convey and assure to the said parties of the second part, their heirs and assigns forever (as agents to the Directors of, and in trust for the persons composing the said Ohio Company of associates, according to their several rights and interests under the said association), and to their heirs and assigns forever, as tenants in common, in fee simple, all that certain tract or parcel of land, *Beginning* at the place where the western boundary line of the seventh range of townships, laid out by the authority of Congress, intersects the Ohio, and extending thence along that river south-westwardly, to the place where the western line of the seventeenth range of townships, to be laid out according to the land ordinance of the 20th May, 1785, would intersect the said river, and extending thence northerly on the western boundary line of the said seventeenth range of townships, so far that a line drawn due east to the western boundary line of the said seventh range of townships will, with the other lines of this tract, include one million and a half of acres of land, besides the several townships, lots and parcels of land hereinafter mentioned, to be reserved or appropriated to specific purposes; thence running east to the western bounds of the said seventh range of townships, and thence southerly along those bounds to the place of beginning; with the rights, members and appurtenances thereof; which said tract of land shall be surveyed by the geographer or some other officer of the said United States, to be authorized for that purpose, who shall plainly mark the said east and west line, and shall render one complete map or plat of the said tract to the Board of Treasury of the United States, for the time being, or such other person as Congress may appoint, and another plat or map thereof to the said parties of the second part, their heirs or assigns. *Provided, always, and it is hereby expressly stipulated,* That in the said grant, so to be executed as aforesaid, a proper clause or clauses shall or may be inserted for the purpose of reserving in each township, or factional part of a township, which, upon such surveys as hereinafter are mentioned, shall fall within the bounds of the tract, so to be granted as aforesaid, lot number sixteen, for the purposes mentioned in the said ordinance of the 20th of May, 1785; lot number twenty-nine to be appropriated to the purposes of religion; and lots number eight, eleven and twenty-six for the use, and subject to the disposition of the Congress of the United States; and also reserving out of the said tract so to be granted, two complete townships to be given perpetually for the purposes of an university, to be laid off by the said parties of the second part, their heirs or assigns, as near the center as may be, so the same shall be of good land, to be applied to the intended object in such manner as the Legislature of the State wherein the said townships shall fall, or may be situated, shall or may think proper to direct. And the said parties of the second part do hereby for themselves, and the Directors, and Ohio Company of associates aforesaid, and every of them, and their and every of their heirs, executors, administrators and assigns, covenant and grant to, and with the said parties of the first part, their heirs, executors and administrators (acting, as aforesaid, for and on behalf of the the United States, by virtue of the authority so as aforesaid to them delegated and assigned), that within the space of seven years, from and after the outlines of the said tract shall have been so, as aforesaid, run out by the geographer, or other officer of the United States to be for that purpose appointed, and the plat thereof given as aforesaid, (if they are not prevented by incursions or opposition from the savages, or if they are so prevented, then as soon as the same can be conveniently thereafter accomplished,) the said Directors and Ohio Company of associates, or some of them, their or some of their heirs or assigns shall and will cause the said tract of land to be surveyed, laid out and divided into townships, and fractional parts of townships, and also subdivided into lots, according to the directions and provisions of the land ordinance of the 20th of May, 1785, issued by Congress, and shall and will make or cause to be made, complete returns of divisions and subdivisions to the Treasury Board of the United States, for the time being, or such other person or persons as Congress shall or may appoint. And, also, shall and will, within one month after the outlines of the said tract shall have been so, as aforesaid, surveyed, well and truly pay, or cause to be paid into the Treasury of the said United States, the sum of five hundred thousand dollars in gold or silver, or in securities of the said United States, without fraud or further delay. And, inasmuch as it was the true intent and meaning of the said parties to these presents, and of the Congress of the United States, that the said Ohio Company of associates should immediately cultivate, if they thought proper, a part of the said tract of land, proportionable to the payment which they have so, as aforesaid, already made; and should have full security for the undisturbed enjoyment of the same. *Now, this indenture further witnesseth,* That the said parties of the first part, by virtue of the power and authority to them given by Congress as aforesaid, have covenanted, promised and agreed, and do hereby covenant, promise and agree to and with the said parties of the second part, their heirs and assigns, that it shall and may be lawful for the said Ohio Company of associates, so called, their heirs and assigns, to enter upon, take possession of, cultivate and improve, at their pleasure, all that certain tract or parcel of land, part of the tract hereinbefore described: *Beginning* at the place where the western boundary line of the said seventh range of townships intersects the Ohio, thence extending along that river southwesterly to the place where the western boundary line of the fifteenth range of townships, when laid out agreeable to the ordinance aforesaid, would touch the said river; thence running northerly on the western bounds of the said fifteenth range of townships, till a line drawn due east, the western boundary line of the said seventh range of townships will comprehend, with the other boundary lines of this tract, seven hundred and fifty thousand acres of land, besides the several lots and parcels of lands hereinafter mentioned to be reserved or appropriated to particular purposes; thence running east to the western boundary line of the said seventh range of townships, and thence along the said line to the place of beginning; with the rights, members and appurtenances thereof, according to the terms of the said association. Reserving, always, and excepting out of the said tract last mentioned, and the permission to cultivate the same in each township and fractional part of a township which shall fall within the same, according to the land ordinance hereinbefore mentioned, lot number sixteen, for the purposes specified in the said ordinance; lot number twenty-nine for the purposes of religion; lots number eight, eleven and twenty-six subject to the disposition of the Congress of the United States, and also reserving and excepting two complete townships for the purposes of an university, to be laid off in the manner hereinbefore mentioned, and to be applied in such manner to that object as the Legislature of the State wherein the said townships shall fall, or be situated, shall or may think proper or direct. And the said parties of the first part do hereby, for and on behalf of the said United States, promise and agree to and with the said parties of the second part, their heirs and assigns, that the said Ohio Company of associates, their heirs and assigns, shall and may, from time to time, and at all times hereafter, freely and peaceably hold and enjoy the said last-mentioned tract of land, except the said lots and parcels of land and townships so, as aforesaid, excepted; *Provided*, that the covenants and agreements hereinbefore contained on the part of the said parties of the second part are observed, performed and fulfilled. And the said parties of the first part do hereby pledge the faith of the UNITED STATES to the said parties of the second part, their heirs and assigns, and to the said Ohio Company of associates, so-called, for the performance of all the grants, promises and agreements hereinbefore contained, which, on the part of the said parties of the first part, or of the said States, are or ought to be kept and performed.

In witness whereof, the parties to these presents have interchangeably set their hands and seals, and the said parties of the first part have caused their seal of office to be hereunto affixed, the day and year first hereinbefore mentioned.

SAMUEL OSGOOD, [L. S.]
MANASSEH CUTLER, [L. S.]
ARTHUR LEE, [L. S.]
WINTHROP SARGENT. [L. S.]

D.

An Act authorizing the grant and conveyance of certain lands to the Ohio Company of Associates.

[Act of April 21, 1792.]

Be it enacted by the Senate and House of Representatives of the United States of America in Congress assembled, That a certain contract expressed in an indenture executed on the 27th day of October, in the year one thousand seven hundred and eighty-seven, between the then Board of Treasury for the United States of America, of the one part, and Manasseh Cutler and Winthrop Sargent, as Agents for the Directors of the Ohio Company of Associates, of the other part, so far as the same respects the following described tract of land, that is to say; " Beginning at a station where the Western boundary line of the seventh range of townships, laid out by the authority of the United States in Congress assembled, intersects the river Ohio; thence, extending along that river, South-westerly, to a place where the Western boundary line of the fifteenth range of townships, when laid out agreeably to the land ordinance passed the twentieth of May, one thousand seven hundred and eighty-five, would touch the said river; thence running Northerly on the said Western bound of the said fifteenth range of townships, till a line drawn due East to the Western boundary line of the said seventh range of townships, will comprehend with the other lines of this tract, seven hundred and fifty thousand acres of land, besides the several lots and parcels of land in the said contract reserved or appropriated to particular purposes; thence running East, to the Western boundary line of the said seventh range of townships, and thence, along the said line to the place of beginning," be, and the same is hereby, confirmed: And that the President of the United States be, and he hereby is, authorized and empowered to issue letters patent, in the name and under the seal of the United States, hereby granting and conveying to Rufus Putnam, Manasseh Cutler, Robert Oliver, and Griffin Green, and to their heirs and assigns, in fee simple, the said described tract of land, with the reservation in the said indenture expressed, in trust for the persons composing the said Ohio Company of Associates, according to their several rights and interests, and for their heirs and assigns, as tenants in common.

SEC. 2. *And be it further enacted*, That the President be, and he hereby is, further authorized and empowered, by letters patent as aforesaid, to grant and convey to the said **Rufus Putnam, Manasseh Cutler, Robert Oliver and Griffin Green**, and to their heirs and assigns, in trust, for the uses above expressed, one other tract, of two hundred and fourteen thousand two hundred and eighty-five acres of land. *Provided*, That Rufus Putnam, Manasseh Cutler, Robert Oliver and Griffin Green, or either of them, shall deliver to the Secretary of the Treasury, within six months, warrants which issued for army bounty rights sufficient for that purpose, according to the provison of a resolve of Congress of the twenty-third day of July, one thousand seven hundred and eighty-seven.

SEC. 3. *And be it further enacted*, That the President be, and he hereby is, further authorized and empowered, by letters patent as aforesaid, to grant and convey to the said Rufus Putnam, Manasseh Cutler, Robert Oliver and Griffin Green, and to their heirs and assigns, in fee simple, in trust for the uses above expressed, a farther quantity of one hundred thousand acres of land. *Provided always nevertheless*, That the said grant of one hundred thousand acres shall be made on the express condition of becoming void, for such part thereof as the said Company shall not have, within five years from the passing of this act, conveyed in fee simple, as a bounty, and free of expense, in tracts of one hundred acres to each male person, not less than eighteen years of age, being an actual settler at the time of such conveyance.

SEC. 4. *And be it further enacted*, That the said quantities of two hundred and fourteen thousand two hundred and eighty-five acres, and of one hundred thousand acres, shall be located within the limits of the tract of one million five hundred thousand acres of land, described in the indenture aforesaid, and adjoining to the tract of land described in the first section of this act, and in such form as the President, in the letters patent, shall prescribe for that purpose.

Approved, *April* 21, 1792.

E.

Patent for 750,000 acres.

[From Records of the General Land Office.]

IN THE NAME OF THE UNITED STATES.
To all whom these Presents may come.

Know ye, that in pursuance of the act entitled " An Act authorizing the grant and conveyance of certain lands to the Ohio Company of Associates," I do hereby grant and convey to Rufus Putnam, Manasseh Cutler, Robert Oliver and Griffin Green, and to their heirs and assigns forever, the following described tract of land, that is to say, beginning at a station or point where the Western boundary line of the seventh range of Townships laid out by the authority of the United States in Congress assembled intersects the River Ohio, thence extending along that river Southwesterly to a place where the Western boundary line of the fifteenth range of Townships when laid out agreeably to the land ordinance passed the twentieth day of May one thousand seven hundred and eighty-five, would touch the said river: Thence running Northerly on the said Western boundary of the said fifteenth range of Townships till a line drawn due East to the Western boundary line of the said seventh range of Townships will comprehend with the other lines of this tract herein specified and described, seven hundred and fifty thousand acres of land beside the several lots and parcels of land in a certain contract executed on the twenty-seventh day of October, one thousand seven hundred and eighty-seven between the then Board of Treasury for the United States of America of the one part, and Manasseh Cutler and Winthrop

Sargent as Agents for the Directors of the Ohio Company of Associates of the other part, reserved or appropriated to particular purposes: Thence running East to the Western boundary line of the said seventh range of Townships, and thence along the said line to the place of beginning, which said tract contains as computed nine hundred and thirteen thousand eight hundred and eighty-three acres, subject however to the reservations expressed in an Indenture, executed on the twenty-seventh day of October, in the year one thousand seven hundred and eighty-seven, between the then Board of Treasury for the United States of America of the one part, and Manasseh Cutler and Winthrop Sargent agents for the Directors of the Ohio Company of Associates of the other part:

To have and hold the said described tract of land with the reservations aforesaid in the said Indenture so expressed as aforesaid, to the said Rufus Putnam, Manasseh Cutler, Robert Oliver and Griffin Green, and to their heirs and asssigns forever, in trust for the persons composing the said Ohio Company of Associates, according to their several rights and interests, and for their heirs and assigns as tenants in common, hereby willing and directing these letters to be made patent.

Given under my hand and the seal of the United States at the city of Philadelphia this tenth day of May, in the year of our Lord, one thousand seven hundred and ninety-two and of Independence the sixteenth.

[L. S.]   G°· WASHINGTON.

By the President:

   TH. JEFFERSON.

F.

Patent for 214,285 *acres.*

[From Records of the General Land Office.]

IN THE NAME OF THE UNITED STATES.

To all to whom these presents shall come:

Whereas, it hath been duly certified to me by the Secretary of the Treasury, in pursuance of the Act entitled "An Act authorizing the grant and conveyance of certain lands to the Ohio Company of Associates," that Rufus Putnam, Manasseh Cutler, Robert Oliver and Griffin Green, have delivered to him warrants which issued for army bounty rights, sufficient for the purposes of the grant and conveyance of two hundred and fourteen thousand two hundred and eighty-five acres of land, in the second section of the above recited act mentioned according to the provision of a resolve of Congress of the twenty-third day of July, one thousand seven hundred and eighty-seven. Now, know ye, that by virtue of the above recited act, I do hereby grant and convey to the said Rufus Putnam, Manasseh Cutler, Robert Oliver and Griffin Green, and to their heirs and assigns, one tract of land, containing two hundred and fourteen thousand two hundred and eighty-five acres, to be located within the limits of the tract of one million five hundred thousand acres described in an Indenture executed on the twenty-seventh day of October, in the year one thousand seven hundred and eighty-seven, between the then Board of Treasury for the United States of America of the one part, and Manasseh Cutler and Winthrop Sargent as agents for the Directors of the Ohio Company of

Associates, of the other part, and adjoining to the tract of land, described in the first section of the above recited act, and in the form herein prescribed, as follows:

Beginning on a line that has been surveyed and marked by Israel Ludlow (a plat or map whereof is filed in the office of the Secretary of the Treasury) as for the North Boundary line of a tract of one million five hundred thousand acres expressed in an Indenture executed on the twenty-seventh day of October, one thousand seven hundred and eighty-seven, between the then Board of Treasury for the United States of America, of the one part, and Manasseh Cutler and Winthrop Sargent, of the other part, at a point which is and shall be established to be the North-west corner of a tract of one hundred thousand acres granted to the said Rufus Putnam, Manasseh Cutler, Robert Oliver and Griffin Green, by letters patent bearing even date with these presents: Thence running westerly on the said line surveyed and marked as aforesaid to a point where the said line would intersect the West boundary line of the eleventh range of townships if laid out agreeably to the land Ordinance passed the twentieth day of May, one thousand seven hundred and eighty-five: Thence running South on the said Western boundary of the said eleventh range of townships if laid out as aforesaid, till it would intersect a westerly continuation of the North boundary line of the third township of the seventh range of townships surveyed by the authority of the United States of America in Congress assembled: Thence running on a further Westerly continuation of the said North boundary line of the said third township to a point, station, or place where the Western boundary line of the sixteenth range of townships would intersect or meet the same, if laid out agreeably to the land Ordinance aforesaid: Thence running South on the said Western boundary line of the sixteenth range of townships if laid out as aforesaid, to a point, station, or place from which a line drawn due East to the West boundary line of a tract of Nine hundred and thirteen thousand eight hundred and eighty-three acres, granted to Rufus Putnam, Manasseh Cutler, Robert Oliver and Griffin Green, by letters patent bearing even date with these presents, will, with the other lines of this tract as herein specified and described, comprehend Two hundred and fourteen thousand two hundred and eighty-five acres: Thence running due East to the Western boundary line of the said tract of Nine hundred and thirteen thousand eight hundred and eighty-three acres: Thence running Northerly on the said Western boundary line to the North-west corner of the said last mentioned tract: Thence running Easterly on the Northern boundary of the said last mentioned tract to the point where the same is touched or intersected by the Western boundary of the aforesaid tract of One hundred thousand acres: Thence Northerly on the said Western boundary of the said last mentioned tract to the place of beginning.

To have and to hold the aforesaid tract of two hundred and fourteen thousand two hundred and eighty-five acres of land to the said Rufus Putnam, Manasseh Cutler, Robert Oliver and Griffin Green, and to their heirs and assigns, in trust for the persons composing the said Ohio Company of Associates, according to their several rights and interests, and for their heirs and assigns as tenants in common, hereby willing and directing these letters to be made patent.

Given under my hand and the Seal of the United States at the city of Philadelphia, this tenth day of May, in the year of our Lord one thousand seven hundred and ninety-two, and of Independence the sixteenth.

[L. S.]   G°· WASHINGTON.
By the President:
   TH. JEFFERSON.

G.

Patent for 100,000 *acres—Donation Tract.*

[From Records of the General Land Office.]

IN THE NAME OF THE UNITED STATES.
To all whom these presents shall come :

Know ye, that in pursuance of the Act intituled "An Act authorizing the grant and conveyance of certain lands to the Ohio Company of Associates" I do hereby grant and convey to Rufus Putnam, Manasseh Cutler, Robert Oliver and Griffin Green, and to their heirs and assigns forever, one hundred thousand acres of land to be located within the limits of the tract of one million five hundred thousand acres of land, described in an indenture executed on the twenty-seventh day of October in the year one thousand seven hundred and eighty-seven, between the then Board of Treasury for the United States of America, of the one part, and Manasseh Cutler and Winthrop Sargent, as Agents for the Directors of the Ohio Company of Associates, of the other part, and adjoining to the tract of land described in the first section of the above recited act, and in the form herein prescribed, as follows : Beginning on the Western boundary line of the seventh range of Townships laid out by the authority of the United States in Congress assembled, at a point which is and shall be established to be the North-east corner of a certain tract of land containing as computed nine hundred and thirteen thousand eight hundred and eighty-three acres by letters patent bearing even date with these presents granted to the said Rufus Putnam, Manasseh Cutler, Robert Oliver, and Griffin Green : Thence running Northerly on the said Western boundary of the said seventh range of Townships to a point or station that has been fixed (pursuant to a survey made by Israel Ludlow, a plat or map whereof is filed in the office of the Secretary of the Treasury) as the North-east corner of a tract of one million five hundred thousand acres, described in an Indenture executed on the twenty-seventh day of October, one thousand seven hundred and eighty-seven, between the then Board of Treasury for the United States of America, of the one part, and Manasseh Cutler and Winthrop Sargent, of the other part: Thence running Westerly on the Northern boundary line of the said tract of one million five hundred thousand acres as surveyed and marked by the said Israel Ludlow to a point from which a line drawn South to the Northern boundary line of the said tract of Nine hundred and thirteen thousand eight hundred and eighty-three acres, will, with the other lines of this tract herein specified and described comprehend one hundred thousand acres : Thence running South to the said Northern boundary line, and thence due East on the said Northern line to the place of beginning.

To have and to hold the said one hundred thousand acres of land to the said Rufus Putnam, Manasseh Cutler, Robert Oliver and Griffin Green and to their heirs and assigns forever, in trust for the persons composing the said Ohio Company of Associates according to their several rights and interests, and for their heirs and assigns as tenants in common.

Provided always nevertheless, that this grant is made on the express condition of becoming void for such part thereof as the said Company shall not have within five years from the passing of the above recited Act, to-wit: from the twenty-first day of April, in the year one thousand seven hundred and ninety-two, conveyed in fee simple as a bounty, and free of expense, in tracts of one hundred acres to each male person not less than eighteen years of age, being an actual settler at the time of such conveyance. And I do moreover will and direct these letters to be made patent.

Given under my hand and the Seal of the United States at the city of Philadelphia this tenth day of May in the year of our

Lord one thousand seven hundred and ninety-two, and of Independence the sixteenth.

[L. S.]   G⁰· WASHINGTON.

By the President:
   TH. JEFFERSON.

H.

CHARGE.

By the Rev. Dr. Manasseh Cutler, at the ordination of Rev. Wm. Story, pastor of the church at Marietta. Given at Hamilton, Massachusetts, August 15th, 1798. [Mr. Story was the first Congregational minister who preached west of the mountains.]

"You are now, sir, by the laying on of hands and solemn prayer to God, set apart to the work of the gospel ministry. To your special care and charge are committed the Church and the Christian Society at Marietta, by whose express desire you are ordained their pastor. In the name of the great Head of the Church, we most solemnly charge you to be a faithful minister of the gospel. Take heed to the ministry which you have received, and fulfill it. Preach the word in its purity and simplicity. Let the most interesting truths contained in the oracles of God be the leading subject of your public discourses. Apply yourself with zeal and industry to the duties of your office. Improve the talent you have received, and bring to the people the beaten oil of the Sanctuary. Shun not to declare the whole counsel of God. As a wise instructor, teach every man. As a true watchman, warn every man. As a faithful shepherd, feed, in all seasons, the flock of God; feed Christ's sheep; feed his lambs. You are engaged in the work of the ministry at a time when infidelity is openly professed—when it is propagated with artful industry. Attend to the internal and external evidences of divine revelation, and be always ready with those substantial arguments in support of the authenticity of the scriptures, which will silence gainsayers and evince the reasonableness of the Christian faith. My Brother, take heed to yourself. Instruct your people by your own example. Live the religion you recommend to them. Let it be your concern that the temper of your mind, as well as the tenor of your conduct, accord with the spirit of the gospel. Feel your dependence, and by ardent and daily supplications look to Heaven for divine influence. In the course of your services at the altar of God, you are to administer the sacraments of the new testament, baptism, and the Lord's supper, to all proper subjects, making the word of God your rule, and strictly adhering to the sacred institutions. You are to preside in the government of the Church with prudence and firmness. You are to dispense the discipline of God's house with faithfulness and impartiality. You are now, sir, vested with power to ordain and separate others to the work of the ministry. In the new and extended country where you are to labor, we hope there will be frequent occasions for the exercise of this part of the ministerial office. We must give it in solemn charge, that you commit this trust to faithful men; to such as are able to teach others; to men whose acquirements and whose characters will not be a reproach to the ministry. Remember you are to lay hands suddenly on no man. To see the many new societies, now forming in your vicinity, supplied with able and faithful ministers, must be an object near your heart. It is, in every view, highly important to them, for it intimately concerns their political and social, as well as their spiritual and eternal interests. There is no description of men capable of doing more in promoting the peace, order, and real prosperity of an infant country, than wise, active and faithful ministers. May it never be forgotten that an unlearned, unskillful and immoral ministry is one of the greatest evils that can befall the Church of God. Sensible that to you the care of souls is committed, you will watch for them as one that must give an account. In the course of your ministry you are to expect to meet with trials and discouragements of different kinds. Providence has cast your lot among a people collected from various parts of the world, bringing with them the sentiments, habits and manners they had previously contracted. Difficult must be the task of rendering yourself useful and acceptable to them all, while you faithfully discharge the duties of your office. To engage their attention, you must endeavor to acquire their confidence. To recommend religion and illustrate its tendency, you must persevere in a constant solicitude to promote their best good. Prudence will be indispensably requisite, and without it every other qualification will be of little avail. You need the wisdom of the serpent and the innocence of the dove. From the assiduous exertions of the people of your charge to obtain and enjoy the stated ministrations of the gospel, and the pleasing unanimity and affection with which they have elected you to be their pastor, after a probationary trial of more than eight years, you must derive the encouraging hope of their cheerful concurrence in rendering your labors agreeable and successful. May you, on your return to them, be received as an ascension gift of our blessed Lord. You have the honor, sir, to be the first regularly ordained and settled minister of the Congregational denomination in that extensive country westward of the Allegheny mountains. We, who are convinced that this denomination is most conformable to the sacred scriptures, and from long experience think it most consistent with the rights of conscience and religious liberty; most congenial with our national government, and most friendly to those numerous municipal advantages which well formed christian societies endeavor to promote, feel much satisfaction in seeing it transplanted into that growing country. You, sir, are going to a country favorable to a high degree of population, which is capable of supporting, and probably will one day, contain inhabitants as numerous as those of the Atlantic states. You are entering on an active scene, and the noblest motives to exertion will continually present themselves to your view. To behold a country which was lately, very lately, a howling wilderness, the gloomy abodes of numerous savage tribes, the haunts and lurking places of the cruel invaders of defenseless frontiers, regardless of age and sex, sporting with the agonies of captives, while expiring under their infernal tortures. A people ignorant of the True God, and devoted to their heathen rites and barbarous superstitions. To see this country so rapidly changing into cultured fields, inhabited by civil and well regulated societies, peaceably enjoying the fruits of their enterprise, industry, culture and commerce, to hear the voice of plenty, urbanity and social enjoyment, above all, to see it illumed by the pure and benevolent religion of the gospel, enjoyed in all its regular ministrations and divine ordinances. To behold scenes and events like these, my Brother, are not merely pleasing contemplations, they are animating motives to zeal and activity in your ministerial labors. It would have afforded great additional happiness to have seen these savage tribes converted to the christian faith. But it gives much satisfaction, and may prepare the way for the introduction of the gospel among them, that a peace, wise and just in its principles, and which promises a permanent duration, has been concluded with them. Government having fairly and honorably purchased of them their right to the soil, they are quietly retreating into distant parts of the wilderness. I can not forbear reminding you, my dear sir, that on the very ground where you are statedly to dispense the gospel, you behold those ancient ruins, those extended walls and elevated mounds which were erected many ages ago. These works must have required, for years, the labors of thousands, and are certain indications that vast numbers of the natives once inhabited this place. When these antiquities are minutely examined, they induce belief that part of them, at least, are the monuments of ancient superstition.

Their temples and their idols were probably placed on the elevated square mounds, where the ceremonies of their gloomy heathenish devotions were performed. On these mounds, in all probability, numerous *human sacrifices* have been offered. May we adore *Providence*, which is now planting on this memorable spot, the evangelical religion of Jesus. Here may it be permanently established, and may its benign influence be extended throughout every part of the American world. Here may you, sir, be long continued a faithful and successful minister. In contemplating the magnitude and importance of the work to which you are this day solemnly consecrated, well may you ask: *Who is sufficient for these things?* Trust not in your own strength, but in Him whose grace is sufficient for you. Feel the influence not merely of those local considerations which your particular situation so naturally suggests, but of those great truths and momentous concerns which the gospel will continually present to your view. You are now about to take your leave, probably a final leave, of your nearest connections. May the painful hour of parting with them be cheered by the reflection that you are going on a great and useful, an honorable and glorious errand—a work which holy angels would, with pleasure, perform. Those benevolent spirits who sang praises to God in the highest, because there was on earth peace and good will toward men, would cheerfully be employed in turning men from the error of their ways and saving souls from death.

Go, then, my Friend, and the God of peace be with you.

I.

Reminiscences furnished by Dr. Chauncey F. Perkins.

Received too late to be inserted in their proper place: Athens Township.

In the spring of 1801, being then about nineteen years old, I left Marietta, in company with a friend, to join my father's family at Athens. Marietta, at that time the largest town in the northwestern territory, had a population of about five hundred. Leaving the town behind us, and crossing an open common bordering "Point Harmar," our course led directly into the dense forest. We traveled on horseback. The rough and difficult road, which was a mere bridle-path, winding over steep hills and through interlying valleys, was skirted on either side by a wilderness, hardly broken by a few log cabins all the way from Marietta to Middletown, as Athens was then generally called. At Amesville, even then celebrated for its thrifty and intelligent population, the names of some of whom are still preserved among the best citizens of the county, we stopped to refresh ourselves and animals, and were most hospitably entertained. Pursuing our way through the still unending forest, we reached, about sunset, the summit of the river hill overlooking the plateau where the site of the town of Athens had been fixed. A few log cabins dotted the scene before us; but, for the most part, the soil was thickly covered with beech, maple, and enormous poplar trees. My father occupied one of the log cabins. Here we soon arrived and were warmly welcomed, and here, for some years afterward, was my home. Among the leading citizens of the future county at this time, I remember Josiah True, Solomon Tuttle, Daniel Weethee, the Rev. Mr. Pugsley,

Elijah Hatch, the Crippens, Hopson Beebe, Mr. Buckingham, Asahel Cooley, Mr. Johnson, Judge Ames, George Ewing, and others whose names I mention elsewhere. At this time, and for many years afterward, the town and vicinity were greatly subject to remittent and intermittent fevers, caused, doubtless, by several ponds and marshes of considerable extent near the town, which diffused a miasma. In the course of fifteen or twenty years these marshes were pretty thoroughly drained and reclaimed, when the endemic diseases in a great degree ceased. A year or two after I went to Athens, the old burying ground was cleared and denuded of trees, my father, Dr. Eliphaz Perkins, superintending and performing a share of the work. The first person buried therein was Mrs. Susanna Anthony, the mother of Dr. Perkins's wife, and aunt of General Nathaniel Greene, of revolutionary memory. During several years, my father was the only physician living anywhere in the extensive region bounded east by Marietta and Waterford, west by Chillicothe, north by Lancaster and Zanesville, and south by Gallipolis and Portsmouth. His rides during this period were accordingly often accompanied with great exposure, fatigue, and danger.

The spring of 1803 was, I presume, one of the most premature ever known in the locality of Athens. I well remember, that, in February, many peach trees were in blossom, and, from that time until the 6th of May, the temperature was like that of summer. At the date last named, peaches and apples, with which the trees were unusually laden, had attained the size of potato balls, or large grapes, and most of the forest trees were in full leaf. Rising, however, on the morning of the 6th of May, we found the temperature greatly reduced. It became rapidly colder, and, before ten o'clock, snow began to fall, and, notwithstanding the warm condition of the ground, it was, before night, completely covered with snow. At that time, my brother Jabez, three years my junior, and I were working on a farm of my father's, about five miles from Athens, where we were living by ourselves in a small cabin. We had been working through the week, and this was a Saturday. The provisions we had, as usual, brought with us from home on Monday, were exhausted, and we had to return for more. We had either worn out our shoes, or left them at home, I am not certain which, and were barefoot. Standing in the door of our cabin we contemplated, with no comfortable feelings, the wintry prospect, and the apparent necessity of walking home through the snow without shoes. However, the case admitted of but one conclusion. We buttoned up our coats, and, stepping out into the snow, started at a "dog trot" for home. We made the trip in pretty good time, crossing the Hockhocking twice in a scow, and suffered no injury from the adventure. During the next night the cold became so intense as to kill all the fruits, strip the leaves from the forest, and entirely destroy the herbage on which the cattle had begun to fatten. Not a peach or apple grew in Southern Ohio, that year, except a few on the islands in the Ohio river.

It was about this time, perhaps in 1805, that the celebrated Aaron Burr visited Athens. He was then, as it afterward appeared, vigorously though secretly pursuing his nefarious schemes for the separation of the Union. He took up his lodgings at the public house kept by Capt. Silas Bingham, and remained there several days. Probably the object of his visit was to sound some of the leading men in the settlement with a view to gaining adherents, but whether he directly approached any one during his stay at Athens I do not know. Burr was at this time a very elegant appearing gentleman, and his manners, studiously fascinating, were in marked contrast to those of the plain, honest people among whom he sojourned. He was arrested very soon after this, and his career brought to a close.

In 1804, I think it was, Governor Tiffin, first Governor of Ohio, spent several days at my father's house in connection with the early efforts to organize the Ohio university. I have a very clear recollection of his fine conversational powers and his easy, graceful manners. He made himself exceedingly agreeable during his stay in our family, especially by his entertaining and instructive talk with the younger members of it. He was deeply interested in the establishment of the university, and took an active part in all matters relating to it. I was studying medicine at that time, and the Governor (who was an accomplished physician and surgeon) gave me many instructive passages and anecdotes of his own experience.

Speaking of Governor Tiffin, reminds me of an anecdote of another early governor of Ohio—Governor Morrow. While visiting Athens at one time as president, *ex officio*, of the board of trustees of the university, sitting down to dinner one day at the village tavern, Governor Morrow found himself in contact with a number of the students. The latter began to help themselves without ceremony to the food before them when the Governor, who was a very pious man, stopped them, saying, "Young gentlemen, you have forgotten to ask the blessing of God on this food," whereupon all paused, and the Governor solemnly performed that ceremony.

I had some acquaintance with Lieut. George Ewing, father of the Hon. Thomas Ewing, of Ames township. As a family they possessed strong natural traits of character. The father was a man of shrewd observation, sound judgment, and considerable reading, and withal an excellent neighbor and citizen. They were poor, and Thomas carved out his own career from the beginning, almost totally unaided. When he came to attend the academy at Athens, in 1811 or '12, he was a handsome and athletic youth, and soon became celebrated scarcely less for his feats of agility and strength than for his rapid intellectual triumphs. While at college, besides working portions of the year in the Kanawha salines, he did " chores " for Dr. Lindley, thus contributing to his support. After the usual period of study he received the degree of A. B., and his subsequent career as lawyer and statesman is well known.

I am reminded here of another statesman and lawyer not

unworthy to be named with Thomas Ewing, and who also made his professional debut at Athens—the late Lewis Cass. His father's family had removed to Marietta in 1800, Lewis being at that time about eighteen years old (he was almost exactly my own age). The family soon left Marietta and settled near Zanesville, but Lewis remained at the former place, where he studied law, and was admitted to the Bar in 1802. I well recollect a speech he made at Athens in 1803, and which I am almost confident was his first effort at the Bar. At that time he was not fluent in speaking, and his manner was somewhat severe. But few men, I imagine, ever improved more rapidly in their oratory than did Mr. Cass. About two years after his admission to the Bar he removed to Zanesville, where he soon became known as a successful lawyer, and his long subsequent career was both brilliant and honorable.

When I went to Athens, and for many years afterward, the forests abounded in wild animals of various sorts. Deer were killed with great ease, and were the principal reliance of the settlers for meat, while smaller game was equally abundant. Panthers, black bears and wolves were also sufficiently plenty. The panther though sometimes extremely ferocious, at others seemed comparatively tame. My father and brother Henry were one day traversing the woods on Stroud's run, when they discovered resting among the limbs of a tree very near them a large panther; he seemed quiet and suffered them to proceed, and they saw him no more. As Captain David Pratt was one day looking for his cows in the woods not far from Athens, he was attracted by the furious barking of his dog at the base of a large tree. Approaching and scanning the trunk, Captain Pratt discovered a large catamount reposing on the very limb under which he had been standing. The animal's eyes were glaring and his sinewy legs were gathered for a spring. Quick as thought Captain Pratt leveled his rifle, fired, and the panther came tumbling down; he measured nine feet from tip to tip. I am persuaded that the black bear (*ursus Americanus*) is naturally a timid animal, though under the influence of hunger he becomes bold, and in self-defense, or if a female, in defending her young, they are very ferocious. I have very often while walking in the forests about Athens, seen bruin emerge into the path I was pursuing, and cantering up the hill before me disappear in the woods, as timid as a hare.

For some years after I went to Athens to live, there were no churches or meeting-houses in the county. Religious services, when any were had, were held in some private dwelling, or barn, or perhaps rude school house with oiled-paper windows to admit the light, and fitted up with rough benches. Such shelter was sought in cold weather. In the summer, the congregation generally assembled in the open air under the spreading branches of the trees, where, seated on benches hastily prepared for the occasion, they listened to the welcome message of the traveling preacher, who was either an independent missionary or sent on a missionary tour by the body to which he belonged. I am speaking of the first years of the century. Shortly after the organization of the county, regular circuits were established by the Methodist bishops, and the circuit rider preached at regular periods at the several stations of his circuit in consecutive order. Thus, with occasional visits from Baptist, Presbyterian or Congregational ministers, the spirit of Christianity was kept alive. Prominent among the Methodist preachers were the Rev. Messrs. Thompson, Joseph and William McMahon, Young, and Thomas Morris; among the Baptists, the Rev. Messrs. Pugsley and Stedman; and among the Congregationalists and Presbyterians, the Rev. Daniel Story, the Rev. Mr. Robbins, and the Rev. Jacob Lindley.

In 1814-15, the county was visited by a terrible epidemic designated then as the "cold plague." I recall with painful emotions the events of that period. My father had, from increasing infirmities, almost wholly retired from the practice of his profession, and I had succeeded in some measure to his business.

Thus it fell to my lot in connection with my professional brethren to participate in the warfare against this dreadful disease. The leading physicians of the county at that time were Dr. Ezra Walker, of Ames, and Dr. Leonard Jewett, of Athens, both of them very skillful practitioners. The disease was not confined to the western regions; indeed it originated in New England, and had, in many instances, baffled the efforts of the best physicians there. We all labored intensely duriug the winter, and I am forced to confess in my own case that I had but little success. The disease raged with terrible violence, and many died in all parts of the county.

Index.

ADELPHIA founded, 87. Origin of name, 87, *note*. Changed to Marietta, 88.
Agriculture, early development of, 75.
Agricultural Society, history of, 183.
Albany settled, 474. Incorporated, 475. Town officers, 475.
Alexander township, organized, 147. Boundaries and extent of, 351. Located and surveyed, 351. First settlers, 352. Population decennially since 1820, 352. Churches, 353. Township trustees since 1829, 353. Justices of the peace, 355. Personal and biographical, 355.
Allison, Samuel and *W. H.*, 540.
Ames, Rev. Edward R., birth, parentage and early education, 420. Licensed to preach, 421. Subsequent career and labors, 422. Summary of character, 422. Amusing narrative by, 424.
Ames, Silvanus, birth, parentage and ancestry, 411. Removal to Athens county, 411. Civil offices held by, 412. Death and descendants, 412.
Ames township, organized, 146. Original extent and first settlement of, 363. Arrival of pioneer settlers, 364. Perilous adventure, 365. First schools, 366. Proposal to found a library in 1803, 367. Scarcity of money, 368. First library in N. W. territory founded, 369. List of stockholders, 370. List of books purchased, 371. Hunting adventures, 374. Great drought, 375. Schools, 376. Early Methodism, 377. Anecdote of a Millerite, 378. Militia organization, 379. Anecdote of John Brown, 379. Ancient land tax duplicate, 381. Township trustees

Index.

Ames Township—Continued.
since 1802, 383. Clerks, 384. Justices of the Peace, 384. Population decennially since 1820, 387. Personal and biographical, 387.

Amesville Academy, 386.

Amesville, postmasters in, since 1821, 177.

Andastes, the, 4.

Armstrong, Elmer, 358.

Armstrong, Thomas, 355.

Asbury, Rev. Bishop, reminiscence of, 199.

Athens county, ante-revolutionary history of, 8. Building of Fort Gower in, 11. Lord Dunmore's march across, 12. Relics of Indian war found in, 13. A part of Ohio company's purchase, 21. Great mineral wealth of, 75. First settlement in, 109. Early emigrants to, 115. First mills, 127. Act organizing county, 143. Alteration in boundaries, 144 to 146. First county commissioners, 146. Extract from their records, 146 to 157. Tax duplicate for 1808, 157. County commissioners since 1805, 158. Other county officers, 159 to 163. Population decennially since 1810, 163 to 166. Products and general statistics, 166 to 172. Vote at various elections since 1836, 172. Post offices, 173 to 182. Agricultural Society, 183 to 187. Topography and minerals, 187. Coal, 188. Iron, 192. Salt, 193. County's services during the rebellion, 193.

Athens, (town), act in relation to laying out in 1799, 124. Act confirming, 125. First houses in, 127. Description of, in 1803, 129. Postmasters in since 1804, 177. First sale of town lots, 200. Incorporating act, 205. Act amended, 206. Population, 207. Town officers since 1811, 209 to 215. Schools, 219. Methodist church, 221. Presbyterian church, 222. Cemetery, 229. Newspapers, 230. Court house, 234 to 243. Early lawyers, 243. Personal and biographical, 249.

Athens township, organized, 146. Indian mounds in, 7. First surveyed, 197. Original extent and boundaries, 198.

Athens Township—Continued.
  Population decennially since 1820, 207. Trustees since 1807, 215. Treasurers and clerks, 217. Justices of the Peace, 218. Early churches and religious movements, 581.
Atwood Institute, the 473.
BAKER, Isaiah, 289.
Baker, Jacob L., 290.
Baker, James, 457.
Baker, Nicholas, 289.
Ballard, John, 307.
Baptist Church, first in Ohio, 471.
Barker, Capt. Isaac, 277.
Barker, Judge Isaac, Jr., birth and parentage, 278. Removal to Ohio in 1788, 278. Arrival at Belpre, 279. Pioneer hardships, 279. Life in a block house, 279. Indian massacres, 280. Novel mode of navigation, 280. Keeps ferry at Athens, 280. Fight with Indians, 281. Amusing anecdote, 282. Tavern keeping in 1815, 284. Public offices held by, 284. A hale old age, 284.
Barker, Michael, 277.
Barnes, Enos, 524.
Barrows, William, George and *Henry,* 445.
Bartlett, Henry, birth and parentage of, 264. Comes to Athens in 1797, 264. Public services, 264. Death and summary of character, 265.
Bayard, James W., 195.
Bear, killed near the college green, 283. Sixty-five killed in one season near Hebbardsville, 352. Killed with a club, 456. Perilous adventure with, 474. Forty-six killed in six weeks, 479. John Holdrens' fight with, 480. Adventure of Henry Bobo with, 486. Timid nature of, 580.
Beardsley, Francis, 298.
Beebe, Captain Hopson, 516.
Belpre, Indian panic at, 103.

Bern township, organization of, 434. Lands and farmers in, 434. Population decennially since 1830, 434. Trustees since 1828, 435. Personal and biographical, 436.
Big Bottom Massacre, 102.
Big Run post office, established, 182.
Bingham, Alvan and *Silas*, 119. Anecdote of, 120. Characters, 121.
Blackstone, Dr. William 303.
Blake, Samuel L. 359.
Bobo, Israel, anecdote of, 352.
Bobo, Joseph, narrative of, 485.
Bobo, Henry, adventure of with a bear, 486.
Boden, Hugh, 539.
Bosworth, James, 524.
Bouquet's Expedition, 72.
Boyd, Daniel, Hugh and *William F.*, 458.
Boyles, Col. Absalom, 416.
Boyles, George, first white child born in the county, 446.
Boyles, John, 447. Hunting adventure of, 375.
Boyles Peter, first white settler in the county, 446.
Boyles, Peter W., 447.
Brice, Barnet and *James*, 293.
Bridges in Athens township, 205. In Rome, 492.
Broadhorns, 111.
Brown, Judge A. G., birth and parentage of, 262. Education, graduation and career, 262. Family of, 263.
Brown, A. Douglas, 261.
Brown, Capt. Benjamin, birth and parentage of, 404. Revolutionary services of, 405. Removal to Ames township, 406. Subsequent career and death, 406.
Brown, Henry T., 195, 263.
Brown, John, birth and parentage of, 406. Removal to Ohio in 1801, 406. Perils of the journey, 406. Settlement in Ames, 407. Public offices held by, 407. Death, 408.

Brown, General John, birth and parentage of, 260. Journey to Ohio in 1797, 260. Voyage down the Ohio river, 260. Settlement in Ames and subsequent career, 261. Public offices held, 261. Anecdote of, 379.
Brown, John, 411.
Brown, Leonard, 474.
Brown, Louis W., 263.
Brown, Oscar W., 261.
Brown, Pearly, 408.
Brown, Pinckney, 409.
Brown, Samuel, 410.
Brown, Samuel H., 409.
Brown, William, 410.
Brown, William L., 261.
Buckingham, Ebenezer, 456.
Buffalo killed on site of Athens, 114. Captured on Raccoon creek, 113.
Burnet, Jacob, narrative of, 133.
Burr, Aaron, visit of to Athens, 578.
CALDWELL, Alexander, 456.
Calvary, post office and postmasters, 179.
Camp meetings, 199 581.
Canaan Township, settlement and organization of, 441. First election, 442. Population decennially since 1830, 442. Trustees since 1819, 442. Justices of the peace, 443. Personal and biographical, 444.
Canaanville post office and postmasters, 178.
Carpenter, Dr. E. G., 302.
Carpenter, Capt. Parker, 449.
Carthage Township, organization of and first election, 451. Early officers, 451. Mills, 452. Churches and school houses, 452. Population and trustees, 452. Clerks and justices of the peace, 453. Personal and biographical, 453.
Case, Eliphalet, 507.
Cass, Lewis, maiden speech at Athens, 580.
Cemeteries, 229.

Chase, John M., 360.
Chase, Gardiner F., 361.
Chauncey, founded and laid out, 462. Post office and postmasters, 179.
Churches, number of in county, 166, 169.
Cincinnati, first settlement of, 96. Population of in 1800, 123. Appearance of in 1796, 134, *note*.
Clark, Samuel, 524.
Coal, vast deposits of, 188. Various veins, 189. Value and importance thereof, 191. Deposits of in Waterloo, 537. Deposits of in York, 541.
Cold Plague, the, 581.
Columbia, Lewis, 433.
Congress, negotiation of with Ohio company, 53 to 69.
Congregational Minister, first in N. W. Territory, 81. Salary and terms of employment, 81, *note*. Ordination and charge, 571.
Cooley, Asahel, settled in Carthage, 453. Pioneer labors, 454. Laid out Coolville, 454.
Coolville post office and postmasters, 177. Village of, 532.
Cotton, Robert H., 539.
Corbley, John, family of, massacred by Indians, 357.
Courts, first established, 94, 95. Courts and judges since 1805, 161.
Court house at Athens, history of, 234 to 243.
Courtney, Neil, 297.
Crary, Archibald, 95.
Culver, Roswell, 506.
Currier, Ebenezer, 288.
Cutler, Judge Ephraim, birth and parentage of, 387. Early education, 387. Removal to N. W. Territory, 388. Toilsome journey to Marietta, 388. Settlement in Ames and subsequent career, 389. Elected to territorial legislature, 389. To constitutional convention, 390. Services there, 391. Elected to State legislature, 392. Labors and services there, 393. Death, 393.

Cutler, Dr. Manasseh, birth and parentage of, 249. Literary attainments, 250. Services in Revolutionary war, 250. Attends meeting to form Ohio company, 47. Drafts articles of association, 48. Appointed a director, 52. Authorized to buy western lands, 52. His negotiation with congress, 53 to 69. Reports success to directors, 69. Conclusion of contract, 70. His amendments to ordinance of 1787, 56. Employs first preacher in N. W. Territory, 81. Ordination charge delivered by in 1798, 571.
Cutler, William P., 391.
DAILEY, David, first settler in Rome, 502. Hunting adventures, 503. Amusing anecdote of, 504.
Dana, Professor Joseph, 291.
Dana, Joseph M., Earl S. and *Capt. W. H.*, 292.
Dare, Nathan, 55, 57, 60.
Dawes, Eliza, 412.
Dawes, Sarah C., 53, *note*.
Davis, Nehemiah, 470.
Dean, Gulliver, 433.
Dean, John N. and *Nathan*, 293.
Deer wantonly destroyed by Indians, 112. Abundance of in Belpre settlement, 285. Killed by a woman, 357. Forty killed for winter stock, 479. Thirty killed in two weeks, 480. Twelve killed by a small boy, 487. Their flesh the main dependence of pioneers, 539.
Delaware Indians, 5.
Devoe, Capt. Charles, 532.
Devoe, Capt. Jonathan, 83.
Dew, James and *Thomas*, 524.
Dickey, A. S., 438.
Dickey, James, 436.
Doan, Charles and *William S.*, 518.

Index.

Dover Township, organization and settlement of, 460. Early settlers, 461. Topography and minerals, 461. Villages and salt works, 462. Population decennially since 1820, 413. Dover library, 464. Trustees since 1825, 464. Justices of the peace, 465. Personal and biographical, 466.

Dunmore's Army, relics of, found, 526.

Dunmore's War, origin, conduct and results of, 9 to 12. Fort Gower built in Troy, 11. March across Athens county, 12. Erroneous account of expedition, 13. Resolutions adopted by Dunmore's officers, 15. His return to Virginia, 17.

ELECTION first in N. W. Territory, 132. First of commissioners in Athens county, 146.

Elliot, Moses, John and *James,* 457.

Ewing, George, first settler in Ames, 394. Revolutionary services, 394. Character and public offices held by, 395, 579.

Ewing, Thomas, autobiographical sketch, 395. Settlement in Ames, 395. Journey through the woods, 396. Boyhood and pioneer life, 396. Early reading, 397. Borrows Virgil's Æneid, 398. Anecdote, 399. Early education, 400. Resolves to attend college, and earns money, 400. Enters academy at Athens, 401. Surveys country roads, 401. Graduates and studies law, 402. First speech at the bar, 403. First fee, 403. Subsequent career, 404. Reminiscence of, 579.

Federalton, post office and postmasters at, 178.

Fee, Abram, 538.

Ferries, early, and ferry rates, 148, 204.

Flint, Timothy, 96. His estimate of Gen. Putnam and Dr. Cutler, 97.

Fortification, Ancient, 7.

Fort Gower, built, 11.

Fort Harmar, established, 84.

Frame, John, 533.

Frost, Abram and *Heman*, 454.

GARDEN, post office established and postmaster at, 181.

German hunter, anecdote of, 283.
Gillett, Samuel, 447.
Gillmore, John, 270.
Glazier, Abel, 417.
Glazier, Walter, 459.
Golden, William, 300.
Golden, William R., 301.
Goodspeed, Joseph, 298.
Gorsline, William, 361.
Grand Juries, from 1805 to 1815, 245.
Greene, M. M., 195.
Greenville, Treaty of, 107, 109.
Gregory's Dam, act authorizing, 202. Mill built, 203.
Grosvenor, Charles H., 305.
Grosvenor, Peter, 517.
Grosvenor, Thomas, 518.
Guysville, post office and postmasters at, 180.
HAMMOND, Peter, 458.
Harmar's Indian Expedition, 101.
Harris, Thaddeus M., 129.
Harrison, William H., 136.
Hartleyville, post office and postmasters at, 181.
Hatch, Judge Elijah, 505.
Hawk, Conrad, 288.
Hebbardsville, post office and postmasters at, 179.
Henry, John, 438.
Henry, William, 450.
Hewitt, John, built first mill in Waterloo, 539.
Hewitt, Moses, fight of with Indians, 281. First white settler in Waterloo, 538.
Hibbards, large family of, 359.
Hockingport, post office and postmasters at, 180. Village of, 531.
Hockhocking, origin and meaning of, 17, *note.*
Holdren, John, early settlement of in county, 478. Success as a hunter, 479. Service in war of 1812, 480. Oldest person in the county, 480.

Hoop snakes, 97.
Hoskinson, Joshua, 449.
House raising in early times, account of, 495.
Hoyt, Benajah, 532.
Huckleberry Knobs, 75.
Hulls, post office and postmasters at, 180.
Hunter, Hocking H., 244, 427, 447.
Huron Indians, the, 3.
INDIAN barbarities, 280, 357.
Indian occupation of Ohio, 3.
Indian fortifications, 7.
Indian war, 100.
Indians, fight with, 281.
Iron ore, deposits of, 192.
JACKSON, William, 444.
James, Daniel and *David,* 440.
Jeffers, William, 456.
Jewett, Dr. Leonard, 272.
Johnson, Azel, 468.
Johnson, John, 266, 509.
Johnson, John B., 525.
Johnson, Dr. W. P., 207, 303, 510.
Jones, Jesse, 539.
Jones, Timothy, 508.
Journal of Manasseh Cutler, 53.
Journal of Mrs. David Pratt, 254.
Juneberries eaten by bears, 397.
KINGS, post office and postmasters at, 182.
Knight, James, 544.
Knowles, Samuel, 306.
Knowles, Samuel S., 306, 533.
LAMPSON, Philip W., 440.
Law, the first in northwest territory, 92.
Lawrence, John and *Edward,* 459.
Lawyers of Athens, 243.
Lee, post office and postmasters at, 178.

Index. 593

Lee Township, organized, 472. Population decennially since 1820, 472. Trustees, 476. Justices of the peace, 477. Biographical and personal, 478.
Legislature, first in northwest territory, 133.
Lewis, Gen. Andrew, connection of with Dunmore's war, 9.
Library, first in northwest territory, 369.
Lindley, Rev. Jacob, 258.
Linscott, Isaac, 414.
Linzee, Robert, 265.
Lodi Township, organization of, 481. First election in and population of, 481. Churches and schools, 482. Trustees and clerks, 483. Justices of the peace, 484. Pioneer times there, 485.
Logan, the Mingo Chief, 9.
Log cabin, how built, 116. Comfort and happiness in, 118.
Lottridge, Bernardus B., 455.
Lottridge, Mrs., adventure of with panther, 455.
Lottridge, post office and postmasters at, 181.
Lovell, Capt. Thomas S., adventures of in war of 1812, 430. Journey to the West, 430. Settles in Ames, 431. Pioneer life there, 431. Takes a ship down the Ohio river, 432. Voyage to Baltimore, 432.
Lowry, Col. William, pioneer adventures of, 538.
MAIL Carrier, perils of in early times, 437.
Mail service early in Ohio, 173.
Mansfield, Martin, 446.
Mansfield, Peter, 446.
Manufactures, 170.
Margaret's Creek, why so called, 119. First mill on, 127.
Marietta settled, 84. Origin of name, 88.
Marshfield, postmasters at, 182. Village of, 537.
Martin, Nathaniel, 458.
Massacre of Ohio Company settlers, 102.
Mayhugh, James, 539.
McCune, Jacob, hunting exploit of, 375.
McCune, John, adventure of, 374.

McDougal, Gilbert, 415.
McDougal, John, 416.
McVey, Abram, 361.
McVey, Jacob, 361.
Meigs, Return J., surveyor of Ohio company, 79. Appointed first clerk of court, 95.
Methodist church, 221, 489.
Miles, Joseph B., 266.
Militia, first law concerning, 92.
Millfield, post office and postmasters at, 179.
Miller, Abel, 448.
Miller, Amos, 515.
Miller Seminary, 491.
Millerite, anecdote of a, 378.
Mills, early, 127. In Athens, 203. In Lodi, 481. In Rome, 493. In Waterloo, 539.
Mill, floating, 538.
Mill, worked by hand, 257.
Mills, William, 459.
Mineral wealth, 188.
Morris, Calvary, 274.
Morrow, Governor, anecdote of, 579.
NEAL, Mrs., perilous adventure of, 467.
Nelsonville incorporated, 542. Postmasters of, 178. Mayors of, 542.
New England, post office and postmasters, 182.
Newspapers, 230.
Newton, Solomon, 524.
Norris, Abraham, 458.
Northrop, Capt. Amos, 559.
Northwestern territory, proposed division of into ten states, 40, *note*. Ordinance for government of, 61. Perpetual freedom secured in, 91. First courts of, 95. First ordained preacher in, 81. First college in, 309. First library in, 369.
Nursery, pioneer, 470.
Nye family, 468.

Index. 595

OFFICERS in Dunmore's army, resolutions of, 15.

Ohio, Indian occupation of, 1. Present greatness and wealth, 2. First settlement of, 84. First territorial legislature, 133. Territorial government of, 138. Contest about state government, 139. Constitution formed, 141. Admitted to the Union, 141.

Ohio Company, origin of, 45. First advertisement of, 46. Articles of agreement, 48. Their adoption, 51. Directors appointed, 52. Agents appointed to buy land, 52. Their negotiation with Congress, 53 to 69. Contract executed, 70. Description of tract purchased, 70. Alleged bad location, 71. Reasons for and against the choice, 71. Ebenezer Zane's advice, 73. Location a good one, 75. Preparations for emigration, 76. Allotment and division of lands, 77. Appointment of surveyors and boat-builders, 78. Superintendent appointed, 80. First party of emigrants, 82. Boats built, 83. Arrival and landing at Fort Harmar, 84. Names of the party, 85. Lots surveyed and laws passed, 86. City founded, 87. Authority of board of treasury to contract with, 551 to 561. Lands authorized to be conveyed, 561. Patent for 750,000 acres, 564. Patent for 214,285 acres, 566. Patent for 100,000 acres, 569.

Ohio University, the first one established west of mountains, 309. Dr. Cutler's efforts to found, 310. Land surveyed and located, 311. Act of 1802 establishing, 312. Accompanying letter of Dr. Cutler, 319. First meeting of trustees, 329. Their early labors, 330. Message of Gov. Tiffin concerning, 331. Academy building erected, 335. Amendatory legislation concerning, 335 to 344. Faculty organized, 345. Useful results of, 345. State aid required, 346. Trustees, 346. Presidents and professors, 349.

Ordination charge, 571.

Ottawa Indians, 6.

PANTHERS, bounty on scalps of, 130.

Parkins, David, 440.

Perkins, Dr. Eliphas, birth and early life of, 252. Migrates to Marietta, 253. Indian barbarities, 253. Flatboat voyage on the Ohio, 255. Walk through the wilderness, 255. Settles at Athens, 256. Summary of characters and death, 257.
Perkins, Dr. Chauncey F., 257. Anecdotes furnished by, 108. Further reminiscences, 576.
Perkins, John, 263.
Perry, Edmund, 440.
Pickering, Simeon W., 195.
Pioneer names of streams, 131.
Pleasanton, post office and postmasters, 181.
Pleasant Valley Seminary, 482.
Point Pleasant, battle of, 10.
Political events, from 1798 to 1805, 132.
Population of county since 1810, 163.
Post offices, 175.
Postmasters, 177.
Post riders, early hardships of, 437.
Post roads, first in Ohio, 174.
Poston, L. D., 546.
Pratt, Capt. David, 290.
Pratt, Mrs. David, journal of, 254.
Pratt, Rev. E. P., 291.
Pratt, Rev. John H., 291.
Pratt, Dr. John, 533.
Pratt, Dr. Robert, 591.
Preacher paid in whisky, 377.
Presbyterian Church, 222.
Price, James, 525.
Prosecuting attorneys since 1805, 163.
Pruden, Samuel B., 296.
Pruden, Silas, 295.
Pugsley, Abraham, 467.
Putnam, Gen. Rufus, life, career and services of, 23 to 43.
QUINN, Rev. James, 199.

RARDIN, William, 440.
Rathburn, David, 428.
Rebellion, volunteers during the, 196.
Recorders since 1805, 160.
Revolutionary patriots, 22.
Rice, Jason, 413.
Rice, Capt. Sabinus, 413.
Robbins, Samuel, 547.
Roberts, Solomon, 547.
Robinett, Ezekiel, 538.
Rock Oak, post office and postmasters, 182.
Rome township, organization and first limits of, 488. Boundaries changed, 489. Population decennially since 1820, 489. First school house, 490. Present schools, 491. First bridges, 492. Mills, 493. Pioneer incidents, 496. Trustees, 499. Clerks, 500. Treasurers and justices of the peace, 501. Personal and biographical, 502.
Root, Norman, 299.
Rowell, Elmer, 506 Reminiscences by, 497.
Ryors, Rev. Alfred, 420.
Ryors, Louisa W., 419.
SALINA, post office and postmasters, 182.
Salt, early scarcity of, 121. First manufacture of in Ohio, 122. High price of, 446. Indian mode of manufacturing, 479. First well bored, 469.
Savannah Academy, 491.
Selby, Dyar, 440.
Seven ranges surveyed, 44.
Shade, post office and postmasters, 180.
Shawanese Indians, 5.
Sheriff, first in Ohio, 95.
Sheriffs since 1805, 160.
Ship built on the Ohio, 431. Built in Rome township, 495. Taken down the Ohio river in 1816, 432. Her arrival at Cincinnati and Baltimore, 432.
Shipman, Charles, 294.

Stanberry, Henry, maiden speech of, 244.
Sickles, William, 360.
Smith, Lot L., 195.
Snowden, Margaret, 119.
Soldiers, Revolutionary, 22. In war of 1812, 498. In war of the rebellion, 196.
Spenser, Joel, 506.
Spinning wheel carried forty miles, 470.
Sproat, Ebenezer, surveyor of Ohio Company. 79. First sheriff in Ohio, 95.
Starr, Capt. Philip, 266.
St. Clair, Gen. Arthur, governor of northwest territory, 88. Arrival at Marietta, 89. Inaugurated governor, 90. Defeat by Indians, 105. Reappointed governor, 137. Anecdote of, 504.
Stedman, Abel, 284.
Stedman, Alexander, 514.
Steenrod, Lewis, 547.
Steuben, Baron, 58.
Stevens, Christopher, anecdote of, 283.
Stewart, Daniel, birth and early life of, 510. Journey to the west in 1802, 511. Settlement in Athens and success there, 511. Summary of character, etc., 512.
Stewart, Daniel B., 513.
Stewart, Ezra, 512.
Stewart William, 512.
Story, Rev. Daniel, first congregational minister in Ohio, 81. Ordained, 571.
Swart, Thornton, 440.
Sweat family, 468.
TAVERN Licenses, early, 149.
Teacher, first in Ohio, 80.
Thompson, John P., hunting incident by, 114.
Tiffin, Governor, reminiscence of, 578.
Torch, post office and postmasters, 181.
Treasurers since 1805, 160.

Trimble, post office and postmasters, 180.
Trimble township, organization of, 519. First settlers in, 519. Churches, schools and mills, 520. Mineral wealth of, 521. Population decennially since 1830, 521. First election in, 522. Trustees, 522. Justices of the peace, 523. Personal and biographical, 523.
Troy township, organization of, 146. Earliest settlement of, 526. Interesting relics found in, 527. First settlers, 528. Early roads, 529. Trustees, 530. Clerks and treasurers, 530. Justices of the peace, 531. Personal and biographical, 532.
True, Jabez, taught school in block house, 310.
True, Josiah, 469.
Tupper, Gen. Benjamin, 43.
UNION school, 220.
VAN VORHES, Abraham, 303.
Van Vorhes, Nelson H., 303.
Vore, John E., 440.
WALKER, Archibald B., 271.
Walker, Dr. Ezra, settlement of, in Ames, 425. Exposure and perils as a physician, 426. Death, and family, 427.
Walker, Ezra, 428.
Walker, Judge George, birth and parentage, 417. Settlement in Ames, 418. Civil offices held by, 419.
Walker, Ralph M., 428.
Walker, William R., 427.
Washington county, first settlement of, 85. Proclamation creating, 93.
Washington, George, letters of, to Rufus Putnam, 27 and 39. Opinion of Ohio Company, 86.
Waterford, Indian panic at, 103.
Waterloo township, organized, 534. Trustees, 535. Clerks, treasurers, and justices of the peace, 536. Population since 1830, 537. Topography and minerals, 537. Personal and biographical, 538.
Watkins, Jonathan, 523.

Wayne, Gen. Anthony, put in command of western army, 106. Indian expedition of, 107. Exhumation of after death, 108.
Weethee College, 463.
Weethee, Daniel, 466.
Welch, Hon. John, settlement of, in Rome, 301. Occupation as a miller, 301. Legal studies and career, 302.
Welch, Thomas, 516.
Wells, Caleb P., 458.
Wells library, 473.
Wildes, Gen. T. F., 307.
Wild turkeys, mode of capturing, 431.
Wilkins, Jonathan, 268.
Wilkins, Timothy, anecdote of, 268.
Williams, E. H., 532.
Wilson, Dr. C. L., 303.
Wolf, killed by a woman, 374.
Wolf hunt, story of a, 424.
Wood yards, post office and postmasters, 181.
Woolen factory, 494, 514.
Wolves, bounty on scalps of, 130. Adventure with, 426.
Wyatt, Joshua, 414.
YORK township. organized, 541. Population decennially since 1820, 541. Topography and mineral wealth, 541. Trustees, 543. Clerks, treasurers, and justices of the peace, 544. Personal and biographical, 544.
Young, Rev. Jacob, 489.
ZANE, Ebenezer, anecdote concerning. 73.

www.ingramcontent.com/pod-product-compliance
Lightning Source LLC
Chambersburg PA
CBHW071132300426
44113CB00009B/948